Futures of International Criminal Justice

This collection identifies and discusses problems and opportunities for the theory and practice of international criminal justice.

The International Criminal Court (ICC) and the project of prosecuting international atrocity crimes have faced multiple challenges and critiques. In recent times, these have included changes in technology, the conduct of armed conflict, the environment, and geopolitics. The mostly emerging contributors to this collection draw on diverse socio-legal research frameworks to discuss proposals for the futures of international criminal justice. These include addressing accountability gaps and under-examined or emerging areas of criminality at, but also beyond, the ICC, especially related to technology and the environment. The book discusses the tensions between universalism and localisation, as well as the regionalisation of international criminal justice and how these approaches might adapt to dynamic organisational, political, and social structures, at the ICC and beyond.

The book will be of interest to students, researchers, and academics. It will also be a useful resource for civil society representatives, including justice advocates, diplomats and other government officials and policymakers.

Emma Palmer is a senior lecturer at the Griffith Law School, Griffith University, Australia. Her teaching and research interests address international criminal law, human rights law, comparative law, and international investment law. She was previously a research assistant at UNSW and has worked an investment analyst. Emma was admitted as a lawyer in New South Wales and is a director for Women's Legal Service NSW.

Susan Harris Rimmer is the Director of the Griffith University Policy Innovation Hub (appointed July 2020). Her research interests address transitional justice, international human rights law, climate justice, and feminist approaches to international law. She was previously the Deputy Head of School (Research) in the Griffith Law School and prior to joining Griffith was the Director of Studies at the ANU Asia-Pacific College of Diplomacy.

Edwin Bikundo is a senior lecturer at the Griffith Law School, Griffith University, Australia. Edwin's teaching and research interests lie in international and comparative law, as well as legal theory.

Martin Clark is an adjunct lecturer at the Faculty of Law, University of Tasmania and Modern Law Review Post-Doctoral Fellow. He completed his PhD in law at the London School in May 2020, where he was a Judge Rosalyn Higgins Scholar and Modern Law Review Scholar (2018 and 2019) and is an assistant editor at the London Review of International Law. He works on the history of legal thought, international law, and public law, and teaches contract and legal theory. His book with Yoriko Otomo, *Eating the World: A Global History of Law and Commodities*, will be out with Counterpress in early 2022.

Routledge Socio-Legal Frontiers of Transitional Justice
Edited by: Chrisje Brants Langeraar, Susanne Karstedt, and Nandor Knust

This series addresses the future potential, developments and success of transitional justice and its multi-faceted approaches. To this end, it focuses on the socio-legal aspects of transitional justice in the widest sense.

Available titles in this series include:

Futures of International Criminal Justice
Edited by Emma Palmer, Susan Harris Rimmer, Edwin Bikundo, and Martin Clark

For more information about this series, please visit: www.routledge.com/law/series/FTJ

Futures of International Criminal Justice

Edited by Emma Palmer, Susan Harris Rimmer, Edwin Bikundo, and Martin Clark

Routledge
Taylor & Francis Group
LONDON AND NEW YORK

First published 2022
by Routledge
2 Park Square, Milton Park, Abingdon, Oxon OX14 4RN

and by Routledge
605 Third Avenue, New York, NY 10158

Routledge is an imprint of the Taylor & Francis Group, an informa business

British Library Cataloguing-in-Publication Data
A catalogue record for this book is available from the British Library

Library of Congress Cataloging-in-Publication Data
A catalog record for this book has been requested

ISBN: 978-0-367-54074-6 (hbk)
ISBN: 978-0-367-54079-1 (pbk)
ISBN: 978-1-003-08753-3 (ebk)

DOI: 10.4324/9781003087533

Typeset in Galliard
by Apex CoVantage, LLC

Contents

Acknowledgements

We would like to acknowledge the support of Mary Keyes and Melanie Davies at the Griffith University Law Futures Centre.

We extend our deep thanks to our reviewers, especially in a pandemic. Thank you to the editorial team at Routledge and to our supportive series editors.

We wish to thank the participants of the Australian International Criminal Law Workshop 2019: International Criminal Justice Futures – a two-day program presented by Griffith's Law Futures Centre. The focus of the wider workshop, held on 28–29 October 2019 at Brisbane's Supreme Court Library Conference Centre, was the exploration and debate of the future of international criminal justice.

The workshop included a keynote speech by McGill University's Professor Frédéric Mégret and sessions on the promise, politics, and future of international criminal justice, as well as future challenges to impunity gaps, future crimes in international criminal law, and futures beyond the trial. We also thank our other key speakers, Melinda Taylor and Chris Sidoti.

We acknowledge that the workshop and editing of this collection occurred on the traditional lands of Jagera and Turubal people, the Bundjalung – Arakwal Bumberlin people, and the muwinina people, and we pay respect to their elders.

Contributors

Edwin Bikundo is a senior lecturer at the Griffith Law School, Griffith University, Australia. Edwin's current teaching and research interests lie in international and comparative law, as well as legal theory. Edwin also practiced as an advocate of the High Court of Kenya and taught at the Faculty of Law at the University of Nairobi and the Faculty of Arts at Egerton University in Kenya. He is a past secretary of the Law Literature and Humanities Association of Australasia and was a visiting lecturer at the Strathmore University Law School in Kenya.

Anna Marie Brennan is a senior lecturer in law at the University of Waikato in New Zealand. Prior to joining the University of Waikato, she held lectureships at University College Cork in Ireland and the University of Liverpool in the United Kingdom. She holds a PhD from University College Cork which was externally funded by an Irish Research Council Postgraduate Fellowship. She teaches and researches in the areas of international criminal Law, international humanitarian law and outer space law. Her book *Transnational Terrorist Groups and International Criminal Law* was published by Routledge in 2019. She has previously worked on the trial and appeal of Radovan Karadzic at the United Nations International Criminal Tribunal for the Former Yugoslavia and for Judge Sylvia Steiner on the trial of Jean-Pierre Bemba Gombo at the International Criminal Court.

Susan Harris Rimmer is the Director of the Griffith University Policy Innovation Hub (appointed July 2020). She was previously the Deputy Head of School (Research) in the Griffith Law School and prior to joining Griffith was the Director of Studies at the ANU Asia-Pacific College of Diplomacy. With Professor Sara Davies, Susan is co-convenor of the Griffith Gender Equality Research Network. Sue also leads the climate justice theme of the new Griffith Climate Action Beacon. Susan is the 2021 winner of the Fulbright Scholarship in Australian-United States Alliance Studies (funded by DFAT) and will be hosted by Georgetown University in Washington, DC.

Philipp Kastner is a senior lecturer at the Law School of the University of Western Australia. He holds degrees from McGill University, Canada (DCL and

LLM) and the University of Innsbruck, Austria (Dr. iur. and Mag. iur.). He researches and teaches in the areas of international criminal law, the resolution of armed conflicts and transitional justice, public international law, and legal pluralism. Publications include *Legal Normativity in the Resolution of Internal Armed Conflict* (Cambridge University Press, 2015) and *International Criminal Justice in Bello?* (Martinus Nijhoff, 2012). He is also the editor of *International Criminal Law in Context* (Routledge, 2018).

Rachel Killean is a senior lecturer in the School of Law at Queen's University Belfast. She has been researching transitional justice and responses to conflict and human rights violations since 2012. She has been an investigator on interdisciplinary research projects exploring a range of transitional justice issues, including processes of restoring cultural property and communities after conflict and representing victimhood in sites of dark tourism. She published her book *Victims, Atrocity and International Criminal Justice: Lessons from Cambodia* with Routledge in 2018 and has published research in the *International Review of Victimology*, *Journal of International Criminal Justice*, and *International Journal of Transitional Justice*, among others.

Eve Massingham is a Senior Research Fellow with the University of Queensland School of Law. Eve's current research focuses on the diverse ways in which the law constrains or enables autonomous functions of military platforms, systems and weapons. She is the co-editor of *Ensuring Respect for International Humanitarian Law* (Routledge, 2020) and has published widely in the field of international humanitarian law (IHL). Prior to joining the University, Eve worked for the International Red Cross and Red Cross Movement, including as the International Committee of the Red Cross' Regional Legal Adviser for East Africa and as an IHL officer for Australian Red Cross. Eve has also served as an Australian Army Reserve Officer. Eve holds an LLB (Hons) from QUT, a Master of International Development from Deakin University, an LLM (Distinction) from King's College London and a PhD from the University of Queensland.

Simon McKenzie is a research fellow at the University of Queensland School of Law. Simon's current research focuses on the legal challenges connected with the defence and security applications of science and technology. He is the author of *Disputed Territories and International Criminal Law: Israeli Settlements and the International Criminal Court* (Routledge, 2020) and his broader research and teaching interests include the law of armed conflict, international criminal law, and domestic criminal law. Prior to joining the University of Queensland, Simon was a policy officer in the Victorian Department of Justice and Community Safety, and he has held roles at the Melbourne Law School, at the Supreme Court of Victoria, and the International Criminal Court. Simon graduated in 2011 from the University of Tasmania with a combined Arts and Law Degree with First Class Honours in Law and was admitted to practice in Victoria later that year. He received his PhD from the University of Melbourne in 2018.

Frédéric Mégret is a professor of law and a William Dawson Scholar at McGill University. He held the Canada Research Chair on the Law of Human Rights and Legal Pluralism from 2006 to 2015. He was promoted to full professor in 2019. He was named co-director of the Centre for Human Rights and Legal Pluralism in 2021. Professor Mégret is currently co-authoring a book on diasporas and international law with Larissa van den Herik (Leiden University). He is the co-editor with Philip Alston of *The United Nations and Human Rights: A Critical Appraisal* (Oxford University Press, 2020); with Immi Tallgren of *The Dawn of a Discipline: International Criminal Justice and its Early Exponents* (Cambridge University Press, 2020); and with Kevin Jon Heller, Sarah Nouwen, Jens David Ohlin, and Darryl Robinson of *The Oxford Handbook of International Criminal Law* (Oxford University Press, 2020). He is also the author of *Le Tribunal pénal international pour le Rwanda* (Pedone, 2002). Prior to joining McGill University, Professor Mégret was an assistant professor at the Faculty of Law of the University of Toronto, a Boulton fellow at McGill University, and a research associate at the European University Institute in Florence.

Natalie J E Nunn is a PhD candidate in international law at the University of Tasmania. Her main research areas include international humanitarian law and arms control law, and her doctoral research is focused on the development of arms control laws for the regulation of lethal fully autonomous weapons. Natalie has previously worked as both an advisor and supervisor for the Kalshoven Grieks Forum and for the Australian Permanent Mission to the United Nations in New York, the Coalition for the International Criminal Court, the International Service for Human Rights, and the United Nations Assisted Tribunal for the Khmer Rouge. Natalie completed her LLB/BA at the University of Melbourne and her LLM at Leiden University.

Emma Palmer has published two books, *Adapting International Criminal Justice in Southeast Asia: Beyond the International Criminal Court* (Cambridge University Press) and, with Sarah Williams and Hannah Woolaver, *The Amicus Curiae in International Criminal Justice* (Hart). She was awarded her PhD for her thesis, 'International Criminal Law in Southeast Asia: beyond the International Criminal Court', from UNSW Law in 2017. She has been a research assistant for two Australian Research Council (ARC) Discovery Projects within the Faculty of Law at UNSW and undertook internships with the Australian Permanent Mission to the United Nations in Geneva and Women's Legal Service NSW. Emma was a senior investment analyst at Macquarie Bank between 2006 and 2011, where she was responsible for coordinating private equity investments, especially in the infrastructure sector. Emma was admitted as a lawyer in New South Wales and is a director for Women's Legal Service NSW.

Shannon Maree Torrens is an international and human rights lawyer, admitted in the Supreme Court of New South Wales, Australia. She was awarded a

PhD in international criminal law from the University of Sydney Law School. Shannon also has a BA (Media and Communications, Government and English) and a Bachelor of Laws (LLB) (Honours), also from the University of Sydney, with a specialisation in public international law, international criminal law, international humanitarian law, international human rights law, and legal theory. Shannon has worked in international criminal law at the international criminal tribunals and courts for Rwanda (ICTR), the former Yugoslavia (ICTY), Sierra Leone (SCSL), and Cambodia (ECCC). In addition, she has worked as a legal advisor for the Marshall Islands Permanent Mission to the United Nations in New York in the UN General Assembly Sixth Committee (Legal) and as an editorial advisor for the *Cambodia Law and Policy Journal*. She has also worked with the UN Food and Agriculture Organisation (FAO), the United Nations Children's Fund (UNICEF), and at the Australian Embassies to Italy and the Holy See (the Vatican). Shannon has lectured, published, and presented papers in the areas of international criminal law and human rights internationally.

1 Introduction

The futures of international criminal justice

Emma Palmer and Susan Harris Rimmer

1 Introduction

There are multiple potential 'starting dates' for international criminal justice[1] – some say from the trial of van Hagenbach, some the Versailles Peace Treaty, or far earlier – such as with the writings of Sun Tzu.[2] Others might focus on a different institutional era, commencing at Nuremberg, with the United Nations establishing international criminal tribunals for the former Yugoslavia or Rwanda, or even 'since Rome' – referring to the diplomatic conference of 1998 that led to the Rome Statute of the International Criminal Court. The International Criminal Court (ICC) has represented the institutionalisation of a norm that has evolved over time,[3] alongside the establishment of internationalised or 'hybrid' mechanisms. It seems that the 'field of international justice has evolved dramatically'.[4] Now, it can be suggested that '[t]transitional justice is an area of study and practice that addresses the question of how societies that experience mass violence or periods of repression should engage these episodes. International criminal law

1 Gerry Simpson, 'International Criminal Law: The Next Hundred Years' in Kevin Jon Heller et al. (eds), *The Oxford Handbook of International Criminal Law* (OUP 2020); Gerry Simpson, 'Linear Law: The History of International Criminal Law' in Christine Schwöbel (ed), *Critical Approaches to International Criminal Law: An Introduction* (Routledge 2014); Emma Palmer, *Adapting International Criminal Justice in Southeast Asia: Beyond the International Criminal Court* (CUP 2020).

2 See Martti Koskenniemi, 'Law, Teleology and International Relations: An Essay in Counterdisciplinarity' (2012) 26 *International Relations* 3; Matthew Craven, Malgosia Fitzmaurice, and Maria Vogiatzi (eds), *Time, History and International Law* (Martinus Nijhoff 2007); Alexander L Hinton, 'Introduction: Toward an Anthropology of Transitional Justice' in Alexander L Hinton (ed), *Transitional Justice: Global Mechanisms and Local Realities After Genocide and Mass Violence* (Rutgers University Press 2010).

3 See Michael J Struett, *The Politics of Constructing the International Criminal Court: NGOs, Discourse, and Agency* (Palgrave Macmillan 2008) 12; Frédéric Mégret, this volume; Emma L Palmer, 'Constructing International Criminal Justice in Time & Space' (2018) 18 *International Criminal Law Review* 958.

4 Jennifer Trahan, 'Views of the Future of the Field of International Justice: A Scenarios Project Based on Expert Consultations' (2018) 33 *American University International Law Review* 843, 843.

DOI: 10.4324/9781003087533-1

occupies a privileged place within that field', even at its 'apex' and possibly 'at the expense of other responses or priorities'.[5]

Yet the ICC and its associated international criminal law 'project' have attracted increasing criticism and critique,[6] leading to accelerating identification and diagnoses of its inequities,[7] anxieties,[8] missed opportunities,[9] and crises.[10] Some point out that typical histories of international criminal law miss or obscure post-colonial, gendered, economic, and politicised experiences[11] and 'a buried history of non-trials'.[12] Indeed, as Gerry Simpson has observed, it may seem that (alongside withdrawals from the Rome Statute and un-prosecuted perpetrators) the project is in some practical senses 'over', even if 'as an intellectual project, [international criminal law] is in its prime'.[13] Meanwhile, earlier courts and tribunals 'wind up' and are the subject of 'legacy' projects, while their relationship to broader transformative and development goals continues to be debated. Trials may follow a trajectory of investigation, trial, conviction, appeal, sentencing or release, reparations, then post-trial issues – including regarding the rights of convicted and released persons. In practice, these issues coincide and are of ongoing concern within courts. The ICC remains relatively

5 Laurel E Fletcher, 'International Criminal Law and the Subordination of Emancipation' in Heller et al. (eds) (n 1) 699.
6 Christine Schwöbel, 'Introduction' in Schwöbel (ed) (n 1).
7 Antonio Franceschet, 'The Rule of Law, Inequality, and the International Criminal Court' (2004) 29 *Alternatives* 23.
8 Frédéric Mégret, 'The Anxieties of International Criminal Justice' (2016) 29 *Leiden Journal of International Law* 197.
9 Therese De Langis, 'A Missed Opportunity, a Last Hope? Prosecuting Sexual Crimes Under the Khmer Rouge Regime' (2014) 3 *Cambodia Law and Policy Journal* 39; Heejin Kim, 'Missed Opportunities in the Judicialisation of International Criminal Law? Asian States in the Emergence and Spread of the Rome Statute System to Punish Atrocity Crimes' (2017) 35 *Netherlands Quarterly of Human Rights* 246.
10 Sergey Vasiliev, 'The Crises and Critiques of International Criminal Justice' in Heller et al. (eds) (n 1); Douglas Guilfoyle 'Lacking Conviction: Is the International Criminal Court Broken? An Organisational Failure Analysis' (2019) 20 *Melbourne Journal of International Law* 401; Mégret, this volume; see also regarding international law Dianne Otto, 'Decoding Crisis in International Law: A Queer Feminist Perspective' in Barbara Stark (ed), *International Law and its Discontents: Confronting Crisis* (CUP 2015); Hilary Charlesworth, 'International Law: A Discipline of Crisis' (2002) 65 *Modern Law Review* 377.
11 Kevin J Heller and Gerry Simpson (eds), *The Hidden Histories of International Criminal Law* (OUP 2013); Michelle Burgis-Kasthala, 'Scholarship as Dialogue? TWAIL and the Politics of Methodology' (2016) 14 *Journal of International Criminal Justice* 921; Hannah Franzki, 'Criminal Trials, Economic Dimensions of State Crime, and the Politics of Time in International Criminal Law: A German – Argentine Constellation' (PhD thesis, University of London, Birkbeck 2018); Telford Taylor, *Nuremberg and Vietnam: An American Tragedy* (Bantam 1971).
12 Gerry Simpson, 'Unprecedents' in Immi Tallgren and Thomas Skouteris (ed), *The New Histories of International Criminal Law: Retrials* (OUP 2019) 12.
13 Simpson, 'The Next Hundred Years' (n 1) 841.

'new' compared to some other tribunals, but at approximately 20 years old, its 'newness' is less obvious.

There is therefore no clear date from which to identify a period of 'future challenges/opportunities' as opposed to 'past challenges/opportunities' in relation to international criminal justice. Moreover, to do so arguably implies a linear, teleological conception of temporal progress – possibly interrupted by episodic disruption – but with a fixed ideal future.[14] Meanwhile, justifications for the application of international criminal justice in a given situation teeter between claims that crimes are 'unprecedented' and that trials for such crimes do have precedents.[15] Understandings of the past and how it relates to the present are therefore contested, just as projections for the future of international criminal justice are 'radically divergent'.[16]

This introductory chapter considers these issues of temporality, newness, and futures in relation to international criminal justice. It assesses what the 'futures' of international criminal justice might mean, or at least what approaches might be made towards considering its 'futures'. It argues that just as it is possible to recognise international criminal justice as holding multiple definitions and histories, there will be multiple futures for international criminal law and its institutions. These include in relation to its mechanisms, scope and subject matter, effects, purposes, challenges, and opportunities. These futures are relational as the understandings and operations of international criminal justice are shaped by state and non-state actors in various locations. Yet drawing on feminist historical institutionalism, they are also nested within existing structures.[17]

The contributions in this book address various visions and analyses of international criminal justice and its futures. They suggest that the histories of prosecuting atrocities and violence are multiple and reverberate now and tomorrow in ways that are neither necessarily predictable nor fixed, linear, or singular. Some problems may be old. Yet we do argue that some questions represent 'new challenges' in the sense that they raise questions for which the answers now seem to be unclear (or less clear than they once were), or they present questions for which international criminal law lacks significant jurisprudence.

Still, very often, the articulation of what is 'new' or of 'future' concern may depend on the level of abstraction and perspective. Outside international criminal law, has COVID-19 been a new challenge or another aspect of an 'old' public health or human rights accessibility issue? Is climate change a new or future emergency, or does it belong to an old category of natural challenges? Are automated technology systems developed in 2021 new, or are they forms of technology or

14 Koskenniemi, 'Law, Teleology' (n 2); Simpson, 'Linear Law' (n 1).
15 Simpson, 'Unprecedents' (n 12).
16 Trahan, 'Views of the Future' (n 4).
17 Fiona Mackay, 'Nested Newness, Institutional Innovation, and the Gendered Limits of Change' (2014) 10 *Politics & Gender* 549.

innovation that law has long struggled with? Is the ICC new at 20 or not, and what are its implications for international criminal law in the next 5, 10, 20 or 1,000 years? Varied spheres of analysis might assist in responding to such questions differently. Further, new institutions of behaviour and practice might be 'nested' in the 'stickiness' of existing, older formal and informal rules.[18] One's understanding and preferred approach(es) to a given issue will depend on the observer's changing and subjective context, which, in turn, may be shaped by dynamic social, political, and cultural structures.

This book therefore proposes to address the plural 'future*s*' *not* because the issues addressed have never arisen in any form before, but because the authors, drawing on their diverse backgrounds and contexts, consider that they are likely to continue emerging as prominent or relatively overlooked topics. Thus, the book incorporates and encourages interdisciplinary perspectives and approaches – including through engagement with international relations, politics, criminology, transitional justice, development, and other concepts and themes. This is also why contributors were not directed to adopt a 'reformist', problem-solving, or diagnostical approach *or* to apply distinctly 'critical' approaches. Instead, they tackle their respective subject matters in an inquiring manner, drawing on their preferred varied frameworks, methodologies, and experiences. As a result, the list of topics addressed is not comprehensive or predictive, but all are in their different ways important and novel and propose something about the variety of international criminal justice's futures.

2 The international criminal justice 'norm(s)' and its institutionalisation

Norms describe standards 'of appropriate behaviour for actors with a given identity'.[19] We consider that norms are dynamic, intersubjective, and shaped by ongoing engagement between agents, structures, and identities, including within institutions. The norms concerning international criminal justice are adapted by various government, military, legal, and other civil society actors. Whether a state's policy should promote ignoring, forgetting, celebrating, memorialising, or prosecuting atrocities is a contested decision and likely always will be. Yet there has been a tendency among scholars to identify a developing or evolving norm, which may really be a set of norms, that favour prosecutions and 'ending impunity' in such cases. These may be promoted alongside, though sometimes with priority over, other 'transitional justice' responses such as truth commissions, reparations, lustration, and memorial initiatives.[20] We see ending impunity through courts and tribunals as international criminal

18 ibid.

19 See Martha Finnemore and Kathryn Sikkink, 'International Norm Dynamics and Political Change' (1998) 52 *International Organization* 887, 891.

20 See Naomi Roht-Arriaza, 'Civil Society in Processes of Accountability' in M Cherif Bassiouni (ed), *Post-Conflict Justice* (Transnational Publishers 2002); Ruti G Teitel, *Transitional Justice* (OUP 2000).

justice's primary 'norm'. Moreover, this norm of international criminal justice gives prominence to particular institutional forms for such prosecution: courts and tribunals with international involvement – especially the ICC, even if as a 'last resort'. These apparent developments in international criminal law have been associated with apparently positive (but indistinct and contested) consequences – such as the promotion of the 'rule of law' or liberal democracy.[21]

As indicated earlier, in this essentially progressive and linear narrative, international criminal justice has evolved from ancient or medieval sources and post–World War II events, which offer it some precedence, towards the 'current' complex institutional network offered by the ICC and other international(ised) tribunals, in which the norm's 'justice cascade' promotes anti-impunity initiatives domestically.[22] Not only that, but specific courts or even individual trials associated with implementing that norm should therefore promote progressive aims (see later in this chapter). At least, that was the hope for many, and for some, the trajectory that was – or maybe still is – appearing to unfold.[23]

From 'here', the ICC's myriad troubles and the quandary of impunity in situations such as Syria or Myanmar are easily viewed as crises, possibly predictable but generally unfortunate, damaging, and at least worthy of ongoing critique. It is as if a bumpy but pleasing plotline has been interrupted by a sorry turn of events that was actually – it can now be seen – indicated by earlier clues but will still ultimately (or hopefully) end much more happily (though, to be sure, some anticipate a tragic finale). In other words, the 'future' of international criminal justice at this gripping moment, maybe even climax(?), *seems* unpredictable but inevitable. Observers can draw on previous events to extrapolate not only what conclusion might result but also how the story might get you there.

Yet notions about international criminal justice have a more complex relationship to history, time, and the future. This section offers five ways that the norm of international criminal justice and its institutionalisation suggest multiple and non-linear histories and trajectories, whereas the next canvasses the possible meaning of 'future' or 'futures' for international criminal law and jurisprudence, trials, and the 'intellectual project'.

21 Alexander Laban Hinton, *The Justice Facade: Trials of Transition in Cambodia* (OUP 2018); Rebecca Gidley, *Illiberal Transitional Justice and the Extraordinary Chambers in the Courts of Cambodia* (Palgrave 2019).

22 Kathryn Sikkink, *The Justice Cascade: How Human Rights Prosecutions are Changing World Politics* (WW Norton 2011).

23 Though many have argued otherwise – e.g., Hannah Arendt, Judith Shklar and, later, Gerry Simpson in 1997: Gerry J Simpson, 'War Crimes: A Critical Introduction' in Timothy LH McCormack and Gerry J Simpson (eds), *The Law of War Crimes: National and International Approaches* (Kluwer Law 1997). See also Simpson 'The Next Hundred Years' (n 1) 843; Mégret, this volume.

The first point is that the 'normalisation' of international criminal justice has never, really, been consistently 'progressive' in the sense of offering something universally positive. For many, there is a normative and instrumental aspect to international law. Martti Koskenniemi has observed that

> [f]or [the late former ICTY President Antonio] Cassese and countless other international lawyers, the field in which we have made our professional careers is more than just another technical discipline. It possesses an inbuilt moral direction to make human rights, justice and peace universal. To 'do' international law is to operate with a teleology that points from humankind's separation to unity.[24]

Similarly, and directed towards international *criminal* law, Frédéric Mégret in this volume notes that:

> In the dominant Kantian narrative, the ICC is primarily seen as the advent of a particular idea whose merit gradually imposes itself on states and becomes embodied in particular institutions. States' will and rationalities are important but seen as mere 'stepping-stones' to the realization of a higher and immanent purpose which fundamentally mandates the creation of the Court.[25]

At Tokyo, Justice Pal was concerned by the selectivity and politicisation of the post–World War II trials that followed and co-existed with colonialism. Accusations of 'victors justice' or partiality remain, even if altered by context so as to – for example – point towards African bias[26] or inequality of arms[27] or political interference (for instance, at the Extraordinary Chambers in the Courts of Cambodia [ECCC]). Shannon Maree Torrens explores the politicisation of the ICC by the United States in her contribution to this volume.[28] Likewise, Third World Approaches to International (Criminal) Law and feminist scholars and practitioners have long directed attention towards

24 Koskenniemi, 'Law, Teleology' (n 2) 4. See, e.g., Antonio Cassese, 'Gathering Up the Main Threads' in Antonio Cassese (ed), *Realizing Utopia: The Future of International Law* (OUP 2012).

25 Mégret, this volume, 28; see also Koskenniemi, 'Law, Teleology' (n 2) 5.

26 Kurt Mills and Alan Bloomfield, 'African Resistance to the International Criminal Court: Halting the Advance of the Anti-Impunity Norm' (2018) 44 *Review of International Studies* 101.

27 See Maria Igorevna Fedorova, *The Principle of Equality of Arms in International Criminal Proceedings* (Intersentia 2012).

28 Shannon Maree Torrens, 'Allegations of Political Interference, Bias and Corruption at the ECCC' in Simon Meisenberg and Ignaz Stegmiller (eds), *The Extraordinary Chambers in the Courts of Cambodia: Assessing Their Contribution to International Criminal Law* (TMC Asser Press 2016); Torrens, this volume.

the silenced, hidden, or overlooked histories and more recent practices of international criminal law that may even harm those it is most overtly tasked with protecting.[29] The jurisprudence of international criminal law might for some fail to support a wider range of convictions – for example, for sexual and gender-based violence – while also equally failing to do enough to protect the rights of the accused.

The second (and related) point is that the norm of international criminal justice is uneven or fragmented. It is enlivened by atrocity, by crimes that shock the conscience of humankind. Yet for political, economic, accessibility, or other reasons, only some atrocities are publicised or are recognised as such in public or political discourse.[30] Only some types of shocking violence or harm are classified as international crimes at a given time;[31] only some fall within the subject-matter, temporal, or territorial jurisdiction of particular courts;[32] and few will be investigated and pursued for reasons described as practical, financial, or discretionary.[33] At the same time, even because of these limits, international criminal justice is further propelled towards claiming only to deal with the exceptional and the 'most serious' – as Gerry Simpson puts it, the '"never before, never again" moment: the unprecedented atrocity, wrenched from history, that ends atrocity'.[34] 'The absence of trial might suggest, for lawyers especially, a past without a history; a history lacking a permanent juridical marker might suggest a past hardly worth remembering. But perhaps the act of not prosecuting or not remembering needs to be understood, too, as a form of international criminal

29 Antony Anghie and BS Chimni, 'Third World Approaches to International Law and Individual Responsibility in Internal Conflicts' (2003) 2 *Chinese Journal of International Law* 77; Burgis-Kasthala (n 11); Charlotte Epstein, 'The Postcolonial Perspective: An Introduction' (2014) 6 *International Theory* 294; Hilary Charlesworth and Christine Chinkin, *The Boundaries of International Law: A Feminist Analysis* (Manchester 2000); Gina Heathcote, *Feminist Dialogues on International Law: Successes, Tensions, Futures* (OUP 2019); Otto (n 10).

30 See the Judgment of Justice Pal in Akira Nakamura (ed), *International Military Tribunal for the Far East: Dissentient Judgment of Justice Pal* (Kokusho-Kankokai 1999).

31 Douglas Guilfoyle, 'Transnational Crimes' in Heller et al. (n 1); see, e.g., 'Co-Prosecutors' Request for the Trial Chamber to Recharacterise the Facts Establishing the Conduct of Rape as a Crime Against Humanity of Rape Rather Than the Crime Against Humanity of Other Inhumane Acts' *Prosecutor v Kaing Guek Eav alias Duch*, ECCC Case No 001, 16 June 2011 ('*Duch* Recharacterisation Decision').

32 'Decision Pursuant to Article 15 of the Rome Statute on the Authorisation of an Investigation into the Situation in the People's Republic of Bangladesh/Republic of the Union of Myanmar, Pre-Trial Chamber' *Situation in Bangladesh/Myanmar*, ICC-01/19–27, 14 November 2019.

33 See, for example, the Pre-Trial Chamber decision overturned in 'Judgment on the Appeal Against the Decision on the Authorisation of an Investigation into the Situation in the Islamic Republic of Afghanistan' *Situation in Afghanistan*, ICC-02/17–138, Appeals Chamber, 5 March 2020. See generally Catherine Gegout, 'The International Criminal Court: Limits, Potential and Conditions for the Promotion of Justice and Peace' (2013) 34 *Third World Quarterly* 800.

34 Simpson, 'Unprecedents' (n 12) 17.

law'.[35] In other words, international criminal justice is itself partial. Further, different states at different times will draft, implement, amend, revoke, and decry particular legal responses to different atrocity 'events'. These approaches can co-exist so that prosecutions for one period of history or one category of crimes or perpetrators might proceed, while others do not.[36] This piecemeal and intersecting reality is not obviously commensurate with an evolution towards one ideal or feared future. Instead, selective approaches co-exist for international criminal justice that lack a clear path.

Third, the institutionalisation of the norm in the form of establishing particular courts or tribunals that carry out trials is non-linear. There may be more numerous courts or tribunals with criminal jurisdiction over 'international crimes' today than, say, 50 years ago, and there may have been more prosecutions and convictions at such courts, but their successes and failures are in the eyes of their beholders. It is fair to say that the ICC has held a prominent role as the preeminent institutionalised protection mechanism to promote the prosecution of individuals for crimes against humanity, war crimes, genocide, and aggression.[37] Scholars have identified a 'justice cascade' associated with prosecutions, apparently correlated with improved domestic human rights practices.[38] Yet as Mégret cautions in this volume, we can also distinguish between the norm against the crimes themselves and the norm of establishing or promoting particular mechanisms for prosecuting them. The latter norm is far more contested than the former, and the range of institutional approaches towards responding to international crimes has been and remains diverse, even when focusing on prosecutorial courts and tribunals, though especially if also considering the full range of transitional justice and 'non' actions. There has also been talk of a 'local turn' or greater recognition and incorporation of 'local' or 'localised' responses to violence, including through the development of internationalised or 'hybrid' court structures,[39] though these have now been in use for many years (including with further decades-long historical reach in the case of the ECCC). Further, we must recall that apparently 'local' (non)responses to violence have been and are the actual norm for the majority, whose experiences of atrocity do not meet the gaze of the international

35 ibid. 24.
36 Lisbeth Zimmermann, 'Same Same or Different? Norm Diffusion Between Resistance, Compliance, and Localization in Post-Conflict States' (2016) 17 *International Studies Perspectives* 98; Palmer (n 1).
37 Struett (n 3).
38 Sikkink, *The Justice Cascade* (n 22); Kathryn Sikkink and Hun Joon Kim, 'The Justice Cascade: The Origins and Effectiveness of Prosecutions of Human Rights Violations' (2013) 9 *Annual Review of Law and Social Science* 26.
39 Philipp Kastner, this volume; Rosalind Shaw and Lars Waldorf, 'Introduction: Localizing Transitional Justice' in Rosalind Shaw, Lars Waldorf, and Pierre Hazan (eds), *Localizing Transitional Justice: Interventions and Priorities After Mass Violence* (Stanford University Press 2010) 3; Adam Kochanski, 'The "Local Turn" in Transitional Justice: Curb the Enthusiasm' (2020) 22 *International Studies Review* 26; Palmer, *Adapting International Criminal Justice in Southeast Asia* (n 1).

architecture. As Philipp Kastner (this volume) points out: 'pigeon-holing these tribunals into four neat phases – from Nuremberg and Tokyo (1) to the *ad hoc* tribunals (2), the hybrid tribunals (3) and the ICC (4) would suggest an unduly linear development that, moreover, does not facilitate a creative and critical consideration of the enforcement dimension of international criminal law'.[40]

Even more recently, hope is placed in expanded centralised UN fact-finding and evidence-gathering mechanisms, such as the International Independent and Impartial Mechanism for Syria (IIIM), Independent Investigation Mechanism for Myanmar (IIMM), and the more temporary Independent International Fact-Finding Mission on Myanmar – the titles of which promote their independence and link it to their internationalism. These bodies might support future trials while also finding precedence in earlier commissions and responses where 'actual courts' were not yet available or likely to prosecute. Arguably, 'Time and again' fact-finding missions document abuses to compel a 'legal or moral conclusion: that these acts are so horrific' that they demand trials, and then such measures are taken.[41] The IIIM and IIMM mandates and policies support international as well as domestic prosecutions and wider non-criminal aims (see later in this chapter).

Meanwhile, some tribunals such as the SCSL, ICTY, ICTR, and ECCC 'wind up' or approach their 'completion'; trials proceed in differently international settings (MICT) or within domestic court settings, alongside a 'new' focus on the 'legacy' of such courts. A debate (sometimes political – in the case of Cambodia, for instance)[42] about what counts or should be considered as a legacy project invites questions about tribunals' impact on post-conflict societies, the rule of law (especially where domestic trials are expected to take over), international criminal law jurisprudence, the rights of those convicted, and the longer-term role of reparations.[43] Alongside the dual historicism and future orientation of 'legacy', the institutionalisation of international criminal justice jumps in multiple directions at once, with a variety of futures already on offer.

40 Kastner, this volume, 78, with reference to Harold Hongju Koh, 'International Criminal Justice 5.0' (2013) 38 *Yale Journal of International Law* 525; Philipp Kastner, 'Hybrid Tribunals: Institutional Experiments and the Potential for Creativity Within International Criminal Law' in Philipp Kastner (ed), *International Criminal Law in Context* (Routledge 2018).

41 Fletcher (n 5) 702.

42 Tessa Bialek, 'Legacy at the Extraordinary Chambers in the Courts of Cambodia: Research Overview' *DC Cam* (2013), <http://d.dccam.org/Tribunal/Analysis/pdf/Legacy_FINAL.pdf> accessed 4 June 2020; Viviane E Dittrich, 'The Legacy of the ECCC' in Simon M Meisenberg and Ignaz Stegmiller (eds), *The Extraordinary Chambers in the Courts of Cambodia: Assessing Their Contribution to International Criminal Law* (Springer 2016).

43 Bialek (n 42); Dittrich (n 42); Office of the High Commissioner of Human Rights, 'Promotion of ECCC Legacy' <https://cambodia.ohchr.org/en/rule-of-law/promotion-eccc-legacy> accessed 4 June 2020; International Criminal Tribunal for Rwanda, 'A Compendium on the Legacy of the ICTR and the Development of International Law' <https://unictr.irmct.org/en/compendium-legacy-ictr-and-development-international-law> accessed 4 June 2020.

This collection was influenced by the work of Jennifer Trahan in relation to futures thinking and international criminal justice. She has interviewed a number of practitioners and scholars working in the 'field' of international criminal law, where she presented possible 'future' scenarios and asked related questions – for instance, 'What would the ICC of the future look like?' and what would be its key challenges.[44] Some (particularly ICC officials) thought that the ICC would remain the dominant institution for prosecuting international crimes, at least in the subsequent 20 years, despite acknowledging its limitations. However, others expected a greater role for '*ad hoc*', hybrid, or domestic trials or a combination of all institutional frameworks (or a retreat from one or all of these). Many interviewees anticipated 'multiple tiers of prosecutions in any country that requires such a robust approach to justice'.[45] Thus, the prominence of various mechanisms for responding to so-called international crimes, both past and emerging, continues to evolve, while the focus and structure of the ICC and other international criminal tribunals remain subject to debate and reconsideration.

The fourth point concerns the relationship between international criminal justice, transitional justice, and notions of transformative justice – as well as development and peacebuilding. In other words, what is the association between international criminal justice and societies? Prosecutions have often been given prominence or even priority over other transitional justice responses, yet there are both reasons for this and reasons to question whether such priority is always accorded. Both relate to how international criminal justice can be understood as a temporal exercise. In terms of the purpose of focusing on prosecutions (and especially convictions), it helps to recall one of the histories of transitional justice, in which this field emerged from events in Latin America and South Africa. There,

> [c]riminal sanctioning of past leaders was to not only remove them from political power, but also to signal an irrevocable break with the past by demonstrating that no one was above the law and providing healing for victims. . . . Countries turned to truth commissions and lustration or vetting when political exigencies precluded criminal prosecutions and thus were seen as second best alternatives.[46]

While concepts of justice were broader and transitional justice gathered a wide range of tools, these origins arguably continued to push criminal justice as at least an essential one of those tools, possibly the 'best' one.[47] But that was not the only reason.

44 Trahan, 'Views of the Future' (n 4).
45 ibid., 935.
46 Fletcher (n 5) 705; Catherine Turner, 'Deconstructing Transitional Justice' (2013) 24 *Law and Critique* 193.
47 Susan Harris Rimmer, *Gender and Transitional Justice: The Women of East Timor* (Routledge 2010) 19.

Criminal prosecutions were also thought to serve other valuable goals for post-conflict societies. They might punish perpetrators, certainly, and remove dangerous individuals from ongoing positions of political power (which might benefit democracy and any peace process), but the trials themselves might contribute to the rule of law,[48] and all this might help 'transition' the society towards a liberal, peaceful, capitalist, and eventually self-reliant, economy.[49] On the other hand, the 'peace versus justice' debate questioned whether amnesties or other responses might produce 'better' – more peaceful or at least stable – outcomes for society.[50] Meanwhile, transitional justice scholars have critiqued these assumptions, pointing out that the outcomes of justice might be illiberal[51] while peace might be associated with 'non-truth and reconciliation'.[52]

The critique of an emphasis upon prosecutions has invited a range of responses,[53] one of which is the promotion of 'transformative justice'. This might redress structural inequalities via reform,[54] whether through adjusted trial processes – for instance, by engaging victims and reparations mandates (though the potential for this is limited)[55] – or a wider and more ambitious approach towards transitional

48 Fletcher (n 5) 70; contrast Peter J Boettke and Christopher J Coyne, 'The Political Economy of Forgiveness' (2007) 44(2) *Society* 53, 59.

49 See Hinton (n 21); Gidley (n 21); Fletcher (n 5) 712; Laurel E Fletcher, Harvey M Weinstein, and Jamie Rowen, 'Context, Timing and the Dynamics of Transitional Justice: A Historical Perspective' (2009) 31 *Human Rights Quarterly* 163; Lisa J Laplante, 'Transitional Justice and Peace Building: Diagnosing and Addressing the Socioeconomic Roots of Violence Through a Human Rights Framework' (2008) 2 *International Journal of Transitional Justice* 331.

50 Palmer, this volume; Rénee Jeffery, 'Amnesty and Accountability: The Price of Peace in Aceh, Indonesia' (2012) 6 *International Journal of Transitional Justice* 60; Louise Mallinder, 'Can Amnesties and International Justice be Reconciled?' (2007) 1 *International Journal of Transitional Justice* 208. On the relationship between peace and international criminal justice, see Frédéric Mégret, 'International Criminal Justice as a Peace Project' (2018) 29 *European Journal of International Law* 835; Janine N Clark, 'Peace, Justice and the International Criminal Court: Limitations and Possibilities' (2011) 9 *Journal of International Criminal Justice* 521.

51 Gidley (n 21).

52 John Braithwaite, Valerie Braithwaite, Michael Cookson and Leah Dunn, *Anomie and Violence: Non-Truth and Reconciliation in Indonesian Peacebuilding* (ANU E-Press 2010); compare Catherine Renshaw, 'Myanmar's Genocide and the Legacy of Forgetting' (2020) 48 *Georgia Journal International & Comparative Law* 425.

53 See Palmer, this volume.

54 Wendy Lambourne, 'Transformative Justice, Reconciliation and Peacebuilding' in S Buckley Zistel, TK Beck, C Braun, and F Mieth (eds), *Transitional Justice Theories* (Routledge 2014); Wendy Lambourne, 'Transitional Justice and Peacebuilding After Mass Violence' (2009) 3 *International Journal of Transitional Justice* 28.

55 See Andrea Durbach and Louise Chappell, 'Leaving Behind the Age of Impunity' (2014) 16 *International Feminist Journal of Politics* 543; Killean, this volume; Sarah Williams and Emma Palmer, 'Transformative Reparations for Women and Girls at the Extraordinary Chambers in the Courts of Cambodia' (2016) 10 *International Journal of Transitional Justice* 31.

justice.[56] 'Transformation' implies a more fundamental 'transformation in structures and institutions that enable the continuation of human rights violations'.[57] Arguably, responses to atrocity in the vast majority of cases have long encouraged weaker interpretations of transformation, including via promoting significant economic and structural reforms alongside prosecutions – but these actions are aimed at producing liberal capitalist goals such as the rule of law and economic growth rather than wealth redistribution.[58]

The approach of some United Nations organs to violence and conflict reveals a wider range of responses than prosecution. For instance, the 2030 Agenda for Sustainable Development promotes a

> comprehensive approach to sustaining peace, particularly through the *prevention of conflict and addressing its root causes*, strengthening the rule of law at the international and national levels, and promoting sustained and *sustainable economic growth* . . . national reconciliation. . . *access to justice and transitional justice*.[59]

In particular, Sustainable Development Goal 16 promotes equal access to justice for all, while Goal 5 aims to end all forms of discrimination against women and girls. These future-oriented development goals are related to justice. In fact, the IIIM for Syria explicitly aims to foster SDG Goals 5 and 16.[60]

Moreover, the United Nations Security Council has not always (recently, notably in relation to Syria and Myanmar) taken tangible steps to ensure the application of international criminal justice as opposed to promoting other goals – even if it has referred some cases to the ICC,[61] though without financial support. For example, UN Security Council resolutions in 2019 (often building on earlier language) suggested a potentially positive relationship (or nexus) between development, peacebuilding, and humanitarian responses. In relation to Afghanistan, the Security Council supported 'regional cooperation . . . to promot[e] stability and

56 Roger Duthie, 'Toward a Development-Sensitive Approach to Transitional Justice' (2008) 2 *International Journal of Transitional Justice* 292.

57 Wendy Lambourne and Vivianna Rodriguez Carreon, 'Engendering Transitional Justice: A Transformative Approach to Building Peace and Attaining Human Rights for Women' (2015) 17 *Human Rights Review* 71.

58 René Urueña and María A Prada-Uribe, 'Transitional Justice and Economic Policy' (2018) 14 *Annual Review of Law and Social Science* 397; Geoff Dancy and Eric Wiebelhaus-Brahm, 'Bridge to Human Development or Vehicle of Inequality? Transitional Justice and Economic Structures' (2015) 9 *International Journal of Transitional Justice* 51.

59 UNSC Res 2282 (27 April 2016) UN Doc S/RES/2282 (emphasis added).

60 UNGA, 'Report of the International, Impartial and Independent Mechanism to Assist in the Investigation and Prosecution of Persons Responsible for the Most Serious Crimes Under International Law Committed in the Syrian Arab Republic Since March 2011' (13 February 2019) UN Doc A/73/741, para. 33.

61 Fletcher (n 5).

peace . . . to advance shared goals of *economic development* across the region'[62] and, for Mali, suggested that 'lasting peace and security . . . will not be achieved without a combination of political, security and development efforts' with a particular focus on 'sustainable development',[63] and similar calls for 'sustainable development and recovery and reconstruction' in Iraq.[64] The Security Council acknowledges that 'social, political, and economic development is crucial to achieving lasting stability', as expressed in another 2019 resolution regarding Haiti.[65]

There is also reference in Security Council resolutions and debates about the 'root causes' of international crimes and human rights violations.[66] Underdevelopment is often posed as a core 'root cause' of conflict and humanitarian catastrophe, which then leads to the commission of international crimes. For instance, a 2019 resolution reaffirmed the Peace, Security and Cooperation Framework for the Democratic Republic of the Congo (DRC), 'in order to address the root causes of conflict and put an end to recurring cycles of violence, and promote lasting regional development'.[67] Likewise, the Security Council affirmed that 'development can support a lasting peace in Darfur'.[68] To do this, the Council indicated, development policies should 'promote reconciliation initiatives'.[69] What was needed in Afghanistan was said to be a 'comprehensive approach to address the security, economic, governance and development challenges', consistent with 'advancing sustainable development and stability', particularly via increasing foreign investment and infrastructure development.[70]

There are fewer Security Council resolutions linking *justice*, particularly international criminal justice, to peace and development. Still, generally, these are presented as complementary goals. For instance, in 2019 the Security Council condemned international crimes[71] in the DRC, '*recognizing* their deleterious effect on the stabilisation, reconstruction and development efforts' and '*emphasizing* that all acts of violence must be investigated and those responsible . . . swiftly brought to justice'.[72] In another resolution, consolidating peace was said to require, together, 'the promotion of socioeconomic development and the fight

62 UNSC Res 2489 (17 September 2019) UN Doc S/RES/2489 (emphasis added). See also UNSC Res 2405 (8 March 2018) UN Doc S/RES 2405.
63 UNSC Res 2480 (28 June 2019) UN Doc S/RES/2480.
64 UNSC Res 2470 (21 May 2019) UN Doc S/RES/2470.
65 UNSC Res 2476 (25 June 2019) UN Doc S/RES/2476.
66 See Palmer, this volume.
67 UNSC Res 2463 (29 March 2019) UN Doc S/RES/2463.
68 UNSC Res 2429 (13 July 2018) UN Doc S/RES/2429.
69 UNSC Res 2448 (13 December 2018) UN Doc S/RES/2448; UNSC Res 2301 (26 July 2016) UN Doc S/RES 2301.
70 UNSC Res 2405 (8 March 2018) UN Doc S/RES/2405. See Daria Davitti, *Investment and Human Rights in Armed Conflict: Charting an Elusive Intersection* (Hart 2019).
71 Such as 'targeted attacks against civilians, widespread sexual and gender-based violence, recruitment and use of child soldiers' and forced displacement.
72 UNSC Res 2463 (29 March 2019) UN Doc S/RES/2463, underlined emphasis added.

against impunity'.[73] Overall, according to various resolutions and statements, 'human rights, the rule of law and democracy'[74] and also 'human rights, peace and security and development, are deeply interlinked and mutually reinforcing'.[75] Conflict is said to 'hinder the transition from relief to stabilization to development activities',[76] disrupting the otherwise apparently natural progression towards development, which would be supported by justice. Thus, as Emma Palmer discusses in this volume, while UN Security Council resolutions do *not* tend to connect international criminal justice or transitional justice to wider reform or transformative (future) aims directly, they *do* tie justice to goals of peace, which are, in turn, linked to development.

In reality, the potential for international criminal justice to achieve the goals of peace, deterrence, redistribution of wealth, and broader 'human development' aims – whether via liberal capitalist *or* more 'transformative' approaches – is beyond the scope of this volume.[77] The relationship between justice and its societal effects is complex. Any doubts about the potential for prosecutions to generate positive transformations might invite what appear to be more practical or 'realist' positions.[78] However, as Kastner discusses in this volume, the 'pragmatic' promotion of societal 'resilience' to violence holds risks. As he argues:

> [I]n the new paradigm of pragmatism and resilience thinking, it has become even more evident that seeking justice cannot be an end in itself; rather, ending a culture of impunity is now considered an instrument to achieve a higher end. In fact, a pragmatic emphasis on the future and on the preparation of individuals and communities for violent events stands in stark contrast to the very idea that engaging with and seeking accountability for past crimes can be useful and, for instance, help envisage a more peaceful future. Disconnecting the past from the future, as promoted by resilience thinking, even risks making every justice-seeking endeavour appear redundant.[79]

A resilience-oriented approach might be contrasted to those aiming to address the 'root causes' of violence via human development–oriented measures. Instead,

73 UNSC Res 2404 (28 February 2018) UN Doc S/RES/2404.
74 'Declaration of the High-Level Meeting of the General Assembly on the Rule of Law at the National and International Levels' UNGA Res 67/1 (30 November 2012) UN Doc A/RES/67/1.
75 United Nations and the Rule of Law, 'Sustainable Development Goal 16' <www.un.org/ruleoflaw/sdg-16/> accessed 11 May 2021; UNSC Res 1016 (5 December 2017) UN Doc S/RES/1016. See also statements in UN Security Council, 'Security Council Stresses Concern at Increasing Global Military Expenditures, Urges States to Devote "As Many Resources as Possible" to Development' (19 November 2008) UN Doc SC/9501.
76 UNSC Res 2302 (29 June 2016) UN Doc S/RES/2302.
77 Mark Drumbl, *Atrocity, Punishment and International Law* (CUP 2007).
78 See Mégret, this volume.
79 See Kastner, this volume, 82.

as Susan Harris Rimmer, Emma Palmer, and Edwin Bikundo conclude in this volume, a focus on *preventing* violence – through a range of policy measures – might be the more transformative approach than justice alone. Yet prevention sits uneasily upon a linear plotline of post-justice futures.

Fifth, the international criminal trial process itself presents different narratives and expressive goals than perhaps anticipated or prescribed by the evolutionary perspective of the international criminal justice norm.[80] As discussed earlier, law – especially for common lawyers – draws upon precedent. Moreover, not only must the application of international criminal law and establishment of related mechanisms be supported by precedent politically, but to do so, the situation also must be arguably 'unprecedented'.[81] Meanwhile, the Rome Statute's sources of international criminal law do not require subservience to earlier jurisprudence, but the principle of legality is to be preserved (which is occasionally problematic for the project),[82] and trials will concern and even seek to remedy past events. In this way,

> [l]aw constructs its universals in an intensely historical way: it looks both backwards and forwards in time so that a prima facie plausible resolution of a legal problem ought to take account of what has taken place in the past (to be used as evidence) and how it might affect the future (as precedent). Legal argument creates a temporal sequence in which the past informs the present, while the future serves as the ideal of the present, its standard of criticism.[83]

On the other hand, international criminal justice does not necessarily redeem the present or future in practice. As discussed, it can fail to address many forms of violence. Still, in rare but notable cases, it might reveal evidence of *other* pasts and of different and ongoing forms of violence, including the harms perpetuated by the trial process itself. Drawing on Walter Benjamin, Hannah Franzki argues that

> [i]mages of the past . . . are either invoked as negative reference in order to authorise the present order, or appear in trials in a way that sheds light on the

80 Maria Elander, *Figuring Victims in International Criminal Justice: The Case of the Khmer Rouge Tribunal* (Routledge 2018); Carsten Stahn, *Justice as Message: Expressivist Foundations of International Criminal Justice* (OUP 2020); Barrie Sander, 'The Expressive Turn of International Criminal Justice: A Field in Search of Meaning' (2019) 32 *Leiden Journal of International Law* 851.

81 Simpson, 'Unprecedents' (n 12).

82 See in relation to prosecuting rape as a crime against humanity, '*Duch* Recharacterisation Decision' (n 31); Rachel Killean, 'An Incomplete Narrative: Prosecuting Sexual Violence Crimes at the Extraordinary Chambers in the Courts of Cambodia' (2015) 13 *Journal of International Criminal Justice* 331; Sarah Williams and Emma Palmer, 'The Extraordinary Chambers in the Courts of Cambodia: Developing the Law on Sexual Violence?' (2015) 15 *International Criminal Law Review* 452.

83 Koskenniemi, 'Law, Teleology' (n 2) 23.

> continuities between past and present, thereby destabilising the claim of the present order to be the non-violent answer to the violent past.[84]

For instance, witness intimidation in Kenya and the former Yugoslavia is exhibited by the trial process. In Cambodia, the ECCC judgments in *Case 002/01* and *Case 002/02* presented a particular version of the Cold War past that contrasted with that offered by the defence.[85] Witness and victim testimony about forced marriages prompted changed prosecutorial approaches while revealing the violence and barriers that had prevented trials from confronting these issues earlier or adequately.[86] In other words, sometimes the persistence of the past – for example, via colonial and heteronormative structures – means that trials have the 'ability to expose the foundational violence of the present juridico-political order' and thereby to 'expose not only the violence of the past, but also that of the present, thereby opening it anew for contestation'.[87] As Koskenniemi observes a little differently, international law 'offers a continuing self-interpretation to society in terms of what has taken place in the past and how society sees its own future'.[88]

Despite these reasons to doubt that the norm of international criminal justice evolves in any linear or progressive manner, and there are surely more,[89] many still hope for a happy end to the ICL story – whatever that may represent for them. The temptation to find its redeeming qualities can be almost 'inescapable' as even critical scholars search for ways that law can be used instrumentally.[90] Again, to draw on Koskenniemi, '[l]aw has a never-ending character (as political decisionmakers sometimes despairingly notice). It makes it possible to constantly produce new interpretations of its rules and prior judgments, thus cultivating the gap between the institutional present and the legal ideal'.[91] Within this 'gap', one may hope for a particular future while recognising that multiple histories persist while multiple futures are both possible and may co-occur.[92] In that context, we now turn to what 'futures' and 'newness' might mean in relation to international criminal justice.

84 Franzki (n 11) 17.
85 'Judgement' *Prosecutor v Nuon Chea and Khieu Samphan*, ECCC Case No 002/01, 7 August 2014; 'Judgement' *Prosecutor v Nuon Chea and Khieu Samphan*, ECCC Case No 002/02, 16 November 2018.
86 See also Rosemary Grey, *Prosecuting Sexual and Gender-Based Crimes at the International Criminal Court: Practice, Progress and Potential* (CUP 2019).
87 Franzki (n 11) 3–4.
88 Koskenniemi, 'Law, Teleology' (n 2) 23.
89 Including the different localised and regional experiences and interpretations of international criminal law and the complexity of defining 'global' and 'local' despite their evident intersections; see discussion in Palmer, *Adapting International Criminal Justice in Southeast Asia* (n 1).
90 Koskenniemi, 'Law, Teleology' (n 2) 6.
91 ibid., 21.
92 See the tendency to combine the list of future options in Trahan, 'Views of the Future' (n 4).

3 The futures and newness of international criminal justice

This section explains how we understand the concept of 'futures' in relation to international criminal justice. The future (in Western thought particularly)[93] can be defined as 'the time that will come after the present or the events that will happen then'.[94] Both aspects are relevant in this volume, and for the reasons described, we consider there to be multiple pasts, presents, and futures, depending on one's perspective.[95]

We consider the concept of 'future' to be related to ideas about what is 'new' and recent, as well as what is 'old'. In that regard, we find it productive to draw upon both Louise Chappell's and Rosemary Grey's feminist historical institutionalist–inspired approaches towards analysing gender justice issues in the ICC.[96] They propose that new rules of behaviour may be situated within older formal and informal 'rules of the game', meaning that futures may be diverse and plural but nested within the 'stickiness' of dynamic structures.[97] Feminist institutionalists consider that

> not only are the formal aspects – the formal 'rules of the game' and their enforcement – crucial but the informal aspects of institutions – the norms, rules, and practices – often less visible or even passing unnoticed or taken for granted by actors inside and outside of those institutions, are also central.[98]

As Fiona Mackay has observed in relation to promoting gender justice, by 'successfully intervening to insert new actors, new values, and new rules into new institutions, reformers may profoundly influence the future developments of an institution'.[99] However, these 'new' occurrences 'must contend with organizational and institutional legacies and path dependencies, with unintended consequences of design decisions, and with ongoing institutional dynamics with

93 See Renshaw (n 52) 447, regarding Buddhist thought concerning how 'the past and future do not exist' discussing the consequences of 'forgetting' atrocities in Myanmar.

94 AS Hornby, M Ashby, and S Wehmeier, *Oxford Advanced Learner's Dictionary of Current English* (OUP 2000).

95 See Annelise Riles, 'The View from the International Plane: Perspective and Scale in the Architecture of Colonial International Law' (1995) 6 *Law and Critique* 39.

96 Louise Chappell, *The Politics of Gender Justice at the International Criminal Court: Legacies and Legitimacy* (OUP 2016); Grey, *Prosecuting Sexual and Gender-Based Crimes at the International Criminal Court* (n 86). See also Louise Chappell, 'Conflicting Institutions and the Search for Gender Justice at the International Criminal Court' (2013) 67 *Political Research Quarterly* 183; Emma Palmer and Sarah Williams, 'A "Shift in Attitude"? Institutional Change and Sexual and Gender-Based Crimes at the Extraordinary Chambers in the Courts of Cambodia' (2017) 19 *International Feminist Journal of Politics* 22.

97 See Mackay (n 17).

98 Georgia Waylen, 'Informal Institutions, Institutional Change, and Gender Equality' (2013) 67 *Political Research Quarterly* 212, 213.

99 Mackay (n 17) 549.

the wider environment'. Thus, '[n]ested newness is a metaphor used to capture the ways in which the new is embedded in time, sequence, and its institutional environment'.[100]

Importantly, 'institution' here does not necessarily refer to the ICC or a particular court but the logics that underlay international criminal justice more broadly. The formal and informal institutions of international criminal justice are influenced by a variety of actors in multiple locations. In that context, we anticipate that considering the 'futures' of international criminal justice involves analysis of various pasts and conceptions of the present – as promoted both formally (in laws and policies) and informally (in common practices and norms)[101] – within which those futures will be situated. As Chappell puts it, '[t]he ICC is nested in both time and space',[102] as is, we think, international criminal justice.

This does not mean that the futures of international criminal justice are predictable or that we or other contributors to this volume offer predictions. We do not, even if here and there, some ideas about possible futures are offered. However, we do propose that those futures will share some relationship to the past, or rather pasts. Yet if the futures on offer are nested within the past, is international criminal law 'over'? 'Of course, new proposals continue to be advanced (the ILC's crimes against humanity draft, a criminal tribunal for Liberia) but international criminal tribunals don't feel like the future'.[103] Rather, such mechanisms might reflect (at least aspects of) 'old' precedents – whether for procedural rules, problems, and forms of domination, despite efforts to inject 'new' policies that, just for instance, promote environmental sustainability or gender equality.[104] Still, we recall the analysis in the previous section to propose that existing structures offer 'stickiness' but not predetermination.

This corresponds to other assessments of the past of international criminal justice in relation to its even earlier precedents. For instance, Simpson observes that, against the history of international criminal law,

> the actual future was a rather haphazard affair. For sure, major Axis leaders were hanged in Tokyo and in Nuremberg . . . and villainous deeds committed during the war were prosecuted. But war crimes trials since then have happened only in jumps and starts, and not often in the places envisaged by the peacemakers at Versailles. No-one in 1919 could have predicted that the future of international criminal law would be found in, among other places, the District Court of Jerusalem or the Bow Street Magistrates' Court or the Rhone Cour d'Assises.[105]

100 ibid., 552.
101 Chappell, 'Conflicting Institutions' (n 96) 184.
102 Chappell, *The Politics of Gender Justice* (n 96) 29.
103 Simpson, 'The Next Hundred Years' (n 1) 842.
104 On the possibility (or not) for crisis to facilitate progressive consequences, see Otto (n 10).
105 Simpson, 'The Next Hundred Years' (n 1) 842.

Observers, then, might have hoped for something like the ICC, and the establishment of that court was embedded in these and subsequent experiences,[106] but the laws, mechanisms, and practices of transitional justice are multiple and subjective. And perhaps this is for the best, if the 'concrete realization' of particular plans 'always involves some distribution of power, and with it, some privileging of preferences and values'.[107]

Thus, we do not offer prescriptions for the future of international criminal justice, and COVID-19 reminds us of the perils of doing so. Rather, our contributors do offer hopes and proposals, derived (openly) from their particular experiences, interests, and perspectives. We do not ask that they 'provide ideas and float proposals which could act as "midwives" for social and legal change'[108] and propose no ' "radiant future" – a future that would never arrive but for which the present would nevertheless be sacrificed'.[109] Nor do we necessarily believe that 'the future of international criminal law is an important matter, closely linked to the development in all sectors of our global village',[110] whereas, for example, we agree that the 'empowerment of women is a precondition for international peace and security – and for justice'.[111] Indeed, we think it possible (and possibly desirable) that a range of futures be imagined in which international criminal law does not form the central focus. Instead, rather than a 'stock-taking' of that history[112] or directions for its future,[113] this volume offers a set of discussions for international criminal justice's challenges and opportunities, for a number of its futures.

4 Overview of the book

In keeping with the idea that international criminal justice has multiple futures, the chapters in this book address a range of issues that are not necessarily consistent with one another and may be more or less likely. They present visions and practical suggestions for international criminal justice that deal with the ICC and its political context, the array of other institutional structures and priorities (including preventing crimes), and jurisprudential developments in the areas of the environment, medical experimentation, technology, and modes of liability. In doing so, the chapters highlight the tensions between 'international' and 'universal' notions of justice and its contexts and subjects, as these evolve over time.

106 See Hans Corell, 'The Future of International Criminal Law Looking Back at Nuremberg' (2016) 49 *Studies in Transnational Legal Policy* 27.
107 Martti Koskenniemi, 'The Subjective Dangers of Projects of World Community' in Cassese (ed) (n 24) 12.
108 Cassese (n 24) 683.
109 See Koskenniemi, 'Projects of World Community' (n 107) 12, referring to Vladimir Zinoviev.
110 Corell (n 106) 43.
111 ibid. 43.
112 Simpson, 'The Next Hundred Years' (n 1) 842.
113 Corell (n 106). See generally the essays in Cassese (ed) (n 24), particularly Jérome de Hemptinne, 'The Future of International Criminal Justice: A Blueprint for Action'.

The first chapters address the ICC and how it engages with states. Mégret argues for a reinterpretation of the ICC's purposes and – consequently – its positioning and even governance. Given the likelihood that the Rome Statute will not be ratified 'universally' (by all states) in the near term, there are advantages to conceptualising the Court as almost a regional-type institution or 'alliance', with greater engagement with and by its states parties. Stepping away from 'universality' and aspirations of representing an 'international community' need not represent a capitulation, but a realistic perspective of its place within a more limited and contested community.

Torrens observes that states, focusing on non-parties and particularly the United States, have engaged and continue to engage politically with the Court. She demonstrates that this can involve adopting the posture of 'the Decider', as if 'they' (states' representatives) control international criminal justice – and, in fact, this may involve exerting some power, such as denying visas. However, this attitude or projection of power – as being 'the Decider' – has an essentially defensive and insecure quality. If states parties and court personnel can understand this posturing in this manner, they might avoid deferring to illusions of power and recognise the opportunity such deflections might present.

Looking beyond the ICC and the institutional forms open to international criminal justice since the 'first wave' of hybrid or internationalised tribunals, Kastner analyses the so-called 'local turn' and more recent generation of adaptive mechanisms said to promote 'resilience', local agency, and self-help, focusing on the Special Criminal Court in the Central African Republic. He argues that while the language of 'resilience' is now pervasive in international development and peacebuilding circles, it has not been an overt focus of international criminal justice scholarship. This is the case even though its institutions are embedded within many of the logics of resilience, including assumptions that internationalised tribunals encourage 'local ownership' and might improve national 'rule of law' capacity. In reality, he argues, the meaning of 'local' and the actual extent of 'local' engagement (which may be symbolic or superficial) with respect to internationalised tribunals is less clear. Likewise, any emphasis on 'resilience' that disconnects the present from past and future international crimes can mask or fail to combat structural drivers of conflict and atrocities.

More broadly, international criminal justice institutions form part of intersecting approaches to situations of past and ongoing violence, including within sites close to the violence, as well as farther away in international fora and United Nations organs. Development approaches are often posed as complementary to typically past-focused prosecutorial initiatives, while – picking up on Kastner's point – prosecutions are sometimes suggested to favour liberal aims, including promoting the rule of law, with wider judicial and governance benefits. Palmer's contribution identifies a 'development and/versus justice' debate with respect to Myanmar, which forms part of the well-known 'peace versus justice' discussion but is distinct in its language and proposals. The relationship between international criminal justice and future-oriented development projects is complex, including (or especially) in the Myanmar context, where conflicts have long roots and persist.

International criminal justice involves the application of international criminal law, which continues to be developed by international criminal courts and tribunals. As hinted earlier, this area of law is both young and has older roots and must deal with apparently 'new' challenges – and be called upon to address persistent forms of violence differently in the future. Several examples of these tensions are explored in this volume. Rachel Killean tackles both aspects, arguing that the ICC's reparations framework could respond to the persistent and growing harms of environmental destruction through several more and less ambitious avenues. This includes considering reparations that recognise environmental harm, as well as adopting an 'eco-sensitive' and transformative approach to the design and (in future) monitoring of reparations for other types of harms.

By contrast, Bikundo addresses another arguably 'old' category of crimes: medical experimentation, which was, however, left out of the explicit categories of crimes against humanity other than 'other inhumane acts' post-Nuremberg. In order to adequately recognise and address this crime in the future, and by analysing the jurisprudence and approach of the ECCC, Bikundo argues this apparent historic oversight might be remedied via the future (re-)alignment of international criminal law with its origins, by the explicit inclusion of a standalone offence in a specialised convention or an amendment to the Rome Statute.

Both the contributions of Eve Massingham and Simon McKenzie and of Natalie Nunn address the challenges of ensuring accountability for potential crimes committed through the use of a new technological development: automated weapons systems that have minimal or no direct human control. Such weapons may operate 'with some distance in space and time' from a human's decision to deploy them[114] while accountability initiatives must necessarily be focused on the intentions and expectations of manufacturers about what the weapons will do or how likely particular outcomes, such as civilian deaths, might be avoided. Massingham and McKenzie argue that an existing legal mechanism, states' obligations under international humanitarian law to carry out weapons reviews, can ensure that such weapons are used effectively and contribute to legal compliance, accountability, and securing evidence (including of the requisite mental elements, such as intent) for international criminal law prosecutions. Nunn suggests that if human control over automated weapons systems is not mandated, and for systems that do not have such control, new forms of liability will be required to ensure accountability for their use. She argues for the extension of a *dolus eventualis*, or recklessness standard, for the commission of war crimes by such systems, alongside a strict liability– (product liability–) type standard for manufacturers and programmers.

It may be challenging to prosecute the crimes of non–human controlled weapons, but there have long been controversies associated with prosecuting international crimes committed by groups of individuals, or 'collective entities'. Anna

114 Massingham and McKenzie, this volume, 184.

Marie Brennan shows how prosecutions have been especially challenging when the members of non-state armed groups do not form part of a clear command structure, or the adaptive and dynamic nature of such groupings renders it difficult to identify which individuals specifically performed particular elements of a crime. While international criminal law has focused on individual liability, in these cases, there may be reason to seek to prosecute the entity itself (as in some domestic jurisdictions that have adopted international crimes laws that explicitly address the liability of corporations, for example). Brennan argues that complexity theory helps explain how collective entities may not be reduced to their individual members. The argument follows that international criminal law must be reoriented to more appropriately address the criminality of groups.

Finally, Harris Rimmer, Palmer, and Bikundo return to the multiple futures of international criminal justice, testing this approach against recent seismic events. While this conclusion argues that the pasts and futures of international criminal justice are plural and intersecting, it seeks to identify what some of these 'futures' might mean or look like. We note the normativity involved in undertaking such a task without promoting linear colonial understandings of time; 'seeing' certain accounts as favouring *particular* futures; and even assuming that any future at all may exist (among climate, conflict, pandemic, and other risks). Indeed, identifying consequent challenges and remedies, including institutions and procedures, for an array of potential futures presents further difficulties, including in the COVID world.

Acknowledgements

Research assistance for this chapter was provided by Chelsey Nichols and Michelle Simpkins.

Futures for institutions

2 Rethinking the International Criminal Court as the court of its state parties

Frédéric Mégret

1 Introduction: the enduring allure of universalism

To think about potential futures for international criminal justice is necessarily to reflect on its past and to connect these dimensions into a compelling account for the present. It would seem that two extreme scenarios possibly await the International Criminal Court (ICC) in years to come. One is that the Court and its supporters succeed in their original bid to make the Court universal, somewhat miraculously convincing the states that have so far studiously stayed outside its realm to join it. A Court with universal membership would be in a position to make a strong claim about its actual universalism beyond appeal to supposedly universal values. What might precipitate such a move is as unclear now as it was in 1998, all the more so because the Court's distributive politics and fault lines have since become increasingly clear. It seems, moreover, that the Court has probably reached its natural size and that there will be fewer and fewer contenders for ratification of the Rome Statute. If anything, there has been recurring talk of states leaving the Court rather than the other way round.

At the opposite extreme, the Court could simply fail, imploding under the weight of its own contradictions and relatively limited membership. It is striking how supporters of the Court seem to assume that whilst its geographic scope may be limited, the Court is there to stay in the long term. One does not need to be a hard-core realist, however, to be mindful that international institutions are hardly eternal and that more universal institutions than the ICC have failed in the past, most notably the League of Nations, whose idealism and formalism doomed it in the end. If enough states parties – notably from Africa – decided that being a party to the ICC was no longer in their interest, then there is a real possibility that the Court could disappear. Furthermore, although broader membership is something that many ICC supporters aspire to, it may complicate the Court's task and make some of the contradictions running through it hard to manage.

Of course, neither of these extremes is particularly plausible. What is more likely is that the Court will continue to hobble along in its current form with a limited membership and therefore as something less than a universal court of the international community. For sceptics of the Court, the fact that it has hit a sort of glass ceiling in terms of its membership is proof that its design is fundamentally

DOI: 10.4324/9781003087533-3

flawed and that it does not have the means of its ambition.[1] But such opponents failed to provide much of an account of why the Court nonetheless is set to persist in this truncated way: how, in other words, it has not imploded yet despite its diminished claim to universality. For proponents of the Court, limited membership is evidently a thorn in their sides, especially for the many who staked so much on its universality.[2] Of course, they can still claim that, despite not being universal, it represents a sizable slice of the international community, one sufficient to sustain the claim that it is at least virtually universal, but, as we will see, this has always seemed a somewhat tenuous claim.

In the meantime, few seem keen to make a compelling case that this middle-of-the road outcome – one that sees the Court proceed fundamentally and perhaps permanently as a less-than-universal institution – has any particular normative appeal, except as a sort of second-best position. Both sides seem to rest their case on how future events will one day settle the argument through the test of time. In this chapter, by contrast, I seek to make the argument that there may be a very real normative merit to conceptualising the Court as an institution of fundamentally and not just contingently limited membership. The main advantage of this argument is that it does not rely on international criminal justice's future to assess whether the Court is the embryo of a world community or a distraction from the underlying reality of the international system. Instead, it provides a defence of the Court *as it is, here and now*, and how it is likely to be for the foreseeable future.

Indeed, one of the hypotheses of this chapter will be that there is significant implicit agreement between critiques and proponents about what a certain essence of the Court is.[3] This then leads the two 'sides' to disagree about whether that model can/should be achieved – but not that this is indeed the model of reference. One might describe this model as the 'cosmopolitan Kantian' model of international criminal justice.[4] The essence of that model is that international

1 Alex George, 'Why the International Criminal Court Can't Serve Universal Justice' [2014] *Medium* <https://medium.com/abstract-magazine/why-the-international-criminal-court-can-t-serve-universal-justice-938ba4b9cd1> accessed 18 January 2021.

2 Campaigns for universal ratification of the Rome Statute began as early as 1998 and have gone unabated since. See, e.g., 'Campaign for the Universality and Effectiveness of the Rome Statute of the International Criminal Court (ICC) System' *Parliamentarians for Global Action – Mobilizing Legislators as Champions for Human Rights, Democracy and Peace* <www.pgaction.org/ilhr/rome-statute/> accessed 18 January 2021.

3 For an example of a treatment of the ICC that is wary of the cosmopolitan claims that are made on its behalf but nonetheless seems to ratify that cosmopolitanism as the framework of choice for the Court, see Victor Peskin, 'An Ideal Becoming Real? The International Criminal Court and the Limits of the Cosmopolitan Vision of Justice' in Roland Pierik and Wouter Werner (eds), *Cosmopolitanism in Context: Perspectives from International Law and Political Theory* (CUP 2010).

4 For explorations of the authority or legitimacy of international criminal justice that invoke that Kantian tradition in defence of rights or the pursuit of peace, see Antonio Franceschet, 'The International Criminal Court's Authority Crisis and Kant's Political Ethics' (2016) 16 *International Criminal Law Review* 201; Alexander Heinze, 'The Statute of the International Criminal Court as a Kantian Constitution' in Morten Bergsmo and Emiliano Buis (eds),

criminal justice, if it is to exist at all, will be a universal institution whose first principles will ultimately be imposed on recalcitrant states, on the basis of the higher, almost metaphysical values of an immanent international community. Although this is largely a theoretical paradigm, it is one that has occasionally been resurrected in actual legal controversies, notably concerning the Court's relations to non–states parties and the vexed issue of immunities. For proponents of the '*ius puniendi*' approach to international criminal justice,[5] the ICC is the incarnation of an already-existing 'right to punish' vested in the international community. Seen from that perspective, the Rome Statute and states' ratification are not so much ordinary manifestations of voluntarism as they are necessary steps in a steady and largely preordained march towards universality. For sceptics of the Court, the argument is that it cannot be this universal version of itself, much more than they are interested in developing an alternative normative account of it.[6]

That conversation is interesting for what it leaves out: the possibility that the Court might be defensible in a strong sense, even as a permanently non-universal jurisdiction. The heart of the reappraisal proposed by this chapter, instead, consists in an at least superficially downward reassessment of the ambition of the universalist ICC, but combined with a realist defence of its actual rather than imagined politics. The realism proposed here is normative rather than descriptive, based on the notion that normative theorising should be plausible and seek to uncover normative foundations on the basis of actual practices. Methodologically, therefore, it starts from the practices that go into making the Court (e.g., joining it, operating it, leaving it) and seeks to understand them normatively in their own terms, rather than being based on a pre-existing blueprint of what the Court can only be. Moving from the ground up, the emphasis is on the best possible normative explanation of why states join the ICC and what they then create.

Philosophical Foundations of International Criminal Law: Correlating Thinkers (TOAEP 2018). On the connection between international criminal justice and cosmopolitan legal thought, see Steven C Roach, 'Value Pluralism, Liberalism, and the Cosmopolitan Intent of the International Criminal Court' (2005) 4 *Journal of Human Rights* 475; Antonio Franceschet, 'Four Cosmopolitan Projects: The International Criminal Court in Context' in Steven Roach (ed), *Governance, Order, and the International Criminal Court: Between Realpolitik and a Cosmopolitan Court* (OUP 2009); Jennifer Biedendorf, *Cosmopolitanism and the Development of the International Criminal Court: Non-Governmental Organizations' Advocacy and Transnational Human Rights* (Rowman & Littlefield 2019).

5 See Kai Ambos, 'Punishment Without a Sovereign? The *Ius Puniendi* Issue of International Criminal Law: A First Contribution Towards a Consistent Theory of International Criminal Law' (2013) 33 *Oxford Journal of Legal Studies* 293; Carsten Stahn, 'The ICC, Pre-Existing Jurisdictional Treaty Regimes, and the Limits of the *Nemo Dat Quod Non Habet* Doctrine – A Reply to Michael Newton' (2016) 49 *Vanderbilt Journal of Transnational Law* 443; Claus Kreß, 'Preliminary Observations on the ICC Appeals Chamber's Judgment of 6 May 2019 in the Jordan Referral re Al-Bashir Appeal' (Occasional Paper, Torkel Opsahl Academic EPublisher 2019) <www.toaep.org/ops-pdf/8-kress>.

6 See, for example, Michael A Newton, 'How the International Criminal Court Threatens Treaty Norms' (2016) 49 *Vanderbilt Journal of Transnational Law* 371.

The gist of this alternative model, then, is that the ICC is better understood, at least at first brush, as a discrete cooperative arrangement between a significant subset of states that maximise their interest and their values through it. In the process, the ICC produces a certain vision of justice. That vision of justice, such as it may be, is not necessarily less defensible simply because it is not universal in the banal sense that universalism is often understood, but it is certainly a *peculiar* vision and one best understood as such. The Court, in short, should be seen as 'the court of its states parties', and a normative vision should be developed from that reality rather than deduced from a certain idealised conception of the international community. This is a paradoxical and unorthodox move in that it proceeds from what many will see as the less-than-ideal predicament within which the Court finds itself. But the chapter will contend that such a view is not only defensible: it may, in fact, make more sense of our intuitions about where international criminal justice is and ought to be going, reconnects to an earlier and productive Nurembergian trajectory, and has been evoked in the context of the Court.

Thinking of the Court in this way can, in particular, clarify what states gain from being parties to the Rome Statute and the kind of institution they have created as a result. It can also significantly and positively 'provincialise' the Court, in ways that relieve it of the burden of 'being universal'. It is thus a view that can help us better make sense of the actual potentialities of the Court, and that is not without its own potential for re-enchantment of the function of international criminal justice in the international legal order, properly understood. Indeed, it can emphasise a sort of 'best case' normative theory of how one might go about justifying the Court, knowing what we know about its conditions of realisation. At the same time, the argument is fully open to the possibility that, if all or even any of the necessary conditions of that best-case scenario are absent, then the Court may come close to being irredeemable.

At any rate, this chapter will suggest that the rationale for the Court needs to be at least 'reimagined' in ways that are politically productive. It begins with a more ontological form of realism, firmly anchoring the creation of the ICC in a vision of the national interest by highlighting the reasons why states may want to join the Court, if at all, and the normative salience of such reasons (Part 2); it then enhances that unit-based model by looking at the Court as the collective project of its states parties, highlighting a best case for what those states might be understood to engage in together (Part 3). It concludes with some thoughts on how one might think about the life of the court going forward, its complex relation to both its states parties, and the distant promise of universalism.

2 A sovereign project: the ICC as grounded in the national interest

In the dominant Kantian narrative, the ICC is primarily seen as the advent of a particular idea whose merit gradually imposes itself on states and becomes embodied in particular institutions.[7] States' will and rationalities are important but seen as mere 'stepping-stones' to the realisation of a higher and immanent purpose which fundamentally mandates the creation of the Court. I suggest that this at the very least reverses the order of things. In this section, I argue instead that the ICC is better seen from a moderate realist lens, as first and foremost a creature of states and as a function of the sort of strategies that they pursue. These strategies not only continue to inform what the Court becomes long after they have seemingly receded, but they also have a certain normative salience of their own, grounded in the national interest and the pursuit of domestic and foreign policy objectives. Understanding them can thus provide the grounds to further develop a normative theory of international criminal justice.

The perspective is a realist one because it foregrounds the state, despite much discussion of the Court being a product of much more, including the work of civil society movements.[8] I do not discount the role that civil society has had, but the assumption here is that this role is derivative and almost entirely directed at getting *states* to support the Court. However much one may present the Court as working for general populations and victims or at the behest of civil society, it is in the end created by sovereigns; provided its jurisdictional foothold by a delegation of states' own jurisdictions; and almost entirely dependent on state support, cooperation, and funding. The lens here is only moderately realist, however, in that it is perfectly conceivable that that the national interest is significantly shaped by normative considerations and that the sum of national interests will yield a whole that is greater than the parts. In adopting this lens, the section seeks to reconstruct the case for the ICC from the ground up. It does so in a theoretical rather than historical way, and in a normative rather than social scientific fashion, by providing a stylised account of the sort of goals that states may be expected to pursue in joining the Court.

a) The case for the national interest

At the heart of the ICC puzzle lies a fundamental mystery that is rarely addressed properly or even taken seriously (perhaps because it raises uncomfortable questions): namely, why states would want to join the ICC in the first place.[9] Although

7 William A Schabas, 'International Justice for International Crimes: An Idea Whose Time Has Come' (2006) 14 *European Review* 421; M Cherif Bassiouni, 'The Time Has Come for an International Criminal Court' (1991) 1 *Indiana International & Comparative Law Review* 1.

8 Marlies Glasius, *The International Criminal Court, a Global Civil Society Achievement* (Routledge 2006).

9 See Frédéric Mégret, 'Why Would States Want to Join the ICC? A Theoretical Exploration Based on the Legal Nature of Complementarity' in Jann K Kleffner and Gerben Kor (eds), *Complementary Views on Complementarity Proceedings of the International Roundtable on the Complementary Nature of the International Criminal Court* (TMC Asser Press and CUP 2005); Yvonne Marie Dutton, 'Treaty Content and Costs: Explaining State Commitment to the International Criminal Court' (PhD thesis, University of Colorado at Boulder 2011).

there is much loose talk about changing global values in the wake of the Court's creation, this often rushes past standard assumptions about what motivates states in international relations. It is not clear, notably, why states would want to join an institution that can (1) make them accountable via some of their leaders; (2) limit their domestic and foreign policy margin of maneuver, including in their military and diplomatic components; and (3) 'pierce the corporate veil' in contempt of long-held assumptions about the answerability of the state as such.[10] In other words, why would states that are otherwise so reluctant to do so – think of how few states recognise the potentially far-less-damaging compulsory jurisdiction of the International Court of Justice – give an international jurisdiction the tools to exact significant costs from them? Or, as Grietje Baars once put it, 'why . . . would state leaders create a body of norms to do something that they do not in fact *want* to do?'[11]

One response is simply that some states *have* joined and that there is not much point in second-guessing their intentions, given that they can now for all intents and purposes be held to that commitment. But this robs us of an explanation of how and why their having joined might inform our understanding of the Court. Another argument proceeds from a sort of categorical imperative that states simply 'should' join the Court because this is the right thing to do. International criminal justice is good for international law and therefore must be good for states. Although, on one level, the Rome Statute is a treaty like any treaty (i.e., based on voluntarism), there is almost an assumption that there is some pre-existing, inchoate obligation to join it, to be part of the realisation of the promise of international justice it portends.[12] Indeed, because of the way in which the ICC has been seen as responding first and foremost to an international ethos, the extent to which its existence has been based on the national interest has tended to be systematically minimised. If anything, the problem has been identified, both historically and in the context of the ICC ratification and activity, as the national interest having an outsize value and the challenge is how to rein it in. Many Court supporters continue to treat the fact that some major powers refuse to join the Rome Statute as somehow incompatible with the spirit of fighting impunity.[13]

But this is highly problematic. An ideal normative case for why states should join the Rome Statute is not a causal explanation of why they do; it risks

10 Rafaëlle Maison, *La responsabilité individuelle pour crime d'État en droit international public* (Bruylant 2004).

11 Grietje Baars, 'Making ICL History: On the Need to Move Beyond Prefab Critiques' in Christine Schwöbel (ed), *Critical Approaches to International Criminal Law: An Introduction* (Routledge 2014).

12 On the idea of a sort of pre-existing obligation to join and even adopt the Rome Statute, see Frédéric Mégret, 'The Rome Conference: Institutional Design and the Constraints of Diplomacy' in Margaret de Guzman and Valerie Oosterveld (eds), *Elgar Companion to the International Criminal Court* (Edward Elgar Publishing 2020).

13 Fadi Haddadin, 'Op-Ed: The US Should Join the ICC – for Humanity's Sake' (*Foreign Policy Blogs*, 30 November 2018) <https://foreignpolicyblogs.com/2018/11/30/op-ed-the-u-s-should-join-the-icc-for-humanitys-sake/> accessed 1 October 2020.

crediting those states who did join with too much. In emphasising system-wide rather than unit-level reasons why states want to join, moreover, this approach fundamentally neglects state agency. States did not suddenly (or even gradually) awaken to the fact that international crimes ought absolutely to be prosecuted always. Everything that they did before or after the ICC suggests a much more ambivalent attitude: highly supportive of international criminal justice in some cases and oblivious or hostile to it in others. There is no pre-existing 'obligation to oblige oneself' when it comes to the Rome Statute, only obligations that flow, at best, from being a party to the Rome Statute once one has consented to be bound by it, presumably for reasons that are at least in part extraneous to the Statute itself. Of course, it might be desirable for the Rome Statute to be universal, and one cannot fault its supporters for trying, but one cannot really hope to do so from an unassailable a priori normative high ground. The Rome Statute is, like any treaty, a peculiar and contingent policy proposal open to those interested but which does not presumptively oblige non-parties.

Note that it would be more problematic if substantive international criminal law treaties of the highest importance were not universally ratified. We would be uncomfortable if the Geneva or the Genocide Conventions, for example, had not been ratified by most states because this would compromise the taboo-like nature of the prohibition of war crimes and genocide as constitutive of the international community. Indeed, we are willing to consider, via customary international law if nothing else, that even non-parties and perhaps even persistent objectors (if there were any obviously) would be bound by those treaties. Yet in principle, even the desirability of certain treaties being universally adhered to does not make it so, and it is possible to imagine international crimes that are not universal. The ICC's less-than-universalism, at any rate, stands to be even less problematic than that of international crimes. The Court is, in the end, not a substantive arrangement: only a peculiar, relatively idiosyncratic way of dealing with the problem of impunity, alongside domestic trials and various *ad hoc* international and hybrid courts, not to mention a vast array of transitional justice mechanisms that use other-than-penal means. The attempt to package such a peculiar jurisdictional arrangement and make it co-extensive with the crimes themselves risks falling flat and ignoring the rather large area of legitimate debate there is about the ICC, even for states that are otherwise committed to repressing the corresponding international crimes.[14]

In fact, there is no reason to assume that the Court necessarily manifests the highest level of commitment to an anti-impunity norm. (For all we know, for example, one of its main roles might be to protect the impunity of its most powerful creators.) One might not be a party to the Rome Statute for legitimate reasons and still be committed to fight impunity within one's ranks. But given that

14 This is an argument long made in particular by Mark Drumbl. See Mark A Drumbl, *Atrocity, Punishment, and International Law* (CUP 2007) 182–183.

states *do* join the Court and that it does have some not-inconsequential powers, some account must be given of this reality that does not fall into the trap of either idealising or trivialising states' motivations. What if the problem, in that context, were not an excess of national interest interfering with how the ICC could and should work, but the inability to provide an account of how states might want to join and support the ICC on purely national interest grounds? Would such a commitment corrupt the ICC, or might it, on the contrary, reinforce it? Instead of focusing on why non–states parties will not join, it may have always been far more interesting to determine why the states who *do join* do so – and not simply as part of a political scientific inquiry as to why states act as they do at all, but as part of a commitment to understanding the normative basis of the Court.

b) A realist and a constitutionalist story

What, then, is the political rationality at work in joining the ICC at the state level, and what promise does it hold for a normative account of international criminal justice? The straightforward answer, from a realist perspective, must be that states have some national interest in joining the Court. For most classical or neo-realists, it may be unfathomable that such an interest exists, but conceptions of the national interest are multiple and include analysis that sees it as well served by subscribing to international jurisdictions.[15] At any rate, it is only upon discovering evidence of such an interest that the ICC can be made sense of. In fact, given the evidence that states *do* join, the problem must be with the sort of dogmatic realism that would exclude any understanding of interest as compatible with the computing of advantages, either relative or absolute, that states may obtain by being party to international institutions.

Let us adopt, then, as a starting point, a simple model that seeks to understand how states may decide that the benefits of joining the Court outweigh the costs. I leave aside for the time being the very real possibility that a number of states have joined the court for trivial reasons or at least reasons not directly connected to what they may get from the ICC, including peer pressure and powerful states strongly inciting them to do so (for example, via conditionality). I also leave aside the possibility that joining the ICC may, for some states, have been a gross miscalculation (e.g., those whose leaders have been investigated) – although that is also a real possibility. I do so not because I think these possibilities are not credible, but because if it is the case that the Court rests on such fragile normative foundations that it would clearly flounder as a normative project (that is, of course, always a possibility).

It is more interesting, in keeping with this chapter's normative ambition, to see how the existence of the Court could be justified in a 'best-case scenario',

15 Laurence R Helfer and Anne-Marie Slaughter, 'Why States Create International Tribunals: A Response to Professors Posner and Yoo Review Essay' (2005) 93 *California Law Review* 899.

in which states do indeed seek to maximise their national interest uncoerced by other states and relatively free of erroneous miscalculation. The cost-averting side of that calculus can, put simply, be articulated such that either (1) states calculate that they have no or only a very small chance of their nationals working in governmental positions being prosecuted, in which case joining the ICC means they conceivably get some advantages without any of the costs; (2) states calculate that those prosecuted will be nationals of other states; or (3) governments calculate that their nationals may be prosecuted, but that the nationals in question will be members of opposition groups rather than governmental elites.

Now, of course, it may be that states get this wrong occasionally, thinking that either (1), (2), or (3) holds true when, in fact, it is their governing individuals who end up being prosecuted. This will be *a fortiori* the case when they have been more or less coerced to join the Rome Statute at the expense of a lucid reckoning of its national interest implications. Did the Kenyan authorities fully anticipate how, in joining the Court, they provided it with a tool that would one day be used against them? Probably not, although they subsequently certainly did a good job of blunting the threat of international criminal justice. I doubt, at any rate, that Kenya would have joined the ICC when it did if it had known then that a few years later, several of its leaders would be prosecuted. But this, in a sense, reinforces the argument that joining the Court must be based on an ongoing interest calculus, albeit one that is sometimes disrupted by unexpected events. Overall, the point is that states that join the ICC must believe that the risk of inconvenience could be minimised. Pushing that logic to its extreme, it is not inconceivable that some states think that, on balance, joining the ICC will provide them with a kind of protection and respectability – perhaps even that it will provide a cover for crimes committed by their nationals, which, for various reasons, they speculate would stand little chance of coming under the Court's scrutiny.[16]

Of course, averting certain harms can only be one prong of a theory of why states join the ICC, and a full theory must also account for how they seek to obtain some non-trivial advantage. That advantage may be the purely reputational one of being seen to be at the vanguard of liberal efforts to deal with excessive violence. But a more plausible notion is that it is a defensive one whereby states protect themselves from the possibility of the commission of crimes on their territory (and, one suspects, against their nationals and possibly against their sovereignty) by providing a measure of deterrence against other states, both parties and non-parties.[17] States parties signal to others that they commit crimes on the states parties' territory at their (relative) peril because the territorial state's

16 On the idea of the ICC as a form of 'planned immunity', see Baars (n 11).

17 This now also includes, as per the Court's jurisprudence, crimes that were committed on the territory of another state but have overspilled into the territory of a state party and affected it as well. 'Decision on the Prosecution's Request for a Ruling on Jurisdiction Under Article 19(3) of the Statute' ICC-RoC46(3)-01/18, Pre-Trial Chamber I, 6 September 2018.

obligation to prosecute certain crimes is henceforth backed by a credible institutional commitment to the ICC.[18]

The fact that the ICC has jurisdiction over the nationals of states parties is a priori more of a self-inflicted wound and therefore harder to explain. Yet a state party may foresee that crimes will be committed by its own nationals and still have a valid case for joining the ICC. If the nationals are members of rebel groups, then the state is merely directing a further international resource against them to considerable effect as had, in fact, probably been foreseen by states at the Rome Conference.[19] It is also not inconceivable that a state would seek some kind of insurance policy against the risk that future regimes would commit international crimes and that the politics of joining the ICC have more to do with binding future governments than binding oneself. Finally, in the most optimistic scenario, states, particularly those that have been marked by violence in the past, may seek to 'protect themselves against themselves' (or at least a version of themselves) by entrenching their commitment to immunity internationally, constitutionalising it, as it were, via membership in an international institution.[20]

In short, it is not particularly difficult to imagine reasons states would want to join the Court that do not involve subscribing to some implausible idealist theory that they are doing so merely as a result of an abstract moral obligation to make good on the ICC's putative universalism. These reasons are, predictably perhaps, a mixed bag but certainly not bereft of any virtue. Shifting the emphasis to states' endogenous rather than exogenous reasons for becoming parties is important because it suggests that, on some deeper level and all other things being equal, states will occasionally welcome ICC interventions, even in relation to matters implicating their own nationals. To be sure, the government that ratified the Rome Statute and the government whose members stand to be prosecuted a few years later by the ICC are not necessarily the same. The latter might be forgiven for not, in the moment, enthusiastically embracing the former's original decision. But the broader framework bears emphasising: namely, that ICC prosecutions can be understood as fundamentally undertaken for the benefit of states that, unless one assumes them to have been profoundly misled, knew what they were getting into when they exposed themselves to international prosecutions. If not (for example, because a number of states were, in fact, coerced to join the ICC against their own interests), then the conclusion must be that the Rome Statute was from the outset destined to play out at the expense of only certain states, which would, in turn, condemn any attempt to mount a normative defence of the Court.

18 Beth A Simmons and Allison Danner, 'Credible Commitments and the International Criminal Court' (2010) 64 *International Organization* 225.

19 See Darryl Robinson, 'The Controversy Over Territorial State Referrals and Reflections on ICL Discourse' (2011) 9 *Journal of International Criminal Justice* 355.

20 Mégret, 'Why Would States Want to Join the ICC?' (n 9).

c) Implications for the ICC

Thinking of the ICC in terms of the national interest, then, helps reconnect its creation to older and often neglected patterns in international criminal justice. It is widely considered, for example, that the Nuremberg and particularly the Tokyo tribunals were primarily tools of their masters in that they were designed, regardless of their attempts to connect to something more immanent, as first and foremost emanations of the states that created them. In the dominant narrative of international criminal justice, this has always been an original sin to be expunged, an inherent limitation that future international criminal tribunals should do their utmost to shed. Yet it did not prevent the tribunals from punishing international crimes on the basis of broadly universal standards. The post-war tribunals would come to be seen as stepping-stones to a more universal international criminal justice. Their groundedness in the national interest of the Allies did not make them irredeemable in the circumstances. In fact, it was in many ways the key to their success, consisting in a particularly effective, relatively swift, and largely enduring form of international justice. In other words, in the trade-off between universal appeal and sovereign anchoring, it would be difficult to argue that the somewhat-parochial support of the Allies as a defining feature of the tribunals was their downfall.

The question, then, is whether a defence of the ICC as rooted, fundamentally, in the particular vision of the 130 or so states that are party to its Statute can be mounted. It is argued that it can and in ways that could be beneficial to the Court. First, such a defence highlights what may be the main source of solidity of the ICC's existence: namely, its basis in treaty consent and an explicit, deliberate, and knowing commitment by state parties. It will be remembered that the creation of the *ad hoc* tribunals by the Security Council rather than by treaty (which was technically possible and, in fact, briefly envisaged) was generally deplored as providing only a second-best grounding in sovereign consent, particularly in relation to the states most concerned, many of which protested adamantly that they did not support either the ICTY or the ICTR. One could, of course, technically bypass such opposition (on the grounds that the states in question were UN members and therefore bound by Chapter VII Security Council resolutions) but only at the cost of the shallowness of these states' commitment. Both the ICTY and ICTR would soon learn at their expense the difficulty of trying to provide justice against the stated wishes of the states most in a position to allow it to proceed. The challenge, to be clear, was not merely one of effectivity but of deep legitimacy.[21] The creation of the ICC by treaty, far from being merely a concession to political reality, in this context can be seen as upholding a vision of international criminal justice as grounded in states' willingness to support and cooperate with it on the basis of freely self-determined consent. It is based on a

21 José E Alvarez, 'Crimes of States/Crimes of Hate: Lessons from Rwanda' (1999) 24 *Yale Journal of International Law* 365.

vision that prioritises the social embeddedness of justice institutions over their sheer moral desirability or at least takes the former as seriously as the latter.

Second, thinking of the ICC as grounded in the interest of its states parties can help lower the temperature of expectations surrounding it and reconcile its cosmopolitan impulse with its Westphalian framework. In particular, it can allow one to relativise the standing of both states that do not join the Rome Statute and those that do. States that do not join cannot be faulted for 'privileging their national interest over international justice', any more than states who do join can claim that they do so because they have 'privileged international justice over their national interest'. That opposition is essentially, under a realist normative framework, a false and misleading one. It seems more relevant to assess why some states, based on their characteristics and their position in the international system, decide that joining the ICC is in their national interest, whereas others do not. States that do not ratify the Rome Statute may have respectable (prudential, symbolic, constitutional, etc.) reasons for doing so, and states that do ratify it may do so for reasons that are not particularly elevated. This suggests a fundamental moral equivalency (all other things being equal) between states parties and non-states parties to the Rome Statute.

It is important, in that respect, to note that states that do not join the Rome Statute may do so from a standpoint that is normatively unassailable. In particular, states that do not ratify the Rome Statute in no way release themselves from their obligation to prosecute international crimes; they simply decide not to avail themselves of a particular mechanism for dealing with such crimes, which, for a range of reasons, is not to their liking. Their reasons for not joining may be debatable, but some are plausible and not ethically beyond the pale. For example, a state might think that it was quite committed to punishing crimes domestically but that doing so under the gaze of an international institution of unknown quantity would not be a particularly good idea or might be incompatible with some of its constitutional protections.[22] Indeed, states today might even be forgiven for thinking that the ICC was not a particularly good idea to fight impunity and enforce ICL, perhaps distracting fundamentally, despite complementarity, from the hard work of focusing on prosecutions and reparations locally or even through *ad hoc* international initiatives. It is also possible to think that some states decided not to join the ICC because, through a sort of surfeit of virtue, they considered the Court would actually be too weak for the task of repressing (at least certain) international crimes.[23]

22 Madeline Morris, 'High Crimes and Misconceptions: The ICC and Non-Party States' (2001) 64 *Law and Contemporary Problems* 13.

23 The example that comes to mind is India, which claimed that it would not join the ICC because it failed to clearly criminalise nuclear weapons. See Devasheesh Bais, 'India and the International Criminal Court' (FICHL Policy Brief Series No 54, Torkel Opsahl Academic EPublisher 2016). Some states also hinted that they might have difficulties joining the Rome Statute if the punishment meted out (notably in terms of length of imprisonment) was not sufficiently severe. This may seem a bit rich, but it is not inconceivable that, had the

Although opponents of the Court, particularly in the US, clearly overextended themselves when they sought to argue that the Court's exercise of jurisdiction over the nationals of non-states parties was illegal,[24] that does not mean that ICC jurisdiction over the nationals of non-states parties, in internationalising the prosecution of individuals whom some states have good reason to want to remain domestically, is not *politically* problematic. In fact, it seems unfair to fault states that do not join the Rome Statute for fostering impunity since some states joined it confident that they would never have to face prosecutions. It is easier to ratify the Rome Statute if one is Liechtenstein than the US, as part of well-worn tradition by small nations of investing in international institutions to compensate for their lack of power. Joining the Court may be rationalised by an abundance of invocations of humanity and history, but this cannot be allowed to obscure the calculated, prudential, and even pedestrian reasons for doing so.

At any rate, the point of this section is that some version of the national interest is necessarily implicated in states joining the ICC. States are not merely bending to some sense of international law's manifest destiny, but engaging, quietly and, in many cases, responsibly, in their own national policies. This can help us, in turn, identify the fundamental political rationale and even normative basis for the Court's existence. The ICC, in that view, merely expresses the particular politics of the states that have joined it, for the reasons that they have joined it. This is not only in the trivial legal positivist sense that the Court is created, no more no less, by the states that ratify its Statute, but also in the normative sense that it is defensible as the Court of those states – in fact, that such a defence succeeds better both descriptively and normatively than the idealist variant in giving us a grounded account of the Court. It is striking how, once that basic fact is acknowledged, it can change how we conceptualise the Court.

The idea that the Court should be primarily understood as the Court of its states parties does not imply that it should blindly do their bidding. It is probably the case that an independent court is, within certain limits, compatible with states parties' well-understood interest. It does, however, lift a taboo about what the Court is doing, portraying it less as a sort of *avant garde* of the international community than as an association based on the interest of its members. In that respect, it particularises what the Court can stand for, relativising the quite

Rome Statute ended up being substantially weaker, some states would have decided not to dignify it with their ratification, lest their membership be understood as validating a shockingly underwhelming court. Few seem to have clearly done so, but even part of the US opposition was always grounded in a kind of idealistic defence of US fair trial guarantees. See Helen Duffy, 'National Constitutional Compatibility and the International Criminal Court' (2001) 11 *Duke Journal of Comparative & International Law* 5. In good faith or not, such a possibility does reinforce the notion that one may have international criminal justice- or human rights-friendly reasons to not join the ICC.

24 Frédéric Mégret, 'Epilogue to an Endless Debate: The International Criminal Court's Third Party Jurisdiction and the Looming Revolution of International Law' (2001) 12 *European Journal of International Law* 247.

common misconception that the Court stands, above all, for universal principles and rights. The Court merely expresses, instead, a particular preference by some states for a way of dealing with the problem of international crimes. That preference then informs a particular politics that is not shameful but not such that it should necessarily command universal assent. Thinking in this way can also help problematise the Court for what it is as an institution both spurred by the collection of these interests and limited by them.

Indeed, one may speculate that therein lies both its strength and vulnerability. On the one hand, I have argued that it is precisely because under one vision, states can and do pursue their national interest when joining institutions of international justice that one can have hope in the relative solidity of the Court. The national interest may be biased and subjective, but we also have reason to think that it is less flimsy than adherence to values as a determinant of foreign legal policy. It puts the Court potentially on solid foundations, as shown, for example, by the fact that even some of the states whose nationals have been targeted have ultimately hesitated to jump ship and leave the Rome Statute. On the other hand, this dependency on the national interest also points to an inherent weakness of the Court. The national interest can evolve over time on the basis of circumstances in which international criminal justice requires stability, if not permanence; it might threaten the life of the Court as states actualise their interest calculations in particular cases; and it is atomistic where it would be appealing to ground international criminal justice in a sense of a shared endeavor.

3 A collective project: the ICC as quasi-regional court

Explaining single-state rationalities for joining the Rome Statute takes us some way towards an understanding of the ICC's true nature as grounded not just technically but in principle in a form of sovereign delegation. On its own, however, it leaves a normative theory of the ICC significantly disjointed and wanting because the Court is bound to be more than the sum of its parts. The key point is that states do not join the ICC alone and unilaterally; rather, they create and support it *with others* (and, crucially, not with some others) as a collective institution that is both a repository of and more than the sum of their respective commitments. The normative distinctiveness of the ICC, then, is that it is a specifically international, multilateral, and collective endeavor. But what collectivity exactly is at work? This section seeks to develop a best normative case for states wanting to be *jointly* part of the ICC, mindful that their reasons for joining may be quite distinct and in tension with each other, even as they partake in a collective endeavor.

In the traditional defence of international criminal tribunals, universality has always featured prominently and excited imaginations. Even at Nuremberg, the Allies, flush with their victory, made sure to enlist the support of other, smaller nations that had fought the war alongside them. The *ad hoc* tribunals were universal in that they were created under the auspices of the Security Council and therefore bound all UN members. In reality, by contrast, the idea that the ICC is defined, even normatively, by its inscription in universality is highly debatable. It seems more helpful to see the ICC, in fact, less as a universal in the making than as the manifestation of a contingent, situated, if potentially powerful and productive, constellation of interests, in the form of a quasi-regional alliance.[25] Contra the Kantian model of international criminal justice, I suggest a more Grotian (or perhaps neo-Grotian) model that relies on a cooperative and transactional rather than an immanent logic.[26] Where the Kantian model assumes a system perspective and infers the need and status of the Court from it, the Grotian model at least takes the relationship of states between themselves and the element of community that they create as being central to what the ICC is and to how it can be defended.

a) Not universal

The irony is that just as international criminal jurisdiction has become more permanent with the ICC, it has also become far less de facto universal, hamstrung by its voluntarist framework. To begin with, the Court does not have global membership, nor is likely to any time soon. It is probably the case, in fact, that its potential for membership expansion has reached a ceiling and that this fact was knowable from the start. After making rapid progress, the narrative of constant ratification has hit its natural limit. If anything, the Court is at risk of the occasional loss of the odd member. No amount of Preambular appeal to the 'fabric of humanity' or even jurisdiction over crimes that are themselves unmistakably universal can bypass the strict voluntarist framework of its founding treaty. Nor is this a contingent feature of the Court soon to be transcended, but what is likely to be the normal path going forward.

In other words, the Court was somehow destined *not* to be universal in terms of membership, given the conditions of the adoption of the Rome Statute and the absence of either a true imperial backer or some temporarily levelling cataclysmic event. Although the Court itself has sought, mimicking the ICJ, to spin this by arguing that it 'represent[s] the vast majority of the members of the international community',[27] that is really in the eyes of the beholder and significant swathes of humanity remain and will remain mostly beyond the Court's reach. The Court, in that significant, descriptive sense is therefore structurally less than universal, or un-universal. Clearly, moreover, courts that claim to deal with universal values or

25 I use the expression 'quasi-regional' here because the list of ICC membership does not overlap with any neat existing geopolitical region, although as I will go on to show that does not mean that it does not overlap with any.

26 For an early exploration of the relationship between a Grotian and Kantian view of the ICC, see Frédéric Mégret, 'Trois paradigmes de la justice pénale internationale' (2012) 32 *Observateur des Nations Unies* 9.

27 'Decision on the Prosecution's Request for a Ruling on Jurisdiction Under Article 19(3) of the Statute' (n 17) para 48.

human rights cannot ipso facto claim exception from the ordinary Westphalian rules that continue to otherwise structure the international order.[28]

But maybe the Court could be thought of more interestingly as *putatively* universal, as a kind of *avant garde* of a universalism in the making. For cosmopolitans, the Court continues to be *imagined* as destined to be a universal project that binds or will eventually bind the international community together in its entirety. Indeed, by analogy, many international lawyers would argue that human rights and at least some international human rights bodies are universal, even if not all states have ratified all human rights treaties or joined all relevant courts or monitoring bodies. Universalism, then, would be less a descriptive than a *normative* claim. This chimes well with the *jus cogens* character of the crimes over which the Court has jurisdiction and the extent to which no degree of 'persistent objection' over such crimes, if it was forthcoming, would nullify their customary and universal character, even for the objectors themselves.

Even that, however, turns out to be an awkward argument, at least when it comes to jurisdictional mechanisms. We have no reason to think that the undoubted universality of certain international crimes should translate automatically into a recognition of the universal character of whatever international criminal jurisdictions are created by various states in the name of repressing them, such that other states would immediately be required to bow to the resulting institutions. Indeed, we have reason to think that non–states parties are legitimately wary of less-than-universal structures being foisted on them as if they were universal. As argued in the previous section, there is no logical incompatibility (although there may be a tension in this or that case) between not wanting to be a party to the ICC and being committed to repressing international crimes. States parties to the ICC do not have a monopoly on what it means to be 'anti-impunity' in the international realm.

Indeed, the question of whether the Court speaks for the world or merely its states parties has arisen very concretely in relation to the prosecution of nationals of non–states parties. Broadly speaking, the issue is whether the ICC can construct its relation to non–states parties on its own exceptional universalist terms or whether these should be dealt with on the basis of the default rules of the international system. No one denies, for example, that a group of states can get together and *inter se* create a court that is not bound by the immunities of their heads of states, but the question is whether they can then impose that arrangement on third states. When the ICC's rules stand to favor non–states parties, as in the case of the applicability of complementarity, there is little doubt that the latter would have little reason to complain. It would, indeed, be quite unfair if

28 For example, regional human rights courts, even though they clearly claim to enforce universal and not merely regional values, have been quite obsessed with the Westphalian limits of their jurisdiction, notably as connected to territory or occupation, even expressing anxiety at the possibility that they might imperialistically impose values that are not those of non-states parties.

complementarity did not apply in relation to them, and surely states parties could not deny to non–states parties an advantage that they consider inherent to the structure of the ICC. But the issue is far more complicated when it comes to immunities, for example, where claims that incumbent heads of states of non–states parties do not have immunity before the Court itself and even before the courts of states parties have been met, unsurprisingly, with scepticism.[29]

This is not the place to discuss the so-called international *jus puniendi* argument on its own legal terms (and its implications, such as, most notoriously, that head-of-state immunities of non–states parties do not apply before the Court), something that I have done separately elsewhere.[30] The idea that the Court derives its authority from a pre-existing top-down right to punish vested in the international community itself is a relatively abstract argument. It relies on a certain preconception of the need for an international criminal jurisdiction and is tempted to see in the ICC its best manifestation. It is true that the ICC is an international court that emerges from a long history of trying to set up a universal court and that meshes particularly well, rhetorically at least, with underlying international themes;[31] however, whether it already represents the international community so that not only its legal personality but also its very claim to universality are opposable to non–states parties is highly contentious. Even if there is such a thing in international law as an a priori *ius puniendi*, it is unclear that the ICC can claim to embody it. The fact that the Court aspires to be universal and connects to international crimes whose universal pedigree is uncontested cannot hide its fundamentally voluntaristic and even transactional nature. The point, for example, is that the ICC stands to prosecute both its nationals and nationals of non–states parties on the basis of states parties' own, incontrovertible territorial and active personal jurisdiction titles (a fact that this chapter has stressed is also part of the political and ideological baggage of the Court). The idea that states, in joining the Court, are merely 'giving back' to an international institution that was only ever granted to them by a supranational authority in the first place would be news to many. The Court and its supporters, having long insisted that it is not usurping the jurisdiction of non–states parties when potentially prosecuting their nationals, are ill placed to then assert that its jurisdiction was based on some descending conferral all along.

29 Dapo Akande, 'ICC Appeals Chamber Holds That Heads of State Have No Immunity Under Customary International Law Before International Tribunals' (*EJIL: Talk!* 6 May 2019) <www.ejiltalk.org/icc-appeals-chamber-holds-that-heads-of-state-have-no-immunity-under-customary-international-law-before-international-tribunals/> accessed 18 December 2020.

30 Frédéric Mégret, 'The International Criminal Court: Between State Delegation and International *Ius Puniendi*' (2020) 23 *Max Planck Yearbook of United Nations Law* 161.

31 For an argument along those lines, see Claus Kreß, 'Article 98 – Cooperation with Respect to Waiver of Immunity and Consent to Surrender' in Kai Ambos (ed), *The Rome Statute of the International Criminal Court, Article-by-Article Commentary* (4th edn, Beck/Hart/Nomos 2021).

If a *ius puniendi* were the ultimate foundation for the ICC's jurisdiction, then states would have based the Court's jurisdiction on some form of universal jurisdiction as was briefly mooted in Rome[32] – but had they done so, they would have almost certainly exposed themselves to legal backlash by non–states parties. Having spared themselves that backlash and not convincingly fought that fight, there is surely something a bit opportunistic about claiming that it has, in fact, been won. When it suits it, the Court has even hinted at a form of substantive separatism from general international law that reinforces the notion that even it does not believe in its universal 'manifest destiny'.[33] Further proof of the Court's relative idiosyncrasy lies in the fact that it is independent from the UN and that, even when the Security Council refers cases to it for its own reasons, it has refused to fund its investigations, as if to make clear that states parties efforts' to finance the court are really only their business.[34] Certainly, the crude instrumentalism involved in Security Council referrals and deferrals does not hint at the Court becoming a sort of necessary feature of the international system in its globality.[35] Note also that the possibility of Article 124 declarations temporarily excepting from the Court's war crimes jurisdiction or the complex rules of recognition involved in the exercise of jurisdiction over aggression suggest that states parties themselves have conceded the possibility of a Court membership that involves differential levels of commitment 'by the menu'. This reinforces the sense of the Court as a malleable tool of complex (although no doubt potentially worthy) national agendas rather than as an ontologically necessary feature of the international legal order.

If the intuition is correct that the Court is not universal even in a limited normative sense, this substantially recasts its promise. The Court is not, important as it may be, 'the Court of the international community' but the 'Court of its states parties', a valuable but fundamentally provincial organisation. It may *aspire* to universalism, but so do many international institutions that we would hesitate

32 The Korean proposal was that the Court would have jurisdiction over any individual a state party had custody over, whereas the German proposal came closer to granting the Court any jurisdiction which any state party might have exercised. The majority in Rome clearly felt that these proposals were too ambitious and would steer the Court in a direction that was undesirable.

33 'Second Decision on the Defense's Challenge to the Jurisdiction of the Court in Respect of Counts 6 and 9' *Prosecutor v Ntaganda*, ICC-01/04–02/06–1707, Trial Chamber VI, 4 January 2017, para 35. (The Rome Statute 'is first and foremost a multilateral treaty which acts as an international criminal code for the parties to it'.)

34 W Michael Reisman, 'On Paying the Piper: Financial Responsibility for Security Council Referrals to the International Criminal Court' (2005) 99 *American Journal of International Law* 615.

35 In particular, whatever 'universality' of obligation arises in the case of Security Council referrals is certainly not the actualisation by the Council of a universal *ius puniendi* that was always there in the ICC, but rather more straightforwardly derives and is entirely dependent on the Security Council's chapter VII powers (although it has sometimes been hinted otherwise; see Yuval Shany, 'In Defence of Functional Interpretation of Article 12(3) of the Rome Statute: A Response to Yaël Ronen' (2010) 8 *Journal of International Criminal Justice* 329.

to describe as such until they have actually become universal. Moreover, we do not operate from the End of History in such a way that we could ascertain which institutions have eventually become fully universal (if any do) and which have turned out to be merely bona fide but transient and local efforts. The Court could end up being more like the Nuremberg or Tokyo tribunals: highly defensible institutions that may very well have articulated relatively universal values but that simultaneously did so from their own localised and grounded point of view. Or it could end up much more like regional human rights courts, whose membership is naturally limited and which only ever claimed to crystallise a particular sensitivity to international problems.

In fact, more fundamentally, the problem with a view of the Court as defined by its universality is not only that the Court, in practice, is highly unlikely to become universal. That is certainly true, but it is also relatively trite and, in the end, not particularly significant from a normative point of view. The deeper problem with the obsession with the Court's universal destiny is that, under the guise of extolling the value of the court, it may actually pass on the opportunity to come up with a strong normative defence of the Court as a court that is certainly less than universal but perhaps defensibly so. What, then, if instead of seeing the court's only possible normative destiny as becoming universal, one were to accept the purely, thoroughly, and permanently regional character of the ICC? What would be lost by letting go of the universalist ambition? What would the discovery of its provincialism do to its work of justice?

b) A defensive and disciplinary alliance

What we can say with a reasonable degree of certainty, in this context, is that the Court is what one might call a quasi-regional or a trans-regional court in that it is less than universal but also not quite regional in the geographic or cultural sense either. The Court is based on a group of 123 states (as of late 2020), mostly found in Europe, Latin America, and sub-Saharan Africa. Geopolitically, the Court is also notable for being an alliance of some medium and small powers, to the exclusion of some of the major economic and military players (the US, Russia, China, and India, for example). Contra a view that sees all Rome Statute ratifications as largely inter-changeable and emphasises the number of ratifications rather than their quality, these factors inscribe the ICC project in a particular political vein, closely aligned with, in particular, Europe's traditional spheres of influence. It should probably not come as a surprise that this is the continent which has historically most imagined itself as standing for a certain conception of universalism associated with international (criminal) law.[36]

36 Martti Koskenniemi, 'Hersch Lauterpacht and the Development of International Criminal Law' (2004) 2 *Journal of International Criminal Justice* 810.

In laying out the case that the ICC may merely be the peculiar project of those states that happen to support it, it may be useful to ponder how regional courts and institutions are sometimes defended. One aspect of such a defence is that groups of states in the international community may wish to forge ahead with more onerous and ambitious regimes. All other things being equal, this is something that the international legal order should want to encourage. It allows experimentation and innovation. The human rights regime is characterised by exactly this sort of push forward by various regional groupings, unsatisfied with the weakness and relative superficiality of the universal system and attracted by the possibility of forging their separate, irreducible path to what one may presume to be a broadly similar goal. In that particular realm, to require states to only opt for the universal system would have diluted the human rights project, deprived persons within the jurisdiction of the relevant states of the benefit of stronger protections, and robbed the international order of the rich reservoir of regional experimentation that is now one of the enduring legacies of various regional courts.

A quasi-regional ICC, then, is one that can allow a subset of states to constitute themselves as an *avant garde* or at least a kind of splinter group within the international community, perhaps experimenting for the benefit of themselves as well as others. This is not incompatible with convincing more and more states to join and perhaps ultimately reaching universality, but it suggests a much more decentralised approach to the development of international institutions, one emphasising their relative and experiential quality rather than a hegemonic claim to the universal. It also highlights the fact that states that decide to join such experiments must have collective reasons of their own to engage in them that go beyond such international institutions' stated aims (e.g., protect human rights or punish international crimes). This, however, is still a fairly idealistic perspective on regional groupings, one that probably glosses over much of the reality and the detail of why the ICC came about, which is also as a function of the exercise of power by a group of states. The emphasis on the Court as a regional mechanism remains vague on the sort of political work that it does and that it might be made to do. What kind of power do the states that join the ICC seek to assert collectively? What brings them together in this venture at a certain point in time? And what kind of quasi-regional court do they thereby produce?

What is well known in this context is that the ICC has served as a mechanism to bring together states that were described as 'like-minded' in the run-up to the Rome Conference. (Rather than the ICC being merely a 'product' of that coalition, the coalition and what it expresses are the key outcomes here.) That there is an identity dimension involved that is hard to disentangle from the logic of interest is evident.[37] However, that raises the question of what, exactly, those

37 For a useful exploration of this dimension, see Itamar Mann, 'International Criminal Law and the Ghost of Politics: Film Review' (2010) 5 *Interdisciplinary Journal of Human Rights Law* 107. See also Mégret, 'Epilogue to an Endless Debate' (n 24).

states were like minded about, how 'unlike minded' other states are, and how the community of states parties might incorporate states that are or have become differently minded. The ICC's existence as a less-than-universal court can be understood as an ongoing struggle to keep a precarious coalition together. In what follows, building and amplifying on states' individual strategies, I argue that the ICC collectively can be conceptualised as both a defensive alliance and a self-ordering community based on solidarity.

More specifically than a regional organisation, then, the ICC might first be conceived as an *alliance* of a certain group of states that happen to share a certain vision of being better protected by being parties to the Court than if they were not.[38] The point of an alliance is that it inscribes, if not quite a friend-enemy distinction, at least a keen sense of an inside and an outside. There are, therefore, two dimensions to any alliance, one more outward and directed at fending off external threats (e.g., NATO) and one more inward and geared towards internal ones (e.g., the OAS's Inter-American Democratic Charter).[39] Outwardly, the ICC can be seen as being set up by states parties to collectively protect themselves from the commission of crimes on their territory by nationals of non–states parties. States seek to protect their population and territory together and use the ICC as one part of wider strategies to deter the commission of crimes against them. Internally, as we have seen, states may also seek to protect themselves from the 'danger within': namely, the commission of crimes by the nationals of other states parties or their own nationals.

What is gained by doing this collectively rather than individually is the crucial question. After all, states might simply commit – for example, as many of them have via the ratification of international treaties – to prosecuting certain crimes domestically. Doing so collectively, however, arguably reinforces and amplifies the guarantee that these crimes will be prosecuted in at least three ways. First, if nothing else, it involves a pooling of resources and expertise. Rather than merely a commitment against impunity (which is arguably shared by all states that have subscribed to international criminal law norms), the ICC manifests a specific, non-trivial commitment to a certain multilateral internationalism in the repression of international crimes.[40] In that respect, when all is said and done, it stands more for a commitment to certain means (punishing crimes internationally) than

38 The term has very rarely been used in relation to the ICC, and when it has, its implications have not been seriously explored. See Tom Malinowski, 'The ICC: An Alliance for Justice' *Washington Post* (9 July 2001) <www.washingtonpost.com/archive/opinions/2001/07/09/the-icc-an-alliance-for-justice/c5c9bae0-b0b0-4af0-bd8d-f1aa05e53a11/> accessed 2 April 2020.

39 See Jerome Slater, *The OAS as Antidictatorial Alliance: The OAS and United States Foreign Policy* (Ohio State University Press 1967). See also Rubén M Perina, *The Organization of American States as the Advocate and Guardian of Democracy: An Insider's Critical Assessment of Its Role in Promoting and Defending Democracy* (UPA 2015).

40 Frédéric Mégret, 'The Case Against Complementarity' in Carsten Stahn and M El Zeidy (eds), *The International Criminal Court: From Theory to Practice* (2nd edn, CUP 2020).

to an end (eliminating impunity). There is an evident financial and logistical dimension to this, but also a political one that is particularly relevant when it comes to cross-border international crimes and the need to punish them through international collaboration (improving on extradition, judicial cooperation, etc.). The ICC may not seem like much of a guarantee of efficiency these days, but it is at least an improvement on the hesitancy of many domestic courts when it comes to international crimes or the obstacles to ordinary state-to-state extradition.

Secondly and relatedly, the collectivisation and institutionalisation of the response to international crime reflects a desire to dissociate decisions to prosecute from the realm of the sovereign wherein the crimes were committed. It vests a power of ultimate guarantee of the anti-impunity regime in a distinct international body that is the repository of interlocking promises and in which all states parties have an interest. It thus represents a powerful effort to externalise, depoliticise, and even sanctuarise that decision by entrusting it to decision makers that are imagined as impartial and disinterested. (Whether they are or not is another question.) This does not mean that states are not primarily responsible for carrying out prosecutions as per the principle of complementarity, but that they are no longer exclusively responsible and that the ICC can step in to prevent states from reneging on their multilateral commitment to prosecutions. It also potentially 'validates' national responses to crimes, reinforcing the case that a response is being monitored by international organs and cannot be suspected of being merely opportunistic or vengeful.

Third and finally, internationalisation includes a strong communitarian signalling function. As a collective, states parties are more credible than as individual states. Making their collective intentions known to their nationals and those of non–states parties is part of the promise of the ICC. When the Court intervenes, it does so not only as the recipient of the relevant state's 'unilateral' commitment to the Court but also as the voice of a collective that is concerned with crimes committed in its midst. Individual states could not default on their commitment to repressing international crimes without weakening the collective guarantee. The ICC materialises the common interest in the punishment of international crimes. It allows states to hold each other accountable for their failures to stand by their commitment to punishing certain crimes or to cooperate with the Court. The intuition is that the Rome Statute is not merely a treaty creating an international organisation (as is typically emphasised) but a solemn commitment *inter se* by states parties to contribute and do 'their share' in the fight against a common problem of impunity. Like all alliances, the ICC at least stabilises expectations between partners, reinforcing the predictability of their behavior and increasing the costs of departure from the norm.

c) A space for solidarity

This defensive dimension is crucial, but it hides a perhaps more compelling account of what is going on within the ICC as an alliance. Evidently, states parties to the Rome Statute are brought together by something else besides a politics of fear and protection or even simply an identity-based differentiation from the approach of non–states parties. They also express something that binds them together more positively. That cement could be a sense of shared values despite their differences, a community of destiny marked by a history of commission of atrocious crimes, or an investment in institutional forms that embody that commitment. But a conception of the Court focused on identity may be too broad brush to explain its *raison d'être*. It neglects the extent to which states parties often start with considerably different experiences and approaches to international crime, as has become only too apparent as a result of some of the rifts that have developed in their midst.

More specifically than identity, then, the ICC might be understood to express a politics of solidarity: the idea that states are not alone in dealing with atrocities and their aftermath. Solidarity is by nature a collective virtue and thus particularly suited to explaining what may hold states parties together.[41] Here, it is premised on the basic notion that crimes committed elsewhere may affect others: if not quite always 'Humanity', at least those states that have decided together to shore up the ICC. It is also based on the quite radical idea that, all other things being equal, no genocide (or crime against humanity or war crime) is less grave than any other or less worthy of international assistance. This was famously one reason why Rwanda had requested the creation of the ICTR: namely, as a validation that the crimes committed on its territory were no less serious than those committed in the former Yugoslavia (and therefore no less deserving of their own tribunal). This, then, is surely one of the most appealing ideas in the ambition that undergirds the project. It delineates a community of states that recognise certain harms as being a priori equally harmful to all of them.

The basic solidarity of international criminal justice then gives rise to a distributive economy of costs and benefits. For states parties that are highly unlikely to be involved in the mass commission of crimes, to join the Rome Statute may be a risk-less move, but it is also one that involves a contribution of resources (political, diplomatic, financial, etc.) to a common cause. For states that imagine

41 There has been an upsurge in the interest in the principle of solidarity in international law. See Abdul G Koroma, 'Solidarity: Evidence of an Emerging International Legal Principle' in Holger P Hestermeyer et al. (eds), *Coexistence, Cooperation and Solidarity* (2 vols, Brill Nijhoff 2012); Karel Wellens, 'Revisiting Solidarity as a (Re-)Emerging Constitutional Principle: Some Further Reflections' in Rüdiger Wolfrum and Chie Kojima (eds), *Solidarity: A Structural Principle of International Law* (Springer 2010); CSR Murthy and Gerrit Kurtz, 'International Responsibility as Solidarity: The Impact of the World Summit Negotiations on the R2P Trajectory' (2016) 30 *Global Society* 38. However, with a few exceptions (see Carly Nyst, 'Solidarity in a Disaggregated World – Universal Jurisdiction and the Evolution of Sovereignty' (2012) 8 *Journal of International Law and International Relations* 36), this has only tangentially been in relation to international criminal justice. See M Cherif Bassiouni, 'Negotiating the Treaty of Rome on the Establishment of an International Criminal Court Symposium: The International Criminal Court: Consenses and Debate on the International Adjudication of Genocide, Crimes Against Humanity, War Crimes, and Aggression' (1999) 32 *Cornell International Law Journal* 443, 469 (briefly mentioning that the ICC 'symbolizes human solidarity' rather than inter-state solidarity).

themselves as relatively more likely to have crimes committed on their territory or by their nationals, becoming a party to the Rome Statute is a way of capturing certain resources and good will in dealing with such crimes. The Court acts as a way of absorbing and distributing the costs of repressing massive international crimes through a collective arrangement. But both types of states are united through a voluntary cooperative framework, and this is one respect in which the ICC is much more conventionally Grotian and intergovernmental. This is a fact only reinforced by the tendency of the Court, via positive complementarity, to act not only as a jurisdiction *stricto sensu* but also as a sort of 'international anti-impunity organisation' normalising both vertical and horizontal cooperation.

There is, of course, a potential dark side to this idea of solidarity if seen in too-abstract terms: the fact that the Court is also at risk of expressing a form of governance of a periphery by a centre, where solidarity provides merely a thin veneer for dominance. The Court could certainly serve as a channel to impose the preferences of one central set of states on others. It might do so, for example, not so much because of its strict enforcement powers but because of its ability to make largely contingent choices appear to be rooted in an iron-clad institutional-legal logic. Many alliances (NATO and the Warsaw Pact, for example) come to mind as having sometimes served that role of consolidating, despite a neutral façade, a sense of the 'responsibilities' of a core towards its periphery in exchange for a certain fidelity of the periphery towards the core. Maybe such was always the design of some states towards the Court, an issue to which I return in the conclusion and which merely underscores the fragility of this sort of 'best-case scenario'.

But there is also potentially an upside. The solidarity of international criminal justice, such as it is, is also one that, in the best of cases, helps construct a community beyond itself. The ICC parties emerge as a collective that has bound itself to an institution meant to reinforce their commitment to an anti-impunity norm. They thus construct a particularly exemplary community which, over time and based on the ICC's institutional record (rather, again, than its sheer authority as an institution that claims to speak for the world), may garner increasing political support and extend its membership until maybe one day that alliance will dissolve any sense of externality in becoming universal. In that respect, the community of states parties could construct its relationship to non–states parties not as one of enmity or hegemony (seeking to subject them to its universalism) but as one based on a mixture of defensive independence (protecting the court) and solidarity (positively contributing to the justice outcomes of non–states parties, despite their indifference or opposition).

Note that states parties are at least producing what is potentially a significant positive externality for others, notably non–states parties, holding themselves to stricter common standards of achievement whilst expecting nothing (much) in return.[42] This may explain why non–states parties have occasionally recognised more or less grudgingly that the Court can be useful, especially when they could

42 On the idea that the ICC creates 'a community where participation carries benefits not only for their citizens but also for humanity as a whole', see Sang-Hyun Song, 'International Criminal Court-Centred Justice and Its Challenges Lecture' (2016) 17 *Melbourne Journal of International Law* 1, 9.

channel – at little cost to themselves – their interests via the Security Council, for example. At the same time, this occasional interest of non–states parties in the Court does point to another, more compelling potential rationale for the universality of the Court than some sort of automatic deferral to its abstract claims to universalism: the fact that non–states parties are, in some cases, essentially 'free riding' on that positive externality (in terms of justice and security) created by other states. That they bear all of the benefits of the self-policing of a large community of 120-plus states whilst providing none of the inputs, then, is a particularly glaring inequity, *a fortiori* when non–states parties have already implicitly acknowledged that the Court does provide these benefits.

The collective framing of the ICC, thus, has a number of normative implications. It suggests that departures from the ICC are rightly understood by states parties as undermining their collective interest in whatever goals the Court is supposed to achieve. For example, maneuvers that undermine the power of the Court, such as Article 98 agreements concluded by states parties with the US, weaken its ability to act as a defensive structure and therefore implicate the interests of the collective.[43] The emphasis on solidarity frames withdrawals from the Court as implicating not only the more-or-less contingent interests of the state deciding to withdraw, but also those of states remaining that had thought they could count on its continued participation.[44] At the same time, that collective interest needs to be weighed against the continued national interest of states parties and the possibility that the latter are not getting what they expected from joining the Court, as well as the need to continue framing the relationship with non–states parties in ways that are reasonably deferential to their legal interests. Alliances can be strong and resilient, but they can also be systemically precarious and even chaotic if they fail to serve their members (equally) – as the life of the Court has confirmed.

4 Conclusion: provincialising the ICC?

Provincialising the Court in the way that has been suggested in this chapter is not, as I hope will have become clear, to give up on its normative ambition but to see it for what it is: a worthwhile, productive arrangement that is nonetheless duly circumscribed by its political limitations, rooted in a sense of real but limited sovereign delegation. The alternative is that the Court will be forever condemned to be a tragic institution, unable to even grasp why it is tragic. It is tragic because it cannot become (at least in the foreseeable future) what it wants to become, understood in the most abstract and categorical cosmopolitan sense. Instead of

43 Harmen Van Der Wilt, 'Bilateral Agreements Between the United States and States Parties to the Rome Statute: Are They Compatible with the Object and Purpose of the Statute?' (2005) 18 *Leiden Journal of International Law* 93.

44 This explains why withdrawals have been framed, perhaps cogently, as 'betrayals'. See Henning Melber, 'Exiting the ICC: South Africa Betrays the World and Its Own History' *The Conversation* (27 October 2016) <http://theconversation.com/exiting-the-icc-south-africa-betrays-the-world-and-its-own-history-67577> accessed 3 April 2020.

evaluating the ICC against this largely imaginary goal, I have suggested that it is more helpful to start from what the ICC effectively already is. I have proposed that the Court is, at best, a regional institution of sorts devoted to promoting the interests of its members, albeit with some vague and promising grand design in mind.

As a result, I hope to have suggested a potentially less tragic destiny for the court: one in which it accepts that it is already the only thing that it can realistically be, but where that provides space to imagine a more robust normative trajectory. In the process of being what it is, the Court encounters and could decide to more directly confront its own politics and engage in a process of reckoning with its underlying distributive outcomes, but this is a topic beyond the scope of this chapter. The goal, at any rate, has been to produce a normative theory backwards from that reality rather than to try to fit the reality of what the ICC is within a theory that cannot countenance it. Note that the result is still a best-case normative theory that only delineates a precarious path through which the Court could thrive: it is highly vulnerable to the Court not living up to that best-case theory. But the point is also that the Court does not have much of a choice given that, as I have argued, the universalist route is not really or defensibly open to it.

This construction can then inform a particular vision of what the Court's politics could be.[45] It can resurrect an agonistic sense that to be *for* the ICC is to be, in some respects, *against* those states that are against it, at least in an adversarial sense bonded by common obligations and an 'agreement to disagree'. At the same time, it can relativise, for example, the sense that certain states not having joined the Court is fundamentally problematic and something that one should tirelessly seek to remedy. There was always something a bit quixotic about the focus on the absolute need for further ratification and making the absentees seem more part of the problem than they are. The vision of the Court suggested in this chapter, instead, is one structured by a sense of the primacy of community, albeit a fraught one, bringing together a number of states that decide, independently and together, to stand for a certain conception of the fight against impunity.

The model proposed in this chapter thus suggests that the Court should not seek to organise its relationship with non–states parties on its own exceptional terms, as if it were not simply one particular amalgamation of states dealing with other states in what is, in the end, a very Westphalian vein. This means that those states parties that seek to continue to organise their relations with non–states parties in ways that conform to traditional rules of immunity (such as the majority of African states), outside the specific case of Security Council referral, cannot easily be faulted for not doing their duty to the Court, let alone violating international law. More respect is due, in that context, to the outsiders and the search for a permanent modus vivendi with them, in a context in

45 This will be the object of a subsequent paper.

which states' identities on the international legal stage are not reduced to their ICC membership.[46]

The main thrust of downgrading the universalist ambition of the ICC, however, is that it can refocus the Court's attention on an inner sanctum of states that are its prime backers as well as its primary targets. This is, no doubt, a paradox – the fact that the Court relies on the very states that it occasionally stands to inconvenience – but it can be productive one. As we have seen, it is states parties that stand to primarily benefit from the Court's trials, although that will necessarily be at the cost of some states being put in a 'worse off' situation, at least on a short-term basis. This has put at the heart of the Court's normative dilemmas the question of its distributive politics when it comes to who should be prosecuted. A legalistic mindset has too often reduced that question to that of computing in the abstract what the 'gravest crimes' are that the Court has to deal with, at the risk of trivialising what should be the central political question of international criminal justice.

More directly tackling the question of who ends up in the crosshairs of international criminal justice as a function of a collective commitment to the Court, by contrast, has never been more urgent. It can put at the heart of the Court's politics a problematisation of what kind of alliance it stands for. In that respect, serious introspection may well reveal some of the misunderstandings on which the ICC as a communal project has always relied (notably its post-colonial and racialising dimensions). But dealing with those politics rather than pontificating about eliminating impunity from international legal heights is inevitable. The Court's success will ultimately depend on its ability not only to nurture its underlying community of reference but also to problematise it. In that respect, the true international justice of the ICC may not be so much its ability to punish international crimes in the abstract as its ability to successfully and convincingly sustain the international alliance that gave rise to that commitment.

The idea of the Court as the Court of its states parties, in that respect, also has some governance implications. In a context in which it remains perennially difficult to decide between competing prosecutorial priorities, the Court should be able to fall back much more heavily on the Assembly of States Parties as a source of general political guidance.[47] This could be in terms of the just-mentioned and

46 On some of the complex push and pull that results in terms of strategising their legal identity, see Frédéric Mégret, 'Peering behind the "Institutional Veil" to Assess State Behaviour in the Security Council: Does/Should ICC Membership Make a Difference?' (2019) 19 *International Criminal Law Review* 938.

47 Although the Report of the Independent Experts has not gone quite as far, it does recommend more strategic involvement of the Assembly of States Parties via a possible 'discussion among stakeholders' and at least encourages the Court not to consider the exercise by the Assembly of its budgetary powers as an inimical interference in its affairs. Independent Expert Review of the International Criminal Court and the Rome Statute System, *Final Report* (30 September 2020) 312–313 <https://asp.icc-cpi.int/iccdocs/asp_docs/ASP19/IER-Final-Report-ENG.pdf> accessed 22 February 2021. See also Douglas Guilfoyle, 'Lacking Conviction: Is the International Criminal Court Broken? An Organisational

ever-sensitive distributive stakes of prosecutions among states parties. But it could also extend to the crucial question of how much the Court should focus on its external cases (crimes committed by nationals of states parties on the territory of non–states parties and crimes committed by nationals of non–states parties on the territory of states parties) as opposed to the ones presenting the most points of connection to that inner sanctum (the classic case of crimes committed by nationals of states parties on the territory of states parties). After all, it is states parties who are likely to most keenly feel the impact of those decisions, which are called upon to withstand the pushback from non–states parties and whose faithfulness to the very institution they have created is constantly tested.

By sharpening the sense that the Court is based on a community that is limited and contested, I hope to have contributed to a theory of its political identity. I have argued that this way of thinking about the Court – unorthodox and running against conventional wisdom as it is – may be one that maximises untapped potentialities in its institutional life. The Court will rise or fall depending on how it confronts the contradictions at its heart, rather than by engaging in a hegemonic agenda beyond its means. Instead of speaking to the intemperate laggards backwards from the End of History, I suggested a logic of coming to terms with and even relishing the particularism of international criminal justice as something that can intensify the Court's inner life and reinforce its interventions. The Court will be no less of a worthwhile institution simply because it is not universal, and it could end up being much less of one if it failed to see the potentialities of its particularism.

Failure Analysis' (2019) 20 *Melbourne Journal of International Law* 401. (However, Guilfoyle seems to anticipate Assembly involvement mostly to deal with organisational and managerial shortfalls, not the Court's absent politics.)

3 The politics of 'the Decider' and the implications of the ICC's response to the Afghanistan and Palestine situations

Shannon Maree Torrens

1 Introduction

In April 2006, three years into the United States' (US) war in Iraq[1] and almost five years after the US invasion of Afghanistan,[2] then US President George W Bush stood in front of the press at the White House.[3] With less conviction than one might imagine would accompany these words, in an attempt to quell further questions and challenges from the press, he announced: 'I am the Decider, and I decide what is best'.[4] Bush's statement responded to the question of whether Donald Rumsfeld would continue on in the role of US Secretary of Defence.[5] There had been calls for Rumsfeld's resignation due to his alleged incompetence in the planning and execution of the war in Iraq, which were rejected by Bush.[6]

The notion of 'the Decider', as used by Bush in this context as a reference to a decision maker, is not grammatically or linguistically conventional.[7] The more common phrasing would have been 'I'm the decision maker', or 'I make the decisions'. The term 'decider' is usually used to describe a sporting play-off or a deciding goal between two teams.[8] I say this not to highlight another 'Bushism',

1 See Jane K Cramer and A Trevor Thrall, 'Introduction: Why Did the United States Invade Iraq?' in Jane K Cramer and A Trevor Thrall (eds), *Why Did the United States Invade Iraq?* (Routledge 2012).

2 Shereena Qazi and Alia Chughtai, 'US War in Afghanistan: From 2001 Invasion to 2020 Agreement' *Al Jazeera* (29 February 2020) <www.aljazeera.com/indepth/interactive/2020/02/war-afghanistan-2001-invasion-2020-taliban-deal-200229142658305.html>.

3 'Bush/Rumsfeld/Fine Job' *CNN* (broadcast 18 April 2006, uploaded 31 March 2016) <www.youtube.com/watch?v=6Z7sg_VwkXw>.

4 ibid; 'Bush: "I'm the Decider" on Rumsfeld' *CNN* (broadcast 19 April 2006) <https://edition.cnn.com/2006/POLITICS/04/18/rumsfeld/>.

5 'Bush/Rumsfeld/Fine Job' (n 3).

6 David S Cloud and Eric Schmitt, 'More Retired Generals Call for Rumsfeld's Resignation' *New York Times* (14 April 2006) <www.nytimes.com/2006/04/14/washington/more-retired-generals-call-for-rumsfelds-resignation.html>.

7 Angus Stevenson (ed), *New Oxford American Dictionary* (3rd ed, OUP 2010); Collins, 'Collins Dictionary' <www.collinsdictionary.com/dictionary/english/decider>.

8 ibid.

DOI: 10.4324/9781003087533-4

but rather to draw attention to Bush's interesting use of the phrase 'the Decider' and his description of himself as such, which comes across as somewhat petulant or childish. This is a compelling self-characterisation on multiple levels, as will be discussed.

This chapter takes this notion of the Decider as Bush intended it to be used and applies it to international criminal law (ICL) to better understand modern international criminal courts and tribunals (ICTs). In doing so, this analysis highlights issues of political interference and power in the work of the ICC with a focus on state responses and engagement with the international criminal justice project. This chapter specifically uses 'the Decider' as a frame to examine state engagement with the International Criminal Court (ICC)'s Afghanistan[9] and Palestine[10] situations.

In doing so, this chapter will look at how the US continues to act out the role of the Decider in the Afghanistan situation, seeking to obstruct the work of the Court and the investigation of international crimes allegedly committed by US citizens.[11] Moving on to the Palestine situation at the ICC, this chapter will then critique the obstructive responses of multiple states, including most notably Israel,[12] all with a view to illuminating the role of the Decider in ICL. In both instances, the key states acting in opposition to the Court in these situations, the US and Israel, are not states parties to the Rome Statute. They are concerned about the vulnerability of their citizens to prosecution and therefore oppose the jurisdiction of the Court.[13]

The notion of the Decider seeks to contribute something new to theorising and critical approaches to ICL, through using the Decider as a frame through which to look at the intersection of decision makers, decisions, and power. This is undertaken in this chapter by identifying the role and effect of the Decider in and on the work of the ICC. The further contribution is in clarifying how and why international criminal law decisions are made and by whom, as well as their broader impact, through better understanding the construction and motivations of those entities that seek to influence these decisions. An examination of the 'politics of the Decider' and the identification of states as acting out the role of

9 International Criminal Court, 'Afghanistan – Situation in the Islamic Republic of Afghanistan – ICC-02/17' <www.icc-cpi.int/afghanistan>.

10 International Criminal Court, 'Preliminary Examination – State of Palestine' <www.icc-cpi.int/palestine>.

11 'US Revokes Visa of International Criminal Court Prosecutor' *BBC* (5 April 2019) <www.bbc.com/news/world-us-canada-47822839>.

12 Israel Ministry of Foreign Affairs, 'PM Netanyahu's Remarks at the Start of the Weekly Cabinet Meeting' (16 February 2020) <https://mfa.gov.il/MFA/PressRoom/2020/Pages/PM-Netanyahu-s-remarks-at-the-start-of-the-weekly-Cabinet-meeting-16-February-2020.aspx> accessed 17 November 2020.

13 'Netanyahu Says ICC Decision Not to Probe US Troops Bodes Well for Israel' *The Times of Israel* (19 April 2019) <www.timesofisrael.com/netanyahu-says-icc-decision-not-to-probe-us-troops-bodes-well-for-israel/>.

the Decider is beneficial in terms of analysing ICL and its future, particularly as it unfolds at the ICC.

Analysis of the individuals and entities who make the decisions in ICL through the labelling of the Decider clarifies the effect of political dynamics on this field and in particular attempts, whether realised or not, to influence modern international criminal courts and tribunals and the dynamics behind those attempts at change. It is this aspect of the Decider, which is also unique – namely, the utilisation of a frame through which to understand attempts to influence in ICL and to then understand how those attempts to influence, even if unsuccessful in their aim – creates ICL. This is pertinent as the ICC moves forward this decade as the world's first permanent response to international crime.[14] These issues will be even more important as the next prosecutor of the ICC is elected and commences work in 2021[15] in a position that often deals with and is impeded by states acting out the role of the Decider in their interactions with the Court.

2 The Decider framework

a) Definition of 'the Decider'

An individual or entity who is 'the Decider' is not a decision maker in the traditional sense. On the surface, these roles may seem deceptively similar, but they are not the same concept. A conventional decision maker gains its authority through mandated powers, such as through a treaty, statute, and rules of procedure at the international level. The decision maker must usually make decisions with reference to principles and processes, pursuant to ideals such as impartiality, professionalism, and expertise. Decision makers thus act with the authority and sanction of those from whom they gain their decision-making power.

In comparison, the Decider is not merely a decision maker, although this may be part of their official role. They may make decisions in the traditional sense and have the mandated power to do so; however, the Decider will normally utilise personal power to exert influence outside this formal structure. In ICL, we see that the Decider often does not have a traditional source of decision-making authority but rather attempts to assert their political power, for example, into the justice process to influence the outcome. Deciders therefore act pursuant to a proclamation of authority, often through action and the enforcement of raw power rather than mandated power, which is accompanied by petulant demands and the derision of external criticism.

The Decider is more akin to a representation or creation by the entity exercising the power, rather than simply being a designated role or position. For

14 Rome Statute of the International Criminal Court (adopted 17 July 1998, entered into force 1 July 2002) 2187 UNTS 90 (Rome Statute).

15 International Criminal Court, 'Election of Prosecutor (2020)' <https://asp.icc-cpi.int/en_menus/asp/elections/prosecutor/Pages/Prosecutor2020.aspx>.

example, with respect to the ICC, the Rome Statute gives states parties a specific role in the Court; however, as the case studies that follow illustrate, states that are external to that official framework attempt to influence the Court's work. This is not just simply political interference or the leveraging of power; it is the self-creation of authority in a situation in which a state does not necessarily have influence and the utilisation of political interference through the creation of that authority that is external to the official judicial and political framework – in this case, the Rome Statute. The impact of this is that it brings into question the legitimacy of the ICC and raises concerns about the influence of forms of authority beyond those contained in official Court instruments.

An individual or entity takes on the role of the Decider for multiple reasons. First, there is the desire to influence a situation or course of events to their advantage, through leveraging politics and power. This action is closely linked to notions of neo-colonialism and hegemony.[16] As Antony Anghie has written, '[t]he empires of our time were short lived, but they have altered the world forever'.[17] Whilst empires are being challenged, power-seeking governments and figures are still influencing the international community and the ICC today, as an extension of their neo-colonial intentions. In labelling himself as the Decider, Bush stated that he was in the position of power. He was a controversial US and world leader, in large part due to his frequent use of US influence globally throughout his presidency, such as with the US invasion of Iraq, in addition to the US war in Afghanistan – all further examples of the US acting in the role of the Decider through failing to act with proper legal justifications and evidence.[18] Therefore, emanating from Bush, the labelling of oneself as the Decider has distinctly hegemonic and authoritative overtones that suggest an interfering power rather than simple facilitation or benevolent intervention in external situations.

An entity may also embody the Decider in order to protect the power that they already hold or to gain further power. The Decider may have some degree of legitimate decision-making power in a situation; however, in acting out the role of the Decider and constructing an image of being the one who will decide, that power is reinforced. If an individual or entity characterises him or herself as the Decider, this encourages the view that no one else is entitled or able to make the decisions that they are making. Thus, embodying this role may enable an entity to simplify and centralise the perception of their power and thus divert challenges to that power from external sources.

The categorisation of the 'self' as the Decider, as occurred in the Bush context, was arguably an avenue for the former president to restate his power and to quell

16 See Antony Anghie, *Imperialism, Sovereignty and the Making of International Law* (CUP 2004).

17 ibid., 1.

18 Gary L Gregg, 'George W Bush: Foreign Affairs' *Miller Center* <https://millercenter.org/president/gwbush/foreign-affairs>.

any challenges to this authority. In the Bush context, he did have the power he protested, which is not always the case in ICL, but it is Bush's defensive posture in asserting that power which lends a similarity to the US engagement with the ICC today. The notion of the Decider thus comprises a self-awareness of a deficit of power, or at least a lack of influential power by the entity and a perception that one's power is either dwindling or uncertain, as was the case with Bush at the time. In making these statements, Bush seemingly felt the need to remind others of his position, perhaps because of the declining influence of his position globally when the statement was made and also due to the increasing tendency of others to criticise the US president, requiring an irrefutable response and an unchallengeable constructed role of the Decider.

b) States as decision makers and Deciders

States are influential and active decision makers and 'Deciders' in the world of ICL. As discussed later in this chapter, the United Nations is a prominent decision maker in ICL in terms of the establishment and work of ICTs. The UN Security Council and its permanent five members also act as an influential decision-making body in ICL and especially with respect to the ICC, due to its role in referring situations to the ICC, if it is a situation over which the ICC does not have jurisdiction.[19] This power invested in the UN Security Council means that high-profile atrocities such as Syria are not able to be prosecuted at the ICC because the 'permanent five' veto-holding states in the UN Security Council can block their referral for political reasons, thus rendering the veto power a form of the Decider.[20] This politicises the process of situation selection at the ICC, as the permanent five members include states that are not states parties to the Rome Statute, such as the US, Russia, and China.[21] This means

19 Rome Statute, art 13(b).

20 United Nations, 'Russia, China Block Security Council Referral of Syria to International Criminal Court' (22 May 2014) <https://news.un.org/en/story/2014/05/468962-russia-china-block-security-council-referral-syria-international-criminal-court>.

21 See United Nations Security Council, 'Current Members' <www.un.org/securitycouncil/content/current-members>; International Criminal Court, 'The States Parties to the Rome Statute' <https://asp.icc-cpi.int/en_menus/asp/states%20parties/pages/the%20states%20parties%20to%20the%20rome%20statute.aspx>. See also, for example, Alana Tiemessen on how state behaviour towards the ICC has politicised prosecutions including through the UN Security Council: Alana Tiemessen, 'The International Criminal Court and the Politics of Prosecutions' (2014) 18 *International Journal of Human Rights* 444. See also Luigi Condorelli and Annalisa Ciampi, 'Comments on the Security Council Referral of the Situation in Darfur to the ICC' (2005) 3 *Journal of International Criminal Justice* 590; Rosa Aloisi, 'A Tale of Two Institutions: The United Nations Security Council and the International Criminal Court' in Dawn L Rothe, James Meernik and Thordis Ingadóttir (eds), *The Realities of International Criminal Justice* (Martinus Nijhoff 2013) (on the disservice done to the implementation of international justice through the reconciling of political and judicial interests); Louise Arbour, 'The Relationship Between the ICC and the UN Security Council' (2014) 20 *Global Governance* 195; Sarah MH Nouwen and Wouter G Werner,

that non–states parties have the ability to formulate the type of justice the ICC disseminates.

States, their leaders, and other actors are therefore influential decision makers in ICL[22] and have a tendency to take on the role of the Decider. Despite ICL focusing on the prosecution of individuals, it relies on states in a number of ways to ensure its establishment and functioning, but that can also result in political interference.[23] Modern ICTs, including the ICC, do not have their own police force; therefore, they rely on states to apprehend accused individuals and facilitate their transportation to the court or tribunal.[24] States are particularly influential at the ICC, which was established pursuant to a multilateral treaty and to date has 123 states parties,[25] which meet every year at the Assembly of States Parties (ASP) to respond to governance issues at the Court.[26] Diplomats and legal officers representing states that drafted the Rome Statute[27] and those who negotiate and vote on behalf of their countries at the ASP[28] every year also play a key role.

The decisions and actions of states therefore shape the type of justice disseminated by ICTs. In fact, multiple levels of decision making and the actors that make those decisions interact in the formulation of international criminal trials and international criminal justice more broadly. However, at times, these actors

---

'Doing Justice to the Political: The International Criminal Court in Sudan and Uganda' (2010) 21 *European Journal of International Law* 941.

22 Regarding the politics of the ICC, see generally Christian De Vos, Sara Kendall and Carsten Stahn (eds), *Contested Justice: The Politics and Practice of International Criminal Court Interventions* (CUP 2015). Regarding the influence of the Assembly of States Parties on the ICC and the risk that the ASP could undermine the ICC's judicial and prosecutorial independence, see Hannah Woolaver and Emma Palmer, 'Challenges to the Independence of the International Criminal Court from the Assembly of States Parties' (2007) 15 *Journal of International Criminal Justice* 641.

23 M Cherif Bassiouni, *Introduction to International Criminal Law* (2nd edn, Martinus Nijhoff 2013) 539. See also the political science scholarship in this area, e.g., Tim Dunn and Jess Gifkins, 'Libya and the State of Intervention' (2011) 65 *Australian Journal of International Affairs* 515; Jason Ralph, 'International Society, the International Criminal Court and American Foreign Policy' (2005) 31 *Review of International Studies* 27; Nicola P Contessi, 'Multilateralism, Intervention and Norm Contestation: China's Stance on Darfur in the UN Security Council' (2010) 41 *Security Dialogue* 323; Jay Goodliffe and Darren Hawkins, 'A Funny Thing Happened on the Way to Rome: Explaining International Criminal Court Negotiations' (2009) 71 *Journal of Politics* 977; Troels Burchall Henningsen and Line Engbo Gissel, 'Non-Cooperation with the International Criminal Court in Gatekeeper States: Regime Security in Deby's Chad' (2020) *Cambridge Review of International Affairs* <www.tandfonline.com/doi/full/10.1080/09557571.2020.1828281>.

24 Bassiouni (n 23) 539.

25 International Criminal Court, 'The States Parties to the Rome Statute' (n 21).

26 International Criminal Court, 'Assembly of States Parties' <www.icc-cpi.int/asp> accessed 1 May 2020.

27 Regarding the negotiations and drafting of the Rome Statute, see Philippe Kirsch, 'The Development of the Rome Statute' in Roy S Lee (ed), *The International Criminal Court: The Making of the Rome Statute: Issues, Negotiations, Results* (Kluwer Law International 1999).

28 International Criminal Court, 'Assembly of States Parties' (n 26).

can veer from being merely decision makers to being 'Deciders', depending on the goals that they want to achieve, as will be explored throughout this chapter. Even beyond the creation of ICTs, states and their leaders can act in the role of the Decider through influencing proceedings and failing to cooperate with the operation of the ICT.[29] The influence of states in the work of the ICC is reflected in, for example, protracted proceedings, as will be discussed later, with the ICC prosecutor's preliminary examination into the Afghanistan situation taking more than ten years.[30] It was difficult for the Office of the Prosecutor to undertake the preliminary examination, and there were potentially political forces that prolonged the process. A number of these issues are replicated in the analysis of the Palestine situation at the ICC, reflecting the interference of the Decider.

c) Decisions in ICL

In understanding what a 'Decider', as discussed here, is, it is important to define what comprises a decision in ICL and what decisions are most commonly made by 'Deciders'. The modern international criminal justice project is formed through the making of decisions at multiple levels. Firstly, there are the decisions that are made to establish each respective ICT, such as through the UN Security Council, as was the case with the Yugoslav and Rwandan tribunals;[31] an agreement, such as occurred with the Sierra Leone and Cambodia hybrid courts;[32] or a treaty, as established the ICC.[33] Prominent decisions also include the delivery of a trial or appeal judgment and decisions by the judges of the court. There is also the decision to select or elect certain individuals to prominent positions at the ICT, such as judges and the chief prosecutor; the decision to prosecute a particular case but not another; and the decision to call certain witnesses and tender certain evidence by the parties or judges, depending on the ICT and its rules of procedure and evidence.

The role of the Decider often focuses on decisions that are made without formal authorisation, meaning they go beyond a law or rule that enables an individual or entity to make a decision. These "decisions" can also be completely outside any formal decision-making framework. The role of the Decider does not, however, always involve explicitly making decisions or a decision that is part

29 For example, Rwanda, which failed to cooperate with the ICTR: Sarah Williams, *Hybrid and Internationalised Criminal Tribunals: Selected Jurisdictional Issues* (Hart 2012) 365.

30 International Criminal Court, 'Situation in the Islamic Republic of Afghanistan' (n 9).

31 See UNSC Res 827 (25 May 1993) UN Doc S/RES/827; UNSC Res 955 (8 November 1994) UN Doc S/RES/955.

32 Agreement between the United Nations and the Government of Sierra Leone on the Establishment of a Special Court for Sierra Leone (signed 16 January 2002, entered into force 12 April 2002) 2178 UNTS 138; Agreement between the United Nations and the Royal Government of Cambodia Concerning the Prosecution under Cambodian Law of Crimes Committed During the Period of Democratic Kampuchea (signed 6 June 2003, entered into force 29 April 2005) 2329 UNTS 117.

33 Rome Statute.

of a legal process, such as takes place at the ICC, but rather, they may act in a way to attempt to influence those decisions. At times, there is an attempt to act in the role of the Decider or to claim Decider status, as will be discussed later in this chapter, which is not necessarily ultimately successful or influential in the final outcome of the Court's processes but which does cast questions on the independence of the Court.

Decisions that are made expressly or covertly without authorisation are often made by those acting out the role of the Decider, when the power to make the decision is merely assumed or undertaken surreptitiously. The ability of the Decider to act in this way is emboldened because power, politics, and decisions are closely linked in ICL. In this field, the state, for example, makes the decision, and their allies will then go on to reinforce the decision. This is particularly so when the decision is made by a 'Decider' that is framing itself as having power in the situation to make an irrefutable decision. Allies reinforce the decision as part of maintaining hegemonic power, alliances, and a global hierarchical structure.

The motivation behind these decisions is significant when analysing the role of the Decider and how this relates to outcomes. It is, of course, challenging to ever truly identify the real motivations behind a decision. We can only speculate through analysing actions and context, the latter of which is relevant in ICL due to the effect of politics on the field.[34] A Decider may believe they know their real motivations, but that may not be the case. There may have been other considerations the Decider did not consciously recognise were included in coming to a particular decision, such as biases and prejudices that were incorporated without recognition. Analysing decisions and those who make them therefore involves considerable interpretation and context analysis, especially those decisions made by Deciders. In the examples outlined next, the focus is predominantly on national self-interest. A number of these decisions can be seen in the Afghanistan and Palestine situations at the ICC as will be discussed in the following sections, serving to illustrate the role of the Decider in ICL.

3 Defining power and politics in international criminal law

In recent years, support for the international criminal justice project has given way to growing critique and an awareness of the powers that inform modern ICTs.[35] The politics of international law more generally was well articulated by

34 See discussion on politics and ICL in Part 3.

35 See, e.g., Gerry J Simpson, *Law, War and Crime: War Crimes, Trials and the Reinvention of International Law* (Polity 2007); Oumar Ba, *States of Justice: The Politics of the International Criminal Court* (CUP 2020); Phil Clark, *Distant Justice: The Impact of the International Criminal Court on African Politics* (CUP 2018); Christopher Rudolph, *Power and Principle: The Politics of International Criminal Courts* (Cornell University Press 2017); Yves Beigbeder, *Judging War Criminals: The Politics of International Justice* (Palgrave Macmillan 1998); William Schabas, *Unimaginable Atrocities: Justice, Politics, and Rights*

Martti Koskenniemi, who wrote that '[i]t is impossible to make substantive decisions within the law which would imply no political choice'.[36] Focusing on the Decider highlights a new angle to the analysis of power in ICL which builds on and refines this existing literature, as discussed later. To examine these issues a range of texts were reviewed, including ICC documents and statements by the ICC prosecutor, as well as political leaders from the states in question. These documents were read with a view to understanding the motivations behind the making of decisions at the ICC and also those decisions made in relation to the Court's operations.

In addition to the theoretical focus of the politics of the Decider and the creation of this frame of reference, what sets this critique apart from the existing, predominantly black-letter scholarship on decision makers and decisions in ICL scholarship[37] is that the notion of the Decider is not merely a decision maker in ICL that is informed by political interests and intent; rather, the Decider attempts to influence particular cases and situations and, in doing so, influences the field as a whole, even if that attempt at influence was not successful.

The Decider as envisaged by this chapter is unique in that it provides a theory and frame to better understand the interactions and tensions between the legal and physical structures and actors of ICTs through the decisions of key actors and an examination of what influences them and how they utilise their own influence on situations. The Decider thus contributes to understanding the ICC and its political nature because it highlights the importance of not just the substance of the Court but also of those who interact with it, often without altruistic but rather self-interested intentions. The notion of authority and understanding those who wield power are also significant in conceptions of international justice and power, as is evidenced in the politics of the Decider.

Applying the discourse of the Decider to an actor's behaviour is important because it gives substance to intangible notions of power that are often difficult to define in concrete terms. This helps us see that political interference in the work of modern ICTs is not an abstract phenomenon, but rather it emanates from a specific concrete entity and thought process which results in a decision, often with political interests. Labelling entities as Deciders, therefore, assists in broadening and deepening our understanding of decisions in ICL, why particular decisions are made, and what effect these decisions have on outcomes of the ICT.

---

at the War Crimes Tribunals (OUP 2012); Cecilia M Bailliet and Nobuo Hayashi (eds), *The Legitimacy of International Criminal Tribunals* (CUP 2017); Kamari Maxine Clarke, *Affective Justice: The International Criminal Court and the Pan-Africanist Pushback* (Duke University Press 2019). See also, more generally, Martti Koskenniemi, *The Politics of International Law* (Bloomsbury 2011).

36 Martti Koskenniemi, 'The Politics of International Law' (1990) 1 *European Journal of International Law* 4, 31.

37 Note also the scholarship on the topic of decision makers and decision making in ICL particularly with respect to the UN Security Council and the ICC: earlier nn 21 and 22.

In terms of wider debates about politics and power in the field of ICL, the notion of the Decider not only labels certain behaviour as being politically driven or self-interested, but it also helps divorce the behaviour from the actor, thus highlighting that context plays an influential role in the formulation and actions of the Decider and in the decisions that are made. The notion of the Decider thus enables us to see that the role of the actor and its impact are distinct and that this is affected by context. This Decider may therefore act in very different ways depending on the particular context. For example, the US is highly supportive of international criminal justice, just as long as it is not itself the subject of prosecutions.

Recalling that the Decider is an entity that takes on a political and defensive posture of power, as did Bush, it is possible to see that there are similar themes in each of the two case studies in this chapter, those of Afghanistan and Palestine. These themes suggest that in certain contexts, such as the interaction of non–states parties with the ICC, when a state's citizens are vulnerable to prosecution, in addition to interactions of the ICC with powerful or at least seemingly powerful states and also in the context of high profile, high stakes situations at the Court, the politics of the Decider is more readily apparent. Finally, the role of the Decider also highlights how bystanders, whether silent or supportive, facilitate the functioning of the Decider, meaning that the Decider is not a unilateral construction.

4 The Afghanistan situation

a) Overview

The preliminary examination into the Afghanistan situation at the ICC began in 2006.[38] It was, however, not until November 2017, over ten years later, when ICC Prosecutor Fatou Bensouda requested authorisation from the ICC Pre-Trial Chamber to open an investigation.[39] The ICC finally decided to open a formal investigation in 2020, on appeal, 14 years after the preliminary examination commenced.[40] This appeal decision came after a 2019 pre-trial decision which rejected the opening of an investigation.[41] The preceding events were controversial to say

38 Fatou Bensouda, 'The Prosecutor of the International Criminal Court, Fatou Bensouda, Requests Judicial Authorisation to Commence an Investigation into the Situation in the Islamic Republic of Afghanistan' *International Criminal Court* (20 November 2017) <www.icc-cpi.int/Pages/item.aspx?name=171120-otp-stat-afgh> accessed 3 May 2002.

39 ibid; 'Public Redacted Version of "Request for Authorisation of an Investigation Pursuant to Article 15", 20 November 2017, ICC-02/17–7-Conf-Exp' *Situation in the Islamic Republic of Afghanistan*, ICC-02/17–7-Red (20 November 2017) (Afghanistan Investigation Request).

40 'Judgment on the Appeal Against the Decision on the Authorisation of an Investigation into the Situation in the Islamic Republic of Afghanistan' *Situation in the Islamic Republic of Afghanistan*, ICC-02/17–138 (5 March 2020) (Afghanistan Investigation Appeal).

41 'Decision Pursuant to Article 15 of the Rome Statute on the Authorisation of an Investigation into the Situation in the Islamic Republic of Afghanistan' *Situation in the Islamic Republic of Afghanistan*, ICC-02/17–33 (12 April 2019) (Afghanistan Investigation PTC Decision).

the least and illustrate the role of states in influencing the justice process at the ICC through embodying the role of the Decider.

In March 2019, the US, which is not a state party to the Rome Statute, said that it would revoke or deny the visas of ICC staff members who were involved in the Afghanistan preliminary examination.[42] US Secretary of State Mike Pompeo unabashedly took up the anti-ICC line of the US government, saying '[t]he ICC is attacking America's rule of law'.[43] In an effort to intimidate the Court's officials into stopping the investigation, he then suggested '[i]t's not too late for the court to change course and we urge that it do so immediately'.[44] At the time, Pompeo also threatened economic sanctions if the ICC investigation went ahead.[45]

Whilst the US is not a state party to the Rome Statute, the ICC has jurisdiction over the Afghanistan situation, because Afghanistan, the territory on which the majority of the crimes were allegedly committed, is a state party.[46] The US is unsurprisingly concerned about an investigation into Afghanistan due to US military engagement in the country. The actions of US citizens who are under scrutiny are not only those crimes allegedly committed in Afghanistan, but also those committed in secret CIA detention facilities in other states parties to the Rome Statute: namely, Poland, Lithuania, and Romania.[47]

In April 2019, it was reported that the US government had indeed revoked the visas in question.[48] As it would be necessary for ICC prosecution staff to collect evidence in both the US and Afghanistan to conduct an effective investigation and trial, preventing them from entering the US would render the job of those working on this situation difficult, if not impossible. Soon after this development, on 12 April, the Pre-Trial Chamber of the ICC rejected the opening of an investigation into the Afghanistan situation,[49] which raises questions about the close timing of the two events and their influence on one another.

The Pre-Trial Chamber decision was then appealed by the prosecutor, and one year later, in March 2020, the ICC Appeals Chamber held that the Pre-Trial Chamber had erred because it was not its role to rule on whether an investigation into Afghanistan was in the interests of justice.[50] The Appeals Chamber held that the Pre-Trial Chamber's only role was to rule on whether there was a reasonable basis to proceed with an investigation and on whether the case was within the jurisdiction of the ICC, which the Appeals Chamber believed the Pre-Trial

42 AFP in Washington, 'US to Deny Visas for ICC Members Investigating Alleged War Crimes' *The Guardian* (15 March 2019) <www.theguardian.com/us-news/2019/mar/15/mike-pompeo-us-war-crimes-investigation-international-criminal-court> accessed 2 May 2020.

43 ibid.

44 ibid.

45 ibid.

46 International Criminal Court, 'Afghanistan – Ratification and Implementation Status' <https://asp.icc-cpi.int/en_menus/asp/states%20parties/asian%20states/Pages/afghanistan.aspx> accessed 2 May 2020; Rome Statute, art 12(2)(a).

47 Afghanistan Investigation Request (n 39) [249].

48 'US Revokes Visa of International Criminal Court Prosecutor' (n 11).

49 Afghanistan Investigation PTC Decision (n 41).

50 Afghanistan Investigation Appeal (n 40) [25].

Chamber had already done.[51] The Afghanistan situation has now moved to the investigation phase. It is, however, uncertain at this point how long the investigation will last. It is doubtful that this process will be swift due to US opposition, as will be discussed in the following section, and the state's embodiment of the Decider.

b) State responses: the US, Afghanistan and others

The extent of US hypocrisy in its engagement with ICL was brought to light with the Afghanistan situation at the ICC, with the US embodying the role of the Decider in its dealings with the Court. US opposition to the ICC is generally motivated by the concern that US citizens may be held accountable for crimes committed in overseas military operations. Secretary of State Pompeo said the ICC Appeal decision which authorised the Afghanistan investigation was 'a truly breathtaking action by an unaccountable political institution, masquerading as a legal body'.[52] That the US sought to revoke the visas of the ICC prosecutor and other staff working on the Afghanistan preliminary examination suggests that there is political interference in the work of the Court or at least attempted political interference by the US. The US has therefore taken on the mantle of the Decider in an attempt to thwart or at least subvert the justice process for its own benefit and protection.

The US has historically been supportive of international criminal justice initiatives, holding itself up as a pillar of ending impunity for international crimes, so long as its citizens are not held accountable. The US has had an influential role in ICL since its inception, going as far back as the Nuremberg trials.[53] The Rwandan and Yugoslav tribunals, the Special Court for Sierra Leone, and the Special Tribunal for Lebanon all received support and funding from the US.[54] Today, however, as one of the permanent five members of the UN Security Council, the US sends situations to and can also block them from going to the ICC[55] but vocally opposes being held accountable for international crimes itself, such as at the ICC. For example, John Bolton, then US national security advisor, said that the US would 'use any means necessary to protect our citizens and those of our allies from unjust prosecution by this illegitimate court'.[56]

51 ibid., [34].

52 ABC News, 'Afghanistan War Crimes Investigation by ICC Goes Ahead Despite US Opposition' (6 March 2020) <https://www.abc.net.au/news/2020-03-06/afghanistan-war-crimes-investigation-goes-ahead-despite-us-oppo/12031926> accessed 17 November 2020.

53 On US leadership at the Nuremberg trials, see David P Forsythe (ed), *Encyclopedia of Human Rights* (vol 3, OUP 2009) 118.

54 Regarding the ICTY and ICTR with the US being the biggest funders of the tribunals, see Annie R Bird, *US Foreign Policy on Transitional Justice* (OUP 2015) 39. Regarding the SCSL and STL, see Marieke Wierda and Anthony Triolo, 'Resources' in Luc Reydams, Jan Wouters and Cedric Ryngaert (eds), *International Prosecutors* (OUP 2012) 113, 149–50.

55 Rome Statute, art 13(b).

56 'Full Text of John Bolton's Speech to the Federalist Society' *Al Jazeera* (10 September 2018) <www.aljazeera.com/news/2018/9/10/full-text-of-john-boltons-speech-to-the-federalist-society> accessed 17 November 2020.

The ICC's response to the Afghanistan situation has not been consistent, suggesting that at times the Court is potentially influenced by US political interference. As noted, in 2019, the Pre-Trial Chamber ruled that it did not believe that it would be in the interests of justice for there to be an investigation into the Afghanistan situation; this was reversed on appeal. This is quite a dramatic shift and interesting in the context of the political storm that surrounded these decisions. It is not at all uncommon for courts to rule differently on appeal; that is not what is controversial about this situation. What is controversial is the timing of the Pre-Trial decision, which occurred soon after the US revoked the visas of ICC staff working on the situation and after considerable US vocalisation of its opposition to the Court.

Also troubling is that the Pre-Trial Chamber said that primary actors in the case (referring to the US) might not cooperate with the proceedings.[57] This pragmatic assessment may be true; however, it is not common for a court of law, particularly an international court of law, to cite difficulties posed by the parties and other interested actors in the potential proceedings as a reason not to proceed with the case. If anything, this should be a reason *to* open an investigation because a domestic trial might not be possible at the national level in any country due to political interference.

Afghanistan itself has increased its interaction with the ICC, notably in April 2020, when the prosecutor of the ICC notified the Court that in March 2020, Afghanistan had requested that the ICC prosecutor defer its investigation of persons the state is investigating or has investigated, pursuant to the complementarity provisions of the Rome Statute.[58] Here, Afghanistan attempted to take back control of the investigation, or at least part of the investigation. Due to the COVID-19 pandemic, it is not yet certain the extent of Afghanistan's investigations.[59] The summary provided by Afghanistan notes that their investigations focus on the Taliban and related groups, Afghan Security Forces and international forces, ISIS (Daesh), and others.[60] It is unlikely the US will respond well to the possibility of Afghanistan attempting to prosecute these individuals if the trials involve US citizens in the reference to 'international forces'. If the US is not supportive of the ICC prosecuting US citizens, it is unlikely to support their prosecution by Afghanistan.

This double standard by which the US proclaims the benefits of international justice on one hand and then opposes it on the other is only possible because its embodiment of the Decider is sanctioned by others, such as Israel's support of US opposition to the Court.[61] This is concerning because it highlights that

57 Afghanistan Investigation PTC Decision (n 41) [94].

58 'Notification to the Pre-Trial Chamber of the Islamic Republic of Afghanistan's Letter Concerning Article 18(2) of the Statute' *Situation in the Islamic Republic of Afghanistan*, ICC-02/17-139 (15 April 2020).

59 ibid., [2].

60 ibid., annex 1.

61 'Netanyahu Says ICC Decision Not to Probe US Troops Bodes Well for Israel' (n 13).

in many ways the US influences international criminal justice and responses to international crime through its own self-characterisation as the Decider, such as through obstructing the justice process. It is interesting that the US can have such an influence on the work of the Court, despite not even being a state party to the Rome Statute. This illustrates that politics and power influence[62] international law and ICL more specifically and that these dynamics create an environment in which the role of the Decider can flourish.

This is common when a country that wants to influence ICL is a powerful nation or an ally of a powerful nation. While the hegemonic clout of the US is declining,[63] the US still exerts influence in the international arena. That the US was once powerful means that at times, countries continue to act with deference to outdated historical power structures that were once far more influential than they are today. This international deference emboldens the US's embodiment of the Decider in its dealings with the ICC and its ability to influence the Court and its situations. Therefore, it is not just the actions and communication of the US that create the role of the Decider; rather, it is often the silent approval of others that enables the US to take on this role without opposition (for example, the failure of states to take a stand against US interference with the ICC). It was only recently that 72 states parties to the Rome Statute offered 'unwavering support' to the ICC in light of US sanctions against ICC staff.[64] This is a positive move, but it will undoubtedly provide the US with another opportunity to state its opposition to the Court and thus act defensively against its operations.

5 The Palestine situation

a) Overview

Alongside the Afghanistan situation at the ICC, the Palestine situation has also been the subject of a lengthy preliminary examination, five years and counting.[65] In 2015, Bensouda decided to open a preliminary examination into the Palestine situation at the Court.[66] This was greeted with praise, at least by those sympathetic to the Palestinian cause[67] as the crimes that have been committed in the Occupied

62 Regarding politics and ICL, see David Bosco, *Rough Justice: The International Criminal Court in a World of Power Politics* (OUP 2014).

63 See Justin Massie and Jonathan Paquin (eds), *America's Allies and the Decline of US Hegemony* (Routledge 2019).

64 'UK, Australia Among 72 Nations Offering ICC "Unwavering Support"' *Al Jazeera* (3 November 2020) <www.aljazeera.com/news/2020/11/3/uk-australia-among-72-nations-offering-icc-unwavering-support> accessed 17 November 2020.

65 International Criminal Court, 'Preliminary Examination – State of Palestine' (n 10).

66 ibid. See generally Seada Hussein Adem, *Palestine and the International Criminal Court* (Springer 2019).

67 See, e.g., Human Rights Watch, 'Palestine: ICC Prosecutor Opens Initial Inquiry' (29 January 2015) <www.hrw.org/news/2015/01/29/palestine-icc-prosecutor-opens-initial-inquiry> accessed 7 May 2020.

Palestine Territory (OPT) have thus far never been prosecuted at an ICT due to the political sensitivity of the Israeli-Palestinian conflict. Furthermore, the ICC has to date focused its prosecutions on Africa;[68] therefore, an investigation into and potential trial of crimes committed in the Middle East would be a welcome development on the Court's docket, reflecting a fleshing-out of the ICC's role as an 'international court'.

The preliminary examination into the Palestine situation at the ICC only focuses on crimes committed since 13 June 2014, which marks the 2014 Gaza conflict.[69] The prosecutor has also considered illegal Israeli settlements in the West Bank since that date and the 2018–2019 Gaza border unrest.[70] Despite there being many other international crimes that have been committed in the OPT that could be prosecuted, they are currently beyond the jurisdiction of the Court. The Rome Statute came into force in 2002; therefore no crimes committed prior to that date can be prosecuted.[71] Further, no crimes committed prior to the date the triggering state joined the ICC can be prosecuted, unless a declaration has been made.[72]

Palestine lodged a declaration accepting the jurisdiction of the ICC in January 2015 and then officially became a state party to the Rome Statute in April 2015.[73] This followed Palestine being recognised as a non-member observer state of the UN in November 2012 by the UN General Assembly.[74] Upon accepting the jurisdiction of the ICC, Palestine then accepted the retrospective jurisdiction of the Court from 13 June 2014.[75] Even though a preliminary examination

68 International Criminal Court, 'Cases' <www.icc-cpi.int/cases> accessed 2 May 2020; Alexandra Zavis and Robyn Dixon, 'Q&A: Only Africans Have Been Tried at the Court for the Worst Crimes on Earth' *LA Times* (23 October 2016) <www.latimes.com/world/africa/la-fg-icc-africa-snap-story.html> accessed 7 May 2020. See also Kamari M Clarke, Abel S Knottnerus and Eefje de Volder (eds), *Africa and the ICC: Perceptions of Justice* (CUP 2016); Gerhard Werle, Lovell Fernandez and Moritz Vormbaum (eds), *Africa and the International Criminal Court* (Springer 2014).

69 International Criminal Court, 'Preliminary Examination – State of Palestine' (n 10); Office of the Prosecutor, 'Report on Preliminary Examination Activities: 2019' *International Criminal Court* (5 December 2019) <www.icc-cpi.int/itemsDocuments/191205-rep-otp-PE.pdf> accessed 6 May 2020 [223].

70 Office of the Prosecutor, 'Report on Preliminary Examination Activities: 2019' (n 69) [220], [226].

71 Rome Statute, art 11(1).

72 ibid. art 11(2).

73 International Criminal Court, 'State of Palestine' <https://www.icc-cpi.int/palestine> accessed 7 May 2020.

74 Status of Palestine in the United Nations, UNGA Res 67/19 (4 December 2012) UN Doc A/RES/67/19; Louis Charbonneau, 'Palestinians Win Implicit UN Recognition of Sovereign State' *Reuters* (29 November 2012) <www.reuters.com/article/us-palestinians-statehood/palestinians-win-implicit-u-n-recognition-of-sovereign-state-idUSBRE8AR0EG20121129> accessed 10 May 2020; Edwin Egede, *Politics of International Law and International Justice* (Edinburgh University Press 2013) 101.

75 Office of the Prosecutor, 'Report on Preliminary Examination Activities: 2019' (n 69) [204].

into the Palestine situation was already underway, in May 2018, the State of Palestine referred the Palestine situation to the ICC prosecutor,[76] which means that the ICC prosecutor did not have to seek the approval of the Pre-Trial Chamber before progressing to an investigation, although that is what actually occurred. In late 2019, Bensouda announced that the preliminary examination into the Palestine situation would come to an end as she believed that a 'reasonable basis' existed to launch an investigation.[77] However, before taking this step, the prosecutor asked the ICC Pre-Trial Chamber to rule on the issue of the territorial jurisdiction of the area under consideration – namely, Palestine – consisting of the West Bank, including East Jerusalem, and the Gaza Strip, otherwise known as the OPT.[78]

The opening of the preliminary examination into the Palestine situation was a positive step forward for the ICC and for crimes committed in the OPT; however, progress towards an actual investigation, let alone a trial, has been lagging. The Pre-Trial Chamber is currently grappling with disagreement as to the existence of the State of Palestine and the territorial jurisdiction of the Court, which has created difficulties for the prosecution in proceeding with an investigation and trial, as numerous states attempt to intervene in the proceedings, at times acting out the role of the Decider, as will be discussed later.

b) State responses: Israel, Palestine, and the US

Like the US, Israel has been vocal about its opposition to the ICC and the Palestine preliminary examination.[79] Also like the US, Israel is not a state party to the Rome Statute and argues that the Court has no jurisdiction to prosecute Israeli citizens.[80] Despite Israel not being a state party to the Rome Statute, the ICC has prima facie jurisdiction over the Palestine situation because the State of Palestine is a state party, and the alleged crimes were committed in the territory of Palestine, a similar situation to the Afghanistan situation.[81] External intervention into

76 International Criminal Court, 'State of Palestine' (n 73); State of Palestine, 'Referral by the State of Palestine Pursuant to Articles 13(a) and 14 of the Rome Statute' PAL-180515-Ref, *International Criminal Court* (15 May 2018) <www.icc-cpi.int/itemsDocuments/2018-05-22_ref-palestine.pdf> accessed 12 May 2020.

77 Fatou Bensouda, 'Statement of ICC Prosecutor, Fatou Bensouda, on the Conclusion of the Preliminary Examination of the Situation in Palestine, and Seeking a Ruling on the Scope of the Court's Territorial Jurisdiction' *International Criminal Court* (20 December 2019) <www.icc-cpi.int/Pages/item.aspx?name=20191220-otp-statement-palestine> accessed 2 May 2020.

78 ibid.

79 Israel Ministry of Foreign Affairs (n 12); Dominic McGoldrick, 'Political and Legal Responses to the ICC' in Dominic McGoldrick, Peter Rowe and Eric Donnelly (eds), *The Permanent International Criminal Court: Legal and Policy Issues* (Hart 2004) 439.

80 Israel Ministry of Foreign Affairs (n 12).

81 See Rome Statute, art 12(2)(a); Yaël Ronen, 'The International Criminal Court and Nationals of Non-Party States' in Gerhard Werle and Andreas Zimmermann (eds), *The International Criminal Court in Turbulent Times* (Springer 2019).

the affairs of states that may not necessarily want to be the subject of international justice mechanisms is, of course, the nature of ICL, where it is not uncommon for a court or tribunal to be established by the UN with a focus on a particular country or situation, even without the support of the state in question. Therefore, this extension of ICC jurisdiction over non–states parties is in alignment with previous international intervention on international criminal justice issues.

Israel's Prime Minister Benjamin Netanyahu opposes this intervention and has said that the ICC is 'a political instrument in the war against Israel'.[82] Israel's opposition to the ICC, therefore, raises questions as to how a potential investigation and trial at the Court would work if Israel refused to cooperate, such as with the collection of evidence in both Palestine and Israel, which would require the cooperation of the respective authorities.[83] This is particularly so when Netanyahu has said '[t]he ICC only has jurisdiction over petitions submitted by sovereign states. But there has never been a Palestinian state'.[84] Along with the Afghanistan situation, the Palestine situation highlights that the ICC requires the cooperation of both states parties and non–states parties to work effectively. Without state support, the ICC is hamstrung or at the least seriously impeded in its operations, especially when there is political interference.

The State of Palestine has cooperated with the Court through firstly joining the Court and then through referring its situation to the prosecutor.[85] Whilst Palestinian individuals can be prosecuted, as has been mentioned by the prosecutor,[86] she has focused her preliminary examination on Israeli settlements in the West Bank and the 2014 Gaza conflict,[87] within which a disproportionate number of Palestinians lost their lives due to Israeli attacks.[88] Just over 2,251 Palestinians, including 1,462 civilians, were killed in comparison to 67 Israeli soldiers and

82 Israel Ministry of Foreign Affairs (n 12).

83 Note that the ICC does not have its own police force: Steven R Ratner, Jason S Abrams and James L Bischoff, *Accountability for Human Rights Atrocities in International Law: Beyond the Nuremberg Legacy* (3rd edn, OUP 2009) 254.

84 Stephanie van den Berg, 'ICC to Probe Alleged War Crimes in Palestinian Areas, Pending Jurisdiction' *Reuters* (21 December 2019) <www.reuters.com/article/us-icc-palestinians-israel-idUSKBN1YO1S9> accessed 17 November 2020.

85 International Criminal Court, 'Preliminary Examination – State of Palestine' (n 10); Office of the Prosecutor, 'Report on Preliminary Examination Activities: 2019' (n 69) [201], [204].

86 See, e.g., Office of the Prosecutor, 'Report on Preliminary Examination Activities: 2018' *International Criminal Court* (5 December 2018) <www.icc-cpi.int/itemsDocuments/181205-rep-otp-PE-ENG.pdf> accessed 4 May 2020 [272].

87 Office of the Prosecutor, 'Report on Preliminary Examination Activities: 2019' (n 69) [220], [223]. Regarding Israeli settlements, see also Simon McKenzie, *Disputed Territories and International Criminal Law: Israeli Settlements and the International Criminal Court* (Routledge 2019).

88 United Nations Office for the Coordination of Humanitarian Affairs, 'Key Figures on the 2014 Hostilities' (23 June 2015) <www.ochaopt.org/content/key-figures-2014-hostilities> accessed 1 May 2020.

6 Israeli civilians.[89] Of the Palestine investigation, the Palestinian Authority has said that 'Palestine welcomes this step as a long overdue step to move the process forward towards an investigation, after nearly five long and difficult years of preliminary examination'.[90]

The US, a strong ally of Israel, has expressed its opposition to the Palestine investigation. Secretary of State Pompeo said: 'We firmly oppose this and any other action that seeks to target Israel unfairly'.[91] This is an interesting statement, given that the US is not a state party to the Rome Statute; however, they are phrasing their opposition to the Palestine situation in a way which suggests that the US believes it has a role to play and a right to intervene in international prosecutions at the ICC. This is an example of the US acting in the role of the Decider, through framing itself as being the one to decide on international criminal justice issues in a context – such as the ICC – in which they do not have a legitimate role of intervention outside the UN Security Council or a role in which such commentary would be warranted. If the US did not think it had an influential role with respect to the ICC, it would not comment on the Palestine issue at the Court. The implication of this is that every time the US takes this stance of the Decider as an external actor to the Court, it undermines the integrity of the ICC.

c) State responses: others

On 28 January 2020, the ICC invited Palestine, Israel, and other interested states, organisations, and experts to submit their observations on the territorial jurisdiction of the Court in relation to Palestine.[92] Bensouda asked the Pre-Trial Chamber to rule on this issue, despite not being required to do so because of Palestine's referral.[93] Bensouda stated that this was because of the 'the unique and highly contested legal and factual issues attaching to this situation, namely, the territory within which the investigation may be conducted'.[94] The prosecutor is, of course, referring to the longstanding conflict and disagreement over the statehood of Palestine, which has gone on for over half a century.

This highlights the importance of states to the work of the ICC and the disruption caused by their interference and obstruction. The prosecutor likely assumes that states will object to the jurisdiction of the Court in the Palestine situation and to the existence of the State of Palestine once the investigation or trial is underway and therefore believes it is best to address these issues at the current moment. Thus, fear of the defensive response of Israel and its acting out the role

89 ibid.
90 van den Berg (n 84).
91 ibid.
92 'Order Setting the Procedure and the Schedule for the Submission of Observations' *Situation in the State of Palestine*, ICC-01/18–14, ICC Pre-Trial Chamber I (28 January 2020).
93 Bensouda, 'Statement on the Conclusion of the Preliminary Examination of the Situation in Palestine' (n 77).
94 ibid.

of the Decider has shaped the operations of the Court through responding to the issue of the existence of Palestine, which, through the Court's cooperation in highlighting this issue, also provides Israel with an opportunity to continue to state its position.

A number of other countries and entities have therefore weighed in on the Pre-Trial Chamber's ruling on territorial jurisdiction, providing amicus curiae briefs, with some states taking on the mantle of the Decider, in a situation that often has very little to do with these states, outside of their being states parties to the Rome Statute. This suggests that the Palestine situation will be a notable case at the Court due to the complex history of Palestine and Israel and the powerful allies and sympathisers of Israel who are brought into the mix.

It is interesting that states took this opportunity to make statements about the existence of Palestine. If this was such a strongly felt opinion, then it likely should have been brought to the attention of the Court formally and earlier than this moment, such as when Palestine became a state party. It seems potentially strategic for this issue to be raised now, years later and after the fact.

These states are not the primary Decider on this issue – that would be Israel – or the ultimate decision maker, which would be the Court and the prosecutor, but they are most definitely vying to be one of the Deciders through attempting to have the ICC rule that it has no jurisdiction on the case. They may have reason to involve themselves in the Court's work as states parties to the Rome Statute, and that intervention was invited by the Court, but the Israel-Palestine conflict and the alleged crimes in question have little to do with them. Yet they are taking a strong stance on this issue, likely because of the influence of Israel and, perhaps more importantly, because of the influence of the US. Thus, these states are enabling Israel to act in the role of the Decider as well as taking up that mantle themselves. More generally, this situation raises the issue of the existence of states and their ability to become states parties to the Rome Statute when there is disagreement by the states parties themselves as to the existence of a state. It further illustrates how the role of the Decider seeks to intervene in whether a state is actually a state, even after that state has become a state party to the Rome Statute, for example.

This also raises the question of the interaction of multiple Deciders as well as decision makers within one situation, particularly when there is no single dominant actor. This can also be seen in the workings of the UN Security Council referrals to the ICC and attempts to send and block these situations by permanent five states (for example, the attempt to send the Syrian situation to the ICC but it being blocked by China and Russia).[95] The Assembly of States Parties more generally is another forum where multiple Deciders interact, such as

95 United Nations, 'Russia, China Block Security Council Referral of Syria to International Criminal Court' (22 May 2014) <https://news.un.org/en/story/2014/05/468962-russia-china-block-security-council-referral-syria-international-criminal-court> accessed 18 November 2020.

through electing the next prosecutor of the ICC and disagreement as to who should be elected.

6 The future

a) Common themes

Common themes run throughout both the Afghanistan and Palestine cases in relation to 'the politics of the Decider' that are relevant to the future of international criminal justice. These include the notion that only certain individuals from certain countries and regions are prosecuted at the international level,[96] and this is controlled by the Decider. There are a number of Deciders active in this process, and, as has been illustrated in this chapter, particular states are the most influential of those Deciders. This selectivity in prosecutions is evident at all the modern ICTs, but it is especially apparent at the ICC.[97] Both the Afghanistan and Palestine situations are focused on developing states with low socioeconomic development and persistent conflict,[98] whilst the non–states parties that are in opposition to the investigations, the US and Israel, are more economically and militarily strong.

This suggests that if a country is more powerful, such as the US with respect to Afghanistan and Israel regarding the Palestine case, then it is less likely that they will be subjected to international prosecutions and, if they are, that they will oppose that intervention through the wielding of various forms of power and the embodiment of the Decider. If such prosecutions of powerful states take place at all, they can alternatively be conducted domestically, such as through the complementarity provisions of the ICC,[99] which are less likely in states struggling with persistent conflict and legal systems that may not be operational or supportive of the rule of law. In the Afghanistan situation, the ongoing conflict and weakness of Afghanistan means that domestic prosecutions are a challenge. In the Palestine context, the continued conflict with Israel and the inability of Palestinians to control their own territory due to the obstruction of Israel render domestic prosecution equally doubtful.

Also reflected in both situations is that non–states parties are influential in the operations of the Court and are at times more influential than the states parties themselves due to their embodiment of the Decider. In this vein, non-state actors are more likely to embody the Decider. Both the Afghanistan and Palestine

96 See, e.g., the focus on Africa in Werle, Fernandez, and Vormbaum (n 68).

97 See, e.g., Hanna Kuczyńska, *The Accusation Model Before the International Criminal Court: Study of Convergence of Criminal Justice Systems* (Springer 2015) 116.

98 World Bank, 'Afghanistan' <https://data.worldbank.org/country/afghanistan?view=chart> accessed 3 May 2020; World Bank, 'Palestine's Economic Update – April 2019' <www.worldbank.org/en/country/westbankandgaza/publication/economic-update-april-2019> accessed 2 May 2020.

99 Rome Statute, art 17.

situations involve the influence of a non–states party in the situation in question. In the case of Afghanistan, it is the US, and with respect to the Palestine situation, it is primarily Israel. This influence occurs because the non–states party does not want to be subject to the jurisdiction of the Court. In order to combat the Court's investigation, they pose as the Decider in opposition to the purported decision-making authority of the ICC and its personnel.

b) The next ICC prosecutor

Going forward, the notion of the Decider will be tested with the decision to appoint the next chief prosecutor of the ICC in 2021.[100] This individual will commence in the role in mid-2021 and will remain in the position for the next nine years, making crucial decisions about the future of the cases under consideration at the Court, including the Afghanistan and Palestine situations.[101] It is not just the decisions the next prosecutor makes that will shape the future of the ICC, but also how states, both states parties and non–states parties will respond to those decisions and prospective decisions that will influence the work of the Court. The prosecutor must be a person of 'high moral character'.[102] They must be unable to be influenced and intimidated by powerful states. However, as was evidenced in the discussions of both the Afghanistan and Palestine situations, there is arguably a degree of attempted political interference in high-profile ICL cases that the prosecutor should be aware of in undertaking the role.

With states parties to the Rome Statute having the authority to appoint the ICC prosecutor,[103] they are able to influence what types of decisions the prosecutor will make in the future because they will choose an individual based on the type of prosecutor they would prefer to have in the position – likely someone with views that will align with the states' own views on key issues, including the role of international criminal justice mechanisms. In doing so, states parties are individually and cumulatively acting as the Decider. They have a legitimate role in selecting the next prosecutor due to their proficiency as a prosecutor, but that role does not extend to choosing someone due to their particular vision of international criminal justice, although that is what actually occurs in practice. The UK, for example, would be unlikely to nominate a candidate with a history of publishing or vocalising support for the prosecution of UK war crimes, lest their own citizens end up in The Hague. The election process of the ICC prosecutor therefore suggests that the role of the ICC prosecutor is not only a role in practice but is also a representative position.

The prosecutor is supposed to be independent, which means that they should not be influenced by any external individuals.[104] Whilst this chapter is not

100 International Criminal Court, 'Election of Prosecutor (2020)' (n 15).
101 Rome Statute, art 42(4).
102 ibid., art 42(3).
103 ibid., art 42(4).
104 ibid., art 42(3) 42(5).

suggesting that this is the case, it *is* highlighting avenues through which states exert their power on figures such as the prosecutor, even if only through their selection, which has an influence on the position and on ICL more generally. The next ICC prosecutor must therefore develop a cautious and productive relationship with both states parties and non–states parties. As was evidenced by the US revoking the visas of the ICC prosecutor and her staff working on the Afghanistan case, there is an interwoven relationship between the prosecutor and even those who are not party to the Rome Statute, particularly when they play out the role of the Decider.

7 Concluding remarks

An understanding of decision makers, Deciders, and their decisions requires the consideration of notions of politics and power, especially with respect to the Afghanistan and Palestine situations at the ICC. The notion of the Decider is not merely a decision maker who uses politics to make decisions, although that is where this starts. The Decider embodies power and politics, utilising historical power structures to influence situations; therefore, the decisions they make are difficult to refute or challenge. This is relevant to ICL because politics is an inherent part of the creation and work of the modern international criminal courts and tribunals. The notion of the Decider helps to better understand that politics is not involved in ICL as an abstract idea, but rather that there are individuals and entities such as states who use politics in their interactions with ICL. The Decider also enables a better understanding of the ICL project and why there are challenges in its effective operation.

A Decider can exert influence because of its perceived or generalised power over others, rather than the Decider solely having specific influence over that particular area. For example, the US is a Decider on issues relating to the ICC even though it is not a state party to the Rome Statute. The Decider derives its influence from being both reinforced and also challenged by others, as those challenges at times give the US position legitimacy. For example, the US is denounced by those who are opposed to US imperialist foreign policy and its selective engagement with international law, but that opposition also provides the Decider with an opportunity to further restate its position. The role of the Decider is also reinforced by those who stand to benefit: for example, Israel supports the US's obstructive engagement with the ICC, likely because the former does not want to be held accountable for international crimes against Palestinians, rather than Israel having a moral or legal opposition to the Court in and of itself. Israel also likely supports the US on ICC matters in return for US support in its own ICC challenges. In short, this opposition by Israel, like that of the US, is strategic.

It is concerning and destabilising to the justice process when states and entities take on roles of obstructive influence in ICL and yet seek to remain impervious to the justice process themselves. At times, these states, for example, do not have the authority to make the decisions they claim to be able to make, and yet these states encourage others to believe that they do have that power. In some instances, the Decider does have some type of power, such as through military, political, or institutional strength, but we live in a changing world where powers are shifting, and the powerful do not have the same degree of influence they once did. The need to believe in the power of these states therefore does not have the same degree of necessity as was once the case, but their influence continues through the collaboration and sanction of others. The Decider, therefore, retains its power as a defensive posture that demonstrates insecurity, not so much because of itself, but because others buy into and facilitate its power in international criminal justice.[105]

105 See Antonio Gramsci's definition of hegemony and power by consent: Joseph A Buttigieg, 'Gramsci on Civil Society' in James Martin (ed), *Antonio Gramsci: Critical Assessments of Leading Political Philosophers* (Routledge 2002).

4 The local, resilience, and the future of hybrid courts in international criminal law

Philipp Kastner

1 Introduction

After a first 'wave' of hybrid criminal tribunals in the late 1990s and early 2000s, the model of hybridity has made a remarkable comeback in recent years. Notably, a Special Criminal Court (SCC) was established in the Central African Republic (CAR) in 2015, and the establishment of such tribunals has been considered in several other countries, such as South Sudan, Sri Lanka, and Syria. This suggests that the idea of hybrid criminal justice, which combines aspects of international criminal tribunals with ordinary domestic courts, is very much alive. Hybrid tribunals are indeed meant to combine elements of, or be a bridge between, the international and the national spheres. One of their main strengths is the ability to draw on international expertise while being closer to the communities most immediately concerned by the violence in question than purely international tribunals.

This chapter examines how this idea of hybridity has been effected in the CAR. The CAR, one of the poorest countries in the world, constitutes an intriguing site of multiple and concurrent approaches to dealing with large-scale violence. As will be discussed, the situation has also been brought before the International Criminal Court (ICC) while the ordinary national courts have started to resume their activities and have tried several alleged perpetrators of crimes committed during the recent episodes of significant violence.

Despite these initiatives, and although the CAR continues to represent one the worst humanitarian crises in the world, with half its population being in need of humanitarian assistance,[1] it must be said that the CAR has received remarkably little international attention. Already as a French colony, the populations living in what constitutes the CAR today experienced high levels of violence, but the remote territory had little geopolitical or economic relevance, and it remains

1 United Nations Office for the Coordination of Humanitarian Affairs, *République centrafricaine: Plan de Réponse Humanitaire 2020* (December 2019) <www.humanitarianresponse.info/en/operations/central-african-republic/document/car-humanitarian-response-plan-2020> accessed 17 December 2020.

DOI: 10.4324/9781003087533-5

a largely overlooked place.[2] It is true that since the late 1990s, numerous peacekeeping and peacebuilding missions have been deployed by France, the former colonial power; the United Nations (UN); and regional organisations, but these missions – criticised as 'quick fixes or low-cost solutions'[3] – have not been able to bring peace or stability to the country. A military coup in 2003, the subsequent emergence of several rebellions – combined with the military involvement of outside actors – and, in particular, the intense violence between and atrocities committed by militia groups known as *Séléka* and *anti-balaka* since the end of 2012 are arguably only the most recent and most visible expressions of these deep-rooted violent dynamics.

When it comes to imagining ways to achieve some form of justice for the serious crimes committed in the CAR, dominant discourses in the field rely on prescriptive universal norms, which are seen as underpinning the exceptionality of international(ised) justice interventions. At the same time, important attempts have been made by experts and advocates, donors, and sponsors of international criminal justice to render such processes more accessible and relevant to local communities. This discursive turn to the local also manifests itself in the context of hybrid tribunals and, as this chapter argues, can usefully be analysed through the concept of resilience. Although the latter is a prominent concept that has pervaded various policy areas, including national security and peacebuilding, international criminal law discourses and scholarship have, so far, remained surprisingly indifferent to it.

Discussing the future of hybrid tribunals like the SCC and relying on a critical approach to resilience that allows exposing common – often neoliberal – assumptions and practices, the chapter highlights some of the shortcomings of the currently dominant approach to dealing with large-scale violence. As the chapter also cautions, adopting, whether consciously or unconsciously, the logic of resilience thinking bears important dangers for hybrid tribunals and for the field of international(ised) criminal justice more generally.

2 Revisiting hybridity and the turn to the local through the lens of resilience

a) The invention of hybrid institutions in international criminal law

Following the establishment of the International Criminal Tribunals for the former Yugoslavia (ICTY) and Rwanda (ICTR), international actors, aware of the

2 Louisa Lombard, *State of Rebellion: Violence and Intervention in the Central African Republic* (Zed Books 2016).

3 Nathaniel Olin, 'Pathologies of Peacekeeping and Peacebuilding in CAR' in Tatiana Carayannis and Louisa Lombard (eds), *Making Sense of the Central African Republic* (Zed Books 2015) 216.

important shortcomings of these purely international criminal tribunals yet still committed to ending impunity by enforcing international criminal law, started to seek other institutional avenues to deal with serious crimes. The idea of establishing hybrid tribunals, which are sometimes also called internationalised or mixed tribunals, led to the creation of a first series of such tribunals in the late 1990s and early 2000s, including the Special Court for Sierra Leone (SCSL), the Extraordinary Chambers in the Courts of Cambodia (ECCC), and the Special Panels for Serious Crimes in the Dili District Court.[4] It was perhaps hoped that the operationalisation of the ICC in 2002 – a court with potentially global jurisdictional reach – would make any *ad hoc* criminal institutions, whether international or internationalised, unnecessary. However, the ICC does not have jurisdiction over crimes committed before 2002, when the Rome Statute entered into force; its substantive jurisdiction is limited to genocide, crimes against humanity, war crimes, and the crime of aggression; and numerous states, including three permanent members of the UN Security Council, have not joined its statute.[5] Moreover, the Court, while controversial from the outset, has encountered significant criticisms and setbacks in recent years.[6]

As a result, other institutions mandated to provide individual accountability for serious crimes continue to be considered and created. Among others, the Special Tribunal for Lebanon was established in 2007, mainly to try those allegedly responsible for the assassination of the former prime minister of Lebanon, Rafiq Hariri, in 2005.[7] More recently, in 2015, the Kosovo Specialist Chambers and Specialist Prosecutor's Office were created in close collaboration with the European Union to try senior leaders of the Kosovo Liberation Army allegedly responsible for grave crimes committed during the 1998–2000 conflict.[8] Finally, and as will be discussed in more detail in this chapter, the SCC was created in 2015 to deal with serious crimes committed in the CAR since 2003. As I have argued elsewhere,[9] these developments confirm that the experimental phase of the institutional enforcement of international criminal law is hardly completed; pigeon-holing these tribunals into four neat phases – from Nuremberg and Tokyo (1) to the *ad hoc* tribunals (2), the hybrid tribunals (3), and the

4 For an overview, see Sarah Williams, *Hybrid and Internationalised Criminal Tribunals: Selected Jurisdictional Issues* (Hart 2012).

5 As of early 2020, the ICC had 123 states parties.

6 See, e.g., Christian De Vos, Sara Kendall and Carsten Stahn (eds), *Contested Justice: The Politics and Practices of International Criminal Court Interventions* (CUP 2015).

7 Nicolas Michel, 'The Creation of the Tribunal in its Context' in Amal Alamuddin, Nidal Nabil Jurdi and David Tolbert (eds), *The Special Tribunal for Lebanon: Law and Practice* (OUP 2014).

8 See, Salvatore Zappalà, 'The Specialist Chambers of Kosovo: Domestic Trials or the First Incursion by the European Union into International Criminal Justice?' (2016) 14 *Journal of International Criminal Justice* 21.

9 Philipp Kastner, 'Hybrid Tribunals: Institutional Experiments and the Potential for Creativity Within International Criminal Law' in Philipp Kastner (ed), *International Criminal Law in Context* (Routledge 2018).

ICC (4)[10] – would suggest an unduly linear development that, moreover, does not facilitate a creative and critical consideration of the enforcement dimension of international criminal law.

Hybrid criminal tribunals hold the promise of being more legitimate and effective than purely international or national criminal tribunals, in the eyes of both international and local actors. Typically, they are also expected to facilitate national capacity building and the penetration of international norms.[11] Given the important criticisms vis-à-vis the ICTY and ICTR regarding their relative lack of local ownership and limited contribution to national capacity building, a hybrid institutional architecture can indeed be expected to be more effective in these regards. A hybrid judicial bench and prosecutorial office, with, respectively, international and national judges and international and national prosecutors working together, probably best illustrates this not only symbolic but also quite tangible hybridity. In other words, these tribunals, which are usually not only staffed with international and local actors but also apply international and national laws, embody the promise of being international in character to a significant extent and of being locally owned at the same time. Operating in close proximity to the national system also means that hybrid tribunals are better placed than comparatively remote international tribunals to contribute to building local capacities and, hence, to be a model for ordinary courts.[12] This is, in fact, related to one of the main justifications for the establishment or involvement of international and internationalised criminal tribunals: namely, that the international community needs to intervene in some way when the national system in question is unwilling or unable to deal with the crimes committed.

It can therefore be said that hybrid tribunals attempt to combine the best aspects of two worlds: on the one hand, they are meant to benefit from international expertise on international criminal law and signal a strong commitment to upholding the international rule of law, including with respect to conducting fair trials; on the other hand, hybrid tribunals are supposed to be closely connected to the local – the meaning of which is, of course, contested – and to allow local actors to assume at least some ownership over the justice process in question.

b) The turn to the local and the rise of resilience thinking[13]

Many influential actors, including international organisations like the UN, specialised non-governmental organisations like Human Rights Watch, and

10 Harold Hongju Koh, 'International Criminal Justice 5.0' (2013) 38 *Yale Journal of International Law* 525.

11 For a critique of such expectations, see Pádraig McAuliffe, 'Hybrid Tribunals at Ten: How International Criminal Justice's Golden Child Became an Orphan' (2011) 7 *Journal of International Law and International Relations* 1.

12 David Cohen, '"Hybrid" Justice in East Timor, Sierra Leone, and Cambodia: "Lessons Learned" and Prospects for the Future' (2007) 43 *Stanford Journal of International Law* 1, 36–37.

13 Parts of this section include a significantly shortened and revised version of a section on the concept of resilience that was published in Philipp Kastner, 'A Resilience Approach to Transitional Justice?' (2020) 14 *Journal of Intervention and Statebuilding* 368.

international criminal justice institutions, continue to rely on prescriptive liberal-universal norms, such as the obligation to prosecute alleged perpetrators of international crimes. However, there is a perceptible trend to turn to the local in the field of transitional justice more generally and also in international criminal law.[14] Especially when compared to the international accountability decade of the 1990s, supposedly local justice processes have received much more attention in recent years.[15] The numerous surveys that have been conducted in conflict and post-conflict communities by international researchers and policymakers to learn about victims' and survivors' priorities and preferences regarding justice processes are another sign of this trend.[16] However, the engagement with the 'local' and the listening to 'local voices' arguably remain very limited and, in particular, constrained by international legal norms.[17]

In fact, the almost ubiquitous – yet often only discursive and superficial – turn to the local has not been accompanied or guided by a lot of critical reflection. First of all, the 'local' is rarely defined, perhaps because so-called local practices and processes are infinitely diverse and often not well understood.[18] However, what emerges is that the local is commonly viewed in an overly positive light and even romanticised, especially by so-called international actors, but also in the context of international(ised) criminal justice.[19] One of the implications is that the benefits of local transitional justice processes are uncritically taken for granted and problems associated with these processes, like the reinforcement of power inequalities, overlooked.[20] In fact, constructing the local as a 'level', as a distinct sphere, implies setting it apart and associating it with something remote and marginal.[21] Yet the local is not a natural and authentic sphere but a social construction;[22] presumably local justice processes have even been described

14 Wendy Lambourne, 'Outreach, Inreach and Civil Society Participation in Transitional Justice' in N Palmer, P Clark and D Granville (eds), *Critical Perspectives in Transitional Justice* (Intersentia 2012).

15 Adam Kochanski, 'The "Local Turn" in Transitional Justice: Curb the Enthusiasm' (2020) 22 *International Studies Review* 26.

16 Rosalind Shaw and Lars Waldorf, 'Introduction: Localizing Transitional Justice' in Rosalind Shaw and Lars Waldorf (eds), *Localizing Transitional Justice: Interventions and Priorities After Mass Violence* (Stanford University Press 2010) 4.

17 ibid., 5.

18 Kochanski (n 15) 27.

19 Oliver P Richmond, 'The Romanticisation of the Local: Welfare, Culture and Peacebuilding' (2009) 44 *International Spectator* 149.

20 Kochanski (n 15) 27.

21 Shaw and Waldorf (n 16) 6.

22 Instead, as it has been suggested in the context of transitional justice, the local should not be approached as a level but as a 'standpoint based in a particular locality but not bounded by it' (ibid., 16). For the argument, in the context of a discussion on international criminal justice in Southeast Asia, that 'spatial designations, such as "local" or "global", may be better understood as dynamic and mutually reinforcing social constructions than firm categories'; see Emma Palmer, *Adapting International Criminal Justice in Southeast Asia: Beyond the International Criminal Court* (CUP 2020) 16.

as neo-traditionalisations by outside – typically Western – actors.[23] Contrary to common assumptions, the 'international', or 'global', and the 'local' should hence not be conceived as clearly separable categories and certainly not as being characterised by binary relations.[24] As Sally Engle Merry has noted, what is considered to be 'global' are often 'circulating locals'.[25] As will be explored later in this chapter, a critical approach to resilience echoes and reinforces such critiques pertaining to the local and its construction and, in particular, the inherently limited, and even cynical, promotion of the agency of local actors.

With respect to international criminal justice institutions, it can be observed that they have also taken up the common – if often only discursive and superficial – turn to the local, notably by making increased efforts to reach out to local communities, which are, after all, most directly affected by the crimes for which accountability is sought. The ICC is a case in point. Intrinsically focused on the individual criminal accountability of those considered most responsible for the most serious crimes, the Court attempts to give a greater voice to victims in the proceedings than other international criminal tribunals did.[26] It also has a novel mandate to provide reparations, including through its Trust Fund for Victims. While this turn to victims has its own problems – among others, it creates a problematic hierarchy among victims and arguably represents an undue justification for the international criminal justice project[27] – it exemplifies that even international institutions committed to upholding liberal-universal norms cannot simply 'intervene' anymore but feel the need to justify their intervention by claiming to be committed to the concerns of local communities. As will be discussed later, hybrid tribunals like the SCC are another manifestation of this turn to what is commonly perceived as the local.

Resilience, despite its malleability and elasticity, is an intriguing concept that sheds new light on these developments. The concept was first developed in the fields of ecology and psychology as well as engineering in the 1970s and has spread rapidly through various policy areas, including national security, disaster risk reduction, climate change, international development, and peacebuilding.[28] While resilience has been described as 'a pervasive idiom of global

23 See, e.g., Adam Branch, 'The Violence of Peace: Ethnojustice in Northern Uganda' (2014) 45 *Development and Change* 608; Phil Clark, *The Gacaca Courts, Post-Genocide Justice and Reconciliation in Rwanda: Justice Without Lawyers* (CUP 2010).

24 Bruno Latour, *Nous n'avons jamais été modernes. Essai d'anthropologie symétrique* (La Découverte 1991).

25 Sally Engle Merry, 'Transnational Human Rights and Local Activism: Mapping the Middle' (2006) 108 *American Anthropologist* 38, 40.

26 Steven Smith Cody and Eric Stover, 'The Role of Victims: Emerging Rights to Participation and Reparation in International Criminal Courts' in Kastner (ed) (n 9).

27 See, e.g., Sara Kendall and Sarah Nouwen, 'Representational Practices at the International Criminal Court: The Gap Between Juridified and Abstract Victimhood' (2014) 76 *Law and Contemporary Problems* 235.

28 Jonathan Joseph, *Varieties of Resilience: Studies in Governmentality* (CUP 2018). There are different, and even conflicting, uses of the term 'resilience'; in the context of disaster

governance',[29] or even '*the* organising principle in contemporary political life',[30] international criminal law discourses and scholarship appear to have remained surprisingly indifferent to the concept.[31] This, as it should be noted at the outset, does not imply that the field of international criminal law is impermeable to the logic of resilience thinking; rather, it seems, quite simply, that a serious and conscious engagement with this concept has not yet occurred in the field.

It can be observed that influential actors in the international domain of capacity-building in conflict and post-conflict situations have started to turn away from liberal concepts like 'accountability' and the 'rule of law' and to privilege instead more pragmatic approaches. The European Union (EU) is a telling example. In the 2016 Global Strategy for its Foreign and Security Policy, the organisation replaced international and transitional justice with 'societal resilience'.[32] As a result, supporting initiatives to provide accountability for political violence and other atrocities, strengthen the rule of law, and reform the domestic legal system must now serve the greater goal of building societal resilience. Arguably, seeking justice for past crimes – via international, internationalised, or national courts or other avenues – has always had multiple and intertwined objectives, including deterring future perpetrators, revealing the truth, and contributing to reconciliation. Yet in the new paradigm of pragmatism and resilience thinking, it has become even more evident that seeking justice cannot be an end in itself; rather, ending a culture of impunity is now considered an instrument to achieve a higher end. In fact, a pragmatic emphasis on the future and on the preparation of individuals and communities for violent events stands in stark contrast to the very idea that engaging with and seeking accountability for past crimes can be useful and, for instance, help envisage a more peaceful future. Disconnecting the

---

management in the United States, for instance, greater emphasis has been placed on engineering understandings of resilience and the associated ability to 'bounce back' than on ecological and psychological understandings: Karl Grove, *Resilience: A Bakhtinian World* (Routledge 2018).

29 Jeremy Walker and Melinda Cooper, 'Genealogies of Resilience: From Systems Ecology to the Political Economy of Crisis Adaptation' (2011) 14 *Security Dialogue* 143, 144.

30 James Brassett, Stuart Croft and Nick Vaughan-Williams, 'Introduction: An Agenda for Resilience Research in Politics and International Relations' (2013) 33 *Politics* 221, 222.

31 Of particular note, however, several articles dealing with resilience and hybrid courts were published as part of a symposium in the *Leiden Journal of International Law* in December 2020 (and hence after the finalisation of this chapter), which illustrate the apparently growing interest in the concept also in the field of transitional justice and international criminal law. See, for instance, Eric Wiebelhaus-Brahm, 'The Concept of Resilience and the Evaluation of Hybrid Courts' (2020) 33 *Leiden Journal of International Law* 1015.

32 Tobias Flessenkemper, 'The EU and Transitional Justice in Former Yugoslavia' (2018) 2 *Südosteuropa Mitteilungen* 88. As a 2019 follow-up report on the EU's Global Strategy states with respect to the engagement of the EU in the Balkans, 'the EU has directly engaged in resilience-building in areas such as rule of law, economic development, employment and connectivity': European Union, *The European Union's Global Strategy: Three Years On, Looking Forward* (2019) <https://eeas.europa.eu/sites/eeas/files/eu_global_strategy_2019.pdf> 23, accessed 17 December 2020.

past from the future, as promoted by resilience thinking, even risks making every justice-seeking endeavour appear redundant.

According to a common definition, resilience describes the 'ability of people, societies, and countries to recover from negative shocks, while retaining or improving their ability to function'.[33] Resilience therefore carries connotations of flexibility and reflexivity, capacity, agency, and empowerment[34] and seems highly desirable from a normative perspective. Moreover, resilience thinking, understood as a reaction to and critique of centralised one-size-fits-all management approaches,[35] resonates with the notion that addressing past and present forms of violence should not be enacted based on certain prefabricated formulas. In line with the critique of a legalistic and technocratic toolbox-oriented approach to transitional justice – echoing, in turn, critiques of the liberal peace[36] – that views different mechanisms as being easily transplantable from one context to another,[37] transitional justice processes should not be imposed from the top or the outside. Rather, they should involve local actors and also be concerned with local priorities and understandings of justice. Such an approach would hence imply more bottom-up than top-down thinking, focusing on facilitating, rather than producing, justice. Relying on international criminal law to hold certain perpetrators accountable may usefully inspire a given society to deal with past and present forms of violence. However, a resilience approach would challenge such liberal ideas and focus on, be driven by, and further support subnational and local processes and actors and would, at least, seek to render centralised justice initiatives more inclusive and accessible.

At the same time, as critical approaches to resilience have highlighted, such a shift can be part of a neoliberal rationality of governance that transfers responsibility from international to local actors, yet without enabling genuine transformation and with the former continuing to govern from the distance.[38] When it comes to establishing and managing justice processes in the Global South, resilience thinking hence also enables ongoing forms of (neo)coloniality. Indeed, focusing on managing threats and adaptation can hide power relations and be, in fact, a distraction that prevents a genuine consideration of the drivers of vulnerability and root causes of violence.[39] It is fundamental to understand the underlying rationale and ramifications of such resilience thinking, which arguably

33 World Bank, *World Development Report 2014: Risk and Opportunity – Managing Risk for Development* (2013) <https://openknowledge.worldbank.org/handle/10986/16092> 12, accessed 17 December 2020.

34 Jonathan Joseph, 'Resilience as Embedded Neoliberalism: A Governmentality Approach' (2013) 1 *Resilience: International Policies, Practices and Discourses* 38.

35 Grove (n 28).

36 See, e.g., Roland Paris, *At War's End: Building Peace After Civil Conflict* (CUP 2004).

37 Kieran McEvoy, 'Beyond Legalism: Towards a Thicker Understanding of Transitional Justice' (2007) 34 *Journal of Law and Society* 411.

38 Joseph, 'Resilience as Embedded Neoliberalism' (n 34).

39 Terry Cannon and Detlef Müller-Mahn, 'Vulnerability, Resilience and Development Discourses in Context of Climate Change' (2010) 55 *Natural Hazards* 621.

challenges the very essence and objectives of justice-seeking endeavours. Instead of trying to address serious crimes, reveal the truth, and have a deterrent effect, the resilient subject, in a Darwinian logic of survival, is made responsible for its own well-being and must have the capacity to continuously adapt to external threats and dangers in an unstable and complex world.[40] In this paradigm, living with danger and under constant threat – rather than attempting to address the danger or prevent the threat – has become the norm.[41] This means that, despite the alleged promotion of the agency of the resilient subject, resilience approaches do not support – but can actually hinder – making any meaningful political claims, including with respect to justice. As a result, with the focus of attention having shifted from addressing causes to preparing for allegedly unknown risks, the bigger sociopolitical dynamics and power structures are left unchallenged.[42] In sum, although resilience discourses often seem to promise progressive change, the implementation of policies that rely on resilience typically has reactionary effects and contributes to keeping in place the political and economic *status quo*.[43]

It can be argued that the dominant approach to transitional justice, which is overly concerned with certain manifestations of violence and with institutional responses to ensure individual accountability, such as international(ised) trials, already does not seek to (or allow) the individuals and communities most immediately affected by the violence in question to challenge the factors that enabled and perpetuate the violence in the first place. Tackling the root causes of violent conflict, or addressing supposedly secondary yet potentially very significant factors, such as a history of colonialism and economic exploitation, has not been high on the agenda of influential actors in the field of international justice.[44] However, it can be argued that resilience thinking, by promoting 'adaptive governance' and 'agential capacities',[45] will push these actors even further away from considering the root causes of violence and from facilitating transitional justice to develop its transformative potential.[46] In fact, the very endeavour of transitional

40 For these critiques, see, e.g., Joseph, 'Resilience as Embedded Neoliberalism' (n 34).

41 Brad Evans and Julian Reid, *Resilience Life: The Art of Living Dangerously* (Polity 2014).

42 As Mark Neocleous has argued, '[r]esilience wants acquiescence, not resistance. . . . [I]t does demand that we use our actions to accommodate ourselves to capital and the state, and the secure future of both, rather than to resist them': Mark Neocleous, 'Resisting Resilience' (2013) 178 *Radical Philosophy* <www.radicalphilosophyarchive.com/issue-files/rp178_commentary_neocleous_resisting_resilience.pdf> accessed 17 December 2020.

43 Grove (n 28).

44 Wendy Lambourne, 'The Idea of Transitional Justice: International Criminal Justice and Beyond' in Kastner (ed) (n 9).

45 Jessica Schmidt, 'Intuitively Neoliberal? Towards a Critical Understanding of Resilience Governance' (2015) 21 *European Journal of International Relations* 402, 406–407.

46 On transformative transitional justice, see, e.g., Pádraig McAuliffe, *Transformative Transitional Justice and the Malleability of Post-Conflict States* (Elgar 2017); Matthew Evans (ed), *Transitional and Transformative Justice: Critical and International Perspectives* (Routledge 2019); Rita Shackel and Lucy Fiske (eds), *Rethinking Transitional Gender Justice: Transformative Approaches in Post-Conflict Settings* (Palgrave 2019).

justice and its most important objectives – revealing the truth, holding perpetrators accountable, and trying to provide some sense of justice to victims – is made redundant in a resilience paradigm: because of increasingly 'future-oriented strategies of resilience', which 'depend upon forms of collective amnesia',[47] the past is disconnected from the future. Seeking to address past – and oftentimes ongoing – forms of violence hence becomes meaningless.

Furthermore, recognising individuals or populations as being resilient, or exhorting them to become more resilient, can be a facile way of disengagement for international actors,[48] including in the field of international(ised) criminal justice. Presumably resilient individuals or populations may never be able to address systemic factors or the responsibilities of external actors, which largely remain beyond their scope of influence and so-called agential capacities. Indeed, mobilising local actors and encouraging them to be part of the solution has always remained partial and limited, with international normative claims to certain forms of accountability and truth being considered universal and consequently unchallengeable[49] – a way of thinking that is arguably embodied in hybrid tribunals like the SCC.

3 Multiplicity and hybridity: justice-seeking endeavours in the CAR

Providing accountability and a sense of justice for the victims of the numerous crimes committed in the CAR is, of course, a significant challenge. The ordinary court system in the CAR can hardly be described as functional, in particular in remote areas, as large parts of the territory of the CAR have been and remain under control by various armed groups.[50] In 2018, a report of the UN independent expert on the situation of human rights in the CAR noted that armed groups remained present in almost 80 percent of the territory.[51] Official institutions, especially outside the capital, Bangui, are hence weak or completely absent. As the UN Stabilisation Mission in the CAR (MINUSCA), deployed since 2014, has noted, because of years of conflict and violence, '[s]tate institutions including the judiciary and prisons were either completely destroyed or seriously weakened'.[52] More specifically, with respect to conducting investigations and prosecutions, the CAR has been considered 'unable to conduct a trial before national courts' by the

47 Evans and Reid (n 41) 24.

48 Jonathan Joseph, 'Governing Through Failure and Denial: The New Resilience Agenda' (2016) 44 *Millennium: Journal of International Studies* 370.

49 Philipp Kastner, 'Transitional Justice and the Challenging Pursuit of Social Justice' (2017) 34 *Windsor Yearbook of Access to Justice* 1.

50 'Report of the Independent Expert on the Situation of Human Rights in the Central African Republic' (13 August 2018) UN Doc. A/HRC/39/70, para 86.

51 ibid., para 72.

52 MINUSCA, 'Activities – Justice and Corrections Section' (2020) <https://minusca.unmissions.org/en/justice-corrections> accessed 17 December 2020.

ICC, which is why the case against Jean-Pierre Bemba Gombo was considered admissible before the ICC[53] and why, more generally speaking, extraordinary justice processes, heavily supported by international actors, have been envisaged to supplement the ordinary courts. The justice initiatives in the CAR, like most transitional justice processes, remain firmly anchored in and committed to the nation-state,[54] even if the state and state authorities are often part of the problem – in the case of the CAR, there have also been calls to partition the territory[55] – and even if the conflict has significant regional dimensions.[56] The SCC exemplifies this logic of supporting the delivery of justice within a supposedly well-defined nation-state. Similarly, the ICC, although an international court, was established by states and, given its institutional architecture, can hardly be seen as transcending this paradigm.

As already noted, influential international actors remain committed to the criminal law avenue, at the international(ised) and national levels. For instance, in a major report on violations of international human rights and humanitarian law committed in the CAR from 2003 to 2015, the UN underscored that although criminal justice is only one pillar of transitional justice, '[c]riminal justice can play an important role in holding those responsible for violations accountable, aiding reconciliation, providing a remedy for the victims and deterring future violations and abuses, particularly in situations where impunity has prevailed for decades'.[57] The work of the United Nations Development Programme (UNDP) in the CAR is also heavily focused on criminal justice. In addition to strengthening the national elections commission and the administration of the territory and, as it

53 'Decision on the Admissibility and Abuse of Process Challenges' *Prosecutor v Bemba Gombo*, ICC-01/05–01/08, 24 June 2010, [246] (*Bemba Gombo Admissibility*).

54 Pierre Hazan, 'Beyond Borders: The New Architecture of Transitional Justice?' (2017) 11 *International Journal of Transitional Justice* 1.

55 See, e.g., 'Report of the Working Group on the Use of Mercenaries as a Means of Violating Human Rights and Impeding the Exercise of the Rights of Peoples to Self-Determination on Its Mission to the Central African Republic' (12 September 2017) UN Doc A/HRC/36/47Add.1, para 47.

56 Over the years, there have been a number of military interventions, including by Chad, and several armed conflicts and humanitarian crises in the region, such as in Darfur and the Democratic Republic of the Congo, have had important spill-over effects on the CAR. For more information, see Carayannis and Lombard (eds) (n 3).

57 UN Office of the High Commissioner for Human Rights, 'Report of the Mapping Project Documenting Serious Violations of International Human Rights Law and International Humanitarian Law Committed Within the Territory of the Central African Republic Between January 2003 and December 2015' (May 2017), <www.ohchr.org/EN/Countries/AfricaRegion/Pages/CARProjetMapping2003-2015.aspx> 292, accessed 17 December 2020. This mapping project was set up by the UN Office of the High Commissioner for Human Rights and MINUSCA and was based on UNSC Res 2301 (26 July 2016) UN Doc S/RES/2301, para 33(b)(i) which mandated MINUSCA to monitor, help investigate, and report publicly and to the Security Council on violations of international humanitarian law and on violations and abuses of human rights committed throughout the CAR, including undertaking a mapping of such violations and abuses since 2003 to inform efforts to fight impunity'.

must be emphasised, to rendering the populations more resilient, UNDP focuses on rendering the national criminal justice system and the SCC operational.[58]

The conflict dynamics in the CAR are, of course, highly complex, and this chapter could not try to do justice to the root causes of the conflict and the factors that are responsible for its perpetuation. However, what can be noted is that there are systemic factors that enable and perpetuate various forms of violence, including in the form of war crimes and crimes against humanity, in the CAR. One may think of colonial violence and its continued effects, ongoing forms of economic exploitation, and extreme poverty: more than 70 percent of the population lives below the poverty line, the average life expectancy is 53 years, and the CAR occupies the penultimate place (188 out of 189 countries) in the UN Development Index.[59] This environment is obviously a fertile ground for the development of further obstacles to achieving peace, justice, and accountability. Two specific issues will be briefly addressed here. The first consists in the profitability, for various actors, of armed conflict, ethnic tensions, and continued instability. For instance, the illegal exploitation and trafficking of natural resources in the CAR, particularly of gold and diamonds, and also of uranium and oil, is fuelled by and further contributes to the instability in the country and the region. The way in which certain individuals benefit from and feed violence and ethnic tensions is illustrated by Abdoulaye Hissène, a warlord and important player in the conflict, against whom sanctions have been imposed by the UN Security Council.[60] Another important factor in the CAR is the use of mercenaries, who are typically recruited abroad and take part in hostilities primarily out of a desire for private gain.[61] As the UN Working Group on the use of mercenaries concluded after its visit to the CAR in 2016,

> the ongoing presence of mercenaries, foreign fighters and multiple armed groups is a serious barrier to the exercise of the right of peoples to self-determination. Their destabilizing effects have hindered the local population from effectively building a peaceful, developed and democratic society.[62]

These systemic problems of the profitability of war and crime cannot, of course, be tackled by international or internationalised tribunals alone. First of all, the

58 United Nations Development Programme, 'Le PNUD en République Centrafricaine' <www.cf.undp.org/content/car/fr/home/about-us/> accessed 17 December 2020.

59 United Nations Development Programme, *Human Development Report 2019* (United Nations 2019) 303.

60 The Sentry, *Fear, Inc: War Profiteering in the Central African Republic and the Bloody Rise of Abdoulaye Hissène* (November 2018) <https://cdn.thesentry.org/wp-content/uploads/2018/11/FearInc_TheSentry_Nov2018-web.pdf>.

61 For the full definition of mercenaries, see International Convention against the Recruitment, Use, Financing and Training of Mercenaries, opened for signature 4 December 1989, entered into force 20 October 2001, 2163 UNTS 7789, art. 1.

62 'Report of the Working Group on the Use of Mercenaries' (n 55) para 66.

ICC and the SCC, just like ordinary courts, need the political support that is necessary to enforce their arrest warrants and other decisions, which is particularly challenging when powerful individuals are targeted. More fundamentally, because of their inherent focus on individual responsibility and certain manifestations of violence, international(ised) criminal tribunals can hardly address the root causes of conflicts and the systemic dimensions of violence. To be clear, this does not make their work completely futile, but pursuing individual criminal accountability must be seen as one strategy among several others to change an unacceptable *status quo*. Moreover, as argued earlier, relying on the logic of resilience thinking, which subordinates the establishment and operation of international(ised) criminal justice institutions and the support for national trials to the higher goal of rendering populations more resilient, risks aggravating the already-significant shortcomings of these justice-seeking institutions by unhelpfully entrenching the current sociopolitical dynamics.

a) The ICC: the limits of liberal interventionism

Given the inability of the national justice system to deal with the manifestly serious crimes committed throughout the country since 2002, the CAR presents itself exactly like a situation for which the ICC was established. The CAR government made two referrals, technically resulting in two situations before the Court. In December 2004, the government first referred to the ICC prosecutor the situation involving war crimes and crimes against humanity committed on its territory since 1 July 2002, the date of entry into force of the Rome Statute.[63] In its letter, the government specifically requested a determination as to whether Ange-Félix Patassé (the former president, ousted by François Bozizé in 2003), Jean-Pierre Bemba Gombo, and/or others should be charged with war crimes and crimes against humanity.[64] Of note, national proceedings considering the violent incidents that occurred between October 2002 and March 2003 had been commenced in 2003. Among others, Bemba was charged with using troops to undermine the security of the CAR and of aiding and abetting murder, rape, and pillage.[65] However, the investigations were suspended a few months later, although the proceedings were not officially terminated. In December 2004, the counsel of the president of the CAR suggested to the Bangui Court of Appeal to refer the situation to the ICC prosecutor, who would be able to conduct investigations 'using means not available to the CAR',[66] which was effected shortly afterwards. One arrest warrant, against Bemba, the former vice president of the Democratic Republic of the Congo, was issued in 2008. It was, among other

63 *Bemba Gombo Admissibility* (n 53) [14]. The letter referring the situation to the ICC prosecutor was received in January 2015.
64 ibid.
65 ibid., [3].
66 ibid., [11].

things, the political power of the accused that was cited as a major obstacle to a national trial in the CAR.[67] Bemba was convicted of war crimes and crimes against humanity by the Trial Chamber but, in 2018, was acquitted on appeal. No further cases have been brought in the situation called 'CAR I'.

The second referral by the CAR government, resulting in 'CAR II', was made in May 2014 and concerned the renewed – and widespread – violence committed in the context of the *Séléka/anti-balaka* crisis. An investigation was opened a few months later, with the prosecutor noting the following:

> The information available provides a reasonable basis to believe that both the *Séléka* and the *anti-balaka* groups have committed crimes against humanity and war crimes including murder, rape, forced displacement, persecution, pillaging, attacks against humanitarian missions and the use of children under fifteen in combat. The list of atrocities is endless. I cannot ignore these alleged crimes.[68]

However, it was only four years later, in November 2018, that Alfred Yekatom, a former *caporal-chef* of the *Forces Armées Centrafricaines*, member of parliament and *anti-balaka* leader, was charged with war crimes and crimes against humanity allegedly committed in this context,[69] arrested, and transferred to the Court. The charges include the crimes against humanity and war crimes of murder, deportation or forcible transfer and displacement of civilian population, torture, pillaging, enlistment of children under the age of 15, persecution, etc.[70] Another *anti-balaka* leader, Patrice-Edouard Ngaïssona, was charged, arrested (by France), and transferred to the Court a few weeks later.[71]

Despite these so-called self-referrals by the CAR government and the latter's apparent cooperation with the Court, the ICC, with its seat in The Hague, was

67 ibid., [246].

68 International Criminal Court, 'Statement of the Prosecutor of the International Criminal Court, Fatou Bensouda, on Opening a Second Investigation in the Central African Republic' (24 September 2014) <www.icc-cpi.int/Pages/item.aspx?name=pr1043> accessed 17 December 2020.

69 'Warrant of Arrest for Alfred Yekatom' *Prosecutor v Yekatom*, ICC-01/14–01/18, 11 November 2018.

70 ibid., [2].

71 'Public Redacted Version of Warrant of Arrest for Patrice-Edouard Ngaïssona' *Situation in the Central African Republic II*, ICC-01/14–02/18, 7 December 2018, [16]. The charges were (partly) confirmed in December 2019, after the two cases had been joined, given that the crimes allegedly committed by Yekatom and Ngaïssona largely correspond: 'Decision on the Joinder of Cases Against Alfred Yekatom and Patrice-Edouard Ngaïssona and Other Related Matters' ICC-01/14–01/18, 20 February 2019, [11]. Another individual, Mahamat Said Abdel Kani, an alleged *Seleka* commander, was surrendered to the ICC in January 2021: International Criminal Court, 'Situation in Central African Republic II: Mahamat Said Abdel Kani Surrendered to the ICC for Crimes Against Humanity and War Crimes' (24 January 2021) <www.icc-cpi.int/Pages/item.aspx?name=pr1559> accessed 4 February 2021.

and remains a remote institution for Central Africans and can hardly be expected to have any significant impact. Moreover, the typical selectivity and limited scope of international criminal justice – so far, one accused in CAR I and two in CAR II – means that the ICC could, at best, set a largely symbolic example of providing accountability and some sense of justice to a necessarily limited number of victims.

More fundamentally, focusing on individual accountability before international institutions, while defensible for various reasons, can hardly promote the agency of local actors and facilitate bottom-up approaches. As I have argued elsewhere,

> trying a few select perpetrators without considering the larger sociopolitical environment, such as socio-economic inequalities and other enablers of serious crimes, hides the root causes of violence and, similar to dominant resilience thinking, obfuscates political solutions to this violence and the quest for political alternatives to the current state of affairs.[72]

b) The SCC: a nod to the local

The establishment of a hybrid tribunal in the CAR, even after the ICC had already been involved and had opened an investigation, illustrates that relying on a purely international court cannot be the only criminal law response to large-scale violence. Moreover, in light of the inherent limitations of an international court and the increasing commitment not only to 'delivering' international justice but also to connecting to the local and to making justice endeavours more relevant to those communities most immediately affected by the violence in question, a hybrid model of criminal justice holds great promise. As mentioned earlier, the very idea behind such hybrid tribunals, which are pictured somewhere between the top-down and the bottom-up, lies in fusing international expertise with local knowledge and legitimacy. In this sense, the SCC can also be seen as taking up at least some elements of resilience thinking. Transcending the logic of liberal interventionism, as embodied in the ICC, it suggests that local actors cannot be ignored; rather, these actors must be actively involved and, ideally, empowered to find their own solutions.

Several institutional elements of the SCC, including the location of the Court, its legal foundation, and applicable law, highlight its close connection – and commitment – to the national sphere. The fact that the SCC has its seat in Bangui[73] means that it is physically closer to those primarily affected by the crimes in question than, for instance, the ICC and the ICTY and ICTR. In this sense, Central Africans, and not an abstract international community, can be seen as the primary

72 Kastner, 'A Resilience Approach' (n 13).

73 *Loi organique no 15/003, portant création, organisation et fonctionnement de la Cour pénale spéciale* (Central African Republic, 3 June 2015) art 2.

constituencies of the Court. Moreover, the SCC's legal foundation – namely, a national law and not, as in the case of other internationalised tribunals, an international agreement between the UN and the host state or a UN Security Council resolution – is telling. Indeed, despite the significant role of the international community, notably via MINUSCA, in the establishment and operationalisation of the Court, the SCC was officially created 'as part of the judicial organisation' of the CAR, as noted in article 1 of the *loi organique* that established the Court.[74] This suggests that the Court was supposed to be 'owned' primarily by Central Africans and that this setup would perhaps also make it more straightforward for the ordinary national courts to eventually continue the work of this *ad hoc* tribunal.[75] It can be observed that important efforts have already been made to explain the Court and its operation to the wider population. An innovative outreach strategy consists in the staging of a theatre play about the SCC, entitled *Kota dati Ngbanga*, in Sango; it was performed 80 times throughout the country in 2019 and seen by more than 80,000 spectators.[76]

Like other hybrid tribunals, the SCC was, from the outset, expected to have a positive impact on the national court system and, hence, to contribute to local capacity building. A specific manifestation of this expectation consists in the pledge of the CAR government, noted in its response to the recommendations made during the 2019 Universal Periodic Review of its human rights obligations, to envisage extending the SCC's strategy on the protection of witnesses and victims to its national courts and tribunals.[77] This does seem more than urgent, as the Code of Criminal Procedure of the CAR does not provide any mechanism to protect witnesses and victims, which is particularly problematic in a context in which numerous alleged perpetrators have not been arrested and have not even laid down their arms.[78] With respect to the applicable law, domestic law plays a preeminent role before the SCC. According to the *loi organique*, the SCC has the competence to investigate and prosecute serious violations of human rights and international humanitarian law as they are defined in the Criminal Code of the

74 ibid., art 1 [author's translation].

75 Note that the initial period of operation of the SCC is five years (to be counted from the start of the effective operationalisation of the Court): ibid., art 70.

76 Cour pénale spéciale de la République centrafricaine, 'Du théâtre pour la justice et contre l'impunité en Centrafrique' (17 July 2019) <https://cps-rca.com/actualites/Du-theatre-pour-la-justice-et-contre-l%E2%80%99impunite-en-Centrafrique./13/> accessed 17 December 2020. The play is available online in French (https://youtu.be/QuefVokYHGo) and in Sango (https://youtu.be/oikyQJkPQyA).

77 'Report of the Working Group on the Universal Periodic Review (Central African Republic), Addendum: Views on Conclusions and/or Recommendations, Voluntary Commitments and Replies Presented by the State Under Review' (8 March 2019) UN Doc A/HRC/40/12/Add.1, para 36.

78 Gaël Grilhot, 'Centrafrique: La justice ordinaire a montré ses dents, pour les crimes à Bangassou' (10 February 2020) <www.justiceinfo.net/fr/tribunaux/tribunaux-nationaux/43745-centrafrique-justice-ordinaire-montre-dents-crimes-bangassou.html> accessed 17 December 2020.

CAR and in light of the CAR's international obligations, notably with respect to the crime of genocide, crimes against humanity, and war crimes.[79] In sum, even if the SCC has a lot in common with previous hybrid tribunals, it appears less international than, for instance, the Special Court for Sierra Leone was.[80]

Having said this, there are important international elements that suggest that the SCC hardly represents a radical break with the logic of liberal international interventionism. Crucially, the Court is funded by international actors.[81] The other probably most visible international element of the institutional setup of the SCC consists in the presence of international judges and prosecutors. The composition varies in the different chambers, but it seems particularly significant that the Appeals Chamber is composed of two international judges and one national judge.[82] Moreover, MINUSCA plays an essential role in the operation of the court, among others, with respect to the selection of international court officials.[83] In this context, it is worth noting that as a formally national court, the SCC does not have jurisdiction over members of MINUSCA, who have immunity from the criminal jurisdiction of the CAR under the Status of Forces Agreement.[84] Another sign of the subordination of the SCC to the international community consists in something like a reverse application of the complementarity principle of the Rome Statute, as the *loi organique* affirms the absolute primacy of the ICC.[85]

In addition to these features of the institutional architecture, it is clear that international actors are supposed to provide technical expertise as well as financial and other resources to the SCC. While understandable and laudable, in particular in the context of a largely dysfunctional national judicial system, the view that it is only the local that can learn from the international(ised) reveals common hegemonic assumptions. In this paradigm, relevant knowledge and expertise are typically associated with international actors, and there is little, if any, space for other kinds of knowledge and expertise or conceptions of justice. The composition of the judicial bench of the SCC and of most other hybrid tribunals, because of the dichotomy of international and national judges, is particularly telling. As has been argued, '[h]ybrid courts may unconsciously reinforce this model by

79 *Loi organique* (n 73) art 3.

80 Patryk I Labuda, 'The Special Criminal Court in the Central African Republic: Failure or Vindication of Complementarity?' (2017) 15 *Journal of International Criminal Justice* 175.

81 *Loi organique* (n 73) art 53.

82 ibid., art 14.

83 ibid., art 24. It is also worth noting that one year before the adoption of the *loi organique*, MINUSCA and the transitional government of the CAR signed a detailed memorandum of understanding on the establishment of the SCC, which has been called a 'quasi-legislative document': Labuda (n 80) 201.

84 This has been called 'the most problematic feature of the SCC law': Labuda (n 80) 202.

85 *Loi organique* (n 73) art 37. Although interesting from a legal perspective, this clause may be of limited practical relevance given the likely cooperation between the ICC and SCC prosecutors: Labuda (n 80) 199.

tacitly supporting an unstated assumption that the role of the international judge is to impart her wisdom on lesser local counterparts'.[86]

In the case of the SCC, the importance of and reliance on international expertise and guidance have been more than obvious. In 2017, for instance, the newly appointed judges were flown to Morocco to receive their first 'training' by international experts on the fundamentals of international criminal law and the investigative phase. This training was organised by the French *École nationale de la magistrature* (National School for the Judiciary) to support the operationalisation of the SCC and included members of the ICC, the Extraordinary Chambers in the Courts of Cambodia and the Special Tribunal for Lebanon.[87] Such exchanges and training sessions can certainly be fruitful and are difficult to criticise, as bringing together different actors from various jurisdictions would seem inherently useful. However, the discourse about 'training' reveals the underlying assumption that knowledge and expertise are to be imparted by international experts on local actors. Such approaches, as Emma Palmer has argued in the context of her discussion on adapting international criminal justice in Southeast Asia, 'represent assumptions about the dominance of external influence and domestic incapacity that diminish agency'.[88] Domestic actors might be respected for their context-specific knowledge and hence at least potentially greater local legitimacy (although the reverse argument might, in fact, also be made). Yet it clearly emerges that they are perceived to be in need of training to be delivered by international experts; otherwise, the SCC could not be operationalised.

It should be recalled that 'the international' and 'the local' are not homogenous entities and that constructing them as such frames the discussion on and analysis of international(ised) criminal justice in unhelpful ways. However, the dominant discourses about – and institutional setup of – hybrid tribunals still operate with this underlying dichotomy. Judges and prosecutors, among other actors, are viewed as either 'international' or 'national', as in the case of the SCC. This hides the fact that national judges are usually part of national elites, have been educated abroad, and may therefore not necessarily be the best representatives of 'local' communities.[89] Furthermore, the complex relationships between the 'international' and the 'local' spheres are typically imagined in a hierarchical and unidirectional manner: the 'international' is inherently more developed, and whereas – in line with the spirit of hybridity – the 'local' is supposed to inform the work of the tribunal in question, it clearly ranks second.

In other words, despite its professed commitment to the local, the SCC remains a product of the dominant (neo)liberal-legalistic paradigm that is focused

86 Harry Hobbs, 'Hybrid Tribunals and the Composition of the Court: In Search of Sociological Legitimacy' (2016) 16 *Chicago Journal of International Law* 482, 519.

87 'L'ENM forme les magistrats de la Cour pénale spéciale en Centrafrique' (23 January 2018) <www.enm.justice.fr/actu-23janvier2018_L-ENM-forme-les-magistrats-de-la-Cour-penale-speciale-en-Centrafrique> accessed 17 December 2020.

88 Palmer (n 22) 239.

89 ibid.

on assigning responsibility for serious crimes to a few individuals. This form of justice cannot capture the systemic dimensions of large-scale violence, and it does not contribute to promoting the transformative agency of local actors. Moreover, while every tribunal can, as one would hope, learn from the experiences of similar institutions, the now well-known challenges of hybrid tribunals are difficult to overcome. Because of its institutional setup and mandate, and because of the political environment in which it operates, the SCC will likely face challenges similar to those of other hybrid tribunals, like the Special Court for Sierra Leone and the Extraordinary Chambers in the Courts of Cambodia, which have not lived up to their promises.[90] The SCC, hence, should not be expected to play a ground-breaking role in delivering accountability for the serious crimes committed in the CAR. In fact, while the SCC can potentially try more cases than the ICC, the first years have not been overly encouraging, in part because of the delay in its operationalisation. Moreover, as the first cases demonstrate, the SCC is unlikely to be able to challenge the existing power structures and arrangements. For instance, nine individuals, presumably members of the armed group *Unité pour la paix en Centrafrique*, were arrested and transferred to the SCC in May 2020.[91] However, these individuals are 'small fry', as a MINUSCA official has noted: '[t]he SCC cannot take issue with the international community which, through the Khartoum Agreement [concluded in February 2019], has granted a kind of impunity to the main perpetrators of the crimes'.[92]

Since it is unlikely that the criminal law avenue will be abandoned in the CAR, it can be expected that most trials will be held at the national level and before ordinary courts. Indeed, rebuilding the national court system and pursuing national trials are heavily supported by international actors. A resilience lens can, once again, help explain why other avenues are difficult to imagine in the CAR: there are few non-governmental organisations, in the Western sense, from which bottom-up initiatives to transitional justice could emerge, and the traditional leaders and authorities are relatively weak.[93]

c) National trials: betting on the faster horse?

With the return of some stability in parts of the country, the national courts have started to resume some of their activities, and several alleged offenders have been

90 McAuliffe, 'Hybrid Tribunals at Ten' (n 11).

91 Cour pénale spéciale de la République centrafricaine, 'Arrestation de 9 éléments de l'UPC' *Press Release* (25 May 2020) <https://www.cps-rca.cf/actualites/Arrestation-de-9-elements-de-l-UPC/53/> accessed 17 December 2020.

92 Gaël Grilhot and Ephrem Rugiririza, 'Why There Is a Wave of Arrests at the Central African Special Court' (5 June 2020) <www.justiceinfo.net/en/tribunals/mixed-tribunals/44493-why-there-is-a-wave-of-arrests-at-the-central-african-special-court.html> accessed 17 December 2020.

93 Stephen W Smith, 'CAR's History: The Past of a Tense Present' in Carayannis and Lombard (eds) (n 3).

tried before these ordinary courts. Notably, Rodrigue Ngaïbona, better known as General Andjilo, a former leader of the *anti-balaka*, and Abdoulaye Alkali-Saïd, a former leader of the *Séléka*, were tried and convicted before the ordinary criminal court in Bangui in 2018 and 2019, respectively.[94] Five *anti-balaka* leaders, along with 23 other members of the militia, were tried and convicted in February 2020 for various atrocities committed against civilians and for attacks against international peacekeepers.[95]

While important procedural differences between trials held before national and international(ised) tribunals in conflict or post-conflict situations are to be expected, among others regarding the length of these trials, comparing the different judicial initiatives in the CAR is still striking. The ICC has terminated one trial, resulting in the acquittal of Bemba in June 2018 – 12 years after the prosecutor opened an investigation in the CAR. As of early 2020, the SCC had not issued any indictments, although it was created in 2015 and became fully operational in 2018. In contrast, the national trial against Alkali-Saïd was opened on 16 September 2019. He was sentenced a week later to six years in prison, after a hearing that lasted a few hours.[96]

Several points are worth noting. First, the national trials have, so far, not targeted those who can be considered most responsible for the most serious crimes committed. Such trials would, of course, be even more sensitive in the still highly volatile political climate, and they also tend to be more complex from a legal perspective. Second, the first trials did not lead to any convictions for international crimes. Andjilo was not even charged with international crimes, and while Alkali-Saïd was charged with war crimes and crimes against humanity, there was not sufficient evidence for a conviction on these counts. This is not to suggest that only convictions matter – the very purpose of a trial being the determination of the individual responsibility of an alleged perpetrator, who may simply not be guilty – or that the only proper charges would have been international crimes. Yet the context of an armed conflict and the widespread attacks against a civilian population mean that the specific charges of war crimes and crimes against humanity are, generally speaking, more appropriate than ordinary crimes, which can hardly capture the particular harm – and the extent of this harm – caused. It is precisely to attempt to make sense, from a legal perspective, of situations like that of the CAR that these concepts were developed. A conviction for war crimes and crimes against humanity arguably also carries greater moral stigma and sends a stronger signal, both to local and international constituencies.[97]

94 'Report of the Secretary-General on the Central African Republic' (15 February 2018) UN Doc S/RES/125, para 41.

95 Grilhot, 'Centrafrique' (n 78).

96 Gaël Grilhot, 'À Bangui, la cour criminelle double la CPI et la CPS' (26 September 2019) <www.justiceinfo.net/fr/tribunaux/tribunaux-nationaux/42466-bangui-cour-criminelle-double-cpi-et-cps.html> accessed 17 December 2020.

97 For these arguments, see, e.g., Robert D Sloane, 'The Expressive Capacity of International Punishment: The Limits of the National Law Analogy and the Potential of International

It is interesting to observe that the national judicial system and other relevant actors seem to have learned important lessons from the first cases and to have reacted quickly in order to bring stronger cases. Notably, the more recent case, terminated in February 2020, against five *anti-balaka* leaders and other militia members included charges of war crimes and crimes against humanity. The trial also lasted significantly longer.[98] Moreover, several human rights organisations, including the *Observatoire centrafricain des droits de l'homme* (OCDH) and the *Fédération internationale pour les droits humains* (FIDH) joined the process as civil parties (*parties civiles*) and submitted extensive information to the Court. Since the defendants were also charged for attacks against international peacekeepers, MINUSCA assumed an investigatory role, too, and provided the Court with abundant material.[99] Finally, from an outreach perspective, and considering the commitment to increasing local ownership of justice processes, it is worth noting that the trial was broadcast on radio and television and seems to have been widely followed by Central Africans.[100]

While the significance of these first national cases dealing with the recent episodes of large-scale violence in the CAR should not be overstated – they are far from perfect from a procedural perspective, remain very limited in scope, and have not targeted high-level perpetrators – they do raise the question of whether the establishment of a specific hybrid tribunal was actually necessary in this situation. The national justice system, with some external support, seems to have been able to bounce back to some extent and also to adjust its practice in order to address some of the violence committed as international crimes. What can be said is that the mere existence of the SCC and the increased presence of international actors in the country seem to have a significant impact. As the spokesperson for the SCC noted after the national trial of several leaders and other members of the *anti-balaka* militia in early 2020, 'the SCC is not intended to replace the national authorities on these issues but the work we are doing can gradually feed the discussions and push the national authorities to integrate new practices'.[101]

More generally speaking, the presence of the international community is clearly felt and has at least some impact on upholding human rights. For instance, although the prosecutor in this trial said in his closing arguments that the defendants 'would have deserved the death penalty', he called for life imprisonment to

Criminal Law' (2007) 43 *Stanford Journal of International Law* 39; Philipp Kastner, 'Domestic War Crimes Trials: Only for "Others"? Bridging National and International Criminal Law' (2015) 39 *University of Western Australia Law Review* 29, 48.

98 Grilhot, 'Centrafrique' (n 78).

99 ibid.

100 ibid.

101 Gaël Grilhot, 'Central African Republic: National Court Gets Tough on Bangassou Crimes' (10 February 2020) <www.justiceinfo.net/en/tribunals/national-tribunals/43747-central-african-republic-national-court-gets-tough-on-bangassou-crimes.html> accessed 17 December 2020.

respect a 'promise' to the international community.[102] In other words, attaining some accountability for the violence in the CAR while respecting fundamental human rights standards seems hardly imaginable without international support. However, as a critical approach to resilience would also suggest, while international involvement remains important, the focus of the dominant liberal model on certain manifestations of violence should not come at the price of preventing those who are primarily affected by the multiple forms of violence from initiating different justice-seeking endeavours and from making meaningful political claims.

4 Conclusion

Instead of attempting to envisage new institutional ways of dealing with large-scale violence, in the CAR or elsewhere, this chapter has tried to provide a constructive critique of hybrid tribunals and, more generally, of institutions seeking to enforce international criminal law by revealing, in particular, some of the dominant assumptions and discourses underlying these institutions. As it has been argued, a resilience lens helps expose some of the shortcomings of hybridity. In fact, hybrid tribunals, like the SCC in the CAR, can be seen as a manifestation of the neoliberal tendencies within resilience thinking: the agency of local actors is not openly denied, as in the case of purely international criminal tribunals, yet this agency remains inherently limited and subject to the dominant neoliberal logic that does not deal with structural or cultural violence or ongoing forms of coloniality. Nor does it offer the space necessary to imagine meaningful change.

Given the ubiquitous – yet superficial – turn to the local and associated resilience discourses, hybrid tribunals would seem to have a bright future ahead, as they promise to involve local actors to a greater extent than purely international institutions. Indeed, the idea that international interventions, such as in the form of *ad hoc* international tribunals or the ICC, can fix complex problems now seems to belong to a bygone age. However, the fundamental proposition that individuals should be held accountable for serious crimes could experience a further push-back, not primarily because of a recognition of the limits of individual criminal accountability for the systemic and collective dimensions of violence, but rather because of the claim of resilience thinking that the past can – and should – be disconnected from the present and the future and that there is therefore little, if anything, that we can learn from the past.

To be clear, international justice interventions, like the Security Council's creation of *ad hoc* tribunals or referrals to the ICC, are deeply problematic. Moreover, as it has been argued, even internationalised tribunals like the SCC in the CAR are not sufficiently innovative to break with the liberal-legalistic paradigm and do not genuinely recognise the agency and transformative potential of those most immediately affected by the violence in question. A resilience lens can usefully

102 ibid.

reveal these underlying assumptions and associated challenges, but uncritically embracing resilience thinking in the context of hybrid tribunals, and in the field of international criminal justice more generally, would represent an unhelpful response to the critique of liberal interventionism. Indeed, relying uncritically on resilience would not only echo the superficial turn to the local but can also frustrate any serious commitment to revealing the truth about or achieving justice for and contribute to preventing further large-scale violence. In other words, even if the model of hybrid tribunals can and should be critiqued for various reasons, jumping to the conclusion that the focus should shift from providing justice to building resilience would appear equally misled.

To end on a more positive note, the establishment of hybrid tribunals has demonstrated that new paths can be taken in the field of international(ised) criminal justice and that there is space for creativity. Seeking to address present and future forms of large-scale violence seems to require even further creative thinking. Perhaps hybridity will at some point take on new forms and meanings and will, for instance, be able to transcend the arguably unhelpful state/non-state divide.[103] And perhaps we will find ways not only to deal with certain manifestations of violence but also – quite contrary to what resilience thinking would suggest – to challenge the factors that enabled and perpetuate this violence.

103 For unofficial tribunals dealing with various violations of international law, see, e.g., Andrew Byrnes and Gabrielle Simm, 'Peoples' Tribunals, International Law and the Use of Force' (2013) 36 *University of New South Wales Law Journal* 711.

Futures for persistent problems

5 Development versus justice

International criminal law and investment in Myanmar

Emma Palmer

1 Introduction

The future of international criminal justice will involve growing attention towards its relationship to economic, social, and sustainable development.[1] Development can play a role as a cause of conflict, as a 'victim' of conflict, and as a challenge to societal recovery post-conflict.[2] Within, but also outside periods of armed conflict, both development initiatives and under-development can contribute to the commission of international crimes, be impeded by such crimes, and inhibit attempts to prevent atrocities and hold perpetrators to account. Proposals for social or economic development – including reformed institutions and justice systems – are sometimes presented as crucial in order to undertake international crimes trials, whether domestically or at the International Criminal Court (ICC). Certain development-oriented projects, including institutional reforms, may also contribute to reparative aims linked to international crimes trials, such as 'guarantees of non-repetition'. The relationship between development and international criminal justice is therefore both wide ranging and deep. This chapter explores the tensions between these concepts – identifying a 'development and/versus international criminal justice' conversation in relation to prosecuting international crimes alleged to have been perpetrated in Myanmar. It analyses how that discussion intersects with the long-recognised 'peace versus justice' debate, arguing that 'development and/versus justice' forms a related but distinct discussion likely to continue in this and other contexts.

'Development' is notoriously difficult to define.[3] Approaches differ by discipline and range from those more concerned with changes in human well-being

1 See generally Sébastien Jodoin and Marie-Claire Cordonier Segger (eds), *Sustainable Development, International Criminal Justice, and Treaty Implementation* (CUP 2013).

2 See also Killean in this volume.

3 See Fabiana Sciarelli and Azzurra Rinaldi, 'Defining Development' in Fabiana Sciarelli and Azzurra Rinaldi (eds), *Development Management of Transforming Economies: Theories, Approaches and Models for Overall Development* (Palgrave Macmillan 2017).

DOI: 10.4324/9781003087533-7

and freedoms (following Amartya Sen)[4] to those focused on 'economic' development through economic growth, typically via investments and consumer activities that increase incomes or gross development product.[5] The former approach is followed by the United Nations Development Programme in its Human Development Reports. These assess 'human development', which 'focuses on improving the lives people lead rather than assuming that economic growth will lead, automatically, to greater wellbeing for all. Income growth is seen as a means to development, rather than an end in itself'.[6] 'Development' may be qualified as 'sustainable', 'social', 'human', or 'economic' development. Development can be, and here is, considered a socially constructed and contingent term, with meanings evolving and diverging, depending on the user, the receiver, and their relative subjective and changing identities. Many statements drawn on in this chapter suggest understandings of development that encompass broader human development aims. They also often imply or assume that these aims are encouraged by economic initiatives, including macro-economic policy, investments (including foreign investments), and overseas development assistance to support growth.

'International criminal justice', along with 'justice' and 'law' alone, also hold multiple meanings, and they are contested concepts. This chapter focuses on *criminal* law investigations and prosecutions of conduct that might fulfil elements of the international crimes of genocide, war crimes, and crimes against humanity, often with international involvement, including via the ICC. It is the pitching of this particular 'normalised' response to atrocities[7] against 'development', broadly understood, that is of interest here. However, responses to other institutions that investigate or respond to alleged international crimes are also relevant, including UN-appointed investigative bodies and institutions. For instance, Myanmar's Ministry of Foreign Affairs responded to a decision by the International Court of Justice to award provisional measures concerning Myanmar's alleged breach of the Genocide Convention by arguing that it had 'hampered Myanmar's ability to lay the foundation for sustainable development in Rakhine'.[8]

4 Amartya Sen, *Development as Freedom* (OUP 1999). See also UN Secretary-General, 'In Larger Freedom: Towards Development, Security and Human Rights for All' UN Doc A/59/2005 (21 March 2005) para 17; Lisa J Laplante, 'Transitional Justice and Peace Building: Diagnosing and Addressing the Socioeconomic Roots of Violence Through a Human Rights Framework' (2008) 2 *International Journal of Transitional Justice* 331.

5 See Michael C Henry, 'Economic Growth and Economic Development: A Distinction without a Difference' (1987) 36 *Social and Economic Studies* 67; Hamid Hosseini, 'Why Development Is More Complex Than Growth: Clarifying Some Confusions' (2003) 61 *Review of Social Economy* 91.

6 UN Development Programme, 'Human Development Reports: About Human Development' <http://hdr.undp.org/en/humandev>.

7 Charlotte Epstein, 'The Postcolonial Perspective: An Introduction' (2014) 6 *International Theory* 294; Frédéric Mégret, 'In Defense of Hybridity: Towards a Representational Theory of International Criminal Justice' (2005) 38 *Cornell International Law Journal* 725.

8 Ministry of Foreign Affairs Myanmar, 'Press Statement on the Decision by the ICJ on "Provisional Measures" in the Case Brought by the Gambia Against Myanmar' (24 January 2020) <www.facebook.com/mofamyanmar/posts/1367204723479819?_rdc=1&_rdr> accessed 29 March 2021.

This chapter addresses four questions. First, how have scholars approached questions of 'development' in relation to international criminal justice issues? Four areas of literature are surveyed that identify potential links between the concepts of development and international criminal justice, including aspects of the 'peace versus justice' debate, alongside discussions about peace and justice in Myanmar. Second, do UN, Myanmar and foreign government, and civil society statements suggest there is (or has been) a 'development and/versus international criminal justice' debate in relation to Myanmar? Third, having identified that there is such a debate, what, if anything, is different about a 'development and/ versus justice' than a 'peace versus justice' debate? Fourth, what are the dangers and opportunities of a 'development and international criminal justice' discussion? These include, among others, the potential to reveal and confront questions about whether or when international criminal justice can contribute to development aims, and vice versa; redirecting attention towards preventative activities and wider 'transformative' justice aims; highlighting the role of economic drivers of conflict and atrocities (including corporate perpetrators); sharpening debates about the interrelationships between peace, development, and international criminal justice; and the risk of development being equated with forms of investment that embed impunity, distract from victims' and survivors' requests, or contribute to inequalities that encourage future violence.

2 Peace versus (international criminal) justice

To begin our review of different approaches towards development and international criminal justice, it is worth noting that official documents establishing international criminal tribunals (and associated reports and government statements) are more likely to propose a positive relationship between justice and peace than mention development. The Security Council resolutions establishing the ICTY and ICTR suggested that establishing an international tribunal would 'contribute to the restoration and maintenance of peace', for example.[9] Still, on the development front, the establishment of the ICTR came alongside requests for 'assistance for the reconstruction of Rwanda'.[10] Reflecting in 2015, the UN Security Council acknowledged 'the substantial contribution of the ICTR to the process of national reconciliation and the restoration of peace and security'.[11]

A perceived connection between peace and development is also evident. To focus on Southeast Asia, the Security Council resolutions mandated for the United Nations Mission in East Timor and the United Nations Transitional Administration in East Timor, UN transitional forces with robust development mandates that created the Special Panels for Serious Crimes in Dili, included to

9 UNSC Res 808 (22 February 1993) UN Doc S/RES/808; see UNSC Res 955 (8 November 1994) UN Doc S/RES/955.
10 UNSC Res 1050 (8 March 1996) UN Doc S/RES/1050.
11 UNSC 'Security Council Press Statement on Closure of International Criminal Tribunal for Rwanda' (22 December 2015) UN Doc SC/12188.

'provide security and maintain law and order' while assisting 'in the establishment of conditions for sustainable development'.[12] They called for support for 'peace-building and development assistance',[13] aiming for a 'smooth transition of the United Nations role towards traditional development assistance'.[14] The group of experts and UN actors assessing the options for Khmer Rouge trials in Cambodia argued that the need for judicial infrastructure, as well as corruption and the lack of an 'impartial criminal justice system', meant that domestic trials could only meet international standards with considerable changes. These included the construction of facilities and training of lawyers,[15] implemented by Cambodia 'alone or with foreign support'.[16] It seemed that some level of development might be a prerequisite for justice. Some governments, including the major donor, Japan, framed their support for the Extraordinary Chambers in the Courts of Cambodia (ECCC) as a contribution towards Cambodia's 'reconstruction and development',[17] which accorded with the Cambodian government's narrative.[18]

In relation to the ICC, the Rome Statute preamble observes that international 'crimes threaten the peace, security and well-being of the world', while the scope in Article 16 for Security Council referral and the prosecutor's discretions provide some ability to consider the impact of justice upon peace or conflict.[19] As discussed in chapter 1,[20] Security Council resolutions have also suggested a relationship between development, peacebuilding, and humanitarian responses. Further, under-development is often posed as a core 'root cause' of conflict and humanitarian catastrophe, which then leads to the commission of international crimes.[21] This situation may result from poor policy making, varied colonial legacies, corruption and crime, natural disasters, and resource distribution – or a combination of these and other factors, as in the case of Myanmar.[22]

12 UNSC Res 1272 (25 October 1999) UN Doc S/RES/1272.
13 UNSC Res 1338 (31 January 2001) UN Doc S/RES/1338.
14 UNSC Res 1410 (17 May 2002) UN Doc S/RES/1410.
15 'Identical Letters Dated 15 March 1999 from the Secretary-General to the President of the General Assembly and the President of the Security Council: Annex: Report of the Group of Experts for Cambodia Established Pursuant to General Assembly Resolution 52/135' UN Docs A/53/850 and S/1999/231, para 129.
16 ibid., para 131.
17 Embassy of Japan in Cambodia, 'Message from Ambassador Kumamaru' <www.kh.emb-japan.go.jp/ambassador/Kumamaru/Amb-Kumamaru-e.htm> accessed 27 February 2020.
18 See Emma Palmer, *Adapting International Criminal Justice in Southeast Asia: Beyond the International Criminal Court* (CUP 2020).
19 Christof Royer, 'International Criminal Justice Between Scylla and Charybdis – The "Peace versus Justice" Dilemma Analysed Through the Lenses of Judith Shklar's and Hannah Arendt's Legal and Political Theories' (2017) 18 *Human Rights Review* 395.
20 See Palmer and Harris Rimmer in this volume.
21 See, e.g., UNSC Res 2463 (29 March 2019) UN Doc S/RES/2463; UNSC Res 2405 (8 March 2018) UN Doc S/RES/2405.
22 See Thant Myint-U, *The Hidden History of Burma: Race, Capitalism, and the Crisis of Democracy in the 21st Century* (Atlantic 2020); Martin Smith, 'Arakan (Rakhine State):

Moving beyond such official documents, there are surely many ways to analyse the relationship between development and international criminal justice, while only some can be canvassed here. Transitional justice 'refers to the ways countries emerging from periods of conflict and repression address large-scale or systematic human rights violations so numerous and so serious that the normal justice system will not be able to provide an adequate response'.[23] It is a broader concept than international criminal justice, which focuses on prosecutions of international crimes, potentially by internationally established or managed courts. This section addresses transitional justice scholarship concerning the relationship between prosecuting international crimes and societal change, alongside more focused international criminal justice literature.

First, much attention is directed towards the relationship between peace and justice, or the 'peace versus justice' debate, which is sometimes shorthand for 'peace versus international criminal justice'. This literature has several aspects, including a more theoretical debate assessing whether justice or peace is preeminent as a normative goal and whether justice should be purely legalistic or take into account its impacts upon peace[24] and empirical research as to whether or in what circumstances prosecutions do contribute to peace, or might undermine it.[25] There is a related discussion in civil society advocacy that pitches the slogans 'no peace without justice' against 'no justice without peace'.[26] Even before the ICC commenced operations, there was debate about whether it might prevent atrocities.[27] There are more recent assessments of the ICC's affect upon peace and deterrence,[28] while others have analysed the relationships between amnesties,

A Land in Conflict on Myanmar's Western Frontier' *TNI* (December 2019) <www.tni.org/files/publication-downloads/tni-2020_arakan_web.pdf> accessed 16 November 2020; International Crisis Group, 'Fire and Ice: Conflict and Drugs in Myanmar's Shan State' (8 January 2019) <www.crisisgroup.org/asia/south-east-asia/myanmar/299-fire-and-ice-conflict-and-drugs-myanmars-shan-state> accessed 16 November 2020; Emma Palmer, 'The Responsibility to Protect and Infrastructure in Myanmar' (2020) 12 *Global Responsibility to Protect* 86. Note that 'root causes' continued to be emphasised by the UN Human Rights Council after the attempted coup; see UNHRC Res S-29/L.1 (12 February 2021) UN Doc A/HRC/S-29/L.1.

23 International Center for Transitional Justice, 'What Is Transitional Justice?' (2019) <www.ictj.org/about/transitional-justice> accessed 20 December 2019.

24 Royer (n 19) 405.

25 Kathryn Sikkink, *The Justice Cascade: How Human Rights Prosecutions Are Changing World Politics* (WW Norton 2011); Kathryn Sikkink and Hun Joon Kim, 'The Justice Cascade: The Origins and Effectiveness of Prosecutions of Human Rights Violations' (2013) 9 *Annual Review of Law and Social Science* 269; James Meernik, 'Justice and Peace? How the International Criminal Tribunal Affects Societal Peace in Bosnia' (2005) 42 *Journal of Peace Research* 271.

26 See Royer (n 19): for example, in the name of the NGO, 'No Peace Without Justice'.

27 See, e.g., Payam Akhavan, 'Beyond Impunity: Can International Criminal Justice Prevent Future Atrocities?' (2001) 95 *American Journal of International Law* 7; Harris Rimmer in this volume.

28 Alyssa K Prorok, 'The (In)compatibility of Peace and Justice? The International Criminal Court and Civil Conflict Termination' (2017) 71 *International Organization* 213;

peace, and transitional justice more broadly.[29] A number of scholars argue that the relationship between peace and justice is always nuanced and requires a practical case-by-case, rather than abstract, approach.[30]

Transitional justice has itself been associated with liberal peacebuilding efforts and an assumption that peace is best delivered via free market economies and democratic structures.[31] To the extent that transitional justice and peacebuilding efforts strengthen justice and constitutional frameworks, including the 'rule of law', these may also encourage investment, including protections for foreign investments. Following atrocities, societies' (new) leaders may, however, face several calculations when determining how best to rebuild trust, secure stability, or 'signal a break with the old regime' that present economic challenges.[32] These might include the challenge of funding or inability to fund compensation, governance systems' reliance on perpetrators' capital and knowledge, and the destruction or repression of economic and justice infrastructures. There may be perceptions that the

> pursuit of justice and reconciliation are beneficial only to the extent that they contribute to the future of the new order. Beyond that, the pursuit of justice will bankrupt the future of the system of cooperation and production and the ability of citizens to break from the past.[33]

In these ways, discussions about how peace relates to justice also concern states' development but are not straightforward.

Benjamin J Appel, 'In the Shadow of the International Criminal Court: Does the ICC Deter Human Rights Violations?' (2018) 62 *Journal of Conflict Resolution* 3; Anna Macdonald, '"In the Interests of Justice?" The International Criminal Court, Peace Talks and the Failed Quest for War Crimes Accountability in Northern Uganda' (2017) 11 *Journal of Eastern African Studies* 628.

29 See, e.g., Rénee Jeffery, *Amnesties, Accountability, and Human Rights* (University of Pennsylvania Press 2014); Rénee Jeffery, 'Amnesties *and* Intractable Conflicts: Managed Impunity in The Philippines Bangsamoro *Peace* Process' (2014) 17 *Journal of Human Rights* 436; Geoff Dancy, 'Deals with the Devil? Conflict Amnesties, Civil War, and Sustainable Peace' (2018) 72 *International Organization* 387; Louise Mallinder 'Can Amnesties and International Justice be Reconciled?' (2007) 1 *International Journal of Transitional Justice* 208; Katerina Mansour and Laura Riches, 'Peace versus Justice: A False Dichotomy' (Contemporary Issues in Conflict Resolution Spring/Summer 2017) <www.sciencespo.fr/psia/sites/sciencespo.fr.psia/files/Peace_versus_Justice-A_False_Dichotomy.pdf> accessed 27 February 2020.

30 Royer (n 19) 407. See, e.g., Mansour and Riches (n 29); Janine Clark, 'Peace, Justice and the International Criminal Court: Limitations and Possibilities' (2011) 9 *Journal of International Criminal Justice* 521.

31 Chandra Lekha Sriram, 'Justice as Peace? Liberal Peacebuilding and Strategies of Transitional Justice' (2007) 21 *Global Society* 579.

32 Peter J Boettke and Christopher J Coyne, 'Political Economy of Forgiveness' (2007) 44(2) *Society* 53, 57.

33 ibid., 59.

Moreover, civil society activists and researchers identify problems with equating development with peace. They offer case studies in which investment initiatives aimed at fostering development in fact exacerbated conflict, including the construction of pipelines, dams, and mines in post-conflict countries.[34] They may recommend the elaboration and implementation of business and human rights frameworks, including in conflict situations.[35] Often such reports pose justice as a necessary, but lacking, response to corporate abuses. This literature focuses on development and peace but at least implicitly distinguishes peace from justice, since development might *not* provide peace, but increased justice offers a solution to any violence.

Second, there are variations of critical international law scholarship that argue that international criminal law is associated, inherently perhaps, with liberal or neoliberal perspectives or corporate indicia.[36] Third World Approaches to International Law and Third World Approaches to International Criminal Law (TWAICL) literature has argued that international law reproduces the exploitation of post-colonial states by the 'West' and the global economy, which also displaces violence to the developing world.[37] Some scholars have argued that, as the 'project' of international criminal justice has expanded, political issues have increasingly been framed as relating to international criminal law, including questions of wealth inequalities.[38] The 'monopolisation' of justice by the ICC in particular may have diminished the scope for alternative conceptions of justice, such as reconciliation, ending violence or conflict, or compensation for harm and

34 See, e.g., Thomas Parks, Nat Colletta and Ben Oppenheim, 'The Contested Corners of Asia' *The Asia Foundation* (7 October 2013) <https://asiafoundation.org/publication/the-contested-corners-of-asia-subnational-conflict-and-international-development-assistance/> accessed 27 February 2020; Michael Likosky, *Law, Infrastructure, and Human Rights* (CUP 2006); Daria Davitti, *Investment and Human Rights in Armed Conflict: Charting an Elusive Intersection* (Hart 2019). Popular works include Antony Loewenstein, *Disaster Capitalism: Making a Killing Out of Catastrophe* (Verso 2017); Naomi Klein, *The Shock Doctrine: The Rise of Disaster Capitalism* (Picador 2007).

35 See, e.g., John Ruggie, 'Report of the Special Representative of the Secretary-General on the Issue of Human Rights and Transnational Corporations and Other Business Enterprises: Business and Human Rights in Conflict-Affected Regions: Challenges and Options Towards State Responses' (27 May 2011) UN Doc A/HRC/17/32.

36 Christine Schwöbel, 'The Market and Marketing Culture in International Criminal Law' in C Schwöbel (ed), *Critical Approaches to International Criminal Law: An Introduction* (Routledge 2014).

37 Antony Anghie and BS Chimni, 'Third World Approaches to International Law and Individual Responsibility in Internal Conflicts' (2003) 2 *Chinese Journal of International Law* 77, 89. See also ibid. 226; Michelle Burgis-Kasthala, 'Scholarship as Dialogue? TWAIL and the Politics of Methodology' (2016) 14 *Journal of International Criminal Justice* 921.

38 Sarah MH Nouwen and Wouter G Werner, 'Monopolizing Global Justice: International Criminal Law as Challenge to Human Diversity' (2015) 13 *Journal of International Criminal Justice* 157; Christine Schwöbel, 'The Comfort of International Criminal Law' (2013) 24 *Law and Critique* 169; Frédéric Mégret, 'What Sort of Global Justice Is "International Criminal Justice?"' (2015) 13 *Journal of International Criminal Justice* 77.

the redistribution of wealth.[39] Similarly, some argue that transitional justice has become a 'dominant language' for transitioning from conflict to peace.[40] Thus, it is suggested that international criminal justice may 'crowd out' human rights law and humanitarian or 'local' responses.[41] Others note the ICC's lack of jurisdiction over corporate entities and the limited – though present – history of international crimes prosecutions of corporate executives.[42] Joanna Kyriakakis observes that 'what unifies [certain] strands of critique is the attention that is given to ways in which ICC situation and case selections manifest a collusion, rather than a confrontation, by the Court with existing hierarchies of state power'.[43] This power structure includes particular financial interests and economic development policies.

This critical literature is diverse but may involve considering the 'project' of international criminal justice to be aligned with particular economic paradigms that favour foreign interventions and investments and then critiquing that relationship. To the extent that international criminal justice is perceived as promoting a particular economic regime, mechanisms for international justice may appear normatively allied with certain perspectives of 'development', particularly those focused on economic (as opposed to human) development. Greater attention towards prosecuting corporate entities may be one response to this challenge, but, particularly if parent corporations are not targeted or are immune from prosecution, some prosecutions may serve to exacerbate TWAICL concerns.[44]

Related scholarship critiques the apparent linearity proposed by '*transitional* justice', which may assume or propose that prosecutions will usher forward a liberal, democratic, capitalist peace. Alexander Hinton points to illustrations in outreach pamphlets for the ECCC of an apparently prosperous Cambodia, complete with distant factories, proclaiming the ECCC slogan 'move forward through justice'.[45] By contrast, the story of the ECCC does not tread a linear path from norm acceptance via establishing a tribunal and prosecutions towards the rule of

39 Nouwen and Werner (n 38). See also Kamari Maxine Clarke, *Fictions of Justice: The International Criminal Court and the Challenges of Legal Pluralism in Sub-Saharan Africa* (CUP 2009); Christian De Vos, 'All Roads Lead to Rome: Implementation and Domestic Politics in Kenya and Uganda' in Christian De Vos, Sara Kendall, and Carsten Stahn (eds), *Contested Justice: The Politics and Practice of International Criminal Court Interventions* (CUP 2015); Carsten Stahn, 'Justice Civilisatrice? The ICC, Post-Colonial Theory, and Faces of "The Local"' in De Vos, Kendall and Stahn (eds), (this note).

40 Catherine Turner 'Deconstructing Transitional Justice' (2013) 24 *Law and Critique* 193, 194. See also Clarke (n 39).

41 See Schwöbel, 'The Comfort of International Criminal Law' (n 38).

42 Joanna Kyriakakis, 'Corporations Before International Criminal Courts: Implications for the International Criminal Justice Project' (2017) 30 *Leiden Journal of International Law* 221.

43 ibid., 226.

44 ibid.

45 Alexander Hinton, *The Justice Façade: Trials of Transition in Cambodia* (OUP 2018). See also Alexander Laban Hinton, 'Transitional Justice Time: Uncle San, Aunty Yan, and Outreach at the Khmer Rouge Tribunal' in Deborah Mayersen and Annie Pohlman (eds), *Genocide and Mass Atrocities in Asia: Legacies and Prevention* (Routledge 2013).

law or liberal democracy.[46] Instead, as Rebecca Gidley argues, the ECCC may represent 'illiberal transitional justice'.[47]

Arguably, transitional justice 'prioritizes building specific institutional arrangements (such as democracy, constitutionalism, and the rule of law) and establishing a market-driven economy, while ignoring other possible arrangement[s] that could also promote social justice and redistribution'.[48] In particular, Gready and Robins assert:

> Transitional justice has been disseminated as an integral part of the globalization of a set of human rights norms linked to liberalism and neoliberalism. Transitional justice has become part of a hegemonic discourse that links development and peacebuilding to a liberal statebuilding project that sees liberal democracy as its endpoint.[49]

This is presented as one of a number of limitations of transitional justice, alongside its association with 'an elite international professional and donor network rather than locally rooted movements'.[50] By contrast, Laurel Fletcher, Harvey Weinstein, and Jamie Rowen propose that '[a]ttention to the underlying socioeconomic disparities and inequalities in the country, in conjunction with structural change in the way that the country is governed, may be the most important first steps in developing an appropriate response to perpetrators of violence'.[51]

Moreover, if – consistent with the 'peace versus justice' literature – 'there may be legitimate arguments that other problems and needs are more important and/or more urgent than seeking justice through trials',[52] then the timing and sequencing of justice initiatives might require careful and context-driven analysis.[53] Yet there are not clear divisions between periods of violence and post-conflict 'periods

46 Palmer, *Adapting International Criminal Justice in Southeast Asia* (n 18).

47 Rebecca Gidley, *Illiberal Transitional Justice and the Extraordinary Chambers in the Courts of Cambodia* (Palgrave Macmillan 2019).

48 René Urueña and María A Prada-Uribe, 'Transitional Justice and Economic Policy' (2018) 14 *Annual Review of Law and Social Science* 397, 400, with reference to Paul Gready and Simon Robins, 'From Transitional to Transformative Justice: A New Agenda for Practice' (2014) 8 *International Journal of Transitional Justice* 339, 341.

49 Gready and Robins (n 48) 341. See also Laplante (n 4) 338, 343.

50 Gready and Robins (n 48) 342.

51 Laurel E Fletcher, Harvey M Weinstein and Jamie Rowen, 'Context, Timing and the Dynamics of Transitional Justice: A Historical Perspective' (2009) 31 *Human Rights Quarterly* 163, 218.

52 Luc Huyse, 'Justice' in David Bloomfield, Teresa Barnes and Luc Huyse (eds), *Reconciliation After Violent Conflict: A Handbook* (International Institute for Democracy and Electoral Assistance 2003) 103.

53 Fletcher, Weinstein, and Rowen (n 51) 218; Hurst Hannum, 'Peace versus Justice: Creating Rights as Well as Order out of Chaos' (2006) 13 *International Peacekeeping* 582.

with reform, justice initiatives and reconciliation'.[54] This challenges understandings of transitional justice involving progression or positive change. Rather, 'new and distinctive sources of criminality and abuse . . . can arise in the post-conflict setting'.[55] This also suggests that the intersections between transitional and international criminal justice approaches with international economic and investment law, including the protections offered to investors via international investment agreements,[56] as well as with other areas of transnational criminal law and corruption, may warrant greater attention.[57]

Third, some might argue that prosecuting individual perpetrators *can* symbolise the rejection of social injustice,[58] or that, at least, transitional justice 'might provide some tools for resisting economic abuses'.[59] Building on some of the previous critiques, scholars have proposed that transitional justice mechanisms should pay greater attention to socioeconomic inequalities.[60] This, it is argued, might better address the prevention of violence in future – where the 'overarching aim of prevention rests on the basic premise that post-conflict recovery entails a holistic approach that should include economic, political and social structural reform'.[61] From that perspective, prosecuting international crimes might seek to prevent violence via promoting peace and responding to violence, but should redress violations of economic and social rights more directly. Mechanisms might do so by explaining the structural and economic context underlying violence and abuses. Truth commissions in Guatemala, Peru, South Africa, Timor-Leste, and a number of other states did incorporate findings concerning economic and social rights, and this approach might be advanced elsewhere or be more directly emphasised.[62] For instance, the International Commission Against Impunity in Guatemala (CICIG) had a mandate not just to investigate but to collaborate with and make recommendations to the state to pursue

54 Jennifer Balint, Kristian Lasslett, and Kate Macdonald, ' "Post-Conflict" Reconstruction, the Crimes of the Powerful and Transitional Justice' (2017) 6 *State Crime Journal* 4, 6.

55 ibid.

56 Urueña and Prada-Uribe (n 48) 406.

57 See Davitti (n 34).

58 Patrick Lenta, 'Transitional Justice and Retributive Justice' (2019) 22 *Ethical Theory and Moral Practice* 385.

59 Geoff Dancy and Eric Wiebelhaus-Brahm, 'Bridge to Human Development or Vehicle of Inequality? Transitional Justice and Economic Structures' (2015) 9 *International Journal of Transitional Justice* 51, 53.

60 See, e.g., Wendy Lambourne, 'Transitional Justice and Peacebuilding After Mass Violence' (2009) 3 *International Journal of Transitional Justice* 28; Zinaida Miller, 'Effects of Invisibility: In Search of the "Economic" in Transitional Justice' (2008) 2 *International Journal of Transitional Justice* 266; Gready and Robins (n 48) 339. See also Lenta (n 58); Laplante (n 4).

61 Laplante (n 4) 332.

62 Laplante (n 4): for example, Timor-Leste CAVR report: Ruben Carranza, 'Plunder and Pain: Should Transitional Justice Engage with Corruption and Economic Crimes?' (2008) 2 *International Journal of Transitional Justice* 310.

prosecutions involving 'illegal security forces and clandestine security apparatus' as well as for 'preventing their reappearance'.[63] Civil society initiatives and peoples' tribunals have also addressed socioeconomic justice issues, including in the case of the Independent People's Tribunal on the World Bank in India, by ' "indict[ing]" the global neoliberal economic system'.[64] This recognises, in part, that 'prosecution in itself may not decisively break the mutually reinforcing walls of impunity built in the pretransition period' if stolen assets and economic crimes are not addressed either at courts or via associated transitional justice mechanisms.[65]

Arguably, an international criminal law–focused trial 'perpetuates an impunity gap by focusing on a narrow range of human rights violations while leaving accountability for economic crimes to ineffective domestic institutions or to a still evolving international legal system that deals with corruption'.[66] The mentioned initiatives suggest that the relationship between transitional justice and preventative reforms *might* be extended to address wider social and economic structures beyond a particular conflict, such as those that contribute to criminal activity. Efforts have included reconsidering the language of 'transition' in favour of 'transformation', 'which implies long-term, sustainable processes embedded in society and adoption of psychosocial, political and economic, as well as legal, perspectives on justice'.[67] Former ICC Prosecutor Luis Moreno-Ocampo thus argued in 2005 that 'we must think about an integrated approach and how to combine justice with other areas, such as rehabilitation and development, in order to produce better communities'.[68] Where transitional justice, including international criminal justice, mechanisms have reparations processes for victims and survivors, there is an argument that such reparations incorporate

63 Comisión Internacional contra la Impunidad en Guatemala (CICIG), 'CICIG Mandate and Agreement' (5 March 2018) <www.cicig.org/cicig/mandato-y-acuerdo-cicig/> accessed 27 February 2020.

64 Gabrielle Simm and Andrew Byrnes, ' "International Peoples" Tribunals in Asia: Political Theatre, Juridical Farce, or Meaningful Intervention?' (2014) 4 *Asian Journal of International Law* 103, 113. See also International People's Tribunal 1965, 'Final Report of the IPT 1965: Findings and Documents of the IPT 1965' (20 July 2016) <www.tribunal1965.org/en/final-report-of-the-ipt-1965/>.

65 Carranza (n 62) 314.

66 ibid., 310.

67 Wendy Lambourne, 'Transitional Justice and Peacebuilding After Mass Violence' (2009) 3 *International Journal of Transitional Justice* 28, 30. 'Transformative justice is defined as transformative change that emphasises local agency and resources, the prioritization of process rather than preconceived outcomes and the challenging of unequal and intersecting power relationships and structures of exclusion at both the local and the global level': Gready and Robins (n 48) 340.

68 Luis Moreno-Ocampo, 'Keynote Address: Integrating the Work of the ICC into Local Justice Initiatives' (2005) 21 *American University International Law Review* 497.

'transformative' aims.[69] These might address the recognition, representation, and redistribution of structural inequalities.[70] Justice initiatives that fail to address the underlying causes of conflict and inequalities are not well positioned to support, particularly, 'guarantees of non-repetition' – a form of reparation promoted by the UN Basic Principles and Guidelines on the Right to a Remedy and Reparation.[71] Some studies suggest that many victims and survivors of violence prioritise economic needs, including employment and housing concerns, over retributive justice.[72] However, while truth commissions might make specific institutional reform recommendations (as do human rights courts), the mandates and focus of international criminal tribunals do not always offer such flexibility, though a number of courts have a reparations function. Moreover, by defining groups of 'victims' and 'non-victims' by connection to particular crimes or perpetrators, alongside the inability of reparations to fundamentally redistribute wealth or shift economic and power structures, reparations might obscure or even exacerbate inequalities.[73]

Others argue that transitional justice – perhaps especially international criminal justice – leads to a misallocation of resources that would be better redirected towards wider development projects or public goods and services or may risk impeding economic and human development goals. For instance, it has been argued that the billions invested by foreign states, the United Nations, and

69 Luke Moffett, 'Reparations for Victims at the International Criminal Court: A New Way Forward?' (2017) 9 *International Journal of Human Rights* 1204.

70 Andrea Durbach and Louise Chappell, 'Leaving Behind the Age of Impunity' (2014) 16 *International Feminist Journal of Politics* 54; Sarah Williams and Emma Palmer, 'Transformative Reparations for Women and Girls at the Extraordinary Chambers in the Courts of Cambodia' (2016) 10 *International Journal of Transitional Justice* 311. See also Catherine Baker and Jelena Obradovic-Wochnik, 'Mapping the Nexus of Transitional Justice and Peacebuilding' (2016) 10 *Journal of Intervention and Statebuilding* 281.

Uruena and Prada-Uribe (n 48) 401; UN Office of the High Commissioner of Human Rights, 'Basic Principles and Guidelines on the Right to a Remedy and Reparation for Victims of Gross Violations of International Human Rights Law and Serious Violations of International Humanitarian Law' adopted and proclaimed by UNGA Res 60/147 (16 December 2005) UN Doc A/RES/60/147.

71 ibid.

72 Nadine Kirchenbauer, Mychelle Balthazard, Latt Ky, Patrick Vinck, and Phuong Pham, *Victims Participation Before the Extraordinary Chambers in the Courts of Cambodia* (Cambodian Human Rights and Development Association 2013) <www.eccc.gov.kh/sites/default/files/Victims-participation-before-ECCC-Baseline-Study-Jan-2013.pdf> accessed 27 February 2020; Simon Robins, *Families of the Missing: A Test for Contemporary Approaches to Transitional Justice* (Routledge 2013) regarding Nepal and Timor-Leste.

73 For example, at the ECCC only 'collective' reparations are available: see Christoph Sperfeldt, 'Collective Reparations at the Extraordinary Chambers in the Courts of Cambodia' (2012) 12 *International Criminal Law Review* 457; Linda Keller, 'Seeking Justice at the International Criminal Court: Victims' Reparations' (2007) 29 *Thomas Jefferson Law Review* 189; 'Observations by the Redress Trust pursuant to Article 75(3) of the Statute and Rule 103 of the Rules' *Prosecutor v Jeanne-Pierre Bemba Gombo*, ICC-01/05–01/08, Trial Chamber, 17 October 2016; Miller (n 60); Clark (n 30) 531.

Cambodian government in supporting the ECCC are yet to significantly contribute to the 'rule of law' in Cambodia.[74] But perhaps, as the former president of the Special Court for Sierra Leone, Geoffrey Robertson, has suggested: 'the money that is being invested in global justice would simply not be made available for infrastructure or policing'.[75]

The extent to which international criminal justice initiatives cannibalise funding for development projects is not necessarily clear. Still, one proposal is that 'transitional justice measures should be designed and implemented in ways that are "development sensitive" ', including through better coordination and integration of economic, social and cultural rights,[76] with or without more 'transformative' aims. Others suggest that the ICC or other international criminal tribunal reparations and assistance programmes might be more effectively delivered by a separate institution or by development agencies with, perhaps, more targeted expertise – especially if they are to deliver on wider economic and social rights aims.[77] As noted earlier, there is a distinction between even 'transformative' judicial reparations and development, since the former 'specifically target[s] victims' of crimes,[78] while the ICC's Trust Fund for Victims' assistance function is not so constrained.

Fourth, in the wider humanitarian, peacebuilding, development, and human rights space, UN organs have long associated development with crime (of all kinds), security, and 'modernisation' initiatives – more recently recognised via the inclusion of crime prevention as a 'global sustainable development priority'.[79] The (then) UN Secretary-General Kofi Annan's 2005 *In Larger Freedom* report tied a broad interpretation of development to security and respect for human rights.[80] The 'Women, Peace, and Security' agenda has drawn attention to the intersections and overlaps between peace, conflict, and gendered violence.[81]

74 Heather Ryan and Laura McGrew, *Performance and Perception: The Impact of the Extraordinary Chambers in the Courts of Cambodia* (Open Society Foundations 2016) <www.justiceinitiative.org/uploads/106d6a5a-c109-4952-a4e8-7097f8e0b452/performance-perception-eccc-20160211.pdf> accessed 20 February 2020.

75 Quoted in Roger Duthie, 'Toward a Development-Sensitive Approach to Transitional Justice' (2008) 2 *International Journal of Transitional Justice* 292, 298.

76 Duthie (n 75) 292.

77 See also Dancy and Wiebelhaus-Brahm (n 59) 54.

78 Duthie (n 75) 299. See OHCHR, *Rule-of-Law Tools for Post-Conflict States: Reparations Programmes* (United Nations 2008) 26–27; Naomi Roht-Arriaza and Katharine Orlovsky, 'A Complementary Relationship: Reparations and Development' in Pablo de Greiff and Roger Duthie (eds), *Transitional Justice and Development: Making Connections* (Social Science Research Council 2009).

79 Laplante (n 4); Jarrett Blaustein, Tom Chodor, and Nathan W Pino, 'Development as a Historical Component of the United Nations' Crime Policy Agenda: From Social Defence to the Millennium Development Goals' [2019] *Criminology & Criminal Justice* <https://doi.org/10.1177/1748895819877453>.

80 Kofi Annan 'In Larger Freedom: Towards Development, Security and Human Rights for All' (26 May 2005) UN Doc A/59/2005/Add.3.

81 See, generally, Sara E Davies and Jacqui True (eds), *The Oxford Handbook of Women, Peace, and Security* (OUP 2019).

Human rights–based approaches to development have promoted participatory development design processes and multi-stakeholder consultations that have also been encouraged as an approach to transitional justice.[82] Particularly after the World Humanitarian Summit in 2016, the UN, the World Bank, and others held workshops and published briefing papers on the 'triple nexus' – the nexus between humanitarian, development, and (when appropriate) peace initiatives.[83] This approach has some support – from the ICRC, for instance.[84] It identifies, and seeks to operationalise better coordination across, tensions between peace and humanitarian goals, as well as development initiatives in practice.

This discussion reflects several implicit models for understanding the relationship between transitional (and international criminal) justice and 'economic structures': viewing justice as a 'roadblock to economic growth', 'vehicle of inequality', or 'bridge to human development'.[85] Human rights activists present cases warning that economic initiatives may require justice responses. Critical international criminal law literature emphasises the relationship between international criminal justice and historic and persistent unequal power structures. The transformative justice literature addresses the perceived relationship between transitional justice and inequality, in order that justice might contribute to broader human development aims.

As for international criminal justice in Myanmar, there are arguments across the peace-justice spectrum from those promoting justice towards those more concerned about the political ramifications and limitations of – in particular – ICC action. For those concerned about the relationship between justice and peace, Morten Pedersen's warning will have rung true, even before the military seized power in 2021:

> By putting not only the Commander-in-Chief but any military officer who served in Rakhine State during the violence on notice that they could someday be held accountable for their crimes, we have essentially ensured that the military-as-an-institution cannot risk letting go of control of the state.[86]

By contrast, Kip Hale and Melinda Rankin supported the ICC Pre-Trial Chamber I's finding that the ICC could have limited jurisdiction on the more legalistic, but also normative, basis that 'Myanmar was not exempt from the non-derogable

82 See Gready and Robins (n 48); Morten Broberg and Hans-Otto Sano, 'Strengths and Weaknesses in a Human Rights-Based Approach to International Development – An Analysis of a Rights-Based Approach to Development Assistance based on Practical Experiences' (2018) 22 *International Journal of Human Rights* 664.

83 International Council of Voluntary Agencies, 'Demystifying the Humanitarian, Development and Peace Nexus' <www.icvanetwork.org/demystifying-nexus> accessed 27 February 2020.

84 State News Service, 'The EU Humanitarian-Development Nexus' (24 July 2019) <https://redcross.eu/positions-publications/the-eu-humanitarian-development-nexus> accessed 27 February 2020.

85 Dancy and Wiebelhaus-Brahm (n 59) 53.

86 Morten B Pedersen, 'The ICC, the Rohingya and the Limitations of Retributive Justice' (2018) 73 *Australian Journal of International Affairs* 9, 12.

legal obligations placed on all states, as well as individuals, to prevent and punish atrocity crimes',[87] while there 'is significant evidence that Myanmar's leadership orchestrated and oversaw atrocity crimes, which demands international action under the Rome Statute (where applicable) and customary international law'.[88] Michal Lubina argues that Myanmar's situation demonstrates that the 'peace versus justice' dichotomy is 'still well and alive' and promoted by the Myanmar government and many in the public, who favour language of 'peace', stability, and reconciliation, including avoiding notions of 'revenge' or potential conflict involving the military or ethnic armed groups.[89] Yet arguably, the situation in Myanmar is more complex than a 'devil's choice' about 'peace versus justice'.[90]

These debates are not new. In 2006, Roman David and Ian Holliday argued that heavily 'qualified amnesties' might be needed for political reform in Myanmar.[91] There has been a failure to prosecute many alleged crimes, alongside the persistence of immunities,[92] and arguably a 'political reality of blanket amnesty'[93] for the period of military control, all of which contribute towards 'everyday impunity'.[94] Meanwhile, Holliday has argued that 'the interface with socioeconomic development needs to be deliberated' in Myanmar,[95] 'where crony capitalism in the junta years underpinned not only individual violations, but also systemic abuse', and '[w]ere this challenge taken seriously, the country's transitional justice agenda would expand to encompass a large programme of development-sensitive

87 Kip Hale and Melinda Rankin, 'Extending the "System" of International Criminal Law? The ICC's Decision on Jurisdiction over Alleged Deportations of Rohingya People' (2019) 73 *Australian Journal of International Affairs* 22, 24.

88 ibid., 25.

89 Michal Lubina, 'Set the Torturers Free: Transitional Justice and Peace vs Justice Dilemma in Burma/Myanmar' (2018) 47 *Polish Political Science Yearbook* 77; Palmer, *Adapting International Criminal Justice in Southeast Asia* (n 18).

90 Catherine Renshaw, 'Myanmar's Genocide and the Legacy of Forgetting' (2020) 48 *Georgia Journal of International and Comparative Law* 425, 446.

91 Roman David and Ian Holliday, 'Set the Junta Free: Pre-Transitional Justice in Myanmar's Democratisation' (2006) 41 *Australian Journal of Political Science* 91.

92 Human Rights Institute, International Bar Association, 'The Rule of Law in Myanmar – Challenges and Prospects' (December 2012) <https://www.burmalibrary.org/sites/burmalibrary.org/files/obl/docs14/IBAHRI-Rule_of_Law_in_Myanmar.pdf> accessed 30 September 2021.

93 Lubina (n 89) 88; Amnesty International, 'Myanmar: Scrap or Amend New Law That Could Grant Immunity to Former Presidents' (28 January 2016) <www.amnesty.org/en/latest/news/2016/01/myanmar-scrap-or-amend-new-law-that-could-grant-immunity-to-former-presidents/> accessed 27 February 2020.

94 Nick Cheesman, Bina D'Costa, and Tyrell Haberkorn, 'Anticipating the Struggle Against Everyday Impunity in Myanmar Through Accounts from Bangladesh and Thailand' (2016) 3 *Asia & the Pacific Policy Studies* 48. See also Palmer, *Adapting International Criminal Justice in Southeast Asia* (n 18); Lubina (n 89).

95 Ian Holliday, 'Thinking About Transitional Justice in Myanmar' (2014) 22 *South East Asia Research* 183, 192.

social justice'.[96] The peace and justice discussion concerning Myanmar therefore includes a development aspect.[97]

These sets of literature point to relationships between peace and justice, between development and peacebuilding, and between transitional justice and its economic underpinnings or inadequacies. The next section reviews UN statements addressing the links between development and justice and then considers whether there is a 'development and/versus international criminal justice' aspect to the debate about prosecuting international crimes in Myanmar.

3 Justice and/versus development in Myanmar

UN, Myanmar and foreign government, and civil society statements reveal a 'development and/versus international criminal justice' debate in relation to Myanmar, though it is not the only focus of the discussion about prosecuting international crimes. The Security Council has been notoriously quiet in relation to Myanmar, with threatened vetoes by China and Russia preventing the passage of related resolutions.[98] However, it has held a number of meetings and briefings, including an August 2019 'Arria-formula' meeting that Germany, Peru, and Kuwait organised on 'Mass Atrocity Crimes in Myanmar: Where Do We Stand on Accountability?',[99] briefings by Special Envoy Christine Schraner Burgener and the chair of the UN fact-finding mission, Marzuki Darusman, and a Security Council delegation's visit to Myanmar in late April 2018. In November 2017, the president of the Security Council condemned violence in Rakhine State, expressed 'grave concern over reports of human rights violations and abuses in Rakhine State, including by the Myanmar security forces', and called for the application of the 'rule of law' and respect for human rights.[100] The statement 'stresse[d] the importance of undertaking transparent investigations into allegations of human rights abuses and violations . . . and of holding to account all

96 ibid., 193.

97 See Lubina (n 89) 84; Impunity Watch, 'Memorialisation as Related to Transitional Justice Processes in Burma/Myanmar: an Exploration' (2014) <www.impunitywatch.org/post/memorialisation-as-related-to-transitional-justice-processes-in-burma-myanmar-an-exploration> 12.

98 Michelle Nichols, 'UN Security Council Mulls Myanmar Action; Russia, China Boycott Talks' *Reuters* (18 December 2018) <www.reuters.com/article/us-myanmar-rohingya-un/un-security-council-mulls-myanmar-action-russia-china-boycott-talks-idUSKBN1OG2CJ> accessed 27 February 2020; UN News, 'China and Russia Veto US/UK-Backed Security Council Draft Resolution on Myanmar' (12 January 2007) <https://news.un.org/en/story/2007/01/205732-china-and-russia-veto-usuk-backed-security-council-draft-resolution-myanmar> 27 February 2020.

99 Security Council Report, 'Chronology of Events: Myanmar' (10 September 2019) <www.securitycouncilreport.org/chronology/myanmar.php> accessed 27 February 2020.

100 United Nations Security Council, 'Statement by the President of the Security Council' (6 November 2017) UN Doc S/PRST/2017/22.

those responsible for such acts to provide justice for victims'.[101] It also welcomed commitments to humanitarian assistance and development work, though this was not a focus of the statement.

The secretary-general, high commissioner for human rights, and special rapporteurs have been more vocal in their calls for accountability. Yet there is also a discussion about development and justice in Myanmar, with three overlapping sides: those favouring development ('no justice without development'), those concerned about a development focus and emphasising accountability ('no development without justice'), and those who – consistent with the Security Council's indications – view peace, development, and justice as correlated (if not causally related).

a) Development vs justice: no justice without development

The civilian government of Myanmar has taken a multi-pronged approach to contesting allegations of international crimes, including genocide.[102] The government has denied the commission of international crimes,[103] deployed rule of law and accountability language to maintain the need for evidence (which it argues is lacking),[104] established investigative bodies that did not focus on securing criminal accountability (though there were limited prosecutions), and proposed an alternative to justice. That alternative continues to be described as a longer-term, broader development approach – though accompanied in practice by instances of violence.

That economic and social development would be a priority for Myanmar's government is unsurprising – Myanmar has been classified as a Least Developed Country since 1987[105] and was ranked 148 of 189 countries and territories (the lowest in Southeast Asia) on the UN Human Development Index in 2017.[106] The government has tended to associate development goals with peace and stability aims. After shifting to a civilian-led government in 2011, President Thein

101 ibid.

102 See *Application of the Convention on the Prevention and Punishment of the Crime of Genocide (The Gambia v Myanmar)* (International Court of Justice) <www.icj-cij.org/en/case/178> accessed 16 November 2020.

103 State Counsellor Office, 'Government Refutes Rights Group Report on Rakhine' (17 November 2016) (copy on file with author).

104 And has reportedly destroyed: see, e.g., Emanuel Stoakes, 'Myanmar Government "Bulldozing Rohingya Mass Grave to Hide Evidence"' *The Guardian* (20 February 2018) <www.theguardian.com/global-development/2018/feb/19/myanmar-government-bulldozing-rohingya-mass-grave-hide-evidence> accessed 16 November 2020.

105 UN Committee for Development Policy, 'List of Least Developed Countries (as of December 2018)' <www.un.org/development/desa/dpad/wp-content/uploads/sites/45/publication/ldc_list.pdf> accessed 27 February 2020.

106 UN Development Programme (UNDP), 'Human Development Reports: Myanmar' <http://hdr.undp.org/en/countries/profiles/MMR> accessed 16 November 2020.

Sein made 'national unity' his 'top priority'.[107] This reflected the history and persistence of subnational conflict, which had entrenched the political dominance of the military.[108] Thein Sein advised that one must 'build roads, railroads and bridges to overcome the natural barriers between regions of national races' and preserve peace.[109] Similarly, Aung San Suu Kyi and her political party, the National League for Democracy (NLD), have preferred a narrative of reconciliation, peace, and the rule of law.[110] In 2012 Aung San Suu Kyi told an International Bar Association (IBA) delegation that she opposed criminal trials as these would be 'unacceptable to the military', with which she needed to cooperate.[111]

Government statements, especially surrounding the 2015 elections, promoted 'peace and stability and development', as well as ethnic and religious harmony.[112] In order to preserve such stability, the Thein Sein government suggested that reform measures, including 'accountability and responsibility', should be gradual.[113] The government asked international actors to appreciate 'the difficulties and challenges which a young democratic State has to face', meaning that 'accountability and responsibility should be progressively developed and matured in proportion so that the goal of democratic society will be achieved smoothly and peacefully'.[114] After the NLD won those elections, Aung San Suu Kyi advised that the government would aim to 'ensure national reconciliation, internal peace, the rule of law, amendments to the constitution and keeping the democratic system dynamic'.[115] This suggested that Myanmar's stability and reform were the priori-

107 Ministry of Foreign Affairs, 'President U Thein Sein Delivers Inaugural Address to Pyidaungsu Hluttaw' (31 March 2011) <https://www.burmalibrary.org/sites/burmalibrary.org/files/obl/docs12/2011-03-30-TS_inaugural_speech_to_Pyidaungsu_Hluttaw.pdf> accessed 27 February 2020.

108 Gerard McCarthy, *Military Capitalism in Myanmar: Examining the Origins, Continuities and Evolution of 'Khaki Capital'* (ISEAS 2019); Independent International Fact-Finding Mission on Myanmar, 'The Economic Interests of the Myanmar Military' (5 August 2019) UN Doc A/HRC/42/CRP.3 (UNFFM Economic Report).

109 'Inaugural Address' (n 107).

110 Renshaw describes this as an approach of 'forgetting': Renshaw (n 90) 389.

111 Human Rights Institute, International Bar Association (n 92) 54. See also Palmer, *Adapting International Criminal Justice in Southeast Asia* (n 18).

112 Myanmar President Office, 'Undertaking Peace and Stability and Development in Rakhine State in Cooperation with UN' (7 November 2015) (copy on file with author); Myanmar President Office, 'Joint Statement on Election Issued' (17 September 2015) (copy on file with author).

113 Myanmar's leaders advised that 'accountability and responsibility should be progressively developed and matured in proportion so that the goal of democratic society will be achieved smoothly and peacefully': Ministry of Foreign Affairs, 2014 (copy on file with author).

114 Ministry of Foreign Affairs, 'Ms Yanghee Lee Expresses Her Recognition and Applause for Progress in Sweeping and Far-Reaching Reforms Dramatically Achieved in Landscape of Political, Economic, Social and Human Rights in Myanmar' (31 July 2014) (copy on file with author).

115 Associated Press, 'Myanmar's Suu Kyi Vows to Amend Junta-Era Constitution' *AP News* (18 April 2016) <https://apnews.com/article/b0e5742a27e44009bc4b22be5f5bc112> accessed 27 February 2020.

ties, rather than international crimes prosecutions. Indeed, foreign direct investment into Myanmar grew rapidly, particularly after 2010, exceeding US$4 billion in 2015 and 2017.[116] Development indicators also continued to improve.[117] Yet reports of violent incidents continued and, in Rakhine State, were increasingly described as amounting to international crimes, including – particularly since 2017 but also before that – as part of an alleged process of genocide.[118] In that sense, foreign investment at least did not prevent atrocity crimes in Myanmar.

Even prior to the political turbulence of 2021, Myanmar's officials critiqued the application of international criminal justice to events within the country. The NLD government 'resolutely rejected the ICC's [2018 jurisdiction] ruling' on the basis that Myanmar is not a party to the Rome Statute and denied any responsibility for deportations,[119] among other, mostly procedural concerns. However, the government also claimed that 'Myanmar is both willing and able to investigate any crimes and violations of human rights in its own territory', and 'the Government has time and again reiterated its principled position of promoting and implementing the rule of law, justice and accountability'.[120]

The NLD government proposed an understanding of 'accountability' as self-directed (taking responsibility for one's own actions), requiring 'acceptable evidence'[121] and, with a nod to the rule of law,[122] applying 'equally to all. Individuals,

116 The World Bank, 'Foreign Direct Investment, Net Inflows (BoP, Current US$) – Myanmar' <https://data.worldbank.org/indicator/BX.KLT.DINV.CD.WD?locations=MM> accessed 16 November 2020.

117 UNDP (n 106).

118 See, e.g., Amnesty International, 'Myanmar: "Caged Without a Roof": Apartheid in Myanmar's Rakhine State' (21 November 2017) <www.amnesty.org/en/documents/asa16/7484/2017/en/> accessed 16 November 2020; Fortify Rights and United States Holocaust Memorial Museum, '"They Tried to Kill Us All": Atrocity Crimes Against Rohingya Muslims in Rakhine State, Myanmar' (November 2017) <www.fortifyrights.org/downloads/THEY_TRIED_TO_KILL_US_ALL_Atrocity_Crimes_against_Rohingya_Muslims_Nov_2017.pdf> accessed 16 November 2020; and earlier with respect to Daniel Feierstein's framework for the stages of genocide: Penny Green, Thomas MacManus, and Alicia de la Cour Venning, *Countdown to Annihilation: Genocide in Myanmar* (International State Crime Initiative 2015) <http://statecrime.org/data/2015/10/ISCI-Rohingya-Report-PUBLISHED-VERSION.pdf> accessed 16 November 2020; Penny Green, Thomas MacManus, and Alicia de la Cour Venning, *Genocide Achieved, Genocide Continues: Myanmar's Annihilation of the Rohingya* (International State Crime Initiative 2018) <http://statecrime.org/data/2018/04/ISCI-Rohingya-Report-II-PUBLISHED-VERSION-revised-compressed.pdf> accessed 16 November 2020.

119 Republic of the Union of Myanmar, 'Press Release' (7 September 2018) (copy on file with author).

120 ibid.

121 State Counsellor Office, 'The State Counsellor Dan Aung San Suu Kyi's Exclusive Interview with Nikkei Asian Review' (22 September 2017) (copy on file with author).

122 See also Republic of the Union of Myanmar, 'Statement by His Excellency U Thaung Tun, National Security Advisor to the Union Government of the Republic of the Union of Myanmar at the ARRIA Formula Meeting of the Security Council on the Situation in Myanmar' (13 October 2017) (copy on file with author).

organizations, national governments *as well as multilateral organizations*, must be held responsible for the consequences of their words and actions'.[123] A series of inquiries and commissions were established to investigate allegations of human rights violations, with international actors invited to participate in some of them. The 'overarching goal' of the domestically managed 2013 Commission of Inquiry concerning Rakhine State 'was to promote peace and development in the region rather than place the blame on a specific group or community'.[124] An advisory commission led by Kofi Annan, with domestic and international participation, was established to identify 'factors that have resulted in violence, displacement and underdevelopment'.[125] When establishing the advisory commission, Aung San Suu Kyi explained that it would 'consider humanitarian and development issues, access to basic services, the assurance of basic rights, and the security of the people in Rakhine'.[126] The aim was therefore not to pursue prosecutions but to attempt a development-based 'innovative approach to peace building in a country undergoing a challenging national peace and reconciliation process'.[127] A Committee for Implementation of the Recommendations on Rakhine State from the Advisory Commission also favoured a long-term perspective focused on infrastructure and other development achievements.[128] Government mechanisms therefore suggest that the 'root causes' of violence are developmental and that justice initiatives should not disrupt this long-term work.

At a 'Rakhine Investment Fair' in 2019, Aung San Suu Kyi gave a speech to encourage sustainable development, arguing that for 'too long the international community's attention has been focused narrowly on negative aspects related to

123 State Counsellor Office, 'Statement by HE U Kway Tint Swe Union Minister for the Office of the State Counsellor and Chairman of the Delegation of the Republic of the Union of Myanmar at the General Debate of the 73rd Session of the United Nations General Assembly New York' (29 September 2018) (copy on file with author).

124 Republic of the Union of Myanmar, 'Final Report of Inquiry Commission on Sectarian Violence in Rakhine State' (8 July 2013) <www.burmalibrary.org/docs15/Rakhine_Commission_Report-en-red.pdf> accessed 27 February 2020.

125 Advisory Commission on Rakhine State, 'Towards a Peaceful, Fair and Prosperous Future for the People of Rakhine: Final Report of the Advisory Commission on Rakhine State' (August 2017) <www.rakhinecommission.org/the-final-report/> accessed 27 February 2020, 12.

126 Myanmar News Agency, 'Establishment of the Advisory Commission on Rakhine State' *The Global New Light of Myanmar* (24 August 2016) <https://www.burmalibrary.org/sites/burmalibrary.org/files/obl/docs23/GNLM2016-08-24-red.pdf> accessed 27 February 2020.

127 Kofi Annan Foundation, 'Advisory Commission on Rakhine State: Lessons Learned Report' (June 2018) <https://www.kofiannanfoundation.org/mediation-and-crisis-resolution/rakhine-lessons-learned/> accessed 27 February 2020.

128 See Committee for Implementation of the Recommendations on Rakhine State, 'Report to the People submitted by the Committee for Implementation of the Recommendations on Rakhine State, on its Activities from September to December 2018' *The Global New Light of Myanmar* (9–12 March 2019) <https://www.burmalibrary.org/en/category/the-global-new-light-of-myanmar-2019?page=2> accessed 27 February 2020.

problems in North Rakhine rather than on the panoramic picture that shows the immense potential of this State for peace and prosperity'.[129] At an earlier summit in Naypyitaw, Rakhine State's Minister of Finance Kyaw Aye Thein argued that the Rakhine 'crisis happened in a small part of the state. We believe when there is economic development, it will lead to stability'. Another official 'admit[ted] there is a problem in Rakhine. We need development in Rakhine'.[130] These statements all posed development as an alternative to – or even replacement for – justice and accountability for the commission of international crimes.

Looking to the future, Myanmar's NLD government had given great prominence to the UN Sustainable Development Goals, including via its Myanmar Sustainable Development Plan.[131] 'Peace and stability' represented the first of the three 'pillars' included in this plan since, according to Aung San Suu Kyi's foreword, the plan is 'fundamental to the sustainment of peace' and 'sustainable and equitable development promotes peace and cements stability'.[132] Indeed, Goal 1 of that pillar poses development as a pathway towards peace.[133] Strategy 1.3 promotes access to justice, respect for human rights 'without discrimination so that no person is above the law', and independent courts that protect the rule of law.[134] Rather than pitching development against human rights, this strategy linked development, peace, human rights, and justice. It reflected the UN and wider tendency to associate justice, peace, and development as mutually reinforcing goals, but with an emphasis on development.

At the time of publication, Myanmar's government was in upheaval, but the 'emergency' leader, Senior General Min Aung Hlaing, was named by the UNFFM as 'one of the persons recommended by the Mission for investigation and prosecution for crimes against humanity, war crimes and genocide'.[135] This suggested an increasingly oppositional stance towards prosecutions, while Min Aung Hlaing's statements exhibited a continued emphasis on development.[136]

129 Simon Lewis, 'Myanmar's Suu Kyi Woos Investors to Crisis-Hit Rakhine, Decries "Negative" Focus' *Reuters* (22 February 2019) <www.reuters.com/article/us-myanmar-rakhine-investment/myanmars-suu-kyi-woos-investors-to-crisis-hit-rakhine-decries-negative-focus-idUSKCN1QB0HO> accessed 27 February 2020.

130 Nan Lwin, 'Major Push for Investment in Rakhine at Invest Myanmar Summit' *The Irrawaddy* (29 January 2019) <www.irrawaddy.com/news/major-push-investment-rakhine-invest-myanmar-summit.html> accessed 27 February 2020.

131 Ministry of Planning and Finance, 'Myanmar Sustainable Development Plan (2018–2030)' (August 2018) <https://themimu.info/sites/themimu.info/files/documents/Core_Doc_Myanmar_Sustainable_Development_Plan_2018_-_2030_Aug2018.pdf> accessed 27 February 2020 (MSDP).

132 ibid., iii.

133 ibid., 8.

134 ibid., 12.

135 UNFFM Economic Report (n 108) para 232.

136 See, e.g., Xinhua, 'China, Myanmar agree to accelerate construction of economic corridor' (12 January 2021) <www.xinhuanet.com/english/2021-01/12/c_139661897.htm>; Chan Mya Htwe, and Kyaw Soe Htet, 'Senior General Min Aung Hlaing to maintain

There are other states and actors that promote development as the most important response to the situation in Rakhine State and decades of violence in Myanmar. For example, although some Chinese-funded, development-oriented projects have been associated with violence,[137] China's view has been clear: 'Development is *the* fundamental way to resolve the issue of Rakhine state, which has abundant resources yet its development lags behind'.[138] China offered a three-stage approach in response to the refugee crisis, involving first, ceasing hostilities to 'restore stability and order'; second 'seek[ing] viable measures . . . through communication and consultations' between Myanmar and Bangladesh; and third, 'resolv[ing] the root causes of poverty through development', with Myanmar government and international support.[139] China does not support criminal accountability initiatives and has previously, alongside Russia, opposed referring the situation to the ICC.

Japan was the main sponsor of a 2019 Rakhine Investment Fair, with the slogan 'Rakhine is open for business to the world'. At this event for foreign investors, the Japanese ambassador proposed that '[s]ome countries have been blaming the Myanmar government for what happened in Rakhine. However, most of the countries – including Japan – want to see Myanmar's economic development, lasting peace and also a peaceful transition'.[140] Instead, despite the violence of previous years, including in Rakhine, Kachin, and Shan states, the Japanese representative's position was that if 'there is economic development, I believe there will be no conflict'.[141] This followed Japan's commitment of US$20.6 million towards two humanitarian projects in northern Rakhine State in 2018, alongside other states such as Indonesia and Myanmar that have funded housing, health, and education projects. For Japan, at least, this funding was tied to development aims, since it aimed to 'improve [the] humanitarian and

---

foreign, economic policies' (9 February 2021) <www.mmtimes.com/news/senior-general-min-aung-hlaing-maintain-foreign-economic-policies.html>.

137 EarthRights International, 'The Burma–China Pipelines: Human Rights Violations, Applicable Law, and Revenue Secrecy' (March 2011) <https://earthrights.org/wp-content/uploads/the-burma-china-pipelines.pdf> accessed 16 November 2020; United States Institute for Peace, 'China's Role in Myanmar's Internal Conflicts' (September 2018) <www.usip.org/sites/default/files/2018-09/ssg-report-chinas-role-in-myanmars-internal-conflicts.pdf> accessed 16 November 2020; John Liu and Kyaw Soe Htet, 'China Projects to Hurt NLD Chances in Ethnic Areas' *Myanmar Times* (25 October 2020) <www.mmtimes.com/news/china-projects-hurt-nld-chances-ethnic-areas.html>; Smith (n 22).

138 UNSC Verbatim Record (28 February 2019) UN Doc S/PV/8477, 6 (emphasis added).

139 UNSC Verbatim Record (13 February 2018) UN Doc S/PV/8179, 8–9.

140 Nan Lwin, 'Japan to Take Leading Role in Pushing FDI in Rakhine' *The Irrawaddy* (8 February 2019) <www.irrawaddy.com/news/japan-take-leading-role-pushing-fdi-rakhine.html> accessed 27 February 2020.

141 Thiha Ko Ko, 'Japan Envoy Says Development Is Solution for Rakhine' *Myanmar Times* (10 February 2019) <www.mmtimes.com/news/japan-envoy-says-development-solution-rakhine.html> accessed 27 February 2020.

development situation in Rakhine State with the approach of the humanitarian-development nexus'.[142]

Some states see under-development and poverty as the, or at least a major, 'root cause' of the violence – as expressed by China, Peru, and other states in 2018.[143] According to the UN High Commissioner for Refugees Filippo Grandi and Sweden's representative, under-development alongside citizenship and rights restoration were together 'root causes' of atrocities, and Ethiopia maintained that restoring rights is the 'root cause' and that 'assigning blame . . . is no longer tenable'.[144] Equatorial Guinea proposed that the international community should 'focus on development by alleviating poverty and seek *peace through development* in order to definitely solve the problem'.[145] These statements also imply that risks of violence remain, so future atrocities might result from a failure to address these 'root causes'. This stress on 'root causes' of violence was continued in a UN Human Rights Council resolution adopted by consensus in February 2021.[146]

Unsurprisingly, elements of the private sector propose that development is crucial for encouraging peace and the end of violence in Myanmar. A letter signed by the European, French, German, Italian, American, Australian, and British Chambers of Commerce noted in 2019 that 'Western' companies are increasingly 'choosing to responsibly participate rather than isolate', passing on their own standards of 'corporate governance and sustainable responsibility'. They argued that 'only through such responsible, sustainable investment and day-to-day engagement on the ground in the country can business usefully assist Myanmar to drive growth, peace and stability'.[147] Anecdotally, one fear had been that an inordinate focus on international justice, at the ICC for instance, risked Myanmar's development trajectory by increasing the government's isolation from (Western) investors.

It is therefore not just Myanmar's government that has presented development as a precursor for justice. Further, the government's policy towards the Rohingya has been a popular one, meaning that it arguably supported the NLD's democratic majority.[148] Investors knew that it was politically risky for the government to change its policy and pursue justice and prosecute perpetrators of violence. While some (possibly many) domestic and international investors and aid providers may have continued to invest in Myanmar without accountability for international

142 Thompson Chau, 'Tokyo's Rakhine Aid Emphasises "Humanitarian-Development Nexus"' *Myanmar Times* (26 February 2018) <www.mmtimes.com/news/tokyos-rakhine-aid-emphasises-humanitarian-development-nexus.html> accessed 27 February 2020.

143 UNSC Verbatim Record (13 February 2018) UN Doc S/PV/8179, 11.

144 ibid., 11.

145 ibid., 16 (emphasis added).

146 UNHRC Res S-29/L.1 (12 February 2021) UN Doc A/HRC/S-29/L.1.

147 EuroCham Myanmar et al, 'Joint Letter: Promoting Foreign Direct Investment in Myanmar' (27 January 2019) <https://www.dica.gov.mm/sites/default/files/news-files/joint_chambers_letter_signatories_as_at_5_feb_2019.pdf> accessed 27 February 2020.

148 Pedersen, 'The ICC, the Rohingya and the Limitations of Retributive Justice' (n 86).

crimes, for others the risk/rewards were unfavourable, even before the military seized power in January 2021. For instance, there was some apparent reduction in investment interest resulting from the government-imposed 'shutdown' of internet services in Rakhine and Chin states in 2019 and 2020.[149] Further, the debate about isolation on human rights grounds versus retaining access in Myanmar is not new.[150] Under the NLD government, the actual relationship between 'no justice' and development remained unclear. On the other hand, there has been a sense of 'no justice without development' in the *position* of Myanmar's government, military, and some states and private actors. In various ways, they suggest that development must come first, whereas international criminal justice is unlikely to resolve the 'root causes' of conflict and violence and – whether via misallocation of resources, distraction, or isolation – may even exacerbate them.

b) Justice vs development: no development without justice

There is a second tension between development and justice. Many civil society and UN actors see the wrong type of development as a threat to justice (broadly understood) – pointing to experiences of impunity across Myanmar, including in the infrastructure and mining sectors.[151] Scholars, the UN's Independent International Fact-Finding Mission (UNFFM), and civil society actors also identify the significant control wielded by the military over economic life in Myanmar, including by military-owned corporations, as undermining international criminal justice aims.

The UNFFM released an important report on the economic interests of the Myanmar military in August 2019.[152] It built on its detailed report on serious violations of human rights in Myanmar, which recommended that no businesses should enter into relationships with Myanmar's armed forces (the Tatmadaw) or any of its many related entities.[153] It named Myanmar holding companies and conglomerates, projects, and individuals involved in

149 John Liu, 'Internet Shutdown Has Been Imposed on Rakhine for Six Months' *The Myanmar Times* (21 December 2019) <www.mmtimes.com/news/internet-shutdown-has-been-imposed-rakhine-six-months.html> accessed 27 February 2020. See also World Bank (n 116).

150 See Morten B Pedersen, *Promoting Human Rights in Burma: A Critique of Western Sanctions Policy* (Rowman & Littlefield 2018).

151 For examples, see Amnesty International, 'Myanmar: Four Years On, Impunity Is the Kachin Conflict's Hallmark' (9 June 2015) <https://www.amnesty.org/en/documents/asa16/1832/2015/en/> accessed 16 November 2020; Vani Sathisan, 'Letpadaung, Daw Khin Win and Impunity' *International Commission of Jurists* (3 November 2016) <www.icj.org/letpadaung-daw-khin-win-and-impunity/> accessed 16 November 2020; Palmer, The Responsibility to Protect and Infrastructure in Myanmar' (n 22). See also Cheesman, D'Costa and Haberkorn (n 94).

152 UNFFM Economic Report (n 108).

153 Independent International Fact-Finding Mission on Myanmar (UNFFM), 'Report of the Detailed Findings of the Independent International Fact-Finding Mission on Myanmar' (17 September 2018) UN Doc A/HRC/39/CRP.2, paras 1708, 1716, and 1717.

the commission of serious human rights violations, including through donations to the Tatmadaw's 'clearance operations' in Rakhine State. The report found that foreign companies have been involved in joint ventures with these companies, including through supplying arms but also through broader commercial ties. The Mission also concluded that private companies with military links were

> financing development projects in northern Rakhine in furtherance of the Tatmadaw's objective of re-engineering the region in a way that erases evidence of Rohingya belonging in Myanmar, and preventing their return to access their homeland and communities. These projects, carried out under the Union Enterprise for Humanitarian Assistance, Resettlement and Development in Rakhine (UEHRD) consolidate the consequences of war crimes, crimes against humanity and acts of genocide.[154]

The UNFFM report drew upon international criminal law modes of liability to discuss the accountability of corporate actors and proposed the retention and expansion of targeted sanctions. It recognised that investments and development projects can contribute to the commission of international crimes in Myanmar, and – by enriching particular groups – prevent accountability for past and future crimes. For its part, the Myanmar government rejected this report.[155]

Likewise, a 2019 application to Argentinian courts to exercise universal jurisdiction over crimes against the Rohingya requested the investigation and prosecution of 'officials of corporations where there are reasonable grounds to believe they participated in the commission of crimes under international law committed in relation to Myanmar's human rights crisis'.[156] Then Special Rapporteur for Myanmar Yanghee Lee has discussed the role of the Sustainable Development Goals in Myanmar and the need for business and human rights principles to be implemented carefully, including via due diligence.[157] She warned that '[d]evelopment is needed for increased prosperity, but it cannot take place at the cost of

154 UNFFM Economic Report (n 108) 4.

155 Agence France-Presse, 'Myanmar "Categorically Rejects" UN Report on Army Business Empire' *The Jakarta Post* (6 August 2019) <www.thejakartapost.com/seasia/2019/08/06/myanmar-categorically-rejects-un-report-on-army-business-empire.html> accessed 27 February 2020.

156 'Certified Translation: Complainant Files a Criminal Complaint of Genocide and Crimes Against Humanity Committed Against the Rohingya Community in Myanmar – Universal Jurisdiction' *Burma Campaign* (11 November 2019) <https://burmacampaign.org.uk/media/Complaint-File.pdf> accessed 27 February 2020, 44.

157 Yanghee Lee, 'Report of the Special Rapporteur on the Situation of Human Rights in Myanmar' (20 August 2018) UN Doc A/73/332, paras 26–27.

human rights',[158] and recognised that 'development and security are pressing priorities for Myanmar currently', but 'also urge[d] Myanmar to recognize human rights as an equal priority, both because human rights are a lynchpin in ensuring that development and security are realized in a balanced and just way' and to help improve daily lives.[159] Put differently, human rights are needed for development and security.

In 2018, the UN High Commissioner for Human Rights Zeid Ra'ad Al Hussein rejected any emphasis on development, directly responding to the slogan, 'Open for Business', adopted at some Myanmar investment fairs.[160] He argued that while the serious need for infrastructure development in Myanmar is 'clear', 'the shocking violations of human rights which have driven hundreds of thousands of people to flee the country should heighten the vigilance of any investor'. He reflected on the history of human rights violations associated with infrastructure development in Myanmar and therefore 'strongly urge[d] those seeking investment opportunities in Myanmar to undertake in-depth, regular human rights due diligence', arguing that '[t]hese measures are vital for informed investments in infrastructure, and for inclusive, sustainable development. They are also *vital for accountability*'.[161] In a related tone, Chair of the UN Fact-Finding Mission Marzuki Darusman argued that the 'international community . . . should not subscribe to a false dichotomy of peace versus justice or of development . . . versus human rights', since, he said, in Myanmar, 'deeply entrenched *impunity is at the root of the problem*'.[162] From this perspective, a lack of accountability embedded the economic and political influence of certain perpetrators and the pattern of human rights violations.

These statements support 'no development without human rights' at least – and in some cases, 'no development without justice'. They recognise the contribution of investment towards violence and recoil from what they see as a 'false dichotomy' between the goals of development and justice. In other words, they argue that development does *not* equal peace, but that justice must support human rights respecting sustainable investments.

158 Yanghee Lee, 'Situation of Human Rights in Myanmar' (26 August 2016) UN Doc A/71/361, para 81.
159 Yanghee Lee, 'Situation of Human Rights in Myanmar' (8 September 2017) UN Doc A/72/382, para 77.
160 Zeid Ra'ad Al Hussein, 'Infrastructure Investment in Myanmar: Open for Business?' *United Nations Human Rights Office of the High Commissioner* (2018) <www.ohchr.org/en/NewsEvents/Pages/DisplayNews.aspx?NewsID=22866> accessed 27 February 2020.
161 ibid. (emphasis added).
162 United Nations Human Rights Council, 'Statement of Mr Marzuki Darusman, Chairperson of the Independent International Fact-Finding Mission on Myanmar to the General Assembly, Third Committee' (23 October 2018) <www.ohchr.org/EN/HRBodies/HRC/Pages/NewsDetail.aspx?NewsID=23800&LangID=E> accessed 27 February 2020 (emphasis added).

c) Justice and development

As indicated already, government mechanisms and some states suggest that the 'root causes' of violence in Myanmar relate – in at least a prominent way – to development issues, whereas the UNFFM and others characterise the core issue as military impunity,[163] acknowledging that this occurs in an environment of under-development. However, most view the issues as interrelated. For instance, the UN Secretary-General has observed that all 'communities in Rakhine state are poor and need sustainable and inclusive development, which is also *essential* for reconciliation and peace', alongside the 'prerequisite' of accountability.[164] Similarly, the Security Council has called upon

> the Government of Myanmar to address the root causes of the crisis in Rakhine State by respecting, promoting and protecting human rights, without discrimination and regardless of ethnicity or religion, including by allowing freedom of movement, equal access to basic services, and equal access to full citizenship for all individuals.[165]

Some propose that development, including trade agreements and financing arrangements, might 'prevent extremism, foster stability and spur economic development' moving forward, too.[166] Sweden's representative has explained that 'it will not be possible to restore peace and stability in Rakhine state without also addressing the conditions that led to the violence and displacement in the first place', naming 'security, reconstruction and livelihood programmes' as possible responses.[167] Indonesia's representative warned that it 'is also imperative to create inclusive and sustainable economic development in Rakhine state in order to ensure the sustainability of the solution'.[168] Many states suggest that development will play a role in sustaining gains and preventing future violence, even if such activities have not always prevented (and may have contributed to) conflict and atrocities in Myanmar.[169]

In terms of what responses are warranted, virtually all states support the implementation of the recommendations made by the advisory commission led by Kofi Annan, which the Myanmar government appointed to review the situation in

163 UNFFM Economic Report (n 108); ibid.

164 António Guterres, 'Remarks to the Security Council on Myanmar' *United Nations Secretary-General* (28 August 2018) <www.un.org/sg/en/content/sg/speeches/2018-08-28/remarks-security-council-myanmar> accessed 27 February 2020 (emphasis added).

165 United Nations Security Council President, 'Statement by the President of the Security Council' (6 November 2016) <www.securitycouncilreport.org/atf/cf/%7B65BFCF9B-6D27-4E9C-8CD3-CF6E4FF96FF9%7D/s_prst_2017_22.pdf> accessed 27 February 2020, 3.

166 UNSC Verbatim Record (13 February 2018) S/PV/8179, 5 (Mr Grandi, UNHCR).

167 ibid., 9.

168 UNSC Verbatim Record (28 February 2019) S/PV/8477.

169 UNFFM Economic Report (n 108).

Rakhine State.[170] Some states, including Canada, the UK, the US, and France, as well as Bangladesh, Malaysia, and The Gambia, have called explicitly for justice – particularly in relation to the Rohingya. UN Human Rights Council resolutions[171] and many NGOs seek international criminal justice, including at the International Criminal Court.[172] Many of the states calling for justice measures are also funding humanitarian assistance in Bangladesh as well as within various conflict-affected areas in Myanmar.[173] States like the US, Canada, many EU states, and Australia that have favoured accountability initiatives have had arms embargoes and targeted sanctions in place. They, too, may nevertheless provide extensive overseas development assistance to Myanmar, focused on encouraging economic growth.[174]

Civil society is diverse and takes multiple perspectives towards violence in Myanmar. Many organisations strongly support sanctions, ICC action (including via Security Council referral) and prosecutions for the commission of international crimes, whether perpetrated in Rakhine State or elsewhere.[175] These calls are often expressed in urgent terms, arguing that '[p]atience is not what we need

170 UNSC Verbatim Record (13 February 2018) S/PV/8179. See also, e.g., Department of Foreign Affairs and Trade, 'Rohingya Crisis – One Year On' (25 August 2018) <https://dfat.gov.au/news/media/Pages/rohingya-crisis-one-year-on.aspx> accessed 27 February 2020.

171 UNHRC Res 40/29 (22 March 2019) UN Doc A/HRC/RES/40/29.

172 See, e.g., Fortify Rights, 'UN Security Council: Refer Myanmar to International Criminal Court' (27 August 2018) <www.fortifyrights.org/mya-inv-2018-08-27/> accessed 27 February 2020; Human Rights Watch, 'UN Security Council: Refer Burma to the ICC' (3 November 2017) <www.hrw.org/news/2017/11/03/un-security-council-refer-burma-icc> accessed 27 February 2020; Forum-Asia and Progressive Voice, 'Joint Statement: Myanmar Must be Referred to International Criminal Court' (22 March 2019) www.forum-asia.org/?p=28501>.

173 See, e.g., Department of Foreign Affairs and Trade, 'Rohingya Crisis' (n 171).

174 See, e.g., US Agency for International Development, 'Our Work' (2019) <www.usaid.gov/burma/our-work> accessed 27 February 2020. In Australia's case, overseas development assistance aims to 'create an environment conducive to inclusive economic growth and increased trade by strengthening government capacity, promoting peace and stability, and supporting the development of an educated and competitive workforce': Department of Foreign Affairs and Trade, 'Development Assistance in Myanmar: Overview of Australia's Aid Program to Myanmar' (2019) <https://dfat.gov.au/geo/myanmar/development-assistance/Pages/development-assistance-in-myanmar.aspx> accessed 27 February 2020.

175 See Department of Foreign Affairs and Trade, 'Rohingya Crisis' (n 171) and see, e.g., Altsean-Burma, 'Burma/Myanmar's Ongoing Refusal to Pursue Accountability: Time for an ICC Referral' (18 October 2018) <http://altsean.org/reports/ICC_Referral-FactsheetOct2018.pdf> accessed 27 February 2020; Forum-Asia and Progressive Voice, 'Joint Statement' (n 173); Kachin Women Association, Thailand, 'Myanmar: UN Security Council Must Act to End Ongoing Crimes Against Humanity in Northern Burma' (4 May 2018) <https://kachinwomen.com/myanmar-un-security-council-must-act-to-end-ongoing-crimes-against-humanity-in-northern-burma/> accessed 27 February 2020; Kachin Women Association, Thailand, Progressive Voice, and Rohingya Women's Welfare Society, 'UN Security Council Must Act Now and Refer the Situation in Myanmar to the International Criminal Court' (25 October 2018) <https://progressivevoicemyanmar.

to resolve the deplorable situation of human rights in Myanmar. . . . The international community must urgently send a strong message'.[176] Others, including ND-Burma, focus more on documenting violence, constitutional and institutional reform, and land and taxation reforms,[177] though sometimes alongside calls for prosecutions.[178] A 2018 report on the desires of 111 victims indicated that the 'most common desire for justice was institutional change to guard against human rights abuses from happening again'; then symbolic satisfaction, such as acknowledgement; compensation or restitution; and many 'asked for justice, but also outlined their lack of confidence in the domestic legal system'.[179]

For both those actors favouring the prosecution of international crimes and those either silent on or apparently opposed to justice responses, development is a valid and important response or activity for Myanmar. Development is often called for alongside other actions, including ending discriminatory practices and even possibly prosecutions, in ways that suggest that both have a positive impact on preventing or responding to violence. However, for others, the relationship between development and justice is more complex. This includes the Myanmar government *and* those concerned about the potential for investments to exacerbate conflict and violence. Despite the general proposal that Myanmar must address under-development to encourage peace, stability, and an end to violence (development *and* justice), there is therefore also an apparent tension between the goals of development and international criminal justice. There are two aspects to this tension. First, the argument that justice initiatives might impede or at least distract from needed development and investment – in other words, the development versus justice perspective. Second, the recognition that investments to encourage development have in the past and might in future contribute to

org/wp-content/uploads/2018/10/Final-PR-Oct-25.pdf> accessed 27 February 2020; Legal Aid Network, 'Seeking Accountability for Ending Impunity in Burma: Analysis of War Crimes' (April 2018) <www.legalaidnetwork.org/Reports%20LAN/Seeking%20Accountability%20for%20Ending%20Impuni.pdf> accessed 27 February 2020.

176 Progressive Voice, Rohingya Women Welfare Society, and Kachin Women's Association, Thailand, 'UN Security Council Must Act Now and Refer the Situation in Myanmar to the International Criminal Court' (25 October 2018) <https://nd-burma.org/un-security-council-must-act-now-and-refer-the-situation-in-myanmar-to-the-international-criminal-court/> accessed 27 February 2020.

177 ND-Burma, 'To Recognise and Repair: Unofficial Truth Projects and the Need for Justice in Burma' (June 2015) <https://nd-burma.org/to-recognize-and-repair/> accessed 27 February 2020; Karen Human Rights Group, 'Dreaming of Home, Hoping for Peace: Protracted Displacement in Southeast Myanmar' (May 2019) <https://khrg.org/2019/05/dreaming-home-hoping-peace-protracted-displacement-southeast-myanmar-0> accessed 27 February 2020.

178 See, e.g., Women's League of Burma, 'The Statement of WLB Welcomes the Report Released by the UN Fact Finding Mission – FFM' (25 August 2019) https://womenofburma.org/statements/statement-wlb-welcomes-report-released-un-fact-finding-mission-ffm>.

179 ND-Burma, 'You Cannot Ignore Us: Victims of Human Rights Violations in Burma from 1970–2017 Outline Their Desires for Justice' (October 2018) <https://nd-burma.org/wp-content/uploads/2018/10/reportupdateOct.pdf> accessed 27 February 2020, 16.

violence and atrocities in Myanmar. Together, this can be termed the 'development and/versus justice debate'.

4 'Development vs justice' vs 'peace vs justice'

If there is a development and/versus justice debate in relation to Myanmar, but arguments lie across the spectrum, is this just an extension of the peace versus justice debate, or is it something different? Section 5 addresses the opportunities and dangers of this debate, but it is worth initially clarifying how this discussion sits in relation to 'peace versus justice'.

First, they are related. Most of the debate in relation to justice initiatives for international crimes in Myanmar involves development and investment being posed as solutions to conflict and necessary steps to encourage peace. This is because so many see the 'root causes' of conflict and the related commission of international crimes (particularly in Rakhine State) as development related. Myanmar's and (for instance) Japan's statements talk about blame and accountability discussions being unhelpful and argue that development will (instead) support peace and stability. In other words, they claim that development is not just an outcome of peacebuilding, but a driver of it. Since justice is being posed against 'development *equals* peace', the debate about development and justice here represents a subset of the peace versus justice debate, rather than an entirely separate one.

Second, development versus justice may form part of a wider peace versus justice debate, partly because development is often equated with peace, but it is still a distinct part of that wider discussion. This is because, as noted earlier, some do not connect development to peace and, in fact, view investments of certain kinds as conflict and violence exacerbators. It also recognises that growing investment and development aid in Myanmar, including from 2015, has not prevented the commission of atrocities. Beyond this, however, rapid investment and economic understandings of development present risks not just to peace, but also to justice. The enrichment of elites and military holding companies, continued use of accused security forces, and displacement of communities (whether voluntary or not) mean that even if armed conflict does not break out because of investment-related violence, there may still be a lack of justice. Certain communities may be disadvantaged, particular projects offer uneven access and impacts, including for access to justice, and impunity for past international crimes may prevail for additionally enriched perpetrators. The history of human rights violations in Myanmar creates very real concern about the potential for this 'development but no justice' outcome.

Third, when Myanmar, China or Japan's governments emphasise the role of development and investment in fostering peace at the implied expense of justice, they are not explicitly claiming that justice would upset the peace and lead to conflict. That is, while the 'peace versus justice' debate is occurring in some quarters concerning Myanmar, posing development as the better pathway towards peace than justice does not propose overtly that ICC action will *cause* conflict in Myanmar, for instance. Instead, Myanmar and some other states are arguing that Myanmar's own development-oriented approach towards securing peace is more appropriate and effective, that its sovereignty should be respected, and that international efforts would be best directed towards supporting its institutional reforms and investing.[180] Myanmar's officials also claim, however unpersuasively, that their own investigations do support the rule of law and accountability and that there is a need for 'evidence' of the commission of international crimes. This suggests a willingness to adopt justice language but *only* to the extent that it supports development initiatives, particularly those of the type proposed in the advisory commission report, rather than international criminal justice.[181] Therefore, it is the relationship between justice and development that Myanmar questions most, rather than the relationship between justice and peace. Still, this position is supported by a belief, shared, in fact, by most other states (but not by all NGOs), that development and investment are the pathway towards peace.

Fourth, the immediate implications of a 'development versus justice' and 'peace versus justice' debate are different. Debating 'development versus justice' more obviously invites topics such as foreign investment and investment law, greater transparency, 'good governance', institutional (including security-sector and parliamentary) reform, anti-corruption initiatives, international 'best practice' and 'do no harm', business and human rights, 'due diligence', corporate accountability, infrastructure redevelopment, and, possibly, 'transformative' approaches to governance. Its aims are reducing poverty, increasing (especially foreign) investment, building roads and schools, etc. It sees justice as still potentially necessary for these tasks – particularly for the 'rule of law' and judicial independence – but views international criminal justice as a distraction, misallocation of resources, or low priority and, at worst, as having the potential to threaten the political stability and reform process necessary to deliver on its development aims. Contrastingly, a 'peace versus justice' discussion is about amnesties, demobilisation, selective personal and temporal jurisdiction, choice of forum considerations, victim participation, legalism versus politics, and wider 'interests of justice' considerations. As mentioned, the former debate arguably fits within the latter, if development is associated with peace, but also has distinct characteristics. Debating development against international criminal justice also holds specific opportunities and dangers.

180 'Decision on the Prosecution's Request for a Ruling on Jurisdiction Under Article 19(3) of the Statute' *Bangladesh/Myanmar*, Case No. ICC-RoC46(3)-01/18, Pre-Trial Chamber I, 6 September 2018, 17 n 54 (*PTC Jurisdiction Decision*).

181 See, e.g., State Counsellors Office, 'Aung San Suu Kyi's Exclusive Interview with Nikkei Asian Review' (n 122).

5 Opportunities and dangers of 'development vs justice'

The situation in Myanmar helps elucidate potential consequences of debating 'development versus justice'. This section first identifies some opportunities in a tentative and hopefully open-minded manner. One prominent reason to 'frame' or approach justice issues with an awareness of development priorities is that it might be more attractive and interesting to the Myanmar government and military. Access has been a problem for international organisations (including civil society) in the past, including a notorious incident when Médecins Sans Frontiers staff were expelled from the country for reporting the treatment of Rohingya people after an alleged massacre.[182] Anecdotal discussions in 2019 suggested that international actors continued to fear losing access, or wanted to avoid isolation tactics, and so found that presenting particular projects as relating to governance, institutional reform, and general training and community peacebuilding could address justice-related aims (such as documentation of violence or improved accountability) in a more palatable manner.[183] This adaptation is often not challenging, since poverty, a lack of infrastructure, misallocation of resources and misgovernment by the military, the effects of many years of Western sanctions, and persistent armed conflict all do present valid and urgent development needs. The advisory commission's recognition, and many states' agreement, that the risk of conflict and violence in Rakhine State was at least exacerbated by under-development – and related issues elsewhere in the country – present good reasons to approach international criminal justice with a wide lens that recognises this material context.

It may be that engaging with a debate about the relationship between development and justice leads to a broader allocation of development assistance and investment resources with wider benefits for communities than specifically justice-oriented (particularly international criminal justice) responses. It is possible, even, that confronting calls for international criminal justice with calls to address poverty, inequality, and other structural impediments to social and economic development would encourage more 'transformative' approaches, including those focused on guarantees of non-repetition. This is arguably both more difficult and more crucial in Myanmar, where severe deprivations of social and economic rights have been linked to the commission of international crimes, including the persecution of Rohingya Muslims, alongside the destruction of evidence.[184] As noted, institutional reform and such guarantees are not side topics but are often

182 Lawi Weng, 'Burmese Govt Reversed MSF Ban Because of 'International Pressure' *The Irrawaddy* (28 July 2014) <www.irrawaddy.org/burma/burmese-govt-reversed-msf-ban-international-pressure.html> accessed 27 February 2020.

183 See Palmer, *Adapting International Criminal Justice in Southeast Asia* (n 18).

184 Green, MacManus, and de la Cour Venning (n 118); 'Decision Pursuant to Article 15 of the Rome Statute on the Authorisation of an Investigation into the Situation in the People's Republic of Bangladesh/Republic of the Union of Myanmar' ICC-01/19, Pre-Trial Chamber III, 14 November 2019; Poppy McPherson, 'Three Years After

central to victim/survivor desires, alongside or sometimes superseding calls for prosecutions. Pursuing these aims will not satisfy all victims, many of whom do want to see perpetrators identified and prosecuted. However, for some, carefully implemented development initiatives leading to stable employment and institutional and infrastructure improvements might be preferable.[185]

International courts have limited jurisdiction and will find prosecuting crimes that occurred within Myanmar challenging (as will national courts with universal jurisdiction, such as in Argentina), while in the near term, domestic prosecutions will be problematic at best. In that context in Myanmar, pursuing a development-oriented institutional reform approach might also be simply more realistic, in the short term at least. Moreover, the temporal framework offered by a 'development' approach has, thus far, been presented as long term and future oriented.[186] As noted, the NLD government repeated that responding to the causes of violence in Rakhine State, in particular, would be a longer-term project, despite requiring action now. While we may hope for faster change, a longer-term perspective in and of itself has potential benefits when approaching international criminal justice initiatives. In particular, it reminds us of future elections, growing infrastructure needs, demographic changes, intergenerational traumas, geopolitical dynamics, and the potential for history to repeat.

While the geopolitical implications of this debate are beyond the scope of this chapter, there may be political benefits (though also risks) for engaging with China (in particular, though also India, Japan, Australia, and other states) on the relationship between development and justice, given the strategic importance of Myanmar, including as a key component of China's Belt and Road Initiative. In other words, if development is thought to be facilitated by international criminal justice, this might be a productive area to push forward discussions about accountability. On the other hand, if doubts remain about the relationship between international criminal justice and development in particular contexts, including beyond Myanmar, this may warrant further research.

These opportunities derive specifically from debating the relationship between development and justice, rather than peace and justice. However, to the extent that these discussions are related, it is worth recalling, as Pedersen warned,[187] that focusing too firmly on prosecutions could risk solidifying military power in Myanmar. This would not help the cause of peace or of preventing international crimes, though Myanmar's history also does show that the military can be capable of limited reform in particular conditions as occurred, to a degree, in later 2008 and from 2011. This context suggests at least the possibility that a discussion

Exodus, Myanmar Erases Names of Rohingya Villages, UN Map Makers Follow Suit' *Reuters* (11 September 2020) <www.reuters.com/article/us-myanmar-rohingya-insight-idUSKBN262058> accessed 16 November 2020.

185 ND-Burma (n 180).

186 See, e.g., State Counsellor Office, 'Rakhine Efforts Need Time and Space' (20 December 2016) (copy on file with author).

187 Pedersen (n 151).

about the role of development in relation to international crimes prosecutions, rather than focusing (only) on the latter, might contribute to peace and stability in Myanmar.

That said, there is limited potential for a truly transparent discussion about the role of development in relation to international criminal justice in Myanmar. Restrictions placed on civil society activities, particularly in the 'emergency' of 2021; growing political complexities; the popularity of the embattled NLD government's stance towards the Rohingya; and enduring and growing military influence narrow the realistic sphere for accessible debate. In particular, approaching an emphasis on development as normatively 'good' or worthy of greater attention than international criminal justice holds real hazard. This chapter arguably contributes to that risk, and so it is necessary to point out some more of these dangers.

A first danger of welcoming a 'development versus justice' discussion is that it may give credence to an argument that has unclear empirical merit in specific contexts – namely, that (particularly economic) development might indeed contribute to 'better' outcomes for societies than justice initiatives – though the reverse proposition is also debatable. At its core, prioritising development is an argument that, if entertained, brings with it the associated risk of fewer investigations or prosecutions and assisting the preservation of 'impunity'. If misunderstood as a focus on foreign investment, rather than on human development aims, deprioritising justice could be counterproductive to rule of law and judicial independence initiatives that form important components of broader development initiatives. It could also facilitate the perpetuation of further violence as has arguably already occurred with devastating consequences in Rakhine State[188] and beyond.

Second, uneven development poses risks for both peace and justice. Focusing on under-development and poverty as the 'root cause' of conflict and violence requires understanding how these factors operate differently across Myanmar – with its diverse issues relating to mining, forestry, land tenure, discriminatory citizenship practices, urban/rural divides, and narcotics. International templates and models may not provide the most effective or useful model in these contexts. Yet emphasising that diverse 'local' issues contribute to community-level inequities and divisions risks overlooking 'top-down' macroeconomic, geopolitical, and – importantly – Myanmar government policy–driven causes of that under-development and separate conflict drivers. In particular, it undermines the alleged criminal responsibility of particular Tatmadaw generals and soldiers and the role of 'conflict entrepreneurs' in fomenting violence, including through social media networks.[189] If development is accepted as the priority, there is a danger that investments contribute to conflict or to the enrichment of elites and military conglomerates that do not necessarily have the public interest (including of victims of violence) in mind. The Myanmar government has environmental and social risk assessment processes in place, but implementation of these has been

188 Renshaw (n 90).
189 UNFFM Economic Report (n 108).

challenging,[190] and reforming the military economy and wider legal system is increasingly complex and problematic.

In conclusion, there are reasons to at least recognise that there is a discussion about the relationship between development and justice that is distinct from, but related to, debates about peace and justice. However, dangers and questions remain in relation to Myanmar, including how it is possible for a government to prioritise human development, institutional reform, and non-repetition of crimes while not actually prosecuting past or recent crimes. It is also worth considering whether certain types of justice present different risks to development than they do to peace and conflict. For instance, would effective domestic trials help a country's development credentials but endanger peace? Or, would ICC activity undermine development via foreign investment but, through its distance and limited powers, have reduced negative impact on peace? How might such questions be resolved? Put more frankly, had certain military leaders actually been investigated and prosecuted for international crimes – whether at the ICC or in Myanmar – in, say, 2020, what effect might that have had on Myanmar's development prospects? Appreciating how the peace versus justice debate has a development versus justice aspect might prompt different questions about the role of international criminal justice in complex societies into the future.

190 Meenakshi Kapoor, Nwe Ni Soe, and Vidya Viswanathan, 'Midcourse Manoeuvres: Community Strategies and Remedies for Natural Resource Conflicts in Myanmar' *Centre for Policy Research & Namati* (June 2018) <https://namati.org/resources/midcourse-manoeuvres-community-strategies-remedies-natural-resource-conflicts-myanmar/> accessed 27 February 2020. See US Agency for International Development et al., 'Draft Guidelines on Public Participation in Myanmar's EIA Processes' (31 May 2017) www.myanmar-responsiblebusiness.org/pdf/2017-05-31-Draft_Guideline_Public_Participation_Myanmar_EIA.pdf>.

6 Imagining future reparations for environmental destruction

Rachel Killean

1 Introduction

From the use of Agent Orange in Southeast Asia to the burning of Kuwaiti oil wells to illegal poaching across the African Great Lakes region, examples of conflict and atrocity-related environmental destruction[1] can be found across the world.[2] As awareness of the interconnections between mass violence and environmental destruction has grown, legal frameworks have expanded to grant greater environmental protections in times of conflict.[3] Examples include the adoption of the Environmental Modification Convention,[4] the Declaration and Protocol on Asphyxiating Gases and Bacteriological Methods of Warfare, and Additional Protocol I to the Geneva Conventions;[5] the drafting of guidelines for the protection of the environment during armed conflict by the International Committee of the Red Cross;[6] and the 2019 legal principles developed by the International

1 i.e., damage to protected species and natural habitats, water damage, and land damage. See Directive 2004/35/CE of the European Parliament and of the Council of 21 April 2004 on Environmental Liability with regard to the Prevention and Remedying of Environmental Damage [2004] OJ L 143, Article 2.

2 Ines Peterson, 'The Natural Environment in Times of Armed Conflict: A Concern for International War Crimes Law?' (2009) 22 *Leiden Journal of International Law* 331; M Schmitt, 'Green War: An Assessment of the Environmental Law of International Armed Conflict' (1997) 22 *Yale Journal of International Law* 19; UNSC, 'Interim Report of the Panel of Experts on the Illegal Exploitation of Natural Resources and Other Forms of Wealth of the Democratic Republic of the Congo' (22 May 2002) UN Doc S/2002/565, para 52.

3 See, e.g., Carsten Stahn, Jens Iverson, and Jennifer S Easterday (eds), *Environmental Protection and Transitions from Conflict to Peace* (OUP 2017).

4 Convention on the Prohibition of Military or Any Other Hostile Use of Environmental Modification Techniques (signed 18 May 1977, entered into force 5 October 1978) 1108 UNTS 151.

5 Protocol Additional to the Geneva Conventions of 12 August 1949, and relating to the Protection of Victims of International Armed Conflicts (Protocol I) (signed 8 June 1977) 1125 UNTS 3.

6 ICRC, 'Guidelines for Military Manuals and Instructions on the Protection of the Environment in Times of Armed Conflict', endorsed by 'United Nations Decade of International Law', UNGA Res 49/50 (9 December 1994).

DOI: 10.4324/9781003087533-8

Law Commission on the Protection of the Environment in Relation to Armed Conflicts.[7]

In this context, the continuing failure of international criminal law to address environmental destruction is notable.[8] The Rome Statute of the International Criminal Court includes only one explicit reference to environmental protection, identifying 'widespread, long-term and severe damage to the environment' as a possible war crime.[9] However, the stringent jurisdictional requirements associated with this provision mean it has yet to be used in practice.[10] Indeed, the anthropocentric nature of the core crimes[11] (genocide, crimes against humanity, war crimes, and aggression) frequently renders invisible the destructive harm that mass violence can have on the natural environment.[12] In recognition of this lacuna, activists, lawyers, policy actors, and academics have long explored different ways to create individual criminal accountability for environmental destruction.[13] Some have campaigned for the establishment of a specific international environmental court,[14] while others have explored how the ICC might be used to respond to this type of harm. Amongst those in the latter camp, two approaches have developed. On the one hand are those who argue in favour of a new international crime against the environment, such as the crime of 'ecocide'[15]

7 Michael Bothe, 'The ILC's Special Rapporteur's Preliminary Report on the Protection of the Environment in Relation to Armed Conflict: An Important Step in the Right Direction' in Pia Acconci er al (eds), *International Law and the Protection of Humanity: Essays in Honor of Flavia Latanzi* (Brill 2017); Doug Weir, Director at the Conflict and Environment Observatory, cited in United Nations Environment Program, 'Why Legal Principles on War and Environment Matter' (20 August 2019) <www.unenvironment.org/news-and-stories/story/why-legal-principles-war-and-environment-matter> accessed 13 April 2020.

8 Notable, but reflective of a broader perception within green criminology that formal institutions of criminal justice fail to take environmental crime seriously. See Rob White, 'Reparative Justice, Environmental Crime and Penalties for the Powerful' (2017) 67 *Crime, Law and Social Change* 117.

9 Rome Statute of the International Criminal Court (adopted 17 July 1998, entered into force 1 July 2002) 2187 UNTS 90 (Rome Statute) art 8(2)(b)(iv).

10 For an in-depth exploration of this article and its limitations, see Jessica C Lawrence and Kevin Jon Heller, 'The First Ecocentric Environmental War Crime: The Limits of Article 8(2)(b)(iv) of the Rome Statute' (2007) 20 *Georgetown International Environmental Law Review* 61.

11 Carsten Stahn, Jens Iverson, and Jennifer S Easterday, 'Introduction' in Stahn, Iverson, and Easterday (eds) (n 3) 16.

12 Audra Mitchell, 'Only Human? A Worldly Approach to Security' (2014) 45 *Security Dialogue* 5.

13 Anastacia Greene, 'The Campaign to Make Ecocide an International Crime: Quixotic Quest or Moral Imperative?' (2019) 30 *Fordham Environmental Law Review* 7.

14 See, e.g., Stephen Hockman, 'The Case for an International Court for the Environment' 3 (2010) *Journal of Court Innovation* 215; Alessandra Lehman, 'The Case for the Creation of an International Environmental Court: Non-State Actors and International Environmental Dispute Resolution' (2015) 26 *Colorado Natural Resources, Energy & Environmental Law Review* 2.

15 Polly Higgins, Damien Short, and Nigel South, 'Protecting the Planet: A Proposal for a Law of Ecocide' (2013) 59 *Crime Law and Social Change* 251; Polly Higgins, *Eradicating*

or 'grave' or 'severe' crimes against the environment.[16] While the urgent environmental challenges facing our planet, the failure of environmental regulation to prevent widespread destruction, and the normative expressive value of prohibiting the loss of ecosystems all make the call for a specific crime against the environment compelling,[17] there are significant barriers to introducing a new crime. These include political resistance,[18] practical challenges surrounding proving intent,[19] the obstacles to recognising the role of corporations in environmental destruction,[20] and the additional resource strains associated with introducing a new type of crime.[21]

Partially as a result of these barriers, others have interrogated the ways in which we might adapt the existing ICC legal framework to incorporate greater awareness of environmental destruction.[22] In addition to exploring the possibilities offered by the explicit reference to the environment in the context of war crimes, scholars have noted the potential for environmental destruction to constitute a genocidal act,[23] a crime against humanity,[24] or an act of aggression.[25] Such explorations are not exclusively academic; the last decade has indicated that the ICC's Office of the Prosecutor (OTP) has also considered the possibility of pursuing prosecutions which encompass environmental harms. Most notably, OTP policy

---

Ecocide: Laws and Governance to Prevent the Destruction of Our Planet (Shepheard-Walwyn 2010); Damien Short, *Redefining Genocide: Settler Colonialism, Social Death and Ecocide* (Zed Books 2016).

16 See, e.g., Sailesh Mehta and Prisca Merz, 'Ecocide – A New Crime Against Peace?' (2015) 17 *Environmental Law Review* 3; Deniz Tekayak, 'Protecting Earth Rights and the Rights of Indigenous Peoples: Towards an International Crime of Ecocide' (2016) 14 *Fourth World Journal* 5.

17 Higgins, Short, and South (n 15).

18 See, e.g., John Bellinger and William Haynes, 'A US Government Response to the International Committee of the Red Cross Study Customary International Humanitarian Law' (2007) 89 *International Review of the Red Cross* 443.

19 Tim Lindgren, 'Ecocide, Genocide and the Disregard of Alternative Life-Systems' (2018) 22 *International Journal of Human Rights* 525.

20 David Scheffer, 'Corporate Liability Under the Rome Statute' (2016) 57 *Harvard international Law Journal* 38.

21 Rosemary Mwanza, 'Enhancing Accountability for Environmental Damage Under International Law: Ecocide as a Legal Fulfilment of Ecological Integrity' (2018) 19 *Melbourne Journal of International Law* 610.

22 Matthew Gillett, 'Eco-Struggles: Using International Criminal Law to Protect the Environment During and After Non-International Armed Conflict' in Stahn, Iverson, and Easterday (n 3); Steven Freeland, 'Human Rights, the Environment and Conflict: Addressing Crimes Against the Environment' (2005) 2 *International Journal on Human Rights* 113.

23 Freeland (n 22).

24 Donald K Anton, 'Adding a Green Focus: The Office of the Prosecutor of the International Criminal Court Highlights the "Environment" in Case Selection and Prioritisation' (Griffith Law School Research Paper No. 17–03, 2016); Alessandra Mistura, 'Is There Space for Environmental Crimes Under International Criminal Law? The Impact of the Office of the Prosecutor Policy Paper on Case Selection and Prioritisation on the Current Legal Framework' (2018) 43 *Colombian Journal of Environmental Law* 181.

25 Gillett (n 22).

papers released in 2013 and 2016 listed 'environmental damage', 'the destruction of the environment', 'illegal exploitation of natural resources', and 'the illegal dispossession of land' as explicit factors to be considered when selecting sites for investigation and cases for prosecution.[26]

The OTP's powers are naturally constrained by the ICC's legal framework: it can only pursue situations and cases in which core crimes appear to have been committed.[27] As a result, some commentators have been sceptical about how the policy papers' indication of an increased environmental awareness will manifest in practice.[28] Yet the ICC Senior Appeal Counsel Helen Brady has stated that the reference to the environment is 'highly important and it's not just symbolic – it means something'.[29] While its possible implications for future case selections and prosecutions have been explored elsewhere,[30] in this chapter, I take a closer look at how other organs of the ICC might build upon and expand this emerging environmental sensitivity. In particular, I focus on the possibilities of incorporating greater environmental awareness into measures of repair, both through the awarding of specific reparations and through the Trust Fund for Victims' (TFV) assistance mandate.

To briefly introduce these measures of repair: reparations may be awarded by the ICC's Trial Chambers following the conviction of an accused.[31] Reparations can be individual, collective, or both, depending on the scope and extent of any damage, loss, or injury, and may include restitution, compensation, and rehabilitation.[32] These orders can be made against the convicted person or through the TFV,[33] an independent, non-judicial institution which can use funds made available by voluntary contributions to complement any money or property collected from the convicted person.[34] In addition to implementing reparation awards,

26 Office of the Prosecutor, 'Policy Paper on Case Selection and Prioritisation' *International Criminal Court* (15 September 2016) <www.icc-cpi.int/itemsDocuments/20160915_OTP-Policy_Case-Selection_Eng.pdf> accessed 14 April 2020.

27 Anton (n 24) 1.

28 William Schabas, 'Feeding Time at the Office of the Prosecutor' *International Criminal Justice Today* (23 November 2016) <www.international-criminal-justice-today.org/arguendo/icc-prosecutors-perpetuation-of-the-fiction-of-objectivity/> accessed 13 April 2020.

29 Phoebe Braithwaite, 'Environmental Crimes Could Warrant International Criminal Court Prosecutions' *Inter Press Service* (1 October 2016) <www.ipsnews.net/2016/10/environmental-crimes-could-warrant-international-criminal-court-prosecutions/> accessed 13 April 2020.

30 Eliana Teresa Cusato, 'Beyond Symbolism: Problems and Prospects with Prosecuting Environmental Destruction Before the ICC' (2017) 15 *Journal of International Criminal Justice* 491; Nadia Bernaz, 'An Analysis of the ICC Office of the Prosecutor's Policy Paper on Case Selection and Prioritization from the Perspective of Business and Human Rights' (2017) 15 *Journal of International Criminal Justice* 527.

31 Rome Statute, art 75(1).

32 International Criminal Court, 'Rules of Procedure and Evidence', adopted 9 September 2002, ICC-ASP/1/3, rr 97–98.

33 Rome Statute, art 75(2).

34 See International Criminal Court, 'Regulations of the Trust Fund for Victims' (3 December 2005) UN Doc ICC-ASP/4/Res.3.

the TFV may also provide more general assistance to victims who have suffered harm as a result of a crime which is within the Court's jurisdiction and linked to a situation under investigation.[35] This can be done prior to any judgment being issued[36] and can include physical and/or psychological rehabilitation and material support.[37]

While reparations and victim assistance are increasingly acknowledged as central aspects of post-conflict and post-atrocity recovery,[38] the understandable prioritisation of severe human rights violations can lead to an overlooking of environmental destruction. However, this arguably overlooks the interconnected relationships that exist between humans and their environments.[39] Environmental degradation and the loss of natural resources can harm livelihoods, place barriers in the way of recovery, and sow the seeds of future human rights violations.[40] Rather than seeing environmental and human welfare as mutually exclusive, it is therefore worth exploring how reparations and measures of assistance which seek to respond to human rights violations might also encompass environmental considerations.

The chapter is written in the knowledge that significant pressures on the ICC's and TFV's reparative mandates already exist[41] and that international criminal institutions cannot in and of themselves prevent and respond to the environmental devastation that so often accompanies conflict and atrocity.[42] However, I argue that the scale of the problem should invite innovative and flexible legal responses whenever possible – including within existing structures – rather than induce paralysis. In that spirit, I argue that there are three interlinked ways that reparations and measures of assistance can contribute to repairing environmental destruction: first, through the incorporation of an 'eco-sensitive' approach to reparations and assistance; second, through the awarding of reparations explicitly responding to environmental destruction that can be appropriately linked to convictions for the core crimes; and third, by exploring the possibilities of environmentally 'transformative' reparations. It should be noted that the recommendations contained within this chapter are necessarily fairly general, as every

35 ibid.

36 Anne Dutton and Fionnuala Ní Aoláin, 'Between Reparations and Repair: Assessing the Work of the ICC Trust Fund for Victims Under Its Assistance Mandate' (2019) 19 *Chicago Journal of International Law* 490, 506.

37 Trust Fund for Victims, 'Assistance Programmes' <www.trustfundforvictims.org/en/what-we-do/assistance-programmes> accessed 13 April 2020.

38 Peter J Dixon, 'Reparations, Assistance and the Experiences of Justice: Lessons from Colombia and the Democratic Republic of the Congo' (2016) 10 *International Journal of Transitional Justice* 88.

39 And, indeed, the value of repairing nature for its own sake.

40 Richard Milburn 'The Roots to Peace in the DRC: Conservation as a Platform for Green Development' (2014) 90 *International Affairs* 883.

41 See, e.g., Luke Moffett, 'Reparations for Victims at the International Criminal Court: A New Way Forward' (2017) 21 *International Journal of Human Rights* 1204.

42 Lindgren (n 19).

experience of conflict or atrocity is different, and there are therefore no specific reparative measures that will always be appropriate.

2 'Eco-sensitive' implementation of reparation and assistance measures

Reparations can take myriad forms and recognise a diverse range of physical, moral, emotional, and social harms, experienced both individually and collectively. Their flexibility allows them to be sensitive to the nature and context of the crimes that have been committed.[43] However, if misconceived or insensitively delivered, reparative measures and measures of victim assistance may exacerbate tensions or undermine the cooperation and reconciliation needed to prevent future violence and harm.[44] In cases in which the environment has been directly targeted or there are tensions around access to resources, a lack of sensitivity to such considerations could have long-term repercussions on the possibilities of long-term peace. Therefore, at a minimum, this chapter argues in favour of an 'eco-sensitive' approach to reparations and victim assistance measures. Adapted from the practice of conflict-sensitivity[45] (which is already implemented by the TFV),[46] I define an eco-sensitive approach as one which (1) attempts to understand how reparations may interact with environmental damage through the use of environmental impact assessments; (2) monitors, evaluates, and mitigates against any unintended environmental effects, and (3) positively influences environmental sustainability wherever possible. Such an approach would prioritise biological diversity and ecological integrity and incorporate an awareness of the possible long-term and inter-generational impacts of reparative projects. Adopting an eco-sensitive approach would signal a further 'mainstreaming' of environmental consciousness in the work of the Court and TFV. It would acknowledge the interconnections between humans and their environment and the need to ensure that projects do not have unintentionally harmful results in the future due to their environmental impacts.

There is some evidence that the TFV is already moving in an eco-sensitive direction. While acknowledging that the ICC does not have a 'going green policy', the Fund claims that it has tried to progressively integrate an environmental

43 Ruti Teitel, *Transitional Justice* (OUP 2000) 127.

44 Merryl Lawry-White, 'Victims of Environmental Harm During Conflict: The Potential for Justice' in Stahn, Iverson and Easterday (eds) (n 3).

45 Adapted from 'Conflict-Sensitive Approaches to Development, Humanitarian Assistance and Peace Building: Resource Pack' <https://www.international-alert.org/publications/conflict-sensitive-approaches-development-humanitarian-assistance-and-peacebuilding> accessed 27 September 2021.

46 Trust Fund for Victims, 'Strategic Plan 2014–2017' (August 2014) www.trustfundforvictims.org/sites/default/files/imce/1408%20TFV%20Strategic%20Plan%202014-2017%20Final%20ENG.pdf>.

dimension into its interventions.[47] For example, in its 2014–2017 Strategic Plan, the Fund identifies as one of its Programming Guiding Principles:

> Work with implementing partners to assess, mitigate and evaluate the likely environmental impact of a proposed project or programme, taking into account inter-related socio-economic, cultural and human-health impacts, both beneficial and adverse.[48]

However, the Fund has acknowledged that its ability to integrate environmental concerns into its activities has been limited by the lack of a monitoring mechanism and limited resources available to dedicate specifically to environmental issues. The 2014–2017 Strategic Plan claimed that the next TFV plan would pay particular attention to putting in place a structured monitoring system that matched its stated priorities and goals for environmental impact. As the Fund has not made subsequent strategic plans public, it is not possible to ascertain whether it has done so. However, while an eco-sensitive approach would, at a minimum, incorporate the monitoring and evaluation highlighted in the Strategic Plan, it would also ideally look beyond 'mitigation' to consider ways in which assistance and reparation projects could positively influence environmental sustainability.[49] Indeed, as noted by Anne Dutton and Fionnuala Ní Aoláin, the TFV's focus on harm requires that its 'services focus on addressing the root causes of the suffering experienced by beneficiaries'.[50] In cases in which experiences of harm are intertwined with environmental destruction or associated resource challenges, an eco-sensitive approach that centered environmental sustainability might better enable effective engagement with those root causes.

The broad scope of the TFV's assistance mandate might prove valuable in this regard as it is designed to enable the delivery of reparative measures to a 'more extensive range of victims who are affected by the broader situations before the Court, regardless of whether the harm they suffered stems from particular crimes charged in a specific case'.[51] However, even in the context of judicially awarded reparations, introducing this level of eco-sensitivity would not rely on or be linked to the OTP's selection of situations and cases which explicitly feature environmental destruction. Rather, it could be implemented throughout the TFV mandate and incorporated into the delivery of measures that respond to human rights violations resulting from the core crimes. For example, if implementing collective

47 ibid., 24.

48 ibid.

49 Peter Woodrow and Diana Chigas, *A Distinction with a Difference: Conflict Sensitivity and Peacebuilding* (CDA Collaborative Learning Projects 2009). <www.cdacollaborative.org/publication/a-distinction-with-a-difference-conflict-sensitivity-and-peacebuilding/> accessed 13 April 2020.

50 Dutton and Ní Aoláin (n 36) 522.

51 Trust Fund for Victims, 'Two Mandates' <www.trustfundforvictims.org/en/about/two-mandates-tfv/assistance> accessed 27 August 2020.

symbolic reparations[52] to acknowledge suffering, the Fund might encompass the establishment of projects that help restore and conserve natural spaces. Drawing from environmental peacebuilding and security studies,[53] this might involve, for example, creating peace parks for use by impacted communities. Examples of peace parks can be found in diverse contexts, and although often used to resolve transboundary conflicts between states, they can also be used to contribute to the rehabilitation of an area after conflict.[54] In Myanmar, a community-based NGO known as KESAN has been involved in the creation of the Salween Peace Park Initiative, described as a 'space that promotes peace, cooperation, cultural preservation, and environmental and natural resources conservation'.[55] The Peace Park's Charter establishes that the war has eroded the bio-cultural practices of local communities and acknowledges that peacebuilding must have both 'ecological and cultural dimensions'.[56]

Reparations or assistance programmes which seek to respond to material harm, such as vocational training and income-generating activities,[57] could also be designed in ways that minimise negative environmental impacts and, where possible, proactively seek to repair environments while restoring the livelihoods of victims. This potential is already acknowledged and pursued by the TFV, which has highlighted 'environmentally-friendly livelihood activities' as a form of material support that can be offered through its assistance mandate.[58] For example, in Northern Uganda, the TFV has supported training in bee-keeping, improved agricultural techniques, and tree-planting.[59] The dependence of much of the population within regions of armed conflict on natural resources means that

52 Modalities previously awarded in the Lubanga and Katanga cases in the DRC situation and the Al Madhi case in the Mali situation. See 'Draft Implementation Plan for Collective Reparations to Victims, Submitted to the Amended Reparations Order of 3 March 2015 in the Case Against Thomas Lubanga Dyilo (ICC-01/04–01/06)' ICC-01/04–01/06–3177-AnxA, 3 November 2015; 'Draft Implementation Plan Relevant to Trial Chamber II's Order for Reparations of 24 March 2017 (ICC-01/04–01/07–3728)' ICC-01/04–01/07–3751-Red, 25 July 2017; 'Corrected Version of Draft Implementation Plan for Reparations, Annex I, 20 April 2018' ICC-01/12–01/15–265-Conf, 30 April 2018, and ICC-01/12–01/15–265-Conf-Corr+Corr-Anx, 18 May 2018.

53 Lesley Evans Ogden, 'Environmental Peacebuilding' (2018) 68 *Bioscience* 157.

54 Examples can be found in the US and Canada, Peru and Ecuador, Costa Rica and Nicaragua, Albania, Greece and Macedonia, and South Africa and Botswana. See Saleem Hassan Ali, *Peace Parks: Conservation and Conflict Resolution* (MIT Press 2007).

55 Salween Peace Park Initiative <https://kesan.asia/salween-peace-park-initiative/>.

56 Shona Loong, 'Notes from the Salween Peace Park' *New Mandala* (27 May 2019) <www.newmandala.org/notes-from-the-salween-peace-park/> accessed 13 April 2020.

57 Modalities previously awarded in the Lubanga and Katanga cases in the DRC situation. See 'Draft Implementation Plan' 3 November 2015 (n 52); 'Draft Implementation Plan' 24 March 2017 (n 52).

58 Trust Fund for Victims, 'Report to the Assembly of State Parties on the Projects and Activities of the Board of Directors of the Trust Fund for Victims for the Period 1 July 2017 to 30 June 2018 Seventeenth Session' ICC-ASP/17/14, 5–12 December 2018.

59 Trust Fund for Victims, 'Two Mandates' (n 51).

initiatives improving the quality and accessibility of such resources could potentially assist a large number of people beyond the direct beneficiaries.[60] Indeed, the TFV describes longer-term sustainability and impact of material assistance as a particularly rewarding and promising aspect of its mandate, noting the potential for community-grown, community-owned, and community-managed interventions in post-conflict settings.[61] Given the long-term nature of the assistance programme and the involvement of local as well as international project implementing partners,[62] introducing an eco-sensitive approach to these measures could arguably entrench practices that are sustainable for both the communities and the environment which they inhabit. Indeed, given the centrality of collaboration to the TFV's mandates, this might have knock-on impacts in the way that implementing partners engage with their own work.

To be effective, eco-sensitivity would need to be applied at each stage of reparation and assistance design and delivery and would be mainstreamed into the TFV's institutional mindset.[63] This would require initial environmental impact assessments of the effects likely to arise from a proposed reparation or assistance project. This would feature both consultation with local experts (when possible) and public participation as integral aspects to ensuring the project proceeded in an eco-sensitive manner.[64] Ongoing monitoring and evaluation would also be required as projects progressed, and the TFV and its implementing partners would need to have the willingness to adjust as necessary. Indeed, an eco-sensitive approach might involve fundamental changes in the way the TFV thinks about the delivery of its reparation and assistance mandates: for example, through the development of eco-sensitive policies and project delivery standards.[65] As with integrating a conflict-sensitivity model, introducing greater eco-sensitivity would have resource implications and require a shift in mindset amongst those responsible for designing and implementing reparations.[66] However, the resource implications of this shift would lessen with time and should be weighed against the risks of environmentally unsustainable or damaging projects, as well as the potential benefits of measures which capture the connections between human and environmental recovery.

60 Richard Milburn, 'Mainstreaming the Environment into Postwar Recovery: The Case for "Ecological Development"' (2012) 88 *International Affairs* 1083, 1088–1089.

61 Trust Fund for Victims, 'Two Mandates' (n 51).

62 Dutton and Ní Aoláin (n 36) 505.

63 Maria Lange, 'Conflict-Sensitive Humanitarian Assistance: Building Capacity for Mainstreaming' in Pat Gibbons and Brigitte Piquard (eds), *Working in Conflict – Working on Conflict: Humanitarian Dilemmas and Challenges* (University of Duesto Publications 2006).

64 Stephen Jay et al., 'Environmental Impact Assessment' (2007) 27 *Environmental Impact Assessment Review* 287.

65 Huma Haider, 'Conflict Sensitivity: Topic Guide' *Governance, GSDRC Applied Knowledge Services* (2014) <www.gsdrc.org/docs/open/gsdrc_cs_topic_guide.pdf> accessed 13 April 2020.

66 'Resource Pack' (n 45).

While this section has focused on the TFV and its implementing partners, it is worth noting that an eco-sensitive approach to reparations delivery could also be supported and further entrenched in practice by the ICC Chambers, through the incorporation of eco-sensitivity into any subsequent reparation principles, awards, or implementation plans produced in future cases.[67] To date, the Court has never adopted institution-wide principles on the delivery of reparations. While this has been critiqued for producing a lack of clarity and inconsistency,[68] it also enables the flexible development of practice through the progressive practices of different Chambers.[69] It also leaves open the possibility of amended or new principles in future as the ICC adapts to new ways of thinking, including the possible future adoption of eco-sensitive approaches. Similarly, as new cases approach the reparations stage, opportunities may arise for Chambers to make awards that specifically address environmental destruction, as explored in the following section.

3 Awarding reparations that address environmental destruction

The ICC's jurisprudence has established the conditions necessary for a victim to claim reparations. A victim must be a natural person or legal entity that has suffered harm, whether directly or indirectly. The harm can be material, physical, or psychological, but it must be personal and must be the result of a crime within the jurisdiction of the Court.[70] The requirement that harm must be 'personal' to a natural or legal person is reflective of the anthropocentric nature of the core crimes and prohibits the Court from responding to environmental destruction outside the context of a related human rights violation. However, in cases in which the OTP successfully brings prosecutions which encompass 'the destruction of the environment, the illegal exploitation of natural resources or the illegal dispossession of land' or which inflict 'environmental damage' on affected communities,[71] the Court's Chambers could award reparations which explicitly respond to the 'damage, loss and injury'[72] caused by that destruction. As noted by Special Rapporteur for environmental protection

67 See Rome Statute, art 75(1): 'The Court shall establish principles relating to reparations. . .'; 'Decision Establishing the Principles and Procedures to be Applied to Reparations' *Prosecutor v Lubanga Dyilo*, ICC-01/04–01/06–2904, 7 August 2012.

68 Alina Balta, Manon Bax, and Riane Letschert, 'Trial and (Potential) Error: Conflicting Visions within the ICC System' (2019) 29 *International Criminal Justice Review* 221.

69 Carla Ferstman, 'Reparations at the ICC: The Need for a Human Rights Based Approach to Effectiveness' in Carla Ferstman and Mariana Goetz (eds), *Reparations for Victims of Genocide, War Crimes and Crimes Against Humanity* (Brill 2020).

70 'Judgment on the Appeals Against the "Decision Establishing the Principles and Procedures to be Applied to Reparations" of 7 August 2012 with AMENDED Order for Reparations (Annex A) and Public Annexes 1 and 2' *Prosecutor v Lubanga Dyilo*, ICC-01/04–01/06–3129-AnxA, 3 March 2015.

71 Office of the Prosecutor (n 26).

72 Rome Statute, art 75.

Marja Lehto, '[n]o reparations entailing environmental remediation have so far been ordered, but the decision on the principles and procedures would seem to allow for such measures as well'.[73] It is possible to 'transpose some of the current provisions on reparations to accommodate justice for non-human life'.[74] As further observed by Lehto, 'the effects of environmental damage are often felt both individually and collectively',[75] thus requiring reparations which are individual or collective in nature, or both. Indeed, environmental destruction in the context of conflict or atrocity can, in some cases, be situated within a deliberate attempt to destroy communities and groups, leading to associated harms that are communal, shared, and with potentially intergenerational impacts. While it may not be possible to meet all demands, the experiences, harms, priorities, and needs of victims should be understood and incorporated into reparation awards to the greatest extent possible.[76] Prior to making an order, the Court may invite representations from victims, which may help in this regard.[77]

In addition to consultation with victims, the Court may wish to consult with appropriate experts to assist in determining the scope and extent of environmental damage, loss, and injury and to suggest various options concerning the appropriate types and modalities of reparations.[78] Repairing the harm caused by environmental destruction undeniably poses specific challenges: complete restitution may be unlikely in many cases.[79] However, potential avenues of restitution could include: (1) orders for restoration of any harm to the environment caused by the commission of the offence, if feasible, and if not, payment of the costs and expenses incurred in restoring the environment; (2) costs for carrying out a specified project for the restoration or enhancement of the environment for the victims' benefit; or/and (3) payment to an environmental trust or environmental organisation for the purpose of a specified restoration project.[80] Examples can be found in the practice of the Inter-American Court of Human Rights (IACtHR), where reparations have previously included environmental

73 Special Rapporteur Marja Lehto, 'Second Report on Protection of the Environment in Relation to Armed Conflicts' International Law Commission, UN Doc A/CN.4/728, 27 March 2019, 32.

74 Mwanza (n 21) 606.

75 Lehto (n 73) 32.

76 John Braithwaite, *Restorative Justice and Responsive Regulation* (OUP 2002) 46.

77 Rome Statute, art 75(3); Rules of Procedure and Evidence, r 97(3).

78 Rules of Procedure and Evidence, r 97.

79 *Gabčíkovo-Nagymaros Project (Hungary v Slovakia)* (Judgment) [1997] ICJ Rep 3, 77–78, [140]: 'The Court is mindful that, in the field of environmental protection, vigilance and prevention are required on account of the often irreversible character of damage to the environment and of the limitations inherent in the very mechanism of reparation of this type of damage'.

80 Eileen Skinnider, *Victims of Environmental Crime – Mapping the Issues* (International Centre for Criminal Law Reform and Criminal Justice Policy 2011) 55.

restitution, clean-up, and reforestation programmes.[81] In domestic systems, the practice of specialist environmental courts may also be instructive. For example, the New South Wales Land and Environment Court in Australia is empowered to order offenders to carry out specified projects for the restoration of the environment, as well as pay compensation.[82] In relation to the practicalities of pursuing restoration, other domestic and regional frameworks may also provide guidance: for example, the US Comprehensive Environmental Response, Compensation, and Liability Act[83] and the European Union Environmental Liability Directive,[84] both of which contain frameworks for the restoration of injured natural resources.[85]

While templates for awarding restitution measures as reparations exist, the reality may be that full restitution is resource intensive and requires specialist expertise and equipment.[86] Depending on the nature of the harm, it may also require state involvement, which the ICC and TFV cannot guarantee. These limitations suggest that other or additional forms of reparation might be required. For example, the Court may consider awarding compensation and ordering fines or forfeitures of property which factor in harm to the environment.[87] In the context of international law, the International Law Commission's commentary to the articles on state responsibility,[88] the International Law Institute,[89] the UN Compensation Commission,[90] the International Court of Justice,[91] and the International Center for Settlement of Investment Disputes[92] have each made clear that environmental destruction is compensable. Certainly, evaluating environmental destruction for

81 *Kichwa Indigenous People of Sarayaku v Ecuador* (Merits and Reparations, Judgment), Inter-American Court of Human Rights Reports (Series C) 245, 27 June 2012, 294.

82 See, e.g., *Chief Executive, Office of Environment and Heritage v Coffs Harbour Hardwood Sales Pty Ltd* [2012] NSWLEC 52; *Chief Executive, Office of Environment and Heritage v Lani* [2012] NSWLEC 115, as discussed in White (n 8).

83 42 USC §9601 et seq (1980).

84 'Directive 2004/35/CE' (n 1).

85 See Kévine Kindji and Michael Faure, 'Assessing Reparation of Environmental Damage by the ICJ: A Lost Opportunity?' (2019) 57 *Questions of International Law* 5.

86 Lawry-White (n 44) 380.

87 Mwanza (n 21) 606.

88 International Law Commission, 'Draft Articles on Responsibility of States for Internationally Wrongful Acts, with Commentaries' (2001) 2 *Yearbook of the International Law Commission* pt 2, 101, para 15 of the commentary to Article 36.

89 Institute of International Law, 'Responsibility and Liability Under International Law for Environmental Damage' (Session of Strasbourg 1997) art 23.

90 Governing Council, UN Compensation Commission, 'Report and Recommendations Made by the Panel of Commissioners Concerning the Fifth Instalment of "F4" Claims' UN Doc S/AC.26/2005/10, 4 April 2005, para 58.

91 *Certain Activities Carried Out by Nicaragua in the Border Area (Costa Rica v Nicaragua)* (Compensation) [2018] ICJ Rep 15. Although note some dissent on the exclusive use of compensation in Judge Cançado Trindade's Separate Opinion, [36]–[37].

92 ICSID, 'Decision on Counterclaims' *Burlington Resources Inc v Ecuador*, Case No ARB/08/5, 7 February 2017.

the purpose of compensation may also pose challenges;[93] valuations are likely to require expert testimony, site visits, and appropriate evidence collection;[94] and a lack of information, scientific certainty, and/or sufficient resources may inhibit the fact finding and analysis necessary to calculate the nature of the harm.[95] Nevertheless, where the practicalities of the situation allow for it, methods of assessment and valuation are possible.[96]

Guidance on this process can be found in recent international law and international human rights law practice. For example, when addressing the environmental damage resulting from Iraq's invasion and occupation of Kuwait, the Environmental Panel of the UN Compensation Commission acknowledged the relative lack of methods for evaluating damage and instead relied on more general principles, 'particularly the principle that reparation must, as far as possible, wipe out all the consequences of the illegal act'.[97] Given the challenges associated with exact restitution, the Commission used an equivalency-based model which valuated the costs of replacing lost natural resources with resources that could supply equivalent ecological services.[98] At the International Court of Justice, judges were called upon to determine compensation for material damage in the case of *Costa Rica v Nicaragua*.[99] The Court adopted an 'overall valuation' approach which took into account 'the perspective of the ecosystem as a whole, by adopting an overall assessment of the impairment or loss of environmental goods and services prior to recovery'.[100] This considered the nature of the harmful acts,[101] harm,[102] and affected area,[103] as well as the area's capacity for natural regeneration.[104] Arguably the most experienced in considering reparations for environmental harms in

93 Tarcisio Hardman Reis, *Compensation for Environmental Damage Under International Law: The Role of the International Judge* (Kluwer Law International 2011) 157.
94 *Burlington Resources* (n 92) 423.
95 Cymie Payne, 'Environmental Integrity in Post-Conflict Regimes' in Carsten Stahn, Jens Iverson, and Jennifer Easterday (eds), *Jus Post Bellum: Mapping the Normative Foundations* (OUP 2014).
96 Kindji and Faure (n 85).
97 UN Compensation Commission (n 90) para 80.
98 Cymie Payne, 'Developments in the Law of Environmental Reparations: A Case Study of the UN Compensation Commission' in Carsten Stahn, Jens Iverson and, Jennifer Easterday (eds), *Environmental Protection and Transitions from Conflict to Peace* (OUP 2017).
99 Diane Desierto, 'Environmental Damages, Environmental Reparations, and the Right to a Healthy Environment: The ICJ Compensation Judgment in *Costa Rica v Nicaragua* and the IACtHR *Advisory Opinion on Marine Protection for the Greater Caribbean*' (*EJIL: Talk!*, 14 February 2018) <www.ejiltalk.org/environmental-damages-environmental-reparations-and-the-right-to-a-healthy-environment-the-icj-compensation-judgment-in-costa-rica-v-nicaragua-and-the-iacthr-advisory-opinion-on-marine-protection/> accessed 13 April 2020.
100 *Costa Rica v Nicaragua* (n 91) [78].
101 ibid., [79].
102 ibid.
103 ibid., [80].
104 ibid., [81].

the context of human rights abuses is the IACtHR, where indigenous communities have sought compensation for the loss of culturally significant land and natural resources.[105] In this context, the Court has previously ordered compensation for material damage caused by 'despoiled subsistence resources' and 'destruction' of forests,[106] as well as the immaterial damage caused to a people's spiritual connection with their territory.[107] While these various examples are distinct from the ICC in terms of their legal frameworks, they demonstrate that the compensability of environmental destruction is well recognised in international law and that valuation approaches exist to enable compensation to be awarded.[108]

The Court may also wish to look to other forms of reparation for environmental destruction, for three reasons. First, compensation alone might not be enough to deliver a sense of justice to victims without accompanying measures of satisfaction.[109] Indeed, a sole focus on compensation has been deemed insufficient in other legal contexts; the ICJ's focus on compensation in *Costa Rica v Nicaragua* faced critiques from judges and academic commentators alike.[110] Second, in line with the eco-sensitive approach advocated earlier, reparations should be delivered with an eye on long term environmental sustainability.[111] As noted by Lee: '[t]he distribution of cash reparations alone will do little to bring about sustainable development, but will simply alleviate poverty temporarily'.[112] And third, the nature of environmental destruction may be such that the harm has been experienced collectively, requiring an appropriately collective response. In addition to those highlighted in the context of eco-sensitivity, examples of additional

105 For a comprehensive overview and critique of the IACtHR's compensation practices, see Thomas M Antkowiak, 'A Dark Side of Virtue: The Inter-American Court and Reparations for Indigenous Peoples' (2014) 25 *Duke Journal of Comparative and International Law* 1.

106 *Kichwa Indigenous People of Sarayaku* (n 81).

107 *Saramaka People v Suriname* (Preliminary Objections, Merits, Reparations, Costs), Inter-American Court of Human Rights Reports (Series C) 172, 28 November 2007.

108 As observed by the Special Rapporteur Marja Lehto, investment arbitration tribunals have also decided a considerable number of environmental cases: see Kate Parlett and Sara Ewad, 'Protection of the Environment in Investment Arbitration – A Double Edged Sword' (*Kluwer Arbitration Blog*, 22 August 2017) <http://arbitrationblog.kluwerarbitration.com/2017/08/22/protection-environment-investment-arbitration-double-edged-sword/>, cited in Lehto (n 73) 63, n 510.

109 Pablo de Greiff, 'Introduction: Repairing the Past: Compensation for Victims of Human Rights Violations' in Pablo de Greiff (ed), *The Handbook of Reparations* (OUP 2006) 1, 13.

110 For an overview of the debate, see Monaliza Da Silva, 'Compensation Awards in International Environmental Law: Two Recent Developments' (2018) 50 *New York University Journal of International Law and Politics* 1417.

111 Pabuda Sachithanandan, 'Reparations for Victims and Sustainable Development' in Sébastien Jodoin and Marie-Claire Cordonier Segger (eds), *Sustainable Development, International Criminal Justice and Treaty Implementation* (CUP 2013).

112 Tsuey-Ping Lee, 'A Welfare Approach to Mitigating Environmental Injustice: Exploring Needs of Pollution Victims' cited in Matthew Hall, *Victims of Environmental Harm: Rights, Recognition and Redress Under National and International Law* (Routledge 2013) 98.

forms of reparation can be found in the practice of the IACtHR. For example, it has previously awarded the creation of community development funds designed to enable eco-tourism developments, access to clean water, and food security.[113] Additional symbolic measures, such as apologies, acceptances of responsibility, and acknowledgements of suffering, could also be structured in a way that incorporated recognition of environmental harms.[114] Awarding a combination of individual reparations in the form of compensation and wider-ranging collective measures would be in keeping with the ICC's developing practice[115] and would increase the possibilities of adequately responding to the harm.[116]

Awarding reparations for environmental destruction would acknowledge the symbiotic relationship between restoring the environment and repairing harm experienced by individuals living in that environment, with potentially wide-ranging impacts.[117] However, if done without sensitivity for local context, dynamics, and inequalities, such reparations would also risk failing to improve the lives of victims or even resulting in further harm and inequality.[118] In the final section, I therefore move to a more ambitious proposal, considering how the potential for long-term positive impacts might be enhanced by the application of an eco-sensitive lens to the 'transformative' reparations discourse.

4 The possibilities of environmentally 'transformative' reparations

Transformative justice has been defined as 'transformative change that emphasises local agency and resources, the prioritization of process rather than preconceived outcomes and the challenging of unequal and intersecting power relationships and structures of exclusion'.[119] Emerging in part as a critique of transitional justice's focus on a relatively narrow range of civil and political issues, transformative justice considers how to address the long-term social, economic, collective, and structural aspects of conflict and authoritarianism.[120] In parallel to the development of transformative justice theories, advocates of transformative reparations

113 *Kichwa Indigenous People of Sarayaku* (n 81); *Saramaka People* (n 107).

114 On the potential of symbolic reparations at the ICC, see Frédéric Mégret, 'The International Criminal Court Statute and the Failure to Mention Symbolic Reparation' (2009) 16 *International Review of Victimology* 127.

115 See 'Order for Reparations pursuant to Article 75 of the Statute' *Prosecutor v Germain Katanga*, ICC-01/04–01/07, Trial Chamber, 24 March 2017; 'Reparations Order' *Prosecutor v Al Mahdi*, ICC-01/12/01-/15, Trial Chamber, 17 August 2017.

116 This has not been without challenges: see Balta, Bax, and Letschert (n 68).

117 Lawry-White (n 44) 376.

118 Barbara Rose Johnston and Holly M Barker, *Consequential Damages of Nuclear War: The Rongelap Report* (Routledge 2008) 225–247.

119 Paul Gready and Simon Robins, 'From Transitional to Transformative Justice: A New Agenda for Peace' (2014) 8 *International Journal of Transitional Justice* 339.

120 Matthew Evans and David Wilkins, 'Transformative Justice, Reparations and Transatlantic Slavery' (2019) 28 *Social and Legal Studies* 137.

have emerged. They note that for marginalised groups, the end of violence may precipitate a continuation of or return to positions of subjugation and that reparations should therefore contribute to 'overcoming structures of inequality and discrimination'.[121] In the context of indigenous peoples and other marginalised groups, advocates and experts have underscored that land restitution and related reparations, while valued and even crucial, are insufficient without the simultaneous addressing of underlying discrimination and oppression.[122]

Within the international criminal law literature, transformative reparations have been advocated for most notably in the context of widespread or systematic sexual violence, 'where the occurrence of the crime reflects more ingrained structural discrimination and marginalisation of certain groups that precipitate such violence'.[123] Feminist transitional justice scholars have critiqued dominant forms of reparation, such as restitution, compensation, and rehabilitation, for risking a return of women harmed during conflict to the positions of gendered inequality that may have preceded and contributed to conflict and endured post-conflict.[124] A significant contribution of transformative justice literature is to argue in favour of representative forms of justice (by increasing the numbers of women in positions of power), redistributive justice (which seeks to enhance economic equality), and recognition (through the designation of social and cultural standing or status).[125]

It is arguable that similar principles are applicable when thinking about reparations for conflict- and atrocity-related environmental destruction. While measures of restitution and compensation may play an important role, an exclusive focus on such relatively narrow measures fails to situate conflict- and atrocity-related environmental destruction in their broader context. This often involves environmental harm pre- and post-conflict, as well as structural inequalities which shape who is able to access and use natural resources.[126] For many targeted communities or marginalised groups, a return to the *status quo* would be a return to limited access to resources and lack of input into how the natural world is used

121 UN Office of the High Commissioner for Human Rights and UN Women, *Guidance Note of the Secretary-General: Reparations for Conflict-Related Sexual Violence* (UN Office of the High Commissioner for Human Rights and UN Women 2014).

122 Antkowiak (n 105) 56.

123 Moffett, 'Reparations for Victims' (n 41) 1211.

124 See, e.g., Ruth Rubio-Marin, *The Gender of Reparations: Unsettling Sexual Hierarchies while Redressing Human Rights Violations* (CUP 2009); Fionnuala Ní Aoláin, Dina Francesca Haynes, and Naomi Cahn, *On the Frontlines: Gender, War and Post-Conflict Process* (OUP 2011); Rashida Manjoo and Calleigh McRaith, 'Gender-Based Violence and Justice in Conflict and Post-Conflict Areas' (2011) 44 *Cornell International Law Journal* 11.

125 Nancy Fraser, *Scales of Justice: Reimagining Political Space in a Globalizing World* (Columbia University Press 2009), cited in Andrea Durbach and Louise Chappell, 'Leaving Behind the Age of Impunity: Victims of Gender Violence and the Promise of Reparations' (2014) 16 *International Feminist Journal of Politics* 543, 548.

126 Lawry-White (n 44) 367.

and protected.[127] The end of conflict may also involve a return to or emergence of unsustainable resource exploitation, environmental degradation, and/or lack of protection for the environment, as states struggle to economically recover from the impacts of conflict.[128] A failure to address these underlying environmental issues and inequalities can make a lasting peace less likely, plant the seeds for future human rights violations, and overlook the challenges facing those who were originally marginalised.[129] Indeed, the environmental justice movement has worked since the 1960s to expose these inequalities,[130] highlighting how disadvantaged groups suffer disproportionately from environmental degradation and unequal distribution of natural resources.[131] Mirroring the calls from proponents of transformative justice, environmental justice is commonly described as requiring distributive justice, procedural justice, and recognition.[132]

The ICC has been identified as an important organ for pursuing transformative reparations.[133] This has been evident in its judgments. As stated in the amended *Lubanga* reparation decision, the principles of dignity, non-discrimination, and non-stigmatisation mean that reparations should address underlying injustices and avoid replicating discriminatory practices or structures that predated the commission of the crimes.[134] The TFV has similarly spoken of the importance of ensuring awards that 'do not exacerbate the root causes of the conflict'.[135] However, the possibilities for a court-ordered reparation to unilaterally fundamentally change underlying structural inequalities are undoubtedly limited, as acknowledged in scholarly critiques of gender transformative justice.[136] As noted by Andrea Durbach and Louise Chappell, achieving equal representation in decision making, a significant redistribution of economic resources, and the removal

127 ibid.

128 David M Ong, 'Prospects for Transitional Environmental Justice in the Socio-Economic Reconstruction of Kosovo' (2017) 30 *Tulane Environmental Law Journal* 217.

129 UN Environment Programme, *Sudan: Post-Conflict Environmental Assessment* (UNEP 2007) 8.

130 See, e.g., Robert Bullard, *Dumping in Dixie: Race, Class and Environmental Quality* (Westview Press 1990).

131 Britta Sjostedt, 'Searching for Environmental Justice in Peacebuilding – Tools Offered by International Environmental Law' *Nature of Peace* (8 January 2018) <natureofpeace.blogg.lu.se/searching-for-environmental-justice-in-peacebuilding-tools-offered-by-international-environmental-law/> accessed 13 April 2020.

132 See, e.g., David Schlosberg, *Defining Environmental Justice: Theories, Movements and Nature* (OUP 2009).

133 Durbach and Chappell (n 125).

134 'Judgment on the Appeals' *Lubanaga* (n 70) 4.

135 'Observations on Reparations in Response to the Scheduling Order of 14 March 2012' *Prosecutor v Lubanga Dyilo*, ICC-01/04–01/06–2872, 25 April 2012.

136 Luke Moffett, 'Reparative Complementarity: Ensuring an Effective Remedy for Victims in the Reparation Regime of the International Criminal Court' (2013) 17 *International Journal of Human Rights* 368; Sarah Williams and Emma Palmer, 'Transformative Reparations for Women and Girls at the Extraordinary Chambers in the Courts of Cambodia' (2016) 10 *International Journal of Transitional Justice* 311.

of socially and culturally embedded bias requires extensive state-sponsored, collective measures.[137] In the context of environmental transformative justice, while one can see the value of increasing the political representation and recognition of, for example, indigenous communities impacted by unequitable natural resource exploitation, this is likely beyond the power of a criminal justice institution, without accompanying state buy-in.[138] Similarly, large-scale redistribution of natural resources and habitat management may require integration into peace agreements and post-conflict policies. The ICC cannot force a state to act and is therefore limited in what it can achieve. There are also significant resource limitations on what the Court can achieve in terms of repairing the environment. Mark Drumbl has highlighted the challenges this poses to implementing environmental change: '[u]nless this criminal law apparatus is hooked into broader restorative remediation efforts, compensation efforts, and scientific expertise . . . the actual hard work of improving the damage to the environment will not take place'.[139]

Such limitations do not mean that the ICC cannot seek to integrate environmental transformative justice to the extent available. For example, guarantees of non-repetition have the potential to become a useful tool in pursuing transformation; as Clara Sandoval has argued, such measures 'remain crucial to realizing the transformative potential of transitional justice'.[140] Guarantees of non-repetition are designed to prevent the reoccurrence of crimes by addressing the structural causes of violations and are more commonly found in the context of human rights violations and state-led reparations.[141] However, the ICC's reparations decision in the case of *Al-Mahdi* demonstrated the Court's willingness to award such reparations in the context of individual accountability. Just as 'effective measures to guarantee non-repetition of the attacks'[142] were considered appropriate in the context of attacks against specific cultural sites in *Al-Mahdi*'s case, so might future Chambers consider the possibility of awarding guarantees against future harmful behaviour directed at the environment. In terms of implementation, the Basic Principles and Guidelines on the Right to a Remedy and Reparation identify eight examples of possible modalities, including training for law enforcement, military, and security forces; promoting mechanisms for conflict resolution; and reforming laws that enabled the violations to take place.[143] Such measures offer the potential to entrench greater

137 Durbach and Chappell (n 125).
138 On the IACtHR's attempts and successes with regards to structural inequalities, see Antkowiak (n 105) 56–59.
139 Mark Drumbl, 'Symposium on "International Responses to the Environmental Impact of War"' (2005) 17 *Georgetown International Environmental Law Review* 623.
140 Clara Sandoval, 'Reflections on the Transformative Potential of Transitional Justice and the Nature of Social Change in Times of Transition' in Roger Duthie and Paul Seils (eds), *Justice Mosaics: How Context Shapes Transitional Justice in Fractured Societies* (ICTJ 2017).
141 ibid.
142 *Al-Mahdi Reparations Order* (n 115) [67].
143 'Basic Principles and Guidelines on the Right to a Remedy and Reparation for Victims of Gross Violations of International Human Rights Law and Serious Violations of

respect for the environment and fairer resource distribution post-conflict, potentially contributing to a more lasting peace. As noted by the Trial Chamber in *Al-Mahdi*, such reparations may require consultation with governmental authorities and would need to be tailored to the individual concerns regarding the natural resources.[144] Again, guidance might be found in the practice of the IACtHR, where guarantees of non-repetition have been awarded in cases involving victim groups' land.[145]

It could be that some of the measures discussed in previous sections could also facilitate this type of environmental transformative agenda. For example, KESAN has described the Salween Peace Park as aiming to contribute to conflict transformation by expanding the conversation around 'governance' to address issues of 'militarization, conflict, displacement, resource capture, and destructive development'.[146] Emerging environmental peacebuilding theory argues that cooperation over environmental resources and biodiversity management can help prevent the outbreak of conflict and enable peacebuilding to promote a transition towards peaceful and sustainable development.[147] Facilitating the treatment, management and development of natural habitats could simultaneously develop biodiversity and human welfare both to meet the needs of the present generation and to improve the standard of living; sanitation; and social, environmental, and political stability for future generations.[148] It might be that a more holistic, eco-sensitive approach to reparations might 'deflect, subsume and eventually even transcend entrenched social conflicts'.[149]

More broadly, representative/procedural justice elements can be incorporated by ensuring that those with an understanding of the specific environmental context in which violence occurred are heard prior to reparation orders being made and during the design and implementation of reparative projects.[150] Steps can be taken to identify the intersections of ethnicity/race/clan, class, sexuality, nationality, dis/ability, and employment status, which influence access to natural resources, to ensure that discriminatory practices of exclusions are not reproduced via the provision of reparations.[151] Adopting an eco-sensitive approach to design and implementation as advocated here could also contribute to mainstreaming environmental concerns into the TFV's

---

International Humanitarian Law' UNGA Res 60/147 (21 March 2006) UN Doc A/RES/60/147.

144 *Al-Mahdi Reparations Order* (n 115) [67].

145 For an analysis of the ICC's awarding of guarantees of non-repetition and the applicability of IACtHR practice, see Francesca Capone, 'An Appraisal of the Al-Mahdi Order on Reparations and its Innovative Elements' (2018) 16 *Journal of International Criminal Justice* 645.

146 Salween Peace Park Initiative (n 55).

147 Ken Conca and Geoffrey D Dabelko, *Environmental Peacemaking* (Johns Hopkins University Press 2002).

148 Milburn, 'Mainstreaming the Environment' (n 60).

149 Ong (n 128) 222.

150 Durbach and Chappell (n 125) 551.

151 ibid.

operations.[152] While likely incapable of natural resource redistribution without state cooperation and involvement, a focus on reparative measures which have the potential to bring about long-term positive impacts on the environment could have lasting benefits for targeted communities that may have historically lacked access to natural resources.

5 Conclusion

With so much already expected of the ICC, it might be fair to query whether there is 'any place within the already congested transitional justice agenda . . . to consider the addition of environmental justice?'[153] One might also question whether a system designed to focus on grave human rights violations such as international criminal law is equipped to protect the environment on its own terms.[154] Certainly, there are both practical and conceptual challenges associated with encompassing environmental destruction into the ICC's remit. The introduction of a new crime against the environment seems far away, if not impossible, and the existing core crimes include little recognition of environmental destruction. The TFV faces resource restrictions and implementation challenges that inevitably impact its ability to deliver meaningful reparation and measures of assistance to victimised communities. These challenges cannot be ignored. Yet this chapter has sought to demonstrate that there are ways and means of adopting greater environmental awareness into the ICC's reparative framework, ranging from an increased eco-sensitivity in human-centric reparation and assistance measures to reparation awards which explicitly respond to environmental harm to pursuing an environmentally transformative reparations agenda.

Even at its most effective, the ICC and TFV are transitional justice mechanisms, with a limited ability to address the broader injustices, inequalities, and structural forms of oppression that may have enabled the perpetration of core crimes and related environmental destruction. Proponents of broader theories of transformative justice have critiqued arguments which focus on addressing broader contexts of violence only inasmuch as existing transitional justice tools can be adapted to do so[155] and would undoubtedly critique my suggestions on that basis. While agreeing that more radical measures are necessary, I nonetheless argue that it is vital that we continue to explore diverse and creative ways to respond to environmental harms wherever possible.[156] The interconnections between conflict, atroc-

152 See Durbach and Chappell (n 125) 555, noting the value of the Trust Fund's 'gender mainstreaming' to the project of gender transformative reparations.

153 ibid.

154 Susanna Borràs, 'New Transitions from Human Rights to the Environment to the Rights of Nature' (2016) 5 *Transnational Environmental Law* 128.

155 Matthew Evans, 'Structural Violence, Socioeconomic Rights, and Transformative Justice' (2016) 15 *Journal of Human Rights* 1.

156 See also Dinah Shelton, 'Legitimate and Necessary: Adjudicating Human Rights Violations Related to Activities Causing Environmental Harm or Risk' (2015) 6 *Journal of Human Rights and the Environment* 139.

ity, and environment mean that the neglect of environmental destruction has potentially long-term and severe implications for individuals and communities recovering from mass violence and human rights violations. The well-being of humans cannot be achieved in isolation from the well-being of nature;[157] indeed, human rights and the protection of the environment are increasingly recognised as interdependent and indivisible.[158] Greater awareness of these interconnections in measures of reparation and victim assistance is therefore a necessary, if modest, first step if the impacts of mass violence are to be meaningfully and sustainably addressed. Furthermore, it is important to note that these interconnections impact all of us. Environmental degradation risks not only the emergence or resurgence of conflict but also larger international security threats through its contribution to global warming and associated changes to the physical and geopolitical world. Integrating environmental considerations into our responses to conflict is therefore not only important to the well-being of victimised impacted communities but also a development and security imperative.[159]

157 Mwanza (n 21) 593.
158 *Environment and Human Rights* (Advisory Opinion), Inter-American Court of Human Rights Reports (Series A) 23, 15 November 2017.
159 Milburn, 'The Roots to Peace in the DRC' (n 40) 876.

7 Unlawful human experimentation in the wake of the trials under Control Council Law No 10 at Nuremberg, in the Rome Statute for the International Criminal Court, and at the Extraordinary Chambers in the Courts of Cambodia

Edwin Bikundo

1 Introduction: defining unlawful experiments under customary international criminal law

Writing in 1981, Cherif Bassiouni, Thomas Baffes, and John Evrard called 'for a specialized convention on human experimentation'.[1] The reasons they gave to justify this included:

> Unlawful human experimentation is a single phenomenon which from the standpoint of the law occurs in two contexts. The first, concerns human experimentation during armed conflict, and the second analogous to torture during peacetime. However, torture in time of peace does not adequately encompass all human experimentation, leaving a need to define the criminal aspects of human experimentation and thereby complete the symmetry between the law of war and the law of peace. Moreover, lawful human experimentation implies certain principles, among which is placing the health and welfare of human subjects foremost.[2]

Not only has no convention on unlawful experimentation been forthcoming, but the limitations noted by Bassiouni et al. regarding unlawful human

1 M Cherif Bassiouni, Thomas G Baffes, and John T Evrard, 'An Appraisal of Human Experimentation in International Law and Practice: The Need for International Regulation of Human Experimentation' (1981) 72 *Journal of Criminal Law and Criminology* 1597, 1655–1656.
2 ibid., 1654.

DOI: 10.4324/9781003087533-9

experimentation during peacetime still persist in the legal framework. This is despite great strides having been made in international criminal law during the intervening period, such as the passing of the United Nations Convention against Torture and other Cruel, Inhuman, or Degrading Treatment or Punishment (CAT). The problem addressed in this chapter is that unlawful human experimentation has been unevenly prosecuted. Its classification, contours, and status remain unclear in the present. On occasion, it is considered both a war crime and a crime against humanity, sometimes only one or the other; sometimes, it is a stand-alone crime; and sometimes, it is included under torture. Moreover, although CAT makes no explicit mention of experimentation, the International Covenant on Civil and Political Rights (ICCPR) only prohibits medical or scientific experimentation under torture. Further, it is clear that vulnerable populations are usually the target of unlawful human experimentation.

This chapter, therefore, sets itself the task of exploring the development and present status of the law on unlawful medical experimentation and, in line with this edited volume's main focus on futures, to outline a clearer future for medical experimentation. Ideally, a stand-alone offence in a specialised convention would be the surest way to address the problems outlined. To be sure, while noting the desirability of creating a stand-alone crime and specialised convention, the difficulty, unlikelihood, and limits of these approaches with regard to international relations are not to be underestimated, even though unlawful medical, biological, and scientific experiments are already repressed under contemporary customary international law.

The chapter begins proper by considering the post-WWII trials at the Nuremberg Military Tribunals under Control Council Law No 10[3] and then turns to the Rome Statute of the International Criminal Court (Rome Statute) and compares both to recent case law coming out of the Extraordinary Chambers in the Courts of Cambodia (ECCC). This analysis will demonstrate certain inconsistencies of approach between the three contexts: while *United States v Brandt et al* (the *Medical Case*)[4] led to convictions for unlawful experimentation under both war crimes and crimes against humanity, the Rome Statute only codifies them as war crimes (inclusive of but not limited to the 1949 Geneva Conventions), while the ECCC only included them under crimes against humanity, although it had the opportunity to include them under grave breaches of the 1949 Geneva Conventions at the time.

Consequently, the argument is that, in the wake of the ECCC Judgement in *Case 002/02*, the law on unlawful experimentation should be clarified to reflect

3 *Control Council Law No 10: Punishment of Persons Guilty of War Crimes, Crimes Against Peace and Against Humanity* (20 December 1945) 3 *Official Gazette of the Control Council for Germany* 50 (1946).

4 *United States v Brandt et al* (United States Military Tribunal, Nuremberg, Case No 1, 20 August 1947) in *Trials of War Criminals Before the Nuremberg Military Tribunals Under Control Council Law No 10* (vols 1 and 2, 1946–9) vol 1, 3 (*Medical Case*).

its uniqueness and gravity, not only as both a war crime and a crime against humanity but also as torture under international human rights law. A definitional outline and structure will progressively appear as we first look at the *Medical Case*.

2 Unlawful medical experiments in the *Medical Case*

Neither the Nuremberg IMT Charter nor the Tokyo IMTFE Charter explicitly mentioned unlawful medical experiments.[5] The first two trials of war criminals before the IMT under Control Council Law No 10, however, provided two cases that addressed unlawful experiments as crimes: the *Medical Case* and *United States v Milch et al* (*Milch Case*).[6] There were, however, no convictions for unlawful experiments in the *Milch Case*; therefore, this analysis focuses on the *Medical Case*. That trial became known as such 'because 20 of the 23 defendants were doctors, and the charges related principally to medical experimentation on human beings'.[7] The three other accused had either administrative or managerial roles over the doctors, which was the basis upon which they were charged and convicted.[8]

With regard to the origin of these prohibitions as being founded on the sort of jurisdiction that the court could employ, the court noted that counts two and three of the indictment – war crimes and crimes against humanity, respectively – were

> identical in content, except for the fact that in count two the acts which are made the basis for the charges are alleged to have been committed on 'civilians and members of the armed forces [of nations] then at war with the German Reich . . . in the exercise of belligerent control', whereas in count three the criminal acts are alleged to have been committed against 'German civilians and nationals of other countries'.[9]

Although they did bear that distinction in mind, the judges otherwise treated both counts as one and discussed them together. With regard to Brandt specifically, the

5 *Agreement by the Government of the United States of America, the Provisional Government of the French Republic, the Government of the United Kingdom of Great Britain and Northern Ireland and the Government of the Union of Soviet Socialist Republics for the Persecution and Punishment of the Major War Criminals of the European Axis* (signed and entered into force 8 August 1945) 82 UNTS 280, annex (*IMT Charter*) and the *Special Proclamation by the Supreme Commander for the Allied Powers: Establishment of an International Military Tribunal for the Far East* (19 January 1946) (*IMTFE Charter*).

6 *United States v Milch et al* (United States Military Tribunal, Nuremberg, Case No 2, 18 April 1947) in *Trials of War Criminals Before the Nuremberg Military Tribunals Under Control Council Law No 10* (vol 2, 1946–9) 353 (*Milch Case*).

7 *Medical Case* (n 4) vol 1, iv, 8–10.

8 ibid.

9 ibid., vol 2, 174.

judges found that '[t]o the extent that these criminal acts did not constitute war crimes they constituted crimes against humanity'.[10]

In the course of the trial, 15 different types of medical experiments were examined: high-altitude experiments; freezing experiments; malaria experiments; lost (mustard) gas experiments; sulphanilamide experiments; bone, muscle, and nerve regeneration and bone transplantation experiments; sea-water experiments; epidemic jaundice experiments; typhus and other vaccine experiments; experiments with poison; incendiary bomb experiments; phlegmon experiments (relating to treating an inflammation of the tissues common in the concentration camps); polygal experiments (a drug tested for its capacity to coagulate the blood); gas oedema (phenol) experiments (phenol was an organic chemical compound suspected of causing fatalities when used in serums); and experiments for mass sterilisation.[11] Sixteen of the defendants, including all the non-doctor administrators, were convicted for their role in the unlawful experiments.[12]

In titling the unlawful experiments as 'crimes committed in the guise of scientific research', the opening statement of the US prosecutor, Brigadier General Telford Taylor, sought to heavily discount the scientific basis or value of those experiments as well as to contextualise their deliberate cruelty to people 'regarded as inferior', although not even he could say they had absolutely no scientific value:

> Mankind has not heretofore felt the need of a word to denominate the science of how to kill prisoners most rapidly and subjugated people in large numbers. This case and these defendants have created this gruesome question for the lexicographer. For the moment we will christen this macabre science 'thanatology', the science of producing death. The thanatological knowledge, derived in part from these experiments, supplied the techniques for genocide, a policy of the Third Reich, exemplified in the 'euthanasia' program and in the wide-spread [sic] slaughter of Jews, gypsies, Poles, and Russians. This policy of mass extermination could not have been so effectively carried out without the active participation of German medical scientists.[13]

Moreover, the *Oxford English Dictionary* gives an alternative etymology of thanatology as 'the scientific study of death' appearing as far back as in 1842 in an American Medical Lexicon.

During the case, not only did the defence compare the experiments to experiments carried out by the Allies, but the defence also argued that the medical experiments alleged to be criminal were useful in furthering medical science, and, in some instances, 'there was no other alternative for the development of

10 ibid., vol 2, 198.
11 ibid., vol 1, 11–16.
12 ibid., vol 2, 189–300.
13 ibid., vol 1, 37–38.

medical science except to conduct experiments on human beings'.[14] The prosecution countered

> that voluntary participation by the subject of experimentation was a prerequisite of legal experiments . . . that the experiments turned out to be entirely useless for medical science and human progress, and that in some cases it was doubtful if considerations of medical science played any controlling role in the decision to conduct the experiments.[15]

The Tribunal began its judgment by outlining what would be 'permissible medical experiments'.[16] The Tribunal found that '[t]he great weight of the evidence before us is to the effect that certain types of medical experiments on human beings, when kept within reasonably well-defined bounds, conform to the ethics of the medical profession generally'.[17] The Tribunal noted the argument that '[t]he protagonists of the practice of human experimentation justify their views on the basis that such experiments yield results for the good of society that are unprocurable by other methods or means of study'.[18] They opposed that approach by the defence with the imperative 'that certain basic principles must be observed in order to satisfy moral, ethical and legal concepts'.[19] The first and by far most fully articulated of these was that '[t]he voluntary consent of the human subject is absolutely essential'.[20] This imposed a 'personal' non-delegable 'duty and responsibility for ascertaining the quality of the consent' resting 'upon each individual who initiates, directs or engages in the experiment'.[21] Not all but only 'unnecessary physical and mental suffering and injury' were prohibited.[22] Moreover, the Tribunal only concerned itself 'with those requirements which are purely legal in nature – or which at least are so clearly related to matters legal that they assist us in determining criminal culpability and punishment'.[23] In so doing, it found:

> Obviously all of these experiments involving brutalities, tortures, disabling injury, and death were performed in complete disregard of international conventions, the laws and customs of war, the general principles of criminal law as derived from the criminal laws of all civilized nations, and Control Council Law No 10. Manifestly human experiments under such conditions are

14 ibid., vol 2, 61.
15 ibid.
16 ibid., vol 2, 181.
17 ibid.
18 ibid.
19 ibid.
20 ibid.
21 ibid., vol 2, 182.
22 ibid.
23 ibid., vol 2, 183.

> contrary to 'the principles of the law of nations as they result from the usages established among civilized peoples, from the laws of humanity, and from the dictates of public conscience.[24]

The Italian philosopher Giorgio Agamben addresses the medical experimentation in concentration and extermination camps in at least two places and makes the point that not only did medical experiments occur in those camps but that those camps in themselves were also, in all probability, a political experiment.[25] Agamben's work – particularly his notion of 'bare life', which is to say humans stripped of all legal protection – is a sound basis for understanding how the vulnerability of populations to unlawful experimentation arises in concrete situations. Although the ICRC's 2016 *Commentary* notes the relevance of the *International Ethical Guidelines for Epidemiological Studies*[26] and the *International Ethical Guidelines for Biomedical Research Involving Human Subjects*,[27] none of these instruments mention criminal culpability at all. Not even the *World Medical Association Declaration of Helsinki Ethical Principles for Medical Research Involving Human Subjects* does.[28] This is why not proscribing unlawful experiments unless a nexus to a state of conflict exists is both unnecessary and undesirable in light of the *Medical Case*. It is unnecessary because even though crimes against humanity were linked to armed conflict in the law of Nuremberg for reasons of the exercise of jurisdiction, they are not subject to the same stipulation in the Rome Statute. It is undesirable because human experimentation occurring in peacetime would be completely outside the purview of the ICC (except insofar as those alleged acts can be classified elsewhere as a crime against humanity: say, torture or inhumane acts). In a sense, this is the result of the *Medical Case*'s failure, as identified by Xavier Aurey, 'to address one of the most difficult issues in clinical trials and human experimentation: the almost unavoidable context of exploitation of any situation where a person is used as an object for the good of others'.[29]

Although he was never tried, Dr Sigmund Rascher's (also spelt Roscher) name is everywhere in the *Medical Case* and with good reason. The experiments were

24 ibid.

25 See especially Giorgio Agamben, *The Open: Man and Animal* (Stanford University Press 2003) 22 and Giorgio Agamben, *Homo Sacer: Sovereign Power and Bare Life* (Stanford University Press 1998) 154–159.

26 Council for International Organizations of Medical Sciences and World Health Organization, *International Ethical Guidelines for Epidemiological Studies* (2009) <https://cioms.ch/wp-content/uploads/2017/01/International_Ethical_Guidelines_LR.pdf> accessed 26 June 2019.

27 ibid.

28 World Medical Association, *World Medical Association Declaration of Helsinki Ethical Principles for Medical Research Involving Human Subjects* <www.who.int/bulletin/archives/79%284%29373.pdf> accessed 26 June 2019.

29 Xavier Aurey, 'The Nuremberg Doctors' Trial: Looking Back 70 Years Later' (2017) 17 *International Criminal Law Review* 1049, 1054.

his brainchild, and he would have been tried had he not already met his death, ironically enough in a concentration camp.[30] In that case – tellingly supportive of Agamben's thesis – both the prosecution[31] and the judges cited the instance of an inmate brought in for experimentation 'whose hair and eyes and figure were pleasing to Dr Rascher', omitting not only precisely *what* was pleasing about her hair, eyes, and figure and *why* it was pleasing, but also that she was actually spared experimentation as a result.[32]

Dr Rascher himself was not so coy, as his letter during the trial, reproduced here in full, makes plain. He put his feelings over and above the scientific value of the experiment were he to proceed with it:

> It hurts my racial feelings to expose to racially inferior concentration camp elements a girl as a prostitute who has the appearance of a pure Nordic and who could perhaps by assignment of proper work be put on the right road.
>
> Therefore, I refused to use this girl for my experimental purposes and gave the adequate reports to the camp commander and the adjutant of the Reich Leader SS.[33]

Holocaust survivor Olga Lengyel observed firsthand that '[s]ince they [Nazi doctors] were free to do whatever they wished, they decided to experiment on these people',[34] the human guinea pigs at Auschwitz and Birkenau. This makes the crucial point that vulnerable populations are an experimental target precisely because they are vulnerable and not because the experiment is either for the good of science or for the advancement of human knowledge. This is an abiding feature of unlawful medical experimentation.

More problematically to contemporary notions of law and justice, those originally proposed medical experiments (which only requested 'that two or three *professional criminals* can be made available for these experiments')[35] would not be triable under the Rome Statute of the International Criminal Court (ICC) as it currently stands, precisely because they lacked the nexus to an armed conflict. Fortunately in these circumstances, however, even the Rome Statute itself in Article 10 reminds us that nothing in the relevant part of the Statute 'shall be interpreted as limiting or prejudicing in any way existing or developing rules of international law for purposes other than this Statute', which would include the classification of unlawful medical experiments as a crime against humanity.

30 *Medical Case* (n 4) vol 1, 38.
31 ibid., vol 2, 45.
32 ibid., vol 1, 71 and 203.
33 ibid., vol 1, 245.
34 Olga Lengyel, *Five Chimneys: The Story of Auschwitz* (Chicago Review Press 2005) 185.
35 *Medical Case* (n 4) vol 1, 92 (emphasis added).

3 Unlawful experimentation under the Rome Statute for the International Criminal Court

There is no mention of experiments in the International Law Commission's Draft Code of Crimes against the Peace and Security, a key precursor to the Rome Statute.[36] Neither is there a single mention of 'experiments' in the official records of the summaries of the plenary meetings or the committee meetings of the United Nations diplomatic conference which led to the establishment of the ICC.[37] The documentary history of experiments in those negotiations is limited to the Draft Statute itself and to texts proposed by participants, including the ICRC and the United States.[38] This history is outlined further later in this chapter.

Experiments are only mentioned thrice in the Rome Statute, once as 'biological experiments' and twice as 'medical or scientific experiments'. Moreover, each of these occasions is within the rubric of war crimes under Article 8. Consequently, these references are always and only in relation to international humanitarian law (IHL)'s conceptualisations, concerns, structure, idiom, and approaches to such an extent that experiments do not feature elsewhere nor in any other context in the statute. Even their division into three types remains very faithful to IHL's disciplinary demarcation between first, the law applicable to *international* armed conflicts – further divided into the so-called 'Geneva law governing the protection of the victims of war' and the 'Hague law governing the conduct of hostilities in war' – and second, the law applicable to *non*-international armed conflicts. That taxonomy is neither dependent on the nature of the experiments, nor, indeed, does it have anything to do with the crime as such, but only with the experiment's classification in relation to whichever conflict it may be connected to.

Antonio Cassese notes, however, that '[n]ot all crimes committed during an armed conflict constitute war crimes. It is widely held in case law and legal literature that, in order to qualify as a war crime, criminal conduct must be "closely related to the hostilities" '.[39] Furthermore, '[t]his relationship between armed conflict and conduct, termed "nexus" (or "link"), serves to distinguish between war crimes, on the one side, and "ordinary" crimes committed during – but unrelated to – an armed conflict, on the other'.[40] Guénaël Mettraux is of the view that the nexus requirement serves first to distinguish 'war crimes from purely

36 International Law Commission, 'Draft Code of Crimes Against the Peace and Security of Mankind with Commentaries' (1996) ii *Yearbook of the International Law Commission* pt 2, and see 54–55 on war crimes.

37 United Nations Diplomatic Conference of Plenipotentiaries on the Establishment of an International Criminal Court, 'Summary Records of the Plenary Meetings and of the Meetings of the Committee of the Whole' UN Doc A/CONF.183/13 (vol 2) 15 June–17 July 1998.

38 ibid., 223.

39 Antonio Cassese, 'The Nexus Requirement for War Crimes' (2012) 10 *Journal of International Criminal Justice* 1395.

40 ibid.

domestic crimes' and second 'to exclude from the realm of the laws of war purely random or isolated criminal occurrences which do not constitute war crimes'.[41] Harmen van der Wilt also agrees that

> [i]n order to qualify as a war crime, an offence must have a nexus with an armed conflict. This contextual element serves to distinguish war crimes from both ordinary crimes and other international crimes such as crimes against humanity and genocide.[42]

The weight of scholarly opinion thus does not support having a link between crimes against humanity and armed conflict. Neither does the law. Rather, the core purpose of the nexus is solely connected to war crimes per se in terms of distinguishing them from domestic crimes with no armed conflict nexus, which are consequently to be dealt with under domestic jurisdiction, as opposed to distinguishing war crimes from crimes against humanity as such. Restricting prosecutions for unlawful medical experiments only to wartime contexts and completely excluding acts in peacetime is thus untenable and unsupported both in doctrine and in theory.

Following a taxonomy borrowed wholesale from IHL (as we shall see established later in this chapter) in the Rome Statute, the first two mentions of experiments are related to international armed conflicts and the third to non-international armed conflicts. To start with the first mention, Article 8(2)(a)(ii) of the Rome Statute codifies 'biological experiments' as criminal and explicitly includes them as a subset of 'torture or inhuman treatment', similarly to how they were already prohibited under the four Geneva Conventions of 1949:

> 2 For the purpose of this Statute, 'war crimes' means:
>
> (a) Grave breaches of the Geneva Conventions of 12 August 1949, namely, any of the following acts against persons or property protected under the provisions of the relevant Geneva Convention:
>
> . . .
>
> (ii) Torture or inhuman treatment, including *biological experiments* . . .[43]

The language used here is virtually identical to an earlier similar provision: namely, Article 2 of the Statute of the International Criminal Tribunal for the former Yugoslavia (ICTY). It needs to be further noted here that in the Rome

41 Guénaël Mettraux, 'Nexus with Armed Conflict' in Antonio Cassese et al. (eds), *Oxford Companion to International Criminal Justice* (OUP 2009).

42 Harmen van der Wilt, 'War Crimes and the Requirement of a Nexus with an Armed Conflict' (2012) 10 *Journal of International Criminal Justice* 1113.

43 Emphasis added.

Statute, crimes against humanity include torture separately under Article 7(1)(f), as well as inhumane treatment under Article 7(1)(k), but not experiments.

The second mention of experiments is in Article 8(2)(b)(x) of the Rome Statute, which codifies 'medical or scientific experiments' as criminal under 'other ['other' here meaning other than under the four Geneva Conventions of 1949] serious violations of the laws and customs applicable in international armed conflict':

(b) Other serious violations of the laws and customs applicable in international armed conflict, within the established framework of international law, namely, any of the following acts:

(x) Subjecting persons who are in the power of an adverse party to physical mutilation or to *medical or scientific experiments* of any kind which are neither justified by the medical, dental or hospital treatment of the person concerned nor carried out in his or her interest, and which cause death to or seriously endanger the health of such person or persons. . .[44]

The language used here is reminiscent of Article 3 of the ICTY Statute, although the ICTY Statute did not actually reference experiments, probably because the drafters of the Statute did not view that as particularly relevant to the Balkan conflicts of the 1990s.

The third mention – and the only one to do with non-international armed conflicts (i.e., 'armed conflicts not of an international character') – is in Article 8 (2)(e)(xi) of the Rome Statute, which codifies 'medical or scientific experiments' as criminal 'within the established framework of international law':

(e) Other serious violations of the laws and customs applicable in armed conflicts not of an international character, within the established framework of international law, namely, any of the following acts:

. . .

(xi) Subjecting persons who are in the power of another party to the conflict to physical mutilation or to *medical or scientific experiments* of any kind which are neither justified by the medical, dental or hospital treatment of the person concerned nor carried out in his or her interest, and which cause death to or seriously endanger the health of such person or persons. . .[45]

Consequently, what distinguishes these 'experiments' in the Rome Statute is not so much the nature or the forms of conduct that are criminalised but rather their precise relationship to an armed conflict. As a consequence, their current criminalisation is strongly influenced by where they were previously

44 Emphasis added.
45 Emphasis added.

codified in IHL. Article 8(2)(a)(ii) utilises the formulation 'biological experiments'[46] while Article 8(2)(b)(x) refers to 'medical or scientific experiments'.[47] They both rely on classic international armed conflict (that is, between states), with the latter focusing on the protection of victims of war, the so-called 'Geneva law', whereas the former focuses on the conduct of hostilities – the so-called Hague law – as codified in the First Additional Protocol to the Geneva Conventions (AP I).[48]

Article 8(2)(e)(xi) also uses the formulation 'medical or scientific experiments', although not with respect to classic international armed conflict but rather in relation to 'non-international armed conflicts'. It references the Second Additional Protocol to the Geneva Conventions (AP II) in its supplementation of GC I, II, III, and IV and AP I, all of which deal with international armed conflicts. However, because 'experiments' appears nowhere in AP II, the Rome Statute here goes beyond the IHL treaties by criminalising unlawful experiments in non-international armed conflicts.[49] There is therefore no better explanation for ICL distinguishing between 'biological experiments' and 'medical or scientific experiments' other than that is what IHL does. Having said that, the codification of unlawful experiments in the Rome Statute is in terms of their relation to an 'armed conflict' and represents, in that sense, a breach of IHL. Because its breach of international human rights law is not explicitly mentioned, it is therefore worth exploring the background and commentary surrounding the relevant IHL provisions in more depth.

GC I and GC II prohibit 'biological experiments'[50] while GC III and GC IV prohibit 'medical or scientific experiments'.[51] According to the ICRC's *Commentary on the Third Geneva Convention on Prisoners of War*, the Convention's authors wanted to prohibit medical and scientific experiments with reference 'only to

46 All of these violations are mentioned as 'grave breaches' in the Geneva Conventions: Geneva Convention for the Amelioration of the Condition of the Wounded and Sick in Armed Forces in the Field (opened for signature 12 August 1949, entered into force 21 October 1950) 75 UNTS 31, arts 12 and 50 (GC I); Geneva Convention for the Amelioration of the Condition of the Wounded, Sick and Shipwrecked Members of the Armed Forces at Sea (opened for signature 12 August 1949, entered into force 21 October 1950) 75 UNTS 85, arts 12 and 51 (GC II); Geneva Convention Relative to the Treatment of Prisoners of War (opened for signature 12 August 1949, entered into force 21 October 1950) 75 UNTS 135, art 130 (GC III); Geneva Convention Relative to the Protection of Civilian Persons in Time of War (opened for signature 12 August 1949, entered into force 21 October 1950) 75 UNTS 287, art 147 (GC IV).

47 GC III art 13 and GC IV art 32. None of these violations are mentioned as 'grave breaches'.

48 Protocol Additional to the Geneva Conventions of 12 August 1949, and Relating to the Protection of Victims of International Armed Conflicts (Protocol I) (opened for signature 8 June 1977, entered into force 7 December 1978) 1125 UNTS 3, art 11(2)(b) (AP I).

49 Protocol Additional to the Geneva Conventions of 12 August 1949, and Relating to the Protection of Victims of Non-International Armed Conflicts (Protocol II) (opened for signature 8 June 1977, entered into force 7 December 1978) 1125 UNTS 609, art 1 (AP II).

50 GC I art 12; GC II art 12.

51 GC III art 13; GC IV art 32.

experiments not justified by the medical treatment of the prisoner concerned'.[52] It was not meant to 'prevent doctors from using treatment for medical reasons with the sole object of improving the patient's condition' and therefore left it 'permissible to use new medicaments and methods invented by science, provided that they are used only for therapeutic purposes'.[53] The basic intention was to ensure that 'prisoners must not in any circumstances be used as "guinea-pigs" for medical or scientific experiments'.[54] What is more, '[t]he intention was to abolish for ever the criminal practices inflicted on thousands of persons during the Second World War'. As we have seen, however, the trials following WWII punished experiments *both* as war crimes and as crimes against humanity.

According to the ICRC's *Commentary on the Convention (I) for the Amelioration of the Condition of the Wounded and Sick in Armed Forces in the Field*,

> [it] was intended, by prohibiting the subjection of wounded and sick to biological experiments, to put an end for all time to criminal practices of which certain prisoners have been the victims, and also to prevent wounded or sick in captivity from being used as 'guinea-pigs' for medical experiments.[55]

They further added that:

> the provision refers only to 'biological experiments'. Its effect is not to prevent the doctors in charge of wounded and sick from trying new therapeutic methods which are justified on medical grounds and are dictated solely by a desire to improve the patient's condition. Doctors must be free to resort to the new remedies which science offers, provided always that such remedies have first been satisfactorily proved to be innocuous and that they are administered for purely therapeutic purposes.[56]

The reference to 'doctors' and, by direct implication, scientists is, as we shall see later, telling of the nature of the crime itself, as is the contention that '[t]his interpretation is in complete accordance with the corresponding provisions of

52 International Committee of the Red Cross, 'Convention (III) Relative to the Treatment of Prisoners of War, Geneva, 12 August 1949, Commentary of 1960: Article 13 – Humane Treatment of Prisoners' <https://ihl-databases.icrc.org/applic/ihl/ihl.nsf/Comment.xsp?action=openDocument&documentId=E34CAB7D3C60B986C12563CD00425C11> accessed 26 June 2019.

53 ibid.

54 ibid.

55 International Committee of the Red Cross, 'Convention (I) for the Amelioration of the Condition of the Wounded and Sick in Armed Forces in the Field, Geneva, 12 August 1949, Commentary of 1952: Article 12 – Protection and Care' <https://ihl-databases.icrc.org/applic/ihl/ihl.nsf/Comment.xsp?action=openDocument&documentId=0117642452D3955AC12563CD004207EE> accessed 26 June 2019.

56 ibid.

the three other Geneva Conventions – in particular Article 13 of the Third Convention'.[57]

The *Commentary* points out that:

> Neither the Geneva Conventions nor the Additional Protocols define the concept of 'biological experiment'. However, in its ordinary meaning, the term 'biological experiment' refers to conduct the primary purpose of which is to study the effects, at that time unknown, of a product or a situation (e.g. extreme cold or altitude) on the human body.[58]

The *Commentary* adds that 'wounded or sick or detained persons cannot validly give consent to a particular biological experiment'; although '[t]he prohibition of biological experiments should not, however, be understood as outlawing therapeutic or clinical research', neither 'does it prevent doctors in charge of wounded and sick persons from trying new therapeutic methods which are justified on medical grounds and are dictated solely by a desire to improve a patient's condition'.[59] Crucially, though, '[p]atients are entitled to freely consent to drug trials aimed at improving their health, provided they are offered in the same manner and under the same conditions as to regular citizens', and 'a biological experiment is outlawed even if it does not cause death or seriously endanger the health of the victim'.[60]

The *Commentary* also states that:

> The Geneva Conventions do not contain a definition of biological experiments. Article 12 of the First and Second Conventions prohibits 'biological experiments', whereas Article 13 of the Third Convention and Article 32 of the Fourth Convention prohibit 'medical or scientific experiments'. The common provisions enumerating grave breaches in the four Conventions list 'biological experiments'. It is understood, however, that there is considerable overlap between these concepts.[61]

57 ibid.

58 International Committee of the Red Cross, 'Convention (II) for the Amelioration of the Condition of Wounded, Sick and Shipwrecked Members of Armed Forces at Sea, Geneva, 12 August 1949, Commentary of 2017: Article 12: Protection and Care of the Wounded, Sick and Shipwrecked' <https://ihl-databases.icrc.org/applic/ihl/ihl.nsf/Comment.xsp?action=openDocument&documentId=0117642452D3955AC12563CD004207EE> accessed 26 June 2019.

59 ibid.

60 ibid.

61 International Committee of the Red Cross, 'Convention (I) for the Amelioration of the Condition of the Wounded and Sick in Armed Forces in the Field, Geneva, 12 August 1949, Commentary of 2016: Article 50: Grave Breaches' <https://ihl-databases.icrc.org/applic/ihl/ihl.nsf/Comment.xsp?action=openDocument&documentId=0117642452D3955AC12563CD004207EE> accessed 26 June 2019 ('2016 Commentary on GC I Article 50').

According to the most recent 2016 *Commentary* on GC I, '[t]he Diplomatic Conference explicitly prohibited biological experiments 'with a view to preventing a recurrence of the cruel experiments which had been made in concentration camps during the last war'.[62] The *Commentary* cites the *Medical Case* in support. That 'judgment outlined 10 basic principles to be observed while performing medical or biological experiments, in order to satisfy moral, ethical and legal principles'.[63] (Although the court solely relied on legal principles when it came to the assessment of guilt in effect discounting moral and ethical as well as, it must be said, scientific principles of which more follow.) The *Commentary* helpfully traverses the *Medical Case* and State practice,[64] which it supplemented with the

62 ibid.

63 International Committee of the Red Cross, 'Convention (III) Relative to the Treatment of Prisoners of War, Geneva, 12 August 1949, Commentary of 2020: Article 13 – Humane Treatment of Prisoners' <https://ihl-databases.icrc.org/applic/ihl/ihl.nsf/Comment.xsp?action=openDocument&documentId=3DEA78B5A19414AFC1258585004344BD> accessed 5 February 2021. These principles were:

> 1 The voluntary consent of the human subject is absolutely essential. 2. The experiment should be such as to yield fruitful results for the good of society, unprocurable by other methods or means of study, and not random and unnecessary in nature. 3. The experiment should be so designed and based on the results of animal experimentation and a knowledge of the natural history of the disease or other problem under study that the anticipated results will justify the performance of the experiment. 4. The experiment should be so conducted as to avoid all un-necessary physical and mental suffering and injury. 5. No experiment should be conducted where there is an a priori reason to believe that death or disabling injury will occur; except, perhaps, in those experiments where the experimental physicians also serve as subjects. 6. The degree of risk to be taken should never exceed that determined by the humanitarian importance of the problem to be solved by the experiment. 7. Proper preparations should be made and adequate facilities provided to protect the experimental subject against even remote possibilities of injury, disability, or death. 8. The experiment should be conducted only by scientifically qualified persons. The highest degree of skill and care should be required through all stages of the experiment of those who conduct or engage in the experiment. 9. During the course of the experiment the human subject should be at liberty to bring the experiment to an end if he has reached the physical or mental state where continuation of the experiment seems to him to be impossible. 10. During the course of the experiment the scientist in charge must be prepared to terminate the experiment at any stage, if he has probable cause to believe, in the exercise of the good faith, superior skill and careful judgment required of him that a continuation of the experiment is likely to result in injury, disability, or death to the experimental subject.

Medical Case (n 4) vol 2, 181–82. In a recent analysis of these principles, Aurey (n 29) 1054 makes two telling and related points: first, that the court moved away from delineating between true or false science and, as a consequence, avoided addressing the more or less unavoidable exploitation of an individual for the good of others in the context of clinical trials and human experimentation.

64 See especially the commentary on Rule 92: 'Rule 92 Mutilation and Medical, Scientific or Biological Experiments' in Jean-Marie Henckaerts and Louise Doswald-Beck (eds), *Customary International Humanitarian Law, Volume I: Rules* (ICRC/CUP 2005) <https://ihl-databases.icrc.org/customary-ihl/eng/docs/v1_rul_rule92> accessed 1 July 2019.

ICC Elements of Crimes and notes that '[t]he grave breach of biological experiments requires the cumulative presence of three material elements, namely:

1 The perpetrator subjected one or more protected persons to a particular biological experiment;
2 The experiment seriously endangered the physical or mental health or integrity of such persons; and
3 The experiment was neither justified by the medical, dental or hospital treatment of, nor carried out in, such person's or persons' interest'.[65]

The jurisdiction of the ICC over unlawful experiments is therefore determined by the origin of the prohibitions in IHL. This aspect is a reversal of the Nuremberg trial processes (where the origin of the offence was driven by the jurisdiction which that Tribunal could exercise). This reversal of the relationship between jurisdiction over the crime driving the origin of the crime (in Nuremberg) to the origin of the crime driving the jurisdiction of the crime (in the Rome Statute) is a key finding of the present inquiry.

4 Unlawful human experimentation at the Extraordinary Chambers in the Courts of Cambodia

On 16 November 2018, judges Nil Nonn (president), Jean-Marc Lavergne, Ya Sokhan, Claudia Fenz, and You Ottara of the Trial Chamber of the ECCC handed down their unanimous decision in *Case 002/02* against Nuon Chea and Khieu Samphan, convicting them of crimes against humanity, grave breaches of the Geneva Conventions, and genocide. This case is important for at least one compelling reason: not only was it the third-ever international criminal trial for unlawful experimentation, but it was also the second-ever conviction and so warrants careful attention, analysis, and contextualisation. In convicting the accused of murder as a crime against humanity, the judges also incorporated unlawful experimentation among the unlawful acts making up that offence as opposed to a stand-alone offence in its own right.[66] Strictly speaking, it is not among the explicit offences provided for in the strict letter of the ECCC law.[67] Additionally, although the Trial Chamber had a sufficient legal-doctrinal foundation as well as factual-evidential basis before them to convict the accused of inhumane treatment as a grave breach of the Geneva Conventions, they did not take the opportunity to do so.[68]

65 '2016 Commentary on GC I Article 50' (n 61).
66 *Case 002/02*, 'Judgement', Case No 002/19–09–2007/ECCC/TC, 16 November 2018, 1296 [2560], 1298 [2564].
67 Law on the Establishment of the Extraordinary Chambers, with Inclusion of Amendments as Promulgated on 27 October 2004 (NS/RKM/1004/006).
68 *Case 002/02* (n 66) 395 [764] – 396 [767], especially note 2310 'medical or scientific experiments not necessitated by medical treatment (see e.g., Geneva Convention (IV), Article 32)'.

Furthermore, although they had the ICCPR before them (and, indeed, referenced it liberally with regard to the right to fair trial, to life, to freedom from torture (not for criminal convictions), etc.), they, however, did not see fit to mention that unlawful experiments are explicitly included under torture in that instrument.[69]

The ECCC Trial Chamber recalled that the first international criminal law convictions for unlawful experimentation were in the *Medical Case*. Indeed, the Trial Chamber was 'satisfied that the *Medical Case* can be considered as one of several authorities for attributing criminal responsibility for intentional killing even if the perpetrator acted with less than direct intent'.[70] The Trial Chamber found that the available evidence established at least one prominent confirmed victim whose high social status led to squabbling among the perpetrators:

> With regard to medical experiments, the Chamber notes that the available evidence is scarce and does not allow a comprehensive finding on the scope of the practice, both with respect to its duration and frequency. The Chamber finds, however, that THACH Chea's wife was detained at S-21 and was subjected to an experiment to allow the medical unit to study the surgical process on a live body. She died as a result of this experiment and SON Sen blamed Duch and Nat for allowing this to happen to the wife of a famous person, saying that a normal person's wife should have been taken.[71]

This relative lack of value attributed to certain human lives, thereby ascribing those vulnerable humans as being the proper subjects of unlawful experimentation, was not unique to *Case 002/02*. Indeed, this point of vulnerable populations being an experimental target precisely because they are vulnerable and not for either the good of science or the advancement of human knowledge was not lost on the Trial Chamber's consideration of the *Medical Case*:

> The factual analysis of the [*Medical*] case shows that while the Nazi doctors had a complete disregard for the life of the individuals subjected to their brutal experiments, or even considered the death of many of them as an expected outcome, in some instances their objective was to assess if it was possible to survive extreme conditions or particularly severe disease. In such situations the intent involved taking the risk of endangering the life of those subjected to the experiments, with the knowledge that this would likely cause their death.[72]

However, in the ECCC case, the vulnerability was based on class, whereas in the *Medical Case*, the vulnerability, as we saw earlier, was on a racial basis. What is more, although the experimental victims' lack of consent was key to the finding

69 ibid., 372 [702].
70 *Case 002/02* (n 66) 346 [636].
71 ibid., 1233–1234 [2447].
72 ibid., 345 [636].

of guilt in the *Medical Case*, this did not feature explicitly with regard to unlawful experimentation in *Case 002/02*, even though the Trial Chamber looked at consent in the context of forced marriage and enslavement.[73] To be fair, it was implicit in the legal finding that it was murder as a crime against humanity:

> Due to the forced nature of the blood drawing, the fact that these deaths were recorded in S-21 documents, and the nature of the surgical medical experiment, the Chamber finds that the direct perpetrators not only intended to cause serious bodily harm to the victims but acted with the knowledge that the blood drawing and the live surgical experiment could lead to death and accepted such outcome. The fact that the perpetrators repeatedly performed blood drawing and observed the physical effects that the procedure had on the prisoners' bodies and at times their resulting deaths confirms their knowledge and acceptance of the result of their acts.[74]

In sum, it is not clear why the ECCC missed an opportunity to convict under war crimes and not just under crimes against humanity (although the court did note that '[w]ith regard to medical experiments . . . the available evidence is scarce and does not allow a comprehensive finding on the scope of the practice, both with respect to its duration and frequency'[75]) while the Rome Statute, as we saw earlier, takes the opposite view and only criminalises unlawful experiments as war crimes but not as crimes against humanity. Had the ECCC recognised that medical experiments can also amount to a grave breach of the Geneva Conventions, this would have been more consistent. Better yet, had the ECCC had the jurisdiction to convict the perpetrators of a stand-alone international crime of medical experimentation, that would have had the consequence of recognising the unique way that this offence exposes vulnerable populations to inhumane acts in the name of advancing knowledge. In any event, the decision affirmed the unlawfulness of the underlying acts that lead to death and the intent to advance knowledge which together make up unlawful experiments, the implicit lack of consent of the victims, and the inhumane nature of the acts.

5 Conclusion: a stand-alone offence in a specialised convention for unlawful experimentation remains overdue

This chapter began by considering the *Medical Case* before the Nuremberg Military Tribunals under Control Council Law No 10. The chapter then turned to the Rome Statute before proceeding to recent case law coming out of the ECCC

73 ibid., 125 [267] and 356 [664], respectively.
74 ibid., 1298 [2565].
75 ibid., 1233 [2447].

in order to outline how and how far unlawful medical, biological, and scientific experiments are describable under contemporary customary international law. This demonstrated inconsistencies of approach regarding the classification, contours, and status of unlawful medical experiments. The analysis also demonstrated the customary international criminal law definition of the offence as conforming to the outline and structure that follow:

> An unlawful human experiment is any act done or intended to be done in order to advance medical, scientific, or biological knowledge in breach of international human rights law and international humanitarian law where that experiment:
>
> a is performed on a human experimental subject without their knowledge, willingness and consent; and
> b leads to the death of, seriously endangers, or damages the physical or mental health or integrity of such human experimental subjects in ways which were reasonably foreseeable but not mitigated; and
> c is not done for the individual therapeutic benefit of that human experimental subject.
>
> This is notwithstanding any claimed benefit of the experiment to humanity as a whole as a justification for the acts perpetrated in that pursuit of experimental knowledge.

Consequent to this, it is clear that a stand-alone offence for unlawful experimentation possibly to be contained in a specialised convention remains overdue because most experiments occur without any nexus to armed conflict, yet only those with a nexus to armed conflict are unlawful under the Rome Statute. At a bare minimum, it could be considered for inclusion in the Rome Statute by the Assembly of State Parties under Article 121 (dealing with amendments to that statute, including to the crimes listed to the Rome Statute) and/or Article 123 (providing for periodical reviewing of the statute). While courts have recognised that the acts that constitute unlawful medical experimentation could be and have been classified, for instance, as murder or torture or inhumane acts and occur during as well as outside of armed conflict, this has been done in an inconsistent way, without due attention to the context of the crimes and their impact upon their subjects. Treating unlawful medical experimentation as a stand-alone offence would recognise the uniqueness of the offence and exposing vulnerable populations to inhumane acts in the name of advancing knowledge would be specifically addressed. In a world where medical experimentation is at the forefront of individuals' experience of COVID-19, it is more important than ever to reassess the future of this crime in order to protect vulnerable populations and individuals.

Futures of responsibility

8 Testing knowledge

Weapons reviews of autonomous weapons systems and the international criminal trial

Eve Massingham and Simon McKenzie

1 Introduction

A recurring theme of the debate about the development and use of autonomous weapon systems (AWS) is how to ensure accountability for their use. There is a fear that in the future, an AWS might be involved in a serious violation of international law but that no one could be held responsible for that violation. This has led many scholars to propose ways to bridge the perceived gap between the decisions of the operator of the system and targets selected by the device.[1]

The concern is partly driven by a lack of confidence that weapon users will have enough knowledge about how AWS will operate and the ways in which they might fail. These concerns often overlook the existing legal, operational, and technical requirements for weapon users to understand how weapons operate and the mechanisms in place in advanced militaries to ensure users have the necessary degree of knowledge for their level of responsibility. This chapter aims to contribute to this discussion by linking these legal, operational, and technical requirements (and challenges) with the high threshold that has been set for individual criminal responsibility for crimes triable before the International Criminal Court (ICC). It shows the importance of testing in the development and acquisition of AWS and how testing is an important way of promoting accountability for the use of AWS.

The ICC is the most widely accepted accountability mechanism for the international community to deal with international crimes. While most agree that the Rome Statute[2] does not allow for prosecution of an individual for reckless use

1 See, e.g., C Grut, 'The Challenge of Autonomous Lethal Robotics to International Humanitarian Law' (2013) 18 *Journal of Conflict & Security Law* 5; Jens David Ohlin, 'The Combatant's Stance: Autonomous Weapons on the Battlefield' (2016) 92 *International Law Studies* 1; Geoffrey S Corn, 'Autonomous Weapons Systems: Managing the Inevitability of "Taking the Man out of the Loop" ' in N Bhuta et al. (eds), *Autonomous Weapons Systems: Law, Ethics, Policy* (CUP 2016); Peter Margulies, 'Making Autonomous Weapons Accountable: Command Responsibility for Computer-Guided Lethal Force in Armed Conflicts' in Jens David Ohlin (ed), *Research Handbook on Remote Warfare* (Edward Elgar 2017).

2 Rome Statute of the International Criminal Court (adopted 17 July 1998, entered into force 1 July 2002) 2187 UNTS 90 (Rome Statute).

DOI: 10.4324/9781003087533-11

of a weapon,[3] it can hold an individual accountable when they use a weapon to intentionally commit a crime. Central to a successful prosecution on this basis would be proving that those operating or deploying a weapon had knowledge about how the weapon was going to operate. In the case of an AWS, this knowledge is likely to be generated by the mechanisms in place to ensure weapon users have a proper understanding of how their weapons work – an understanding that is both strategically and legally necessary.

The chapter proceeds in three parts. Part 2 begins with a definition of an AWS and identifies the relevant sources of international law. Part 3 outlines how the mental element of offences under the Rome Statute sets a high threshold for criminal responsibility, requiring evidence that an AWS user knew that the use of the weapon was 'virtually certain' to fail to comply with the principle of discrimination in target selection. This standard makes evidence of knowledge of the operation of the AWS critical to international criminal accountability. Part 4 discusses how those operating or deploying a weapon need to have knowledge of the capabilities of a weapon for both strategic and legal reasons and that this knowledge, obtained through information generated by extensively testing the weapon, could be used as evidence of intent in an ICC trial. The analysis provides an opportunity to reflect on the importance and limitations of the international humanitarian law (IHL) requirement to conduct a weapons review and shows how a more comprehensive weapons review will both assist with the efficient use of AWS and promote accountability for the misuse of these weapons.

2 Defining and regulating AWS

a) There are different views about what amounts to an AWS

There is no agreed definition of what capabilities a weapon system must have before it can be classified as an AWS. This often complicates discussion about these weapons systems and results in people talking at cross-purposes when discussing how they should be regulated.[4] The terminology used includes the distinctions between 'partially autonomous', 'semi-autonomous', and 'fully autonomous'. In the armed forces context, the phrases 'man-in-the-loop', 'man-on-the-loop', and 'man-out-of-the-loop' are often used to demarcate the different levels of

3 See Elies van Sliedregt, *Individual Criminal Responsibility in International Law* (OUP 2012) 49–50; Sarah Finnin, 'Mental Elements Under Article 30 of the Rome Statute of the International Criminal Court: A Comparative Analysis' (2012) 61 *International & Comparative Law Quarterly* 325; Alex Whiting, 'Recklessness, War Crimes, and the Kunduz Hospital Bombing' *Just Security* (2 May 2016) <www.justsecurity.org/30871/recklessness-war-crimes-kunduz-hospital-bombing/> accessed 28 February 2020. More will be said on this in Part 2.

4 Carrie McDougall, 'Autonomous Weapon Systems and Accountability: Putting the Cart Before the Horse' (2019) 20 *Melbourne Journal of International Law* 58, 60.

autonomy.[5] The idea of varying levels of autonomy has been used across many fields to describe and categorise autonomous systems;[6] the discussion of AWS is no exception. One of the most widely cited definitions of AWS was proposed by the International Committee of the Red Cross (ICRC), which describes an AWS as having autonomy in 'critical functions' such that it can 'select and attack targets without human intervention'.[7] The ICRC argues that AWS can be distinguished from other weapon systems for which the user chooses the timing, location, and target when it is launched or activated.[8]

Others have written extensively about where we might draw the line between AWS and other weapons systems.[9] These discussions have to take account of a wide range of weapons systems with different degrees of automation for different functions such as navigation and targeting.[10] Such weapons include air defence systems and active protection systems (for tanks and other military vehicles) with autonomous modes capable of destroying incoming projectiles such as missiles or mortar shells.[11] In addition, some loitering weapons can autonomously target objects – like radars – with an identifiable electronic signature.[12] There are many weapons that have some autonomous capability: a 2017 study by the Stockholm International Peace Research Institute into existing technology found 277 military systems that can 'govern and direct [their] own motion' without direct human control and 154 weapons systems for which some parts of the targeting process are automated.[13]

Many experts believe that future robots with artificial intelligence 'will be capable of improvising in the battlefield', coping with 'unforeseen events', and

5 See, e.g., Yoram Dinstein, 'Autonomous Weapons and International Humanitarian Law' in Wolff Heintschel von Heinegg, Robert Frau and Tassilo Singer (eds), *Dehumanization of Warfare: Legal Implications of New Weapon Technologies* (Springer 2018) 18.

6 Using levels to define different levels of automation is first credited to Thomas B Sheridan and William L Verplank, 'Human and Computer Control of Undersea Teleoperators Man-Machine Systems Laboratory' (Report, Department of Mechanical Engineering, MIT, 14 July 1978). See also Dale Richards and Alex Stedmon, 'To Delegate or Not to Delegate: A Review of Control Frameworks for Autonomous Cars' (2016) 53 *Applied Ergonomics* 383, 385–386.

7 International Committee of the Red Cross, 'International Humanitarian Law and the Challenges of Contemporary Armed Conflicts – Recommitting to Protection in Armed Conflict on the 70th Anniversary of the Geneva Conventions' (Report, November 2019) 29.

8 ibid.

9 See, e.g., Vincent Boulanin and Maaike Verbruggen, *Mapping the Development of Autonomy in Weapon Systems* (SIPRI 2017) <www.sipri.org/publications/2017/other-publications/mapping-development-autonomy-weapon-systems> accessed 20 April 2020; International Committee of the Red Cross, 'Autonomy, Artificial Intelligence and Robotics: Technical Aspects of Human Control' (August 2019) <www.icrc.org/en/download/file/102852/autonomy_artificial_intelligence_and_robotics.pdf> accessed 20 April 2020.

10 Boulanin and Verbruggen (n 9).

11 International Committee of the Red Cross, 'Autonomy, Artificial Intelligence and Robotics' (n 9).

12 ibid.

13 Boulanin and Verbruggen (n 9).

operating 'free in every respect from human intervention'.[14] This sort of hypothetical weapon system could use machine learning to adapt to its environment and use this 'knowledge' to select and engage targets without human intervention. This could make a system unpredictable to the programmer or user, a potential outcome that is one of the central concerns of those campaigning against the development and use of AWS.[15] The reality is that AWS of this nature do not yet exist. There is some debate about how long it will take to develop this capacity and whether it, in fact, will ever be possible.[16]

Not everyone accepts that autonomy means unpredictability. Schmitt contests the idea that AWS will be unpredictable in a way that is radically different from other weapons; he says that while an AWS might 'fall out of parameters', it will not take on a life of its own.[17] Indeed, as Stewart explains, 'the premise underpinning automation is that the operation of the relevant device is capable of being accurately predicted based on the programming and commands inputted'.[18] In any event, as is discussed later in this chapter, if a weapon or weapons system is known to be genuinely unpredictable, it is hard to imagine a viable military use.

There is a tendency amongst some international organisations and commentators to talk about AWS as if they were persons by, for example, focusing on whether an AWS could 'apply' the law. It is better to avoid anthropomorphising AWS: the legal framework does not allow for the 'outsourcing' of the responsibility to a machine for the use of a weapon. The focus should not be on whether these systems can 'apply' the law, but whether the AWS can be ***used by human operators*** in compliance with the law.[19]

While the use of AWS in warfighting may pose some profoundly challenging ethical and strategic questions, this chapter does not seek to intervene in that debate. Rather, it is sufficient for the purposes of our argument to adopt the view that autonomy exists on a spectrum. Weapons designed and deployed to date have had varying levels of autonomous functionality and are used by military personnel when they decide it is operationally useful; humans are ultimately responsible for what happens when they are used.

14 Robin Geiß and Henning Lahmann, 'Autonomous Weapons Systems: A Paradigm Shift for the Law of Armed Conflict?' in Ohlin (ed), *Research Handbook on Remote Warfare* (n 1) 371.

15 Dinstein (n 5) 19.

16 Charles James Dunlap, 'Accountability and Autonomous Weapons: Much Ado About Nothing?' (2016) 30 *Temple International & Comparative Law Journal* 71.

17 Michael N Schmitt, 'Autonomous Weapon Systems and International Humanitarian Law: A Reply to the Critics' (2013) 4 *Harvard National Security Journal* 1, 7.

18 Darren Stewart, 'New Technology and the Law of Armed Conflict' in Raul A Pedrozo and Daria P Wollschlaeger (eds), *International Law and the Changing Character of War* (Naval War College Press 2011) 289–290.

19 For a succinct explanation of this point, see Estonia and Finland, 'Categorizing Lethal Autonomous Weapons Systems: A Technical and Legal Perspective to Understanding LAWS' (24 August 2018) UN Doc CCW/GGE2/2018/WP2, para 12.

b) AWS are not specifically prohibited by international law

There is no current legal framework that specifically regulates the use of AWS, but there are some suggestions that one might be developed. Since around 2007, a group of advocates, today led by Human Rights Watch and the Campaign to Stop Killer Robots, has been arguing that AWS should be banned.[20] In 2013, the Special Rapporteur on extrajudicial, summary, or arbitrary executions, Christof Heyns, in discussing 'weapons systems that, once activated, can select and engage targets without further human intervention', recommended that states:

> declare and implement national moratoria on at least the testing, production, assembly, transfer, acquisition, deployment and use of [them] until such time as an internationally agreed upon framework on the future of [these weapons systems] has been established.[21]

Since 2014, discussions on potential regulation of AWS have been taking place in the United Nations framework with groups of experts on lethal autonomous weapons.[22] In 2016, the Fifth Review Conference of the *Convention on the Prohibitions or Restriction on the Use of Certain Conventional Weapons Which May Be Deemed to Be Excessively Injurious or to Have Indiscriminate Effects* (CCW) led to the establishment of the Group of Government Experts on Emerging Technologies in the Area of Lethal Autonomous Weapons Systems (known as the GGE).[23] One of the guiding principles that has been repeatedly endorsed by the GGE is:

> The CCW offers an appropriate framework for dealing with the issue of emerging technologies in the area of lethal autonomous weapons systems within the context of the objectives and purposes of the Convention, which seeks to strike a balance between military necessity and humanitarian considerations.[24]

20 Campaign to Stop Killer Robots, 'All Action and Achievements' <www.stopkillerrobots.org/action-and-achievements/> accessed 20 April 2020.

21 Christof Heyns, 'Report of the Special Rapporteur on Extrajudicial, Summary or Arbitrary Executions' (9 April 2013) UN Doc A/HRC/23/47, para 113.

22 United Nations, 'Background on Lethal Autonomous Weapons Systems in the CCW' <www.unog.ch/80256EE600585943/(httpPages)/8FA3C2562A60FF81C1257CE600393DF6?OpenDocument> accessed 20 April 2020.

23 The GGE met in 2017, 2018, and 2019. 'Report of the 2019 Session of the Group of Governmental Experts on Emerging Technologies in the Area of Lethal Autonomous Weapons Systems' (25 September 2019) UN Doc CCW/GGE.1/2019/3 (2019 GGE Report).

24 Guiding Principle (k) was most recently endorsed in 2019 GGE Report (n 23).

Notwithstanding these efforts, although some doubt whether the CCW is the best forum to discuss these issues and instead call for action outside the CCW mechanism.[25]

The lack of specific regulation of the use of AWS means that their use will usually be governed by the general rules and principles of IHL and international criminal law (ICL).[26] It is not a breach of IHL as such, much less a war crime, to deploy a weapon system with some autonomous functions; the lawfulness of the use of an AWS (indeed, any weapon system) depends on the features of the system, its technical capabilities, and its use. IHL prohibits the use of a weapon that is inherently indiscriminate, causes unnecessary suffering, or causes widespread, long-term, and severe damage to the natural environment.[27] It is also prohibited to use any weapon in a way that causes excessive damage to protected persons and objects that is not justified by military necessity.[28] These principles apply to all types of weapons – including AWS – and to all targeting decisions and will apply to any new technological development. As Eric Talbot Jensen explains, 'to the extent that weapon systems use technological advances, such as machine learning or artificial intelligence, to select and engage targets', the systems must be capable of being deployed in full compliance with IHL, 'including minimizing civilian deaths and injury and damage to civilian objects'.[29]

It is a reality of armed conflict that weapons will not always work as intended.[30] This does not necessarily mean someone should be held criminally responsible. As Timothy McFarland explains, the unintended consequences following the use of a weapon have never been the basis for criminal responsibility under IHL, provided reasonable steps have been taken to avoid such unintended results.[31] There is, however, a clear argument that deploying a weapon known to be unpredictable could be a breach of IHL (even if, as discussed later in this chapter, it may not amount to an international crime).[32] This is because if a weapon (an AWS or otherwise) is entirely unpredictable, then it is very hard to see how it could be

25 Michael T Klare, 'Autonomous Weapons Systems and the Law of War' (*Arms Control Association*, March 2019) <www.armscontrol.org/act/2019-03/features/autonomous-weapons-systems-laws-war> accessed 20 April 2020.

26 Note that it is also possible for an AWS to be designed to operate a weapon system subject to a specific arms control treaty to which a deploying state might be party.

27 Protocol Additional to the Geneva Conventions of 12 August 1949, and Relating to the Protection of Victims of International Armed Conflicts (Protocol I) (opened for signature 8 June 1977, entered into force 7 December 1978) 1125 UNTS 3, arts 35, 51(4)(b) and (c) (Additional Protocol I); Jean-Marie Henckaerts and Louise Doswald-Beck, *Customary International Humanitarian Law* (vol 1, CUP 2015), rules 45, 70, 71.

28 Additional Protocol I, art 51.

29 Eric Talbot Jensen, 'The (Erroneous) Requirement for Human Judgment (and Error) in the Law of Armed Conflict' (2020) 96 *International Law Studies* 26, 28–29.

30 Timothy McFarland, 'The Status of Autonomous Weapon Systems Under International Humanitarian Law' (PhD thesis, University of Melbourne 2017) 195.

31 Dunlap (n 16) 71.

32 ibid.

used in compliance with the principles of distinction and proportionality. Neil Davison argues that lawful use of an AWS would require the weapon user to have a very high level of confidence that, once activated, it would predictably and reliably operate as intended.[33] Similarly, McFarland explains that 'an attack planner must be sufficiently certain about the targets which an AWS is likely to engage to be confident that the chosen AWS is a better choice (in legal terms) than another means or method of attack'.[34] He adds that using a weapon system 'when it is not possible to take sufficient precautions to ensure that only legal targets are struck is an illegal act in itself, in violation of the principle of distinction'.[35] This is not limited to the moment when the weapon is deployed: if a weapon user became aware an AWS was unpredictable after it was deployed, they would have to cease its operation.

3 The problem of intent in international criminal trials for the use of an AWS

The use of an AWS is not in itself a crime under the Rome Statute. The Rome Statute has only a few specific crimes for deploying a particular kind of weapon, all of which are based on pre-existing prohibitions. For example, it is a war crime to use poison or poisoned weapons in armed conflict[36] or to use expanding bullets.[37] The Rome Statute also criminalises using weapons that 'cause superfluous injury or unnecessary suffering or which are inherently indiscriminate' but only when they are subject to a comprehensive prohibition and included in an annex to the Statute.[38] States have not managed to agree on the annex, which means that Article 8(2)(b)(xx) is inoperative.

Like any weapons systems, an AWS could be used by a person to commit many of the war crimes covered by the Rome Statute. A person could also use an AWS to carry out genocide, a crime against humanity, or the crime of aggression,[39] each of which has different mental and physical elements. The appropriate crime will depend on the conduct, the circumstances, and how it fits in with any broader policies of the state or armed group. A few examples illustrate this point. The crime of intentionally directing an attack against civilians[40] requires the perpetrator to direct an attack against civilians while *intending* to make civilians the object of the attack. The crime of intentionally directing attacks against buildings 'dedicated to religion, education, art, science, or charitable purposes, historic

33 Neil Davison, 'A Legal Perspective: Autonomous Weapon Systems Under International Humanitarian Law' (UNODA Occasional Papers No 30, November 2017) 10.
34 McFarland (n 30) 195.
35 ibid.
36 Rome Statute, arts 8(2)(b)(xvii) and 8 (2)(e)(xiii).
37 ibid., arts 8(2)(b)(xix) and 8 (2)(e)(xv).
38 ibid., art 8(2)(b)(xx).
39 McDougall (n 4) 65.
40 Rome Statute, art 8(2)(b)(i).

monuments, hospitals and places where the sick and wounded are collected'[41] requires the perpetrator to *intend* to target a building falling into one of those categories. Murder as a crime against humanity[42] requires the killing occur *intentionally* and as 'part of a widespread or systemic attack directed against any civilian population'. In all these cases (and in the case of many other crimes) it is the mental element – the intention of the perpetrator – that may be particularly difficult to prove in the case of AWS use due to a lack of clarity about whether the potential perpetrator understands the operation of the weapon.

Importantly, the crime will not be committed by the AWS itself; as a machine, it is not an appropriate subject for criminal law and cannot be held responsible for its actions.[43] The decision of whether to deploy an AWS will be made by a human (even if this decision occurs with some distance in space and time). Given this, the most obvious person (or people) will be the commander and operators who triggered the operation of the AWS. In addition, in some situations, the developer of the weapon may be liable.[44] These people are (potentially) responsible for what happens when the system is used, and it is their conduct, intent, and knowledge that will determine whether a crime has been committed. Of course, individual criminal responsibility is only one form of liability, and different types of legal accountability in both international and domestic law (including those discussed by Natalie Nunn in this volume) have different rules for the attribution of responsibility.

a) *The requisite mental element for criminal responsibility under the Rome Statute is strict*

Article 30 of the Rome Statute establishes the principles for the mental element in the Statute and sets a particularly high knowledge and intent threshold for criminal responsibility. Article 30 is a difficult provision to apply and has been widely recognised to be a challenging mix of common law and civil law concepts.[45] Article 30 allows for two gradations of intent: direct intent (*dolus directus* in the first degree) or oblique intent (*dolus directus* in the second degree.)[46]

It is useful to briefly set out the precise words of this provision. Paragraph 2(a) of Article 30 provides that a person has intent in relation to conduct if they 'mean to' engage in the conduct, and paragraph 2(b) provides that a person has

41 ibid., art 8(2)(b)(ix).
42 ibid., art 7(1)(a).
43 Marco Sassòli, 'Autonomous Weapons and International Humanitarian Law: Advantages, Open Technical Questions and Legal Issues to Be Clarified' (2014) 90 *International Law Studies* 308, 313–14; McDougall (n 4) 61.
44 Tim McFarland and Tim McCormack, 'Mind the Gap: Can Developers of Autonomous Weapons Systems Be Liable for War Crimes?' (2014) 90 *International Law Studies* 361. See also Nunn in this volume.
45 Finnin (n 3); McDougall (n 4) 66.
46 McDougall (n 4) 66.

intent in relation to a consequence if they 'mean to cause that consequence or is aware it will occur in the ordinary course of events'.[47] Paragraph 3 of the same article provides that knowledge means 'awareness that a circumstance exists or a consequence will occur in the ordinary course of events'.[48] The ICC Trial Chamber has held that awareness that something will occur in the 'ordinary course of events' requires knowledge that the outcome is a 'virtual certainty'.[49] The Rome Statute does not require the perpetrator to physically carry out the crime; they may act through other people or through the bureaucratic machine of the state or the armed forces.[50] This means that in order to be held criminally responsible under the Rome Statute, the prosecution must prove the accused either deliberately engaged in the conduct and intended that the prohibited consequence occur (direct intent), or they engaged in the conduct knowing that the consequence was 'virtually certain' to occur but were ambivalent about whether it did (oblique intent).[51]

Other forms of individual criminal liability are not covered by this provision. Many scholars have concluded that Article 30 does not generally provide for individual criminal responsibility for recklessness[52] (often compared to *dolus eventualis*, despite there being some differences between the concepts[53]). Liability on the basis of recklessness is less strict than direct or oblique intent; it applies when a person engages in conduct knowing the consequence is foreseeable but not necessarily that it is 'virtually certain'.[54] The view that Article 30 does not include recklessness is supported by the drafting history of Article 30. While this form of liability was included in earlier drafts of the Rome Statute, it was removed from the final version.[55] In these circumstances, it would be inappropriate to read it into Article 30. It should be accepted that the Rome Statute does not generally provide for criminal liability for recklessness.[56]

47 Rome Statute, art 30.
48 ibid.
49 'Judgment Pursuant to Article 74 of the Statute' *Prosecutor v Katanga*, ICC-01/04–01/07, Trial Chamber II, 7 March 2014, [776] (*Katanga Judgment*).
50 Ohlin, 'The Combatant's Stance' (n 1) 6–11.
51 See Finnin (n 3) 328.
52 ibid., 346–348 for a good overview of the different positions taken on recklessness in the Rome Statute. See also Whiting (n 3); William Schabas, *The International Criminal Court: A Commentary on the Rome Statute* (2nd edn, OUP 2016) 630; Ohlin, 'The Combatant's Stance' (n 1) 21–29.
53 Finnin (n 3) 330.
54 See *Katanga Judgment* (n 49) [776].
55 'Decision on the Confirmation of Charges' *Prosecutor v Lubanga*, ICC-01/04–01/06, Pre-Trial Chamber I, 29 January 2007, 121 [355] n 438; 'Decision Pursuant to Article 61(7)(a) and (b) of the Rome Statute on the Charges of the Prosecutor' *Prosecutor v Bemba Gombo*, ICC-01/05–01/08, Pre-Trial Chamber II, 15 June 2009, [360].
56 There are exceptions to this general rule and a small number of crimes that have a lower mental element not relevant in the AWS context, such as conscripting or enlisting children: McDougall (n 4) 67.

b) Proving the requisite mental element when dealing with a crime involving the use of an AWS will be difficult

That there is no international criminal liability for recklessness has important consequences for the potential liability of the use of an AWS. It will make it very difficult to prosecute an individual for an AWS that has 'gone rogue' or where a machine has engaged in self-learning and rewritten its code to override, for example, a prohibition on targeting civilians.[57] For many scholars, this potential lack of individual criminal responsibility is an unacceptable outcome, and different proposals have been made to address this gap,[58] including modifying the doctrine of command responsibility to include responsibility for AWS[59] or arguing that the developers and programmers should be the focus of attention.[60] Some propose lowering the mental element in situations where an AWS is used recklessly or negligently (or lowering the mental element required for international crimes more generally), a move justified by the high risk and potential unpredictability of the use of these systems.[61] Others contest this view, drawing the analogy with other weapons systems to argue that finding there is no criminal liability for an AWS behaving in an unexpected way is not necessarily a problematic conclusion.[62] Some argue that the lack of accountability means AWS should be banned altogether.[63]

But assuming they are not banned, the central challenge that scholars have identified is that the autonomous nature of the weapon means the operator might not be 'virtually certain' of the factual circumstances establishing the victims as protected or that an AWS was going to target them. The crucial difficulty is, as Stewart explains, that

> [n]either the programming nor the command data inputted to [the AWS] prior to their deployment on a particular operation will necessarily result in a specific outcome in response to any given set of circumstances.[64]

57 ibid., 74.
58 See ibid., 76–82, for more detail.
59 Stewart (n 18) 292; Thilo Marauhn, 'An Analysis of the Potential Impact of Lethal Autonomous Weapons Systems on Responsibility and Accountability for Violations of International Law' (CCW Expert Meeting on Lethal Autonomous Weapons Presentation, Geneva, 13–14 May 2014) <www.reachingcriticalwill.org/images/documents/Disarmament-fora/ccw/2014/statements/15May_Marauhn.pdf> accessed 24 September 2021; Margulies (n 1).
60 McFarland and McCormack (n 44).
61 Ohlin, 'The Combatant's Stance' (n 1) 21–29.
62 Dunlap (n 16) 71; Ian S Henderson, Patrick Keane, and Josh Liddy, 'Remote and Autonomous Warfare Systems: Precautions in Attack and Individual Accountability' in Ohlin (ed), *Research Handbook on Remote Warfare* (n 1) 361, 363, 369.
63 See, e.g., Bonnie Lynn Docherty, 'Mind the Gap: The Lack of Accountability for Killer Robots' (Human Rights Watch, Report 2015) <www.hrw.org/report/2015/04/09/mind-gap/lack-accountability-killer-robots> accessed 28 February 2020. However, note McDougall's persuasive critique of this position: McDougall (n 4) 85.
64 Stewart (n 18) 290.

As it stands, the drafters of the Rome Statute made a policy decision to limit criminal accountability to situations when a person directly or obliquely intended the unlawful outcome.[65] This limitation does not mean that anything goes when it comes to AWS. There are several scenarios in which it would be possible to hold a person criminally responsible for a crime perpetrated through an AWS.[66] For example, the requisite mental elements for intent and knowledge for the crime of intentionally targeting civilians are likely to be satisfied where civilians are attacked because:

- The operator deliberately provided the system with unlawful targeting parameters for the purpose of attacking civilians.[67]
- The operator knew that the AWS was unable to properly distinguish civilians from combatants and was not authorised to be deployed where there were civilians but nevertheless deployed the weapon to an area with a large number of civilians.[68]
- The operator became aware there was an error in the programming of the AWS that caused it to target indiscriminately and continued to use the weapon.[69]
- The developer deliberately programmed the AWS to target civilians (either in cooperation with the operator or by acting through the innocent operator responsible for deploying the weapon).[70]

To convict someone of an international crime under the Rome Statute, the prosecution will have to adduce evidence that goes to what the perpetrator knew about the operation of the weapon to show that the high mental element threshold has been met.

4 AWS users will know something about how they work

In order to effectively command, military leaders must know certain things about their forces.[71] Some of the most important pieces of information relate to the effects of the means and methods of warfare at their disposal. Deciding on a particular means or method of attack requires a commander to take into account a range of factors including, for example, selecting a weapon that will limit damage to essential infrastructure that would be required post-conflict.[72] Military personnel will not

65 Not all scholars agree that the decision to delete recklessness from the Statute is determinative of the policy rationale. See Finnin (n 3) 344–345.
66 McDougall (n 4) 68–70.
67 ibid., 69.
68 ibid.
69 ibid.
70 ibid.
71 Martin van Creveld, *Command in War* (Harvard University Press 1985) 7.
72 ibid., 316.

use weapons without knowing the potential implications of the use of the weapon, both for their achievement of their military goal and for the protection of their troops. This includes, for example, whether the weapon could be subsequently turned against them. The more complex the weapon system and the wider the range of outcomes that could occur from its use, the more information a commander will require in order to be satisfied that the use of the weapon is appropriate. Understanding how an AWS will operate is, therefore, an operational necessity.

In addition, this knowledge will be essential for commanders to have the capacity to comply with IHL. For example, the commander has a duty under customary IHL to take 'all feasible precautions, in the choice of means and methods of attack, to minimise collateral damage'.[73] Commanders have an obligation under IHL to take all necessary and reasonable measures to prevent war crimes, which, as Charles James Dunlap observes, 'implicitly requires a reasonable understanding of the foreseeable consequences'.[74] This will not be possible without an understanding of the capabilities and limitations of the AWS.

Indeed, advanced militaries operate on the basis that different types of weapons are available to commanders at different levels, each of which has 'corresponding obligations within the confines of the area of their competence'.[75] If a commander needs greater firepower, they request this support from a higher level of command.[76] For example, a platoon commander calls in support from a company commander and a company commander from a battalion commander. The system is predicated on appropriate training at each level so as to ensure they understand the capabilities of the weapons they are authorised to use. Weapon users need to know technical details, including the blast and fragmentation range and accuracy of the weapons, in order to deploy them in accordance with IHL.

This approach is reflected in the command structure of the partially autonomous systems currently in use, such the AEGIS missile defence system used on warships. AEGIS connects the ship's radar with its defensive weapons systems and provides a central control interface for operators.[77] AEGIS can function with different levels of automation from a high degree of human control over tracking

73 Henckaerts and Doswald-Beck (n 27) vol 1, rule 15. See, e.g., Australian Defence Force, 'ADDP 06.4 Law of Armed Conflict' (11 May 2006) [5.61] <www.onlinelibrary.iihl.org/wp-content/uploads/2021/05/AUS-Manual-Law-of-Armed-Conflict.pdf> accessed 24 September 2021.

74 Dunlap (n 16) 70–71.

75 Jean Pictet et al., *Commentary on the Additional Protocols of 8 June 1977 to the Geneva Conventions of 12 August 1949* (ICRC 1987) [3558].

76 See, e.g., Irish Defence Forces, 'Army Weapons' <www.military.ie/en/who-we-are/army/weapons/> accessed 20 April 2020.

77 See US Navy, 'Fact File: AEGIS Weapon System' <www.navy.mil/Resources/Fact-Files/Display-FactFiles/Article/2166739/aegis-weapon-system/ > (20 September 2021) accessed 24 September 2021. For a concise overview of how the AEGIS system operates, see Paul Scharre, *Army of None: Autonomous Weapons and the Future of War* (WW Norton & Company 2018) 162.

objects and deploying defensive systems to automatically firing against threats that meet pre-set criteria.[78] The AEGIS system is highly customisable for different situations, and, in the US, naval commanders adjust the settings of the system by selecting the appropriate mix of pre-developed programs (referred to in the US Navy as 'doctrine') for the operating environment.[79] The officers and senior enlisted personnel responsible for the ship's AEGIS system develop different doctrines, taking account of the mission goals and any relevant intelligence.[80] This group makes recommendations to the ship's captain about the doctrine for final approval.[81] Designing and operating the doctrine for this system of 'staggering complexity'[82] can only be done by individuals with appropriate expertise. The US Navy's approach to managing the AEGIS system suggests that if states use complex AWS, they are likely put in place thorough training and deployment processes to guard against error. After all, without such precautions, the use of the system risks harming one's own forces and leading to other outcomes that do not accord with the military strategy.

a) The weapons review process generates information about the weapon system to examine its compliance with IHL

One way that advanced militaries gather the necessary information about the operation of new weapons to inform commanders and their subordinates is through conducting weapons reviews. An effective review involves 'understanding the weapon's capabilities and foreseeing its effects, notably through verification and testing'.[83] This testing includes assessing the operation of the weapon in environments where it is expected to be used.

A weapons review satisfies the legal requirement that new methods and means of warfare (including new weapons) be checked prior to deployment to ensure they can be used in compliance with IHL. Additional Protocol I (API) adopts a principled approach to ensure that weapons of a nature to cause unlawful consequences are prohibited even where there is no weapon-specific prohibition in place.[84] The weapons review obligation requires states to determine that a weapon is capable of being used lawfully in armed conflict. Article 36 of API provides:

> In the study, development, acquisition or adoption of a new weapon, means or method of warfare, a High Contracting Party is under an obligation to determine whether its employment would, in some or all circumstances, be

78 ibid., 163–164.
79 ibid., 163–165.
80 ibid., 164.
81 ibid.
82 ibid., 163.
83 Davison (n 33) 10.
84 Additional Protocol I, arts 35 and 36.

> prohibited by this Protocol or by any other rule of international law applicable to the High Contracting Party.[85]

This obligation is not onerous: it does not prescribe a particular process for carrying out the review, and there is no agreed format for their conduct.[86] This makes it difficult to ascertain whether states are engaging in a meaningful review process of their weapon systems. States do not need to make the results of these reviews public, and the decisions of states are not binding on other states.[87] As the 2019 report of the GGE observed, 'States are free to independently determine the means to conduct legal reviews although the voluntary exchange of best practices could be beneficial, bearing in mind national security considerations or commercial restrictions on proprietary information'.[88]

The reality is that few states, whether party to API or not, actually have a formal process that reflects any possible interpretation of Article 36.[89] However, even states not party to API have a customary international law obligation not to use weapons that will inherently violate IHL and not to use weapons in violation of IHL. This results in their having to undergo a process of understanding the capabilities of their weapons and testing to ensure that the weapon, when used appropriately, does not violate IHL. The standard it sets is still a pragmatic one: the commentary to API explains that a state 'is not required to foresee or analyse all possible misuses of a weapon, for almost any weapon can be misused in ways that would be prohibited'.[90] The obligation concerns the normal use of the weapon and not any possible misuse.[91]

85 ibid., art 36.

86 For a suggested approach to reviews, see William H Boothby, *Weapons and the Law of Armed Conflict* (2nd ed, OUP 2016) ch 19. Boothby's approach adds a couple of additional considerations – although these go to practical considerations rather than lawful ones – such as future legal developments: at 346. Daoust, Copeland, and Ishoey provide some guidance on the process for conducting a review, noting that the provision 'implies, as a first step in the review, an examination of the specific prohibitions found under international law to which the reviewing State is a party and which bans or restricts the use of a weapon or method of warfare': Isabelle Daoust, Robin Copeland, and Rikke Ishoey, 'New Wars, New Weapons? The Obligation of States to Assess the Legality of Means and Methods of Warfare' (2002) 846 *International Review of the Red Cross* 345, 349. See also Michael W Meier, 'Lethal Autonomous Weapons Systems (LAWS): Conducting a Comprehensive Weapons Review' (2016) 30 *Temple International & Comparative Law Journal* 14; Justin McClelland, 'The Review of Weapons in Accordance with Article 36 of Additional Protocol I' (2003) 85 *International Review of the Red Cross* 397.

87 See Pictet et al. (n 75) [1469].

88 2019 GGE Report (n 23) 4.

89 International Committee of the Red Cross, *A Guide to the Legal Review of New Weapons, Means and Methods of Warfare* (ICRC 2006) 5. See also Boothby (n 86) 341; Jensen (n 29) 49–53. For a list of the approach some states take to weapons reviews, see PREMPT, 'Legal Review of Weapons' (4 August 2019) <www.premt.net/resources/legal-review/> accessed 9 June 2020.

90 Pictet and others (n 75) [1469].

91 ibid., [1469] and [1480]; Duncan Blake and Joseph Imburgia, '"Bloodless Weapons"? The Need to Conduct Legal Reviews of Certain Capabilities and the Implications of Defining Them as "Weapons"' (2010) 66 *Air Force Law Review* 157, 168; Boothby (n 86).

b) States have recognised that AWS testing will be more complicated and require a different approach

There is no agreed standard for testing an AWS, but there is widespread acceptance that it will pose real difficulty. The US Defense Science Board acknowledged in 2016 that 'current testing methods and processes are inadequate for testing software that learns and adapts' because it 'exhibits different behaviour as it incorporates more data'.[92] Michael Meier notes that the 'complexity' and unpredictability of these systems has led to concern by delegates at the GGE that the increased risk of IHL non-compliance shows the need for 'rigorous' review.[93]

AWS that are able to change their operation in response to their environment will be the most difficult to review. The possibility that a weapon can change itself means that testing will invariably be more complex. Justin McClelland, in reference to the evolution of weapons technology, observes 'up-to-date reports on the testing of the weapon in its final configuration will be essential to demonstrate that the predicted performance is matched by the results of the tests'.[94] When changes to a weapon are made, the weapon may need to be reassessed to determine if the changes have impacted the ability of the weapon to comply with IHL.[95] The challenge this would pose for continued compliance with the weapons review obligation was recognised during the GGE process, during which states questioned 'whether a self-learning system would need to be reviewed every time it changed itself'.[96]

It is unclear what level of change to the weapon necessitates reassessment. The ICRC speaks of modifications that 'alter its function'.[97] James Farrant and Christopher Ford note other phrasing includes 'changes its combat function' (citing William Boothby) and 'significant changes' (using the Tallinn Manual language). They observe that there is some support in state practice for 'the idea that "significant" or "material" changes to a weapon triggers a legal requirement for a new review'.[98] They conclude that the appropriate test is to consider whether (1) the changes cause the weapon to operate in a manner not contemplated by the first weapon review, and (2) the changes potentially affect the ability to use the weapon in compliance with applicable legal standards.[99] An added complication

92 US Defense Science Board, 'Defense Science Board Summer Study on Autonomy' (*US Department of Defense*, June 2016) 30 <https://fas.org/irp/agency/dod/dsb/autonomy-ss.pdf> accessed 24 January 2020.

93 Meier (n 86) 122.

94 McClelland (n 86) 411.

95 See further ibid., 404.

96 'Report of the 2018 Session of the Group of Governmental Experts on Emerging Technologies in the Area of Lethal Autonomous Weapons Systems' (28 October 2018) UN Doc CCW/GGE.1/2018/3, [32] (2018 GGE Report).

97 International Committee of the Red Cross, *A Guide to the Legal Review of New Weapons, Means and Methods of Warfare* (ICRC 2006) 10; James Farrant and Christopher M Ford, 'Autonomous Weapons and Weapon Reviews: The UK Second International Weapon Review Forum' (2017) 93 *International Law Studies* 35, 405.

98 Farrant and Ford (n 97) 405.

99 ibid., 406.

is that, in contrast to modifications made to conventional weapons, the operators might not always be aware when a self-learning AWS makes changes to itself.

Two further problems that arise in relation to AWS (but are also relevant to some other weapon systems) are the technical difficulty and cost of carrying out the necessary testing. States cannot just rely on the claims of the weapon manufacturer or developer, nor can they rely on the claims of other states or private entities that sell them the weapons. However, as Stewart noted in relation to the testing of un-crewed vehicles, the nature of AWS technology 'will mean that not all States will even have the capacity to conduct adequate testing were they to acquire the technology'.[100] Although more economical computer and simulated testing may be possible to some extent, the cost of carrying out appropriate testing may be beyond the reach of some states.[101]

Some proposals for AWS testing standards do exist. Australia submitted a statement on its System of Control and Applications for Autonomous Weapon Systems to the 2019 GGE.[102] This statement, in which Australia argues for a 'system of control' applicable to all weapons, including those with 'limited and with near-fully autonomous functionalities', speaks to '[c]omprehensive testing and evaluation . . . on designs and concepts during the design and development stage'.[103] Specifically, the evaluation of AWS would include 'software verification, performance reliability testing, compliance with commands, and operational permissions and limitations' and would be carried out on 'both the system as a whole, as well as its subsystems'.[104]

Similarly, the United States Department of Defense has published a specific directive for the development and use of autonomous weapons. The directive notes that '[s]ystems will go through rigorous hardware and software verification and validation . . . and realistic system developmental and operational test and evaluation'.[105] This process will include testing after initial test and evaluation to catch any 'degraded' features, 'regression' testing (that is, ensuring that the systems functions are still as expected following any changes or updates) to 'identify any new operating states and changes', as well as 'integrated' testing to 'characterize the system behavior'.[106] In 2016, the United States Defense Science Board recommended 'creating new test and evaluation and modeling and simulation paradigms',[107] as well as 'regression testing of system software'.[108]

100 Stewart (n 18) 284.
101 McClelland (n 86) 412.
102 Australia, 'Australia's System of Control and Applications for Autonomous Weapon Systems' (26 March 2019) UN Doc CCW/GGE.1/2019/WP.2/Rev.1.
103 ibid., 3, 13.
104 ibid., 14.
105 US Department of Defense, 'Directive 3000.09 21' (21 November 2012) 4(a)(1) <www.esd.whs.mil/Portals/54/Documents/DD/issuances/dodd/300009p.pdf> accessed 20 April 2020.
106 ibid., enclosure 2.
107 US Defense Science Board (n 92) 29–32.
108 ibid., 21.

Commentators have also made some observations about the AWS review process. Farrant and Ford propose that:

> [A] forward-looking review of what the machine might learn and in what circumstances could be supplemented by a program of re-reviews, tailored to the system, which might be periodic (time-based) or substantive (after each operational or exercise use) as discussed between the system engineers, the user community and the legal reviewer.[109]

Vincent Boulanin observes the importance of starting the process as early as possible, making the process as multidisciplinary as possible, and providing the legal personnel doing the review with technical training. He argues that interaction between 'lawyers, systems developers, technical experts and end-users' during the review will help everyone involved better understand the testing and evaluation procedures and how the results should be interpreted.[110] He adds that:

> [w]hen automation supports the targeting process, it is essential to assess technical and operational performance of the systems, and define restrictions on their use accordingly. These restrictions could relate to the context of deployment (time frame of the action of the weapon and environment in which it is being used) and the types of targets (materiel or personnel).[111]

Jensen expresses confidence that 'a thorough and well-designed weapons review' will 'force' states to make sure that the development or employment of AWS will comply with IHL.[112] He says that while states would be required to design the review process recognising 'the unique aspects of the weapons that use machine learning or artificial intelligence', a new kind of weapons review is not necessary:

> Rather, the standard of a weapon review remains constant, but the rigor of the testing, evaluation, and analysis might have to increase to ensure the weapon system meets the generally accepted requirements of a weapon review.[113]

For Jensen, such a review will 'satisfy the concerns not only of predictability' but also ensure that 'whatever the means of human control', the AWS can comply with IHL.[114] His conviction is that 'the current concerns and claims of inferred illegality should dissolve in the face of a thorough and rigorous weapon

109 Farrant and Ford (n 97) 407.
110 Vincent Boulanin, 'Implementing Article 36 Weapon Reviews in the Light of Increasing Autonomy in Weapon Systems' [2015] (1) *SIPRI Insights on Peace and Security* 16–17.
111 ibid., 17.
112 Jensen (n 29) 52.
113 ibid.
114 ibid.

review'.[115] This is probably too optimistic: Jensen's view is premised on the fact that states will be carrying out weapons reviews that go beyond what is required by Article 36.

The adoption of new standards, methods, and protocols for testing and validation has been identified as an issue of importance to states in the GGE process.[116] Meier correctly asserts that '[a]n outcome document that sets forth what is necessary in a comprehensive weapons review would have a tangible and beneficial impact on the development of new weapons'.[117] Such an approach would provide clarity regarding the testing of AWS. While the GGE process seems to be continuing the discussion in this direction, given the reluctance to date of states to conduct Article 36 processes and, when they do, to share the results of those processes, it seems unlikely that any agreement will be binding.

c) Information about the operation of an AWS would be relevant to an international criminal trial related to its use

In order to make a decision to deploy an AWS lawfully and strategically, it will be necessary for the weapon user to have confidence that it can comply with IHL and is useful for achieving a military goal. Given this, and despite the limitations of the weapons review process, there is some information that we can say with more confidence will be generated by the review of a weapon. The ICRC[118] and others, including Boothby,[119] have articulated a long list of information that should be collected by weapons reviews. As discussed earlier, this information is necessary for determining both the legal uses of the weapon and the uses that will be strategically productive. The kind of information that we could be expected from a review of a conventional weapon includes, for example:

- the range of the weapon;
- the effect of a weapon (penetration, blast, fragmentation, and/or incendiary effect);
- the destruction radius of the weapon's munition(s);
- the failure rate of the weapon's munition(s);
- medical reports on the types of injuries caused by the weapon;

115 ibid.
116 2018 GGE Report (n 96) [9].
117 Meier (n 86) 132.
118 International Committee of the Red Cross, *A Guide to the Legal Review of New Weapons, Means and Methods of Warfare* (n 89) s 1.3.
119 Boothby (n 86) 19.5.5. See further Eve Massingham, 'The Obligation to Respect and to Ensure Respect in All Circumstances Pursuant to Common Article 1 of the Four Geneva Conventions of August 1949 and Additional Protocols I and III: An Australian Weapons Law Perspective' (PhD thesis, University of Queensland 2016) 73–80.

- casualty reports on the number of people who could be impacted by the weapon; and
- whether information contained in the manufacturer's documentation about the weapon is borne out by the tests.

In addition, depending on the level of autonomy, the review of an AWS would also need to include information about:

- the data used to program or teach the system (for example, if the system is programmed to attack only enemy tanks and all enemy tanks are one of three shapes, the imagery of these three shapes);
- the predictability of the AWS – i.e., data that shows how many times it correctly selected a military target;
- any safety or anti-tamper mechanisms that are a part of the weapon;[120] and
- evidence (if any) of self-learning and how a user might ascertain whether any changes to the weapon have taken place.

Of course, not everyone deploying a weapon will have full access to this information. It is very unlikely that commanders and weapons operators will read the actual weapons review document, and there will be security considerations that necessitate limiting the availability of some of the information. Instead, commanders and operators will be given necessary and relevant information about the capabilities of the weaponry in their arsenal through doctrine, training, and manuals. The level of detail about the operation of an AWS that should be made available to different levels of the military hierarchy will depend on the nature of the weapon system, the level of risk, and the weapon's intended use.

The production and dissemination of this information will be key to promoting accountability for the use of AWS. The way this information is distributed throughout the armed forces is likely to be documented and, should the need arise, be available to investigators. In the event that there is an investigation or prosecution relating to the operation of an AWS, this information, as well as the underlying documentation of the review, would theoretically be accessible (noting, of course, the challenges that any investigation into government wrongdoing faces). This will allow for the identification of the information available to the commander or weapon user about the AWS, information that will be crucial to ascertaining their level of knowledge about the operation of the weapon and directly relevant to the question of intent.

In the event that the evidence from the review and the information available to the weapon user is enough to satisfy a panel of judges at the ICC that the user either intended to commit a crime or used the weapon while being 'virtually certain' that a criminal consequence would ensue, they would be found guilty. For example, if someone uses an AWS knowing that it will lead to the unlawful death

120 Boulanin and Verbruggen (n 9) 23.

of civilians, they will be committing a crime punishable under the Rome Statute. In addition, if it could be proved that a commander equipped their forces with an AWS knowing that it was incapable of selecting and engaging targets consistently with the principle of distinction, they could be held liable for directing an attack against civilians or civilian objects.

Evidence that this information was available to the commander or weapon operator would demonstrate whether or not they deserved to be punished for their conduct. ICL does not punish individuals for unforeseen failures in weapon technology or other accidents. The intent and knowledge of the perpetrator are key components of their moral culpability for the most serious of international crimes. Just as it could help a prosecution, the evidence from a weapons review could also be critical to a defence case, showing that the commander or weapon user did not intend or foresee the criminal consequence. A thorough review could provide evidence that despite rigorous testing, the AWS acted in an unexpected fashion, and that operator should not be held responsible for the consequence.

5 Conclusion

To ensure compliance with IHL, weapons operators must understand the capabilities of their weapons prior to using them in an attack. This extends to an AWS. The requirement to exercise precautions in attack requires knowledge that the AWS will comply with the principles of IHL when used in its normal, intended way. Those operating or deploying a weapon must also then ensure that their actual use of the AWS is within those normal, intended, and IHL-compliant parameters of use for that weapon. Advanced militaries generate the knowledge needed to properly understand a weapon through a weapons review process. This has both legal and strategic implications. This knowledge is necessary to make good strategic decisions about how to use an AWS. It could also inform a criminal trial.

In the case of an ICC proceeding, the information generated and gathered by a weapons review process would be evidence that could help identify what the commander or weapon operator knew about how the AWS worked, an important part of satisfying the intent requirements of the Rome Statute. This is not to say that having a weapons review of an AWS makes the conduct of an ICC proceeding easy: meeting the strict mental element set by Article 30 of the Rome Statute would require proof that the perpetrator either intended the criminal consequence or knew that it would occur in the 'ordinary course of events'. Insufficient review of the operation of an AWS would increase the likelihood that the weapon operator was not equipped with the information necessary to make lawful and strategically sound decisions. Depending on the facts, this could be evidence of a failure to take reasonable precautions or evidence of a lack of intent. Conversely, clear information that the weapon could not be used in a particular way amounting from the review could be demonstrative of intent.

This demonstrates that developing a robust weapons review mechanism for AWS is an important aspect of promoting accountability for the use of this complex and potentially risky technology. If militaries decide that it is acceptable to use AWS in armed conflict, then ensuring the appropriate testing and that reviews of these machines are reliable will not only help minimise the risk of the weapon acting in unexpected ways, but may also provide evidence that the person deploying or operating the weapon has acted consistently with IHL. Conversely, a failure to carry out these tests of an AWS may be part of the evidence that shows the commission of an international crime.

Figuring out how to do the testing will not be easy and, above all, will depend on the type of weapon and the intended context of use. It is not a problem that can be solved through legal mechanisms, but instead will require substantial investment in better understanding how the reliability of autonomous systems can be assessed. States should continue to work to promote greater clarity about testing and ensure that proper weapons review mechanisms are in place prior to using an AWS.

Acknowledgements

The research for this chapter received funding from the Australian Government through the Defence Cooperative Research Centre for Trusted Autonomous Systems. The views and opinions expressed in the chapter are those of the authors, and do not necessarily reflect the views of the Australian Government or any other institution. The authors wish to thank Rain Liivoja, Renato Wolf and Kate Devitt for their helpful comments and feedback in drafting this contribution, as well as Emma Palmer and her colleagues for their editorial assistance and the anonymous reviewers for their useful suggestions.

9 Creating legal frameworks to afford human accountability for AI decisions in war

Natalie J E Nunn

1 Introduction

We are at the dawn of a new era of weaponry in which armaments using artificial intelligence (AI) are in the early stages of being researched and developed.[1] AI allowing superior detection and faster analysis and response times,[2] and lacking physically limiting factors such as exhaustion or hunger, make lethal autonomous weapon systems (LAWS) a potentially desirable option for military operations.[3] They also raise serious ethical concerns.[4]

These developments impact international humanitarian law (IHL) to varying degrees, depending on how the weapons are ultimately developed. If development requires meaningful human control (MHC) to be maintained over the critical functions of LAWS, as a number of experts and states are currently advocating for,[5] IHL frameworks will not be significantly challenged, and the implications for IHL are negligible.[6] In this instance, mandating MHC 'would resolve many

1 Commonwealth of Australia, 'The Potential Use by the Australian Defence Force of Unmanned Air, Maritime and Land Platforms' (25 June 2015) <www.aph.gov.au/Parliamentary_Business/Committees/Senate/Foreign_Affairs_Defence_and_Trade/Defence_Unmanned_Platform/Report/c05> para 5.24, accessed 17 December 2020.

2 'Statement of Hon Julie Bishop MP, Minister for Foreign Affairs' (1 March 2018) <www.cse.unsw.edu.au/~tw/ciair/julie.pdf> accessed 17 December 2020.

3 ibid.

4 For an overview of the ethical concerns raised by utilising AI in life-and-death decisions in battle, see Robert Sparrow, 'Killer Robots' (2007) 24 *Journal of Applied Philosophy* 62; Jai Galliott, *Military Robots: Mapping the Moral Landscape* (Routledge 2017).

5 Discussions at the 2018 Convention on Certain Conventional Weapons (CCW) Group of Governmental Experts (GGE) meetings on LAWS reaffirmed the essential importance of MHC in the use of force. It was stated that MHC must be retained since accountability cannot be transferred to machines. 'Report of the 2018 Session of the Group of Governmental Experts on Emerging Technologies in the Area of Lethal Autonomous Weapons Systems' (23 October 2018) UN Doc CCW/GGE.1/2018/3 (2018 GGE Report).

6 In 2019, the International Committee for the Red Cross provided commentary at the CCW GGE exploring how 'human supervision, and the ability to intervene and deactivate' are key elements of maintaining respect for IHL in human-machine interaction. This position was mirrored by the European Union which provided that '[h]uman control over lethal

DOI: 10.4324/9781003087533-12

of the moral and legal concerns that fully autonomous weapons raise',[7] rendering LAWS akin to drones and other semi-autonomous, less legally challenging arms. If weapons are developed that do not require MHC to be maintained or that make decisions too rapidly for MHC to be effective, LAWS will take full control of targeting cycle decisions. If this occurs, existing IHL frameworks will not be sufficient, and a legal vacuum will be created. In this instance, questions relating to the principles of distinction and proportionality will arise; however, the most significant implication for IHL is that a new framework addressing human accountability for machine-made decisions will be required.[8]

Currently, machines are not considered the subject of law,[9] and using them to make decisions with legally regulated consequences has the potential to create an unacceptable accountability gap.[10] Generally speaking, the need for human judgment to be present to establish accountability is paramount in existing legal structures, and there are conflicting views on whether LAWS are fundamentally unable to fulfil this requirement.[11]As a result, creating novel frameworks to clearly

---

autonomous weapons systems is essential to ensure their compliance with international law, including IHL'. This was further supported in a number of formal statements given by Brazil, Estonia, Germany, India, Israel, the Netherlands, Poland, and the United Kingdom. See 'Statement of the International Committee of the Red Cross (ICRC) under Agenda Item 5(b) Further Consideration of the Human Element in the Use of Lethal Force; Aspects of Human-Machine Interaction in the Development, Deployment and Use of Emerging Technologies in the Area of Lethal Autonomous Weapon Systems' (26–29 March 2019) <https://docs-library.unoda.org/Convention_on_Certain_Conventional_Weapons_-_Group_of_Governmental_Experts_(2019)/CCW%2BGGE%2BLAWS%2BICRC%2Bstatement%2Bagenda%2Bitem%2B5b%2B26%2B03%2B2019.pdf> accessed 17 December 2020; European Union, Group of Governmental Experts, 'Further Consideration of the Human Element in the Use of Lethal Force; Aspects of Human-Machine Interaction in the Development, Deployment and Use of Emerging Technologies in the Area of Lethal Autonomous Weapons Systems' (26–29 March 2019) <https://docs-library.unoda.org/Convention_on_Certain_Conventional_Weapons_-_Group_of_Governmental_Experts_(2019)/ALIGNED%2B-%2BLAWS%2BGGE%2BEU%2Bstatement%2BHuman%2BElement.pdf> accessed 17 December 2020.

7 Human Rights Watch, 'Killer Robots and the Concept of Meaningful Human Control: Memorandum to Convention on Conventional Weapons (CCW) Delegates' (11 April 2016) 2 <www.hrw.org/news/2016/04/11/killer-robots-and-concept-meaningful-human-control> accessed 17 December 2020.

8 Bonnie Docherty, 'The Need for and Elements of a New Treaty on Fully Autonomous Weapons' (*Human Rights Watch and International Human Rights Clinic*, June 2020) 4 <www.hrw.org/sites/default/files/media_2020/06/202006arms_rio_autonomous_weapons_systems_2.pdf> accessed 17 December 2020.

9 Swati Malik, 'Autonomous Weapon Systems: The Possibility and Probability of Accountability' (2017–2018) 35 *Wisconsin International Law Journal* 609, 620.

10 The ICC only has jurisdiction over natural persons: Rome Statute of the International Criminal Court (adopted 17 July 1998, entered into force 1 July 2002) 2187 UNTS 90, art 25(1) (Rome Statute).

11 Jack M Beard, 'Autonomous Weapons and Human Responsibilities' (2014) 45 *Georgetown Journal of International Law* 617 at 621. See generally MN Schmitt, 'Autonomous Weapon Systems and International Humanitarian Law: A Reply to the Critics' (2013) 4 *Harvard National Security Journal* 1.

assign human accountability in the absence of traditional human involvement in decision making may prove to be imperative.

This chapter will focus on LAWS that do not require MHC, as this is where the main friction with IHL exists and will focus solely on the issue of accountability. This chapter will begin by looking briefly at the concept of MHC and the impact of LAWS on modern warfare. It will then analyse the effect these impacts have on accountability under international criminal law (ICL) and will suggest a new framework for responsibility that utilises and extends upon existing law to safely regulate AI in battle. It will conclude with two findings:

1 The development of LAWS that do not maintain MHC over their critical functions will require the creation of new regulations to determine where accountability for their use lies.
2 The accountability gap is best answered by a two-pronged approach of (1) codifying the extension of the principle of *dolus eventualis* to allow the assignment of a reckless liability under IHL to the military commander responsible for fielding the weapons, and (2) creating a state-imposed strict liability for manufacturers and programmers of LAWS.

2 Meaningful human control (MHC)

While it has been proposed that MHC could provide the conceptual framework for regulating LAWS,[12] the term itself is unsettled. The concept of MHC was first introduced by civil society in early discussions at a conference of the Convention on Certain Conventional Weapons (CCW),[13] and while it has garnered a great deal of support,[14] the international community is struggling to determine how it should be defined and implemented.[15] It is clear from more recent CCW meetings that most governments agree human control will be necessary over the critical functions of LAWS;[16] however, there are still key states who apparently believe that a human control framework is an 'overly simplistic construct

12 Vincent Boulanin, Neil Davison, Netta Goussac, and Moa Peldán Carlsson, 'Limits on Autonomy in Weapon Systems: Identifying Practical Elements of Human Control' (*SIPRI and ICRC*, 2 June 2020) 3 <www.sipri.org/sites/default/files/2020-06/2006_limits_of_autonomy.pdf> accessed 17 December 2020.

13 Richard Moyers, 'Key Elements of Meaningful Human Control' (Article 36 Background Paper, April 2016) <www.article36.org/wp-content/uploads/2016/04/MHC-2016-FINAL.pdf> accessed 17 December 2020.

14 Ray Acheson, 'It's Time to Exercise Human Control over the CCW' (2019) 7(2) *Reaching Critical Will* 1 <https://reachingcriticalwill.org/images/documents/Disarmament-fora/ccw/2019/gge/reports/CCWR7.2.pdf> accessed 17 December 2020.

15 Merel Ekelhof and Giacomo Persi Paoli, *The Human Element in Decisions About the Use of Force* (United Nations Institute for Disarmament Research 2019) <https://unidir.org/publication/human-element-decisions-about-use-force> accessed 17 December 2020.

16 Acheson (n 14).

that fails to capture the various human touchpoints throughout the life-cycle' of LAWS.[17]

MHC will only provide a useful basis for discussions if states decide on a common meaning of 'human control'.[18] To date, what discussions of MHC have successfully achieved is directing the focus of discussions on the regulation of LAWS to a central concern: 'the loss of control over the use of force'.[19]

To clarify the term, a recent publication by the Campaign to Stop Killer Robots[20] proposed a framework for characterising MHC using three categories. These are:

> Decision-Making Components: The decision-making components of meaningful human control give humans the information and ability to make decisions about whether the use of force complies with legal rules and ethical principles. In particular, the human operator of a weapon system should have: an understanding of the operational environment; an understanding of how the system functions, including what it might identify as a target; and sufficient time for deliberation.
>
> Technological Components: Technological components are embedded features of a weapon system that can enhance meaningful human control. They include: predictability and reliability; the ability of the system to relay relevant information to the human operator; and the ability for a human to intervene after the activation of the system.
>
> Operational Components: Operational components make human control more meaningful by limiting when and where a weapon system can operate and what it can target. Factors that could be constrained include: the time between a human's legal assessment and the system's application of force; the duration of the system's operation; the nature and size of the geographic area of operation; and the permissible types of targets (e.g., personnel or material).[21]

These components are understood to be used cumulatively rather than individually to create the basis for MHC. While this classification is just one example of

17 Karl Chang, 'Intervention by the United States' (*CCW GGE LAWS*, 22 September 2020) <https://reachingcriticalwill.org/images/documents/Disarmament-fora/ccw/2020/gge/statements/22Sept_US2.pdf> accessed 17 December 2020.

18 Australia, 'Australia's System of Control and Applications for Autonomous Weapon Systems' (26 March 2019) UN Doc CCW/GGE.1/2019/WP.2/Rev.1, 5.

19 Boulanin, Davison, Goussac, and Carlsson (n 12) 3.

20 The Campaign to Stop Killer Robots is the primary coalition of non-governmental organisations working to ban LAWS. Founded in 2012, the coalition's main goal is to retain meaningful human control over the use of force.

21 Campaign to Stop Killer Robots, 'Key Elements of a Treaty on Fully Autonomous Weapons' (November 2019) <www.stopkillerrobots.org/wp-content/uploads/2020/04/Key-Elements-of-a-Treaty-on-Fully-Autonomous-WeaponsvAccessible.pdf> accessed 17 December 2020.

how MHC can be defined, it is preferred as it creates a clear accountability chain between the commanders fielding weapons and the actions of the weapons. It also allows traditional IHL and ICL accountability frameworks to be applied to LAWS use, as lethal decisions are ultimately overseen with full control by human operators.

While it is ideal to expect MHC will be clearly defined and mandated over the use of LAWS and that such mandate will be adhered to, until there is greater understanding as to how LAWS will be developed, it is necessary to explore avenues for accountability in instances when such high levels of human control are not realised. Until further understanding of how LAWS will be developed exists, LAWS that lack MHC cannot be discounted. Understandably, the primary example of LAWS that lack MHC are those programmed to disallow human interjection in the targeting cycle. In addition to these, however, LAWS that lack MHC would also include 'systems that become too complex for human users to understand and thus produce . . . inexplicable effects'[22] or complex systems that 'might apply force based on prior machine learning or allow critical system parameters to change without human authorization'.[23] If this is the case, MHC over LAWS is extinguished, and current IHL and ICL frameworks will not be sufficient to assign human accountability, as will be discussed later in this chapter. In that instance, novel accountability frameworks will need to be created to ensure adherence to the existing body of IHL. It is this unique situation that this chapter will address.

3 Impacts of LAWS on warfare

> They don't get hungry. They're not afraid. They don't forget their orders. They don't care if the guy next to them has just been shot. Will they do a better job than humans? Yes.
>
> – Gordon Johnson, Pentagon Joint Forces Command[24]

LAWS that do not require MHC to be maintained over critical functions will remove humans from the battlefield both physically and mentally. The main practical impacts of replacing humans in the battlefield are clear: faster data collection, analysis and action will be accessible to militaries, and human soldiers will be spared. LAWS will be able to process greater amounts of incoming sensory information without discarding or distorting it to fit preconceived notions,[25] enhanc-

22 ibid., 6.
23 ibid.
24 Tim Weiner, 'New Model Army Soldier Rolls Closer to Battle' *New York Times* (New York, 16 February 2005).
25 Amitai Etzioni and Oren Etzioni, 'Pros and Cons of Autonomous Weapons Systems' [May–June 2017] *Military Review: The Professional Journal of the US Army* <www.armyupress.army.mil/Journals/Military-Review/English-Edition-Archives/May-June-2017/Pros-and-Cons-of-Autonomous-Weapons-Systems/> accessed 23 March 2020.

ing their ability to dispassionately select targets and make decisions within the boundaries of their programming. Their use will also allow commanders to send fighters on more hazardous missions, those which previously would not have been pursued due to the risk to human life, thus changing the face of military operations.[26] In short, LAWS will operate with greater speed, agility, accuracy, persistence, and reach and better mass coordination than current lethal weapons or human soldiers.[27]

Despite a tendency to anthropomorphise them, LAWS would not make decisions in the same way humans do[28] due to their lack of emotional capacity, which, in turn, would eradicate human irrationalities from decisions in battle. As with defensive fully autonomous weapons, which are in active use and considered non-controversial,[29] their efficiency and the precision with which they react[30] will render them superior to human soldiers in nearly all practical respects. LAWS will also allow access to high-skill capabilities that until now vested with only highly trained human soldiers. Consequently, LAWS will replace the need for high-level human training and will reduce the expertise required to execute attacks.[31]

Notwithstanding these seductive advantages to fielding LAWS, given the lack of human involvement they facilitate, their use creates several legal impacts for IHL that require addressing before LAWS can be fielded legally. The most important of these issues to address is the question of accountability: whether LAWS themselves can be held accountable and, if not, how human accountability can be created.

Ignoring momentarily that LAWS do not meet the natural persons standards required for accountability to be assigned under ICL,[32] LAWS also do not have human cognitive function, meaning their ability to act intentionally or recklessly is non-existent. Under the current regime, the requisite mental element for criminal liability is not satisfied, and responsibility is unable to be assigned

26 Paul D Sharre, 'The Opportunity and Challenge of Autonomous Systems' in Andrew P Williams and Paul D Scharre (eds), *Autonomous Systems: Issues for Defence Policymakers* (NATO 2015).

27 Vincent Boulanin and Maaike Verbruggen, 'Article 36 Reviews: Dealing with the Challenges Posed by Emerging Technologies' (*SIPRIS*, December 2017) 19 <www.sipri.org/sites/default/files/2017-12/article_36_report_1712.pdf> accessed 17 December 2020.

28 Kathleen McKendrick, 'Banning Autonomous Weapons Is Not the Answer' *Chatham House* (2 May 2018) <www.chathamhouse.org/expert/comment/banning-autonomous-weapons-not-answer> accessed 12 August 2019.

29 Examples of active fully autonomous weapons include the Iron Dome Missile Defence System utilised by the Israeli defence force and the US Phalanx close-in weapon system.

30 David Akerson, 'The Illegality of Offensive Lethal Autonomy' in D Saxon (ed), *International Humanitarian Law and the Changing Technology of War* (Martinus Nijhoff Publishers 2013) 72–73.

31 Future of Humanity Institute, *The Malicious Use of Artificial Intelligence: Forecasting, Prevention and Mitigation* (20 February 2018) <https://maliciousaireport.com/>.

32 Rome Statute, art 25(1).

to the weapons themselves. Given that LAWS will take over a number of the targeting decisions that usually vest with humans, this has sparked concern that no person will be held accountable for the 'decisions' made by the weapons systems. Given that the 'effective implementation of individual criminal liability' for violations of IHL is essential to ICL,[33] this has caused concern as to the legitimacy of LAWS.

To close this accountability gap, LAWS must be treated as non-human inorganic objects and not be considered independent actors with free agency. In traditional command structures, it is the role of the military commander to order an operation be carried out. It is then the obligation of the soldier to carry out those orders. In effect, the human soldier is treated as a unit with no agency. At this juncture, and with the state of AI as it is,[34] LAWS will act within their programmed parameters as set by humans, without free agency. So it is arguable that decisions concerning the use of force are not delegated to machines but that LAWS are simply effectuating the human intention of their programmer and military commander.[35]

If LAWS are categorised as weapons acting under the control of humans, then the mental element of the military commander fielding the weapons would once again be incorporated into the accountability chain, allowing more traditional analysis to ensue. In this instance, the mental element of the commander becomes central to assigning responsibility.

4 Human accountability

> There can be no justice in war if there are not, ultimately, responsible men and women.
>
> – Michael Walzer[36]

There are two unique aspects of LAWS that cause current legal frameworks for accountability to collapse: (1) the question of whether the mental element required to establish a punishable breach of ICL by the military operator is reached and (2) the introduction of a programmer/developer third party who has significant influence over the outcome of the weapon's behaviour without having any active involvement in its fielding. Both will be explored next.

33 Tim McFarland and Tim McCormack, 'Mind the Gap: Can Developers of Autonomous Weapons Systems Be Liable for War Crimes?' (2014) 90 *International Law Studies* 361.

34 Future of Life Institute, 'Podcast: AI Breakthroughs and Challenges in 2018 with David Krueger and Roman Yampolskiy' (31 January 2019) <https://futureoflife.org/2019/01/31/fli-podcast-ai-breakthroughs-and-challenges-in-2018-with-david-krueger-and-roman-yampolskiy/> accessed 3 May 2019.

35 2018 GGE Report (n 5) 36.

36 Michael Walzer, *Just and Unjust Wars: A Moral Argument with Historical Illustrations* (2nd edn, Basic Books 1992) 288.

a) The mental element of the military operator

i) Current frameworks for the mental element of the military commander in ICL

Under existing laws, breaches of IHL are punishable as war crimes[37] and must consist of a serious breach of IHL, along with 'individual criminal responsibility of the person breaching the rule'.[38] At an international level, the main bodies dealing with breaches of IHL for individual responsibility are ICL institutions: namely, the United Nations–mandated *ad hoc* tribunals[39] and assisted tribunals[40] and the International Criminal Court (ICC). Under the jurisdiction of the *ad hoc* tribunals, to establish responsibility, the perpetrator must act willfully,[41] that being intentionally (*dolus directus*) or recklessly (*dolus eventualis*).[42] Under the jurisdiction of the ICC, the mental standard is narrower, allowing repercussions only for perpetrators who act with 'intent and knowledge' (*dolus directus*).[43] Within the ICC jurisdiction, there is no direct codified provision made for recklessness.[44] And while recklessness has been discussed in several judgments of the ICC,[45]

37 Antonio Cassese, *Cassese's International Criminal Law* (3rd revised edn, OUP 2013) 65.

38 'Decision on the Defence Motion for Interlocutory Appeal on Jurisdiction' *Prosecutor v Tadić*, IT-94–1-AR72, ICTY Appeals Chamber, 2 October 1995, [141].

39 These are the International Criminal Tribunal for the Former Yugoslavia and the International Criminal Tribunal for Rwanda, both created by resolutions of the United Nations Security Council.

40 These are the Extraordinary Chambers in the Courts of Cambodia and the Special Court for Sierra Leone.

41 Rebecca Crootof, 'War Torts: Accountability for Autonomous Weapons' (2016) 164 *University of Pennsylvania Law Review* 1350.

42 'Judgement' *Prosecutor v Delalic and Landzo*, IT-96–21-T, ICTY Trial Chamber II, 16 November 1998, [437] and [439]; 'Trial Judgement' *Prosecutor v Bisengimana*, ICTR-00–60-T, ICTR Trial Chamber, 13 April 2006, [71].

43 Rome Statute, art 30.

44 The wording of the Rome Statute, Article 30, which outlines the mental element, specifies that an individual will only be held responsible if the material elements of a crimes are 'committed with intent and knowledge'. This suggests at a doctrinal level that *dolus directus* is the only standard of *mens rea* available before the ICC.

45 Discussion of *dolus eventualis* has appeared in several judgments of the ICC. In *Lubanga* in 2007, the Pre-Trial Chamber I held that there are three levels of *dolus* under Article 30, those being *dolus directus* in the first and second degree and *dolus eventualis*: 'Decision on the Confirmation of Charges' *Prosecutor v Lubanga Dyilo*, ICC-01/04–01/06, Pre-Trial Chamber I, 29 January 2007 (*Lubanga Confirmation*). Subsequently, in *Bemba* in 2009, Pre-Trial Chamber II held that there were only two levels of *dolus*, those being *dolus directus* in the first and second degrees: 'Decision Pursuant to Article 61(7)(a) and (b) of the Rome Statute on the Charges of the Prosecutor Against Jean-Pierre Bemba Gombo' *Prosecutor v Bemba Gombo*, ICC-01/05–01/08, Pre-Trial Chamber II, 15 June 2009, [369]. This decision was upheld by the *Lubanga* Trial Chamber I in 2012: 'Judgment Pursuant to Article 74 of the Statute' *Prosecutor v Lubanga Dyilo*, ICC-01/04–01/06, Trial Chamber I, 14 March 2012, [1011]. This supports the notion that under existing jurisprudence, there is no *dolus eventualis* standard applicable under the Rome Statute.

the resulting jurisprudence cements that a reckless standard, or *dolus eventualis*, is not recognised by the court.[46] This exclusion of *dolus eventualis* in the Rome Statute has drawn criticism,[47] and this chapter now seeks to identify an interpretation of *dolus eventualis* specifically in relation to the regulation of LAWS.

Taking this current standard for the mental element of crimes into account, when evaluating the mental state of the military commander in the hypothetical situation of fielding LAWS and breaching IHL, two possibilities arise:

1 the military commander fields LAWS *with the intention* to breach IHL; or
2 the military commander fields LAWS *without the intention* to breach IHL, but a breach occurs due to the commander's reckless fielding of the weapon.

ii) The military commander fields LAWS with the intention to breach IHL

If the military commander can be shown to have fielded LAWS with the intention to breach IHL, and the LAWS have simply actioned their intended outcome, this would fulfil the well-established and requisite mental element of *dolus directus* as expressed under Article 30 of the Rome Statute. For example, if a commander were to have directed a LAWS attack against a medical unit[48] with intention to attack the unit and knowledge that the target was, indeed, a medical unit, this would be sufficient to establish a *dolus directus* mental element under ICL. In this instance, the actions of the LAWS would be attributable to the military commander responsible, and individual criminal responsibility is easily established. There are no issues in attributing accountability. Cases such as these could be handled under the jurisdiction of the ICC or the related state-imposed military law. Alternatively, these breaches could be codified in a new mechanism for completeness. But the salient point is that when there is a provable mental state of

46 Geert-Jan Alexander Knoops, *Mens Rea at the International Criminal Court* (Brill 2017) 39.

47 Antonio Cassese, 'The Statute of the International Criminal Court' (1999) 10 *European Journal of International Law* 144, 153–154.

48 Attacks against medical units during international armed conflicts directly contravene the Geneva Convention for the Amelioration of the Condition of the Wounded and Sick in Armed Forces in the Field (opened for signature 12 August 1949, entered into force 21 October 1950) 75 UNTS 31, art 19; Geneva Convention Relative to the Protection of Civilian Persons in Time of War (opened for signature 12 August 1949, entered into force 21 October 1950) 75 UNTS 287, art 18; Protocol Additional to the Geneva Conventions of 12 August 1949, and Relating to the Protection of Victims of International Armed Conflicts (Protocol I) (opened for signature 8 June 1977, entered into force 7 December 1978) 1125 UNTS 3, art 2. Their protection during non-international armed conflicts is outlined in Protocol Additional to the Geneva Conventions of 12 August 1949, and Relating to the Protection of Victims of Non-International Armed Conflicts (Protocol II) (opened for signature 8 June 1977, entered into force 7 December 1978) 1125 UNTS 609, art 11(1). These IHL provisions are reflected in the Rome Statute under Article 8(b)(ix) for international armed conflicts and Articles 8(2)(e)(ii) and (iv) for non-international armed conflicts.

intent and knowledge, or *dolus directus*, of the military commander fielding the weapons, attributing accountability for the misuse of LAWS is not contentious.

iii) The military commander fields LAWS without the intention to breach IHL

Complications arise when the recklessness of the military commander combines with the capabilities and decision-making aspects of the LAWS, eventuating in a breach of IHL. Given the unique nature of LAWS, it is foreseeable that a breach of IHL may occur due to the autonomous behaviour of the weapons coupled with the reckless fielding of the weapons rather than the military commander having a direct intention to commit a crime. If the military commander can be shown to have fielded LAWS without a provable explicit intention[49] to breach IHL, but a breach has occurred due to that commander employing the weapon recklessly, currently, under Article 30 of the Rome Statute, the requisite *mens rea* will not have been established, meaning that individual responsibility cannot be assigned.

When analysing traditional human-operated weapons, this has not caused much issue; however, the increased decision-making capabilities of LAWS make this scenario much more problematic. Should a commander field LAWS knowing, or having ought to have known, that the weapons may act in an illegal way, the situation is similar to (although still distinct from[50]) that of fielding a soldier not fit for battle. In this instance, a reckless standard must be established to allow for individual liability to be assigned. To illustrate this point, take a hypothetical situation wherein a military commander is aware that the LAWS they intend to field have shown difficulty differentiating between combatants carrying assault weapons and civilian children playing with toy weapons. In the weapons review process, to be discussed next, this particular system accurately identifies, targets, and kills anywhere between four and eight of ten combatants and mis-targets and kills two to six civilian children. If the commander then chooses to deploy the LAWS in an area densely populated with both combatants and civilian children, and several children are murdered as a result, it is arguable that by engaging the

49 This could occur if the commander fielded LAWS without an intention to breach IHL or if the intention to breach cannot be proven.

50 Under the Command Responsibility Doctrine, commanders should have known the likelihood that their subordinates would commit breaches of IHL and then have failed to prevent or punish those breaches. While some commentators have suggested the Command Responsibility Doctrine be used to close the accountability gap with LAWS, it is problematic. In the instance of LAWS, commanders may not have the technical knowledge to know the LAWS would commit a certain crime, or if they do, they may not have the ability to prevent that crime from occurring, thus making the doctrine inapplicable in many cases. Furthermore, the Command Responsibility Doctrine requires that a crime be committed by a subordinate, and for that to be the case, the 'primary perpetrator', which in this instance is the LAWS, would require a level of intent, which it is incapable of possessing, to fulfil the *mens rea* requirements for the underlying crime to be established. See generally Guénaël Mettraux, *The Law of Command Responsibility* (OUP 2009).

weapon despite the known risks, they have employed a reckless standard to their decision making that has resulted in an unlawful killing under IHL.

The primary alteration of the current regulations required to ensure robust accountability of military commanders in this or similar instances is to extend the existing standard for *mens rea* under a new mechanism to include a codified principle of *dolus eventualis*. This would ensure the reckless fielding of LAWS is sufficient to satisfy the mental element required for liability.

The concept of *dolus eventualis* is an unsettled one[51] with numerous, competing understandings.[52] Furthermore, as briefly outlined earlier, its application in ICL has been inconsistent. Despite its uncertain inclusion within existing ICL frameworks, the liability for risk-taking behaviour that *dolus eventualis* represents[53] makes it an appealing framework when dealing with LAWS. The creation of a legal framework wherein the mental element explicitly includes a *dolus eventualis* standard would help create part of the necessary human accountability framework. For this to be workable, *dolus eventualis* for the misuse of LAWS would need to be carefully and thoroughly defined. In doing so, the law would allow accountability for the human military commander in the instance of reckless harm occurring.

Drawing on the *Lubanga* Confirmation of Charges decision, a concise classification of *dolus eventualis* in an ICL context, and that favoured by this chapter, reads as:

> situations in which the suspect (a) is aware of the risk that the objective elements of the crime may result from his or her actions, and (b) accepts such an outcome by reconciling himself or herself with it or consenting to it.[54]

This definition is preferred for application to LAWS as it clearly shows a level of disregard for the risk associated with making a decision in battle. To make this definition applicable to military commanders fielding LAWS, the spotlight is put on the commander and what level of understanding they had of the predictability of the weapon when deploying it. To ascertain this, robust weapons review processes would need to be in place to ensure commanders are aware of the risks of fielding LAWS and their level of unpredictability. Weapons review processes are broadly required for any new weapon acquired by a military.[55] They are regulated

51 Kjølv Egeland, 'Lethal Autonomous Weapon Systems Under International Humanitarian Law' (2016) 85 *Nordic Journal of International Law* 89.

52 Jens David Ohlin, 'Targeting and the Concepts of Intent' (2013) 35 *Michigan Journal of International Law* 79, 83.

53 ibid., 89.

54 *Lubanga Confirmation* (n 45) [352] (ii).

55 Signatories to Additional Protocol I of the Geneva Conventions (1977) are bound to review weapons before deployment under Article 36. There is not sufficient state practice to confirm this yet constitutes customary law, the implication being that Article 36 reviews are not yet universally required.

by Article 36 of Additional Protocol I to the Geneva Conventions which mandates that:

> In the study, development, acquisition or adoption of a new weapon, means or method of warfare, a High Contracting Party is under an obligation to determine whether its employment would, in some or all circumstances, be prohibited by this Protocol or by any other rule of international law applicable to the High Contracting Party.[56]

The applicability of Article 36 reviews to regulating LAWS has created its own significant body of academic discourse that will not be explored in this chapter.[57] What is salient however is that:

1. Article 36 review processes are not universally obligatory,[58] meaning that they cannot be solely relied upon to create a universal basis for oversight or accountability of LAWS; and
2. If relied upon to any extent, Article 36 review processes would need to be robust enough to ensure that the military commanders in question understood the general predictability and risks associated with fielding LAWS.

Given the anticipated machine learning aspects of LAWS and their speculated ability to adapt and evolve with experience,[59] if Article 36 reviews were to be relied upon by states as a means to provide commander understanding of LAWS' behaviours, such reviews would need to be carried out regularly. Commentary suggests that new reviews would be required each time the machine learning capabilities of the weapons led to 'a change in the programming such that it would make the system operate in a way not considered by the first review'[60] or when machine learning capabilities change 'the system's or end user's ability to comply with legal standards'.[61] While appealing, it is unknown whether this standard would be possible to maintain, given the potentially rapid changes machine-learning algorithms allow for. More pragmatically speaking, such constant need for new weapons reviews may also prove to be financially and practically

56 Article 36 of Protocol Additional to the Geneva Conventions of 12 August 1949, and relating to the Protection of Victims of International Armed Conflicts (Protocol I) (adopted 8 June 1977, entered into force 7 December 1978)1125 UNTS 3 (Additional Protocol I).

57 For more detailed discussion of Article 36 reviews in relation to LAWS, see Massingham and McKenzie in this volume.

58 McFarland and McCormack (n 33) 383.

59 Shin-Shin Hua, 'Machine Learning Weapons and International Humanitarian Law: Rethinking Meaningful Human Control' (2019) 51 *Georgetown Journal of International Law* 117, 120.

60 Boulanin and Verbruggen (n 27) 24.

61 ibid.

prohibitive for some governments.[62] As a result, periodic weapons reviews may not be sufficient to oversee LAWS.

Technical commentators have proposed that one possibility for maintaining a sufficient standard of weapons reviews over LAWS is the creation of a 'method for continuous testing and evaluation',[63] wherein LAWS would report on their learning and modifications, 'allowing the end user to understand whether a new legal review might be needed'.[64] This would potentially streamline the responsibility of governments in carrying out Article 36 reviews; however, it would require governments to develop new methods for testing and evaluation.[65] It would also require a deep level of trust in the reporting mechanisms of LAWS to report accurately and in a timely manner. Whether these limiting factors make such a system of review unachievable is open to debate. However, if realised, this would help ensure that commanders were sufficiently educated as to the up-to-date performance parameters and risks of fielding LAWS, which, in turn, would facilitate assigning accountability.

Whichever way weapons reviews for LAWS eventuate, the human commander fielding the weapons must stay abreast of the predictable behaviours of the systems. It is in this understanding that their mental element is based; thus, the review process will be integral to identifying when a commander has acted recklessly. If the commander is aware of the risks and deploys the weapons irrespective of them, resulting in a breach of IHL, the *mens rea* standard of 'intent and knowledge' will not be sufficient in many cases to assign accountability to the commander. Except in the case of a commander intentionally fielding LAWS to commit a crime, the lowering of the *mens rea* standard to include a reckless, or *dolus eventualis*, standard is integral to assigning sufficient human accountability for breaches of IHL actioned by LAWS.

In briefly looking at the mental element of the military commander mentioned earlier, what becomes apparent is that the behaviour of the weapons system will play an important factor in ascertaining whether a commander has fielded LAWS recklessly and can be held accountable. So, for completeness, it is necessary to look at the role and responsibility of the third-party developers of LAWS.

b) The third-party developer

While responsibility of military commanders is the obvious starting point for closing the accountability gap, as the level of autonomy programmed into LAWS increases, commanders and developers begin to share various forms of control of and responsibility for the behaviours of the systems.[66] The unique influence these

62 ibid.
63 ibid.
64 ibid.
65 ibid.
66 McFarland and McCormack (n 33) 376.

third-party developers will have on the discretionary decision making of LAWS through their programming will be effectuated when they are fielded. The result is the introduction of a possibly civilian third party with significant influence over the outcome of fielding a weapon. To maintain legitimacy in the law, they must be incorporated into the accountability framework.

Firstly, it is important to acknowledge that, in using the term 'developers', this chapter seeks to simplify the various parties required to develop novel LAWS technology. Although many actors will be ultimately involved in the production of the software and hardware required to create LAWS, in using the term 'developer', this chapter is referring to the business entity ultimately responsible for producing the final product and passing the weapons on to militaries. These are the end-seller corporations that have coordinated the various contributors required to produce LAWS and under whose banner the finished product is distributed.[67]

As LAWS are developed to have autonomous functions, the behaviour of those weapons will be heavily influenced during the development stages. It is at these various stages of development, those being the 'design, testing, and verification' stages, that human control and supervision are most meaningful to the eventual outcomes in battle.[68] Developers build algorithms 'defining the behavior of a weapons system',[69] and it is this behaviour that will ultimately be relied on during armed conflicts. They also determine which information is passed back to human operators, who, in turn, use this information to make command decisions. Given the reliance on this programmed behaviour and that autonomous systems 'can return potentially incorrect, unjustified, or unfair results',[70] it is relevant to ensure developers are held responsible for any programmed behaviours that result in breaches of IHL.

i International humanitarian law/international criminal law

With the influence developers have on battle in this context, the intuitive starting point to investigate their accountability is under ICL frameworks. However, despite their increased influence over the behaviour of LAWS, the accountability of developers does not sit comfortably within existing ICL frameworks. The primary issues surrounding the ability to hold developers accountable under

67 This broad categorisation is borrowed from directives on AI accountability from the European Union, wherein the 'producers' of AI hold ultimate liability for products. See: Commission to the European Parliament, the Council and the European Economic and Social Committee, 'Report on the Safety and Liability Implications of Artificial Intelligence, the Internet of Things and Robotics' COM(2020) 64 (19 February 2020), <https://ec.europa.eu/info/sites/info/files/report-safety-liability-artificial-intelligence-feb2020_en_1.pdf> accessed 10 March 2021.

68 Hua (n 59) 146.

69 McFarland and McCormack (n 33) 375.

70 Joshua A Kroll et al., 'Accountable Algorithms' (2017) 165 *University of Pennsylvania Law Review* 633.

ICL rest in three areas, as discussed in detail by McFarlane and McCormack and briefly outlined here.

The first hurdle to accessing ICL remedies for accountability in this context is 'the threshold requirement of the existence of an armed conflict'.[71] This is the issue of contemporality of LAWS development. For IHL to apply to conduct, that conduct must occur during an armed conflict.[72] While it is possible that some development of LAWS will occur during the existence of an armed conflict, it is also highly likely that much of their development will be done during times of peace, when IHL does not apply.[73] If an armed conflict does not exist at the time of the act in question, it becomes a hurdle to accessing ICL remedies for IHL breaches[74] and could hinder the chances of successfully holding developers accountable.

If the contemporality threshold outlined here is met, the next issue that arises is whether the developers can meet the *mens rea* threshold required to instigate ICL proceedings. As discussed earlier in relation to the military commanders, Article 30 of the Rome Statute outlines a high threshold for *mens rea* – that being 'intent and knowledge'. Given the complexity of developing LAWS and the numerous parties responsible for programming and building them, determining whether the developer of the weapons had a requisite level of intent and knowledge would make the mental element impossible to satisfy. Furthermore, given that the developers do not make the choice of when to deploy LAWS, assigning their intent to carry out specific acts is tenuous at best.

Lastly, the prosecution of corporations as juridical persons under the current ICL framework is not possible at the ICC, and complex amendments to the Rome Statute would be required to facilitate such prosecution.[75] This is not to say that such liability will never exist,[76] but under current frameworks, the developer corporation, as defined in this chapter, is unable to be prosecuted under ICL.

Given the limitations briefly outlined here, trying to assign accountability to developers for breaches of IHL under existing ICL frameworks is currently nearly impossible. The existing frameworks create a system with a remarkably low chance

71 McFarland and McCormack (n 33) 383.

72 Common Article II of the Geneva Conventions. In relation to war crimes, this is codified in International Criminal Court, 'Elements of Crimes' (2011) ICC-PIDS-LT-03–002/11_Eng, art 8.

73 A widely adopted standard for the existence of an armed conflict is outlined by the ICTY as: 'an armed conflict exists whenever there is a resort to armed force between States': 'Decision on Defence Motion for Interlocutory Appeal on Jurisdiction' *Prosecutor v Tadić*, IT-91-I-1, ICTY Appeals Chamber, 2 October 1995, [70].

74 'Elements of Crimes' art 8.

75 David Scheffer, 'Corporate Liability Under the Rome Statute' (2016) 57 *Harvard International Law Journal* 35.

76 See generally Joanna Kyriakakis, 'Corporations Before International Criminal Courts: Implications for the International Criminal Justice Project' (2017) 30 *Leiden Journal of International Law* 221.

of prosecutorial success, so, to be able to assign accountability to developers, solutions must be sought outside the traditional ICL framework. The question then becomes how we can assign accountability to these new third parties to ensure the production and programmed behaviour of LAWS are sufficiently regulated. One possible response, and that favoured in this chapter, is the introduction of an internationally mandated and state-imposed strict product liability on developers. Such a liability would not form part of ICL but would instead act as a complementary state-imposed law governed by international agreement to help bridge the gap of accountability in the unique instance of LAWS. Although individual liability for torts does not exist in the international sphere,[77] ICL has opened the door to constructing new international legal regimes grounded in individual responsibility,[78] and this rationale could be extended in the ways explored next. While applying a tortious strict product liability to actions taken within armed conflicts is a novel approach, the introduction of a civil law strict product liability lends useful frameworks to the issue of accountability for AI-programmed weapons.

ii Strict liability

General principles of product liability have emerged at the state level to regulate artificial intelligence in non-military fields.[79] This is intuitive, given that AI in the civilian sector is available in the form of consumer products, such as self-driving cars and medical equipment. Within product liability frameworks, a civil negligence standard[80] is usually applied, and the question of assigning liability, for the most part, rests on whether the harm suffered by using a product was 'foreseeable'. This sits uncomfortably with the idea of AI, wherein AI-controlled products presuppose an expectation to perform, at least to some extent, in an unforeseeable way.[81] In order to circumvent this, a civil strict liability framework could be applied. Strict liability removes the negligence a standard from questions of

77 Crootof (n 41) 1390.

78 ibid.

79 The application of product liability frameworks to the regulation of AI is most readily seen across discussions of autonomous vehicles. For discussion in the Australian context, see Mark Brady, 'Is Australian Law Adaptable to Autonomous Vehicles?' [2019] *Griffith Journal of Law & Human Dignity* 35; Tom Mackie, 'Proving Liability for Highly and Fully Automated Vehicle Accidents in Australia' (2018) 34 *Computer Law & Security Review* 1314. For discussion of product liability frameworks in the regulation of autonomous vehicles under European Union laws, see, e.g., Expert Group on Liability and New Technologies, 'Liability for Artificial Intelligence and Other Emerging Digital Technologies' (2019) <https://ec.europa.eu/transparency/regexpert/index.cfm?do=groupDetail.groupMeetingDoc&docid=36608> accessed 17 December 2020 ('EU AI Liability Report').

80 The remainder of this chapter will focus on a civil negligence standard as found in the civil laws of torts dealing with product liability. This is distinct from a criminal negligence standard, which will not be discussed further in this chapter.

81 Omri Rachum-Twaig, 'Whose Robot Is It Anyway? Liability for Artificial-Intelligence-Based Robots' [2020] *University of Illinois Law Review* 1141, 1152.

responsibility and is the most onerous standard of product liability able to be imposed on manufacturers. This would impose a civil liability on developers that would sit alongside the ICL accountability just discussed. There is no one classification of strict liability across jurisdictions or, indeed, even within the one jurisdiction,[82] with the result being that discussion of it is often generalised. It could be used to impose a civil liability on developers that would sit alongside the ICL accountability just discussed, working together to create a robust liability framework.

iii General principles of strict liability

The core tenet of strict liability required for this discussion is that should any harm occur outside the realm of expected use, accountability would lie with the developer regardless of any negligence. Assigning responsibility for product faults regardless of negligence creates a strict liability that evaluates the condition of the product, rather than the conduct of the manufacturer.[83] This is an important aspect in discussing LAWS as it eliminates the need to determine that a developer had a certain mindset when developing the weapon. Given that weapons may take decades to be developed and brought to market and that there may be a significant lag between when a weapon is brought to market, acquired by a military, and ultimately fielded, having to establish a certain mental state of a developer could be impossible. A strict product liability framework would ensure that only the behaviours of the product and its effects are evaluated in assigning responsibility for harm.

A strict liability regime is typically applied to 'lawful but inherently dangerous activities' and is thus most suitable to address the trouble with tracing the causal chain of injuries caused by LAWS.[84] It also accounts for the complexity of LAWS as it covers situations in which programming errors cause unanticipated results.[85] Strict liability makes engaging in activities with a higher risk of causing harm costlier to injurers,[86] and its application to developers of LAWS creates the highest standard of responsibility possible. Though this would be a significant development of current law, it could be deemed appropriate given the high threshold for civilian protection afforded by IHL and the need to mirror this in the regulation of LAWS.

While this places a severe burden on the developers of LAWS, at this juncture, if implemented properly, the severity of the liability and its strict application could have further, more practical benefits. First, a strict liability imposed on developers could act as a way of deterring developers from releasing LAWS that they do not

82 Douglas N Husak, 'Varieties of Strict Liability' (1995) 8 *Canadian Journal of Law and Jurisprudence* 189.

83 JW Wade, 'Strict Product Liability: A Look at Its Evolution' (1989) 19 *The Brief* 8.

84 Crootof (n 41) 1395.

85 Paul Scharre, *Autonomous Weapons and Operational Risk* (Centre for New American Security 29 February 2016) <www.cnas.org/publications/reports/autonomous-weapons-and-operational-risk> accessed 17 December 2020.

86 Jules L Coleman, 'The Structure of Tort Law' (1987) 97 *Yale Law Journal* 1233, 1235.

have sufficient trust in. This, in turn, may help limit the proliferation of poorly designed and dangerously programmed weapons.[87] Secondly, given that it would fall to the relevant state to enforce a strict liability regime, states may be incentivised to carefully oversee LAWS development and encourage additional care in designing them.[88] It may also provide incentive for states to increase security measures to avoid hacking or to minimise the deployment of LAWS overall.[89] In doing so, they could slow the introduction of LAWS onto the battlefield, giving developers and militaries the necessary time to adapt to the use of new technologies.

With these points in mind, it is necessary to see how strict product liability is being used in relation to AI currently. While many states have not begun the lengthy process of discussing appropriate frameworks for the regulation of AI as a product, the European Union (EU) is at the forefront of such discussions. The centralised nature of the EU policies that are emerging on AI and the expressed need for an AI liability scheme that is uniform across member states mirror the need for a uniform liability scheme internationally for LAWS. To avoid the myriad differences in product liability frameworks that exist globally and affect the application of an accountability regime for LAWS, a centralised scheme that is imposed on states at the international level is preferred. This is reflected in the EU rationale behind requiring a unified liability scheme to account for incongruent national rules creating obstacles for developers selling or operating AI solutions across country borders. The EU regulations, therefore, make a worthwhile case study in the evaluation of applying strict liabilities to LAWS.

iv Strict liability for AI in the European Union

The EU position on strict liability for the regulation of AI is presented in its 'Liability for Artificial Intelligence' paper.[90] This document was published in 2019 by the EU to give members guidance on how best to regulate AI in the civilian sector under product liability laws, but its principles can be useful in exploring the application of strict product liability in the military context. As per the EU guidance:

> [p]roducers, whether or not they incidentally also act as operators . . . should have to: (a) design, describe and market products in a way effectively

87 It is widely accepted that the technology required to build LAWS, once created, could be cheap to access and easy to assemble, resulting in the proliferation of lethal robots without relevant military controls. See further Justin Haner and Denise Garcia, 'The Artificial Intelligence Arms Race: Trends and World Leaders in Autonomous Weapons Development' (2019) 10 *Global Policy* 331.

88 James Igoe Walsh, 'Political Accountability and Autonomous Weapons' (2015) 2 *Research and Politics* <https://doi.org/10.1177/2053168015606749>.

89 Crootof (n 41) 1396.

90 'EU AI Liability Report' (n 79) 42.

> enabling operators to comply with the duties . . . and (b) adequately monitor the product after putting it into circulation.[91]

In addition,

> [t]he producer should be strictly liable for defects in emerging digital technologies even if said defects appear after the product was put into circulation, as long as the producer was still in control of updates to, or upgrades on, the technology.[92]

This strict liability framework is brief, but it provides significant guidance. This framework creates a double-pronged duty for developers that requires cautious development of AI before it is released to market and then vigilant oversight of AI once it is in market. This careful approach pays respect to the increasingly powerless position of the user/injured party when AI is deployed, given their decreased control over the injurious outcome. It also reflects the need to place more stringent boundaries on product developers to account for the greater influence they have over the behaviour of the product. While these frameworks are a work in progress within the EU currently, the Liability for Artificial Intelligence paper is one of the first high-level papers released worldwide that begins to address the complicated task of adapting existing product liability laws to AI products. It provides a thoughtful perspective on the novel issue of how best to regulate AI with reference to existing laws. It further highlights the additional caution required in assigning liability and the need to think beyond traditional analysis of product liability to maintain the relevance of existing legal frameworks in an AI world. These additionally cautious aspects make it a desirable foundation for considering accountability for AI in weapons.

For a similar framework to be realised in relation to LAWS, developers of LAWS would need to be incorporated into the maintenance and oversight of the weapons systems. How this would be done practically would be ultimately determined by the forum in which new LAWS regulations are settled, whether that be as a novel stand-alone treaty, an annexed Protocol to the CCW, or an alternative codification process. While there are possible practical considerations that speak to this point, this rationale supports the notion for the need to maintain expert oversight of weapons to ensure their ongoing compliance with existing laws. From a technical perspective, this could be achieved in several ways: for instance, by the employment of software verification,[93] cryptographic commitments,[94] or

91 ibid., 7 [17](a) and (b), see further 44ff.

92 ibid., 6 [14], see further 42ff.

93 Software verification provides a set of techniques for 'proving mathematically that software has certain properties, either by analyzing existing code or by building software using specialized tools for extracting proved correct invariants': Kroll et al. (n 70) 662.

94 Cryptographic commitments are digital objects that bind the 'prover to a certain statement' that is then verifiable at a later date to maintain a form of accountability: see Ariel T Hamlin

zero-knowledge proofs.[95] While this chapter will not delve into the technical aspects of developer oversight, these are detailed to highlight that ongoing technical oversight is possible and should be a minimum expectation of developers producing LAWS. Given the machine-learning aspects anticipated to be present in some LAWS, this strict liability would require that developers maintain proximity to the weapons, regularly overseeing their behaviours and how they have adapted to ensure they are behaving within the intended scope of their original programming and continue to be fit for deployment in battle.

The introduction of product liability to IHL is highly unconventional. So, too, however, was the idea of fully autonomous weapons with lethal function, at least until recently. Overall, while a strict liability framework in IHL would seem controversial, it may well provide the necessary extension of the law to help navigate the uncharted waters of regulating AI in battle. A strict liability framework would place an onerous responsibility on developers and would require a high standard of oversight to be maintained by the developer. This makes it the preferred framework to maintain respect for the principles of IHL. With the financial incentives of developing LAWS and the military advantages to fielding them, it is important that the legal framework ensures due care is taken when developing the systems to allow a thorough risk analysis, ample testing, and the creation of weapons that can behave in a way that adheres to legal requirements. A strict product liability framework not only allows human accountability for wrongful AI decisions but also acts as a limitation on LAWS proliferation. When used in conjunction with the ICL frameworks suggested in this chapter for the accountability of military commanders, such liability closes the gap created by the introduction of a civilian third party with significant influence over the behaviour of LAWS.

5 Conclusion

While this chapter gives a brief overview of a possible option for extending the law to attach human responsibility to machine-based actions, it aims to highlight that finding sufficient frameworks for accountability of military AI is not an impossibility. While the current law is not sufficiently equipped to handle this new wave of military technologies, building on existing legal frameworks and extending the law in some uncontentious and other more creative ways will allow lawmakers to reach appropriate outcomes.

The main objective of this overview is to highlight that for LAWS to be able to fall within the realms of human accountability as required by the law, they must

et al., 'Cryptography for Big Data Security' in Fei Hu (ed), *Big Data: Storage, Sharing, and Security* (CRC Press 2016).

95 Zero-knowledge proofs are a 'cryptographic tool that allows a decisionmaker, as part of a cryptographic commitment, to prove that the decision policy that was actually used (or the particular decision reached in a certain case) has a certain property, but without having to reveal either how that property is known or what the decision policy actually is': Kroll et al. (n 70) 668.

not be considered individual agents. They are and will remain weapons fielded by military commanders who have the ultimate control over whether they exist on the battlefield. Consequently, the accountability for their use and behaviours rests primarily on the military commanders fielding them and, to a lesser extent, on the developers who produce them.

Ideally, LAWS will only be developed with MHC being maintained over their critical functions as such development helps respond to the raft of other legal and ethical concerns raised by the introduction of AI into the battlefield. However, if this is not to be the case, then having considered the potential legal frameworks that could adapt the law accordingly will help ultimately protect IHL from being surpassed by rapid technological changes.

10 Future-proofing international criminal law

Complexity theory perspectives on collective entity accountability

Anna Marie Brennan

1 Introduction

From its inception, international criminal law (ICL) has had very little to do with collective entities, how to think about them, or how to hold them accountable for international crimes.[1] This is, without doubt, because of ICL's focus on individuals. That focus is even more important now as questions emerge about whether collective entities should be brought within ICL's ambit.[2] Some collective entities are adaptive, meaning they consist of dynamic networks of interactions between individuals with a loosely organised command structure. As a result, it can be difficult to pinpoint which individuals within the entity are responsible for the perpetration of international crimes. This ambiguity raises questions about whether it is still appropriate to only prosecute individuals or whether we should be pursuing the collective entity as well. This chapter aims to invigorate the debate on this dilemma by contending that systems theory – in particular complexity theory – may boost the argument that ICL needs to be revamped to include a mode of liability for collective entities. By taking this dilemma seriously, this chapter will utilise complexity theory to make sense of our varied intuitions about the scope of justice, persisting problems within ICL, and its future direction.

Complexity theory aims to explain the behavioural pattern of objects, actors, and agents and has gained attention in legal scholarship, reflecting its potential to be a distinct methodology to resolve some of law's most deep-rooted

1 Gerhard Werle, *Principles of International Criminal Law* (TMC Asser Press 2005) 35.
2 Andrew Clapham, 'Extending International Criminal Responsibility beyond Individuals to Corporations and Armed Opposition Groups' (2008) 6 *Journal of International Criminal Justice* 899; Annyssa Bellal and Stuart Casey-Maslen, 'Enhancing Compliance with International Law by Armed Non-State Actors' (2011) 3 *Goettingen Journal of International Law* 175; Jann Kleffner, 'The Collective Accountability of Organized Armed Groups in System Crimes' in Andre Nollkaemper and Harmen van der Wilt (eds), *System Criminality in International Law* (CUP 2009).

DOI: 10.4324/9781003087533-13

dilemmas.[3] In particular, it has been utilised to explain the workings of the global macroeconomic network, international relations, and the operation of manufacturing companies.[4] More recently, complexity theory has started to consider the system features of other types of collective entities such as non-state armed groups.[5] Complexity theory concerns the study of individuals' interactions and the system-wide effects they produce. In particular, it posits that the interactions of individuals within the collective entity can lead to bifurcations and new self-sustaining phenomena which the individuals could not have reasonably foreseen. By harnessing complexity theory, this chapter proposes that collective entities have such causal effects on their environment that they should be regarded as ontologically distinct and separate from their individual members. Therefore, they should be regarded as a subject upon which responsibility for international crimes could be imposed. With this insight, this chapter will explore the argument that there is a need to develop ICL to embrace a principle of collective entity responsibility.

Of course, ICL is no longer a new field of inquiry, but its scope of moral and legal inquiry has been dominated by approaches that emphasise the criminal responsibility of natural persons, not collective entities. While Andrew Clapham and others have written on the prospects for holding corporations and non-state armed groups accountable under international criminal law as collective entities, this growing interest in collective entities lacks any contextual analysis and understanding of the environment in which their crimes are planned and perpetrated.[6] This chapter provides that foundation since it is the first dedicated piece of research to examine complexity theory's implications for the accountability of collective entities under ICL. In particular, this chapter will claim that the theory frustrates the central premise of ICL: that the natural person as such is the most appropriate bearer of responsibility. In other words, the theory posits that the collective entity, as an emergent phenomenon, is not a proxy for the individuals that act on its behalf, nor is it merely an extension of the individual. Instead, it

3 Steven Wheatley, 'The Emergence of New States in International Law: The Insights from Complexity Theory' (2016) 15 *Chinese Journal of International Law* 579; Mark Chinen, 'Complexity Theory and the Horizontal and Vertical Dimensions of State Responsibility' (2014) 25 *European Journal of International Law* 703, 704. Game theory also studies individuals in bilateral strategic interactions. For further analysis, see Martin Shubik, 'Game Theory, Complexity and Simplicity Part II: Problems and Applications' (1998) 3 *Complexity* 36, 37.

4 Fremount Kast and James Rosenzweig, 'General Systems Theory: Applications for Organizations and Management' (1972) 15 *Academic of Management Journal* 451.

5 David Kilcullen, 'Counter-Insurgency Redux' (2006) 48 *Survival: Global Politics and Strategy* 111; Teresa Beck, *The Normality of Civil War: Armed Groups and Everyday Life in Angola* (Campus Verlag 2012) 64ff; Lars Skyttner, 'Systems Theory and the Science of Military Command and Control' (2005) 74 *Kybernetes* 1240.

6 Clapham (n 2) 899; Bellal and Casey-Maslen (n 2); Kleffner (n 2) 238; Liesbeth Zegveld, *Accountability of Armed Opposition Groups in International Law* (CUP 2002).

should be regarded as a distinct entity which can perpetrate international crimes.[7] Thus, development of ICL is needed to embrace a principle of collective entity responsibility.

Ultimately, this chapter will contend that there should not only be a principle of individual criminal responsibility under ICL but also a principle of collective entity responsibility. Complexity theory highlights that there is a gap between the collective entity and the latent individual interactions from which it has emerged, which correlates to a gap that is starting to become more apparent in international law. This gap separates the responsibility that collective entities, in particular non-state armed groups, have to ensure their compliance with international humanitarian law (IHL) norms from its accountability for violations of those same norms. ICL has overlooked the significance of this element and has put aside questions about the ontology of collective entities; therefore, it would appear insignificant whether or not a non-state armed group is a complex adaptive system. It is natural persons who must bear the burden of responsibility under ICL, and certainly, if there is a legal and ontological segregation between the collective entity and the individual member, it is debatable why only individual members should bear that responsibility. ICL could be further developed to tackle this problem; however, it could also be the case that the gap between the conduct of collective entities like non-state armed groups and their individual members who are ultimately held accountable for the group's crimes will never be fully overcome.[8] If so, ICL's distribution of responsibility for international crimes to individuals only is deficient. Thus, complexity theory imparts an ontological elucidation of why the dilemma of distributing criminal responsibility to the individual only is so problematic.

The majority of the chapter is dedicated to defending these ideas, with specific reference to non-state armed groups, and to highlighting their implications for the future of ICL. Building on existing accounts of international criminal justice, I delineate an ontology of the non-state armed group that undermines the individual-centric focus of international criminal law. I argue that if ICL is to be effective in achieving its central goal of suppressing impunity for international crimes, it must have a legal means of investigating and prosecuting collective entities, especially non-state armed groups. By taking this dilemma seriously, we can make sense of both our varied intuitions about the scope of justice and persisting problems within ICL.

This chapter contributes to the exploration of this argument in two parts. Part 2 considers the friction between the objective of ICL to investigate and prosecute

7 *Prosecutor v Tadić*, IT-94-1-A, Appeals Chamber, 15 July 1999, [191] (*Tadić Appeal*).

8 For further academic commentary on the concept of collective responsibility, see the seminal works of Hans Kelsen, 'Collective and Individual Responsibility in International Law with Particular Regard to the Punishment of War Criminals' (1942) 31 *California Law Review* 530; Hans Kelsen, 'Collective and Individual Responsibility for Acts of State in International Law' (1948) 1 *Jewish Yearbook of International Law* 226; Shane Darcy, *Collective Responsibility and Accountability Under International Law* (Brill 2007); Daryl Levinson, 'Collective Sanctions' (2003) 56 *Stanford Law Review* 345.

those most responsible for international crimes on the one hand and its failure to address collective entities on the other.[9] Part 3 introduces complexity theory to explain why the problem has been so difficult to resolve. As will be explored, complexity theory argues that, as complex adaptive systems, collective entities such as non-state armed groups are not always reducible to their individual members. One consequence is that it will be difficult to explain ICL's distribution of responsibility for international crimes to individuals only.[10] This is clearly problematic, and the chapter thus responds to the literature that encourages that ontology be set aside and that a consideration of purely legal conceptions of the collective entity be embraced.

2 The dilemma of collective entity responsibility in international criminal law

a) Contextualising the dilemma

An effective international legal system endeavours to impose repercussions for breaches of the norms it seeks to protect. This was the premise behind the Articles on the Responsibility of States for Internationally Wrongful Acts of 2001 adopted by the UN International Law Commission (ILC), which to a significant extent codified customary international law.[11] It took the best part of 50 years for the ILC to conclude its work on the draft. However, scholars have been highly critical of it since by the time it was adopted, it was already out of date with regard to contemporary challenges.[12] Indeed, in a globalised world with many different types of actors there continues to be no legal mechanism to investigate and prosecute international crimes by collective entities.[13] That is that – apart from a short-sighted and dubious decision handed down by the Special Tribunal for Lebanon in the case of *Akhbar Beirut S.A.L and Ibrahim Mohamed Al Amin*, in which a corporate entity was found guilty of interfering with the administration of justice – individuals remain the primary focus of ICL.[14] This is perplexing since

9 Clapham (n 2) 899.

10 Mark Drumbl, *Atrocity, Punishment and International Law* (CUP 2007). See also K Heller, 'Review Essay: Deconstructing International Criminal Law' (2007) 106 *Michigan Law Review* 975.

11 International Law Commission, 'Draft Articles on Responsibility of States for Internationally Wrongful Acts, with Commentaries' (2001) ii *Yearbook of the International Law Commission* pt 2. For a seminal analysis of the Draft Articles, see James Crawford, *The Law of International Responsibility* (OUP 2010).

12 Edith Brown Weiss, 'Invoking State Responsibility in the Twenty-First Century' (2002) 96 *American Journal of International Law* 798, 799.

13 Jutta Brunnée, 'International Legal Accountability Through the Lens of the Law of State Responsibility' (2005) 36 *Netherlands Yearbook of International Law* 21, 23.

14 *In the Case Against Akhbar Beirut S.A.L. and Ibrahim Mohamed Al Amin*, STL-14–06/1/CJ, 31 January 2014, [27].

international crimes are archetypically perpetrated by collective entities.[15] Indeed, as the Appeals Chamber of the International Criminal Tribunal for the Former Yugoslavia has enunciated in *Prosecutor v Tadić* 'most of the time these crimes do not result from the criminal propensity of single individuals but constitute manifestations of collective criminality: the crimes are often carried out by groups of individuals acting in pursuit of a common criminal design'.[16] Yet ICL continues to pursue a model of individual culpability only.

Certain individuals in the joint criminal plan may physically perform the crime while others may have acted in other ways that were vital towards the commission of the offence. ICL involves evaluating the culpability of individuals in each category, which involves considerable resources to investigate the contribution of individuals to mass atrocity. However, '[w]here the organization of the social whole largely determines the character and conduct of its parts, exclusive attention to these constituent components risks missing everything of significance to moral judgment and social understanding'.[17] This has led commentators to raise concerns about the potential for discord between ICL's objective to bring those most responsible for international crimes to justice on the one hand and its perceived failure to address collective entities on the other.[18]

Non-state armed groups highlight the nature of this dilemma quite acutely. Pursuant to Common Article 3 to the Geneva Conventions 1949 as supplemented by Additional Protocol II, non-state armed groups are obliged to comply with and, to some extent, further IHL.[19] Rules that non-state armed groups must obey when conducting hostilities include a prohibition from carrying out direct and indiscriminate attacks against civilians and a duty to take all feasible precautions to avoid civilian casualties as far as possible. Duties are not always absolute, and in particular, under the Geneva Conventions, the application of some are limited by the resources available during hostilities. Nevertheless, such duties continue to evolve; some non-state armed groups have endeavoured to adopt them as part of their internal rules of operations, and the feasible precautions principle implies that duties can take on a harder cast as such resources do, in fact, become more available.[20]

15 George Fletcher, 'The Storrs Lectures: Liberals and Romantics at War: The Problem of Collective Guilt' (2002) 111 *Yale Law Journal* 1499; Larry May, 'Collective Punishment and Mass Confinement' in Tracey Isaacs and Richard Vernon (eds), *Accountability for Collective Wrongdoing* (CUP 2011).

16 *Tadić Appeal* (n 7) [191].

17 Mark Osiel, *Making Sense of Mass Atrocity* (CUP 2009) 188. See also Chrisje Brants, 'Guilty Landscapes: Collective Guilt and International Criminal Law' in Cecilia Bailliet and Katja Aas (eds), *Cosmopolitan Justice and its Discontents* (Routledge 2012).

18 Clapham (n 2) 899.

19 Christopher Greenwood, 'Scope of Application of Humanitarian Law' in Dieter Fleck (ed), *The Handbook of Humanitarian Law in Armed Conflict* (2nd edn, OUP 2007).

20 Anna Brennan, 'Exploring the Accountability of Leaders of Armed Opposition Groups Under International Law' (2010) 23 *Hague Yearbook of International Law* 223, 236.

The growth of IHL has accompanied a more general concern about how non-state armed groups can be held accountable for breaches of humanitarian norms since there continues to be no formal international judicial mechanism with jurisdiction to investigate and prosecute them.[21] This is reflected in criticisms about the reality deficit in ICL, as well as the critique by some scholars that ICL has been used to impose particular political structures on the international community, with resulting doubts about ICL's legitimacy.[22] Scholars have voiced their disquiet about the possible impact of only prosecuting individuals for crimes arising from the conduct of the non-state armed group. Andrew Clapham, in particular, notes that:

> [w]hile the practice concerning criminalization of individual members of rebel groups under international law is now well-established (with regards to inter alia war crimes and crimes against humanity), the question of whether the groups as such can be said to have violated international criminal law remains, however, under explored.[23]

So ICL's failure to embrace the accountability of the collective entity needs to be further examined.[24]

However, what precisely is impeding the reform of ICL to embrace collective entity accountability? One argument is that modes of collective entity responsibility that have been adopted in domestic law systems have not garnered universal acceptance and, as a result, have not been included in ICL.[25] Of course, ICL can from time to time be quite innovative; why this inventiveness has not expanded to embrace the accountability of collective entities needs to be explored. A second argument advanced is that there is simply no rationale for a principle of collective entity responsibility under ICL. Indeed, Article 25 of the Rome Statute already provides for various modes of individual liability within the jurisdiction of the ICC, and it is on this basis that the argument has been presented that ICL in its current form is more than adequate to punish those responsible for international crimes. Finally, are there broader political reasons which have impeded the

21 The Uppsala Conflict Data Program has estimated that the number of armed conflicts worldwide has increased by nearly 20 percent from 41 in 2014 to 50 in 2015. Of these 50 armed conflicts, only one can be described as purely international in character (India-Pakistan). See Department of Peace and Conflict Research, 'Uppsala Conflict Data Program' <https://ucdp.uu.se/encyclopedia> accessed 5 February 2021.

22 Carsten Stahn, *A Critical Introduction to International Criminal Law* (CUP 2019) 159–174.

23 Clapham (n 2) 920.

24 Mark Drumbl, 'Collective Violence and Individual Punishment: The Criminality of Mass Atrocity' (2005) 99 *Northwest University Law Review* 539, 570.

25 Shachar Eldar, 'Exploring International Criminal Law's Reluctance to Resort to Modalities of Groups Responsibility: Five Challenges to International Prosecutions and Their Impact on Broader Forms of Responsibility' (2013) 11 *Journal of International Criminal Justice* 331, 335.

development of a doctrine of collective entity responsibility? If there are, does this ultimately hinder ICL's objective of investigating and prosecuting those most responsible for international crimes?

Perhaps one manifestation of this dilemma is the intense debate concerning a comprehensive definition of the term 'non-state armed group'. This debate was provoked by the intricacies of modern warfare and the ambiguity about whether they should satisfy a minimum set of criteria with regard to their size, organisation, and power to qualify as international legal subjects. There is also the apprehension that recognising a doctrine of collective entity responsibility under ICL would somehow place the non-state armed group on an equal legal footing with states and give their political/quasi-political objectives legitimacy.[26] Despite these concerns, the potential for ICL to be utilised to prosecute them has been explored in a piecemeal fashion.[27]

Prompted by Article 9 of the Charter of the International Military Tribunal at Nuremberg, which criminalised organisations such as the Leadership Corps of the Nazi Party, the Gestapo, and the SS, the ICC Working Group did consider the possibility of prosecuting corporations, political parties, and even racist groups. But according to James Owen: '[t]he French and the Soviets had grave concerns [during the Nuremberg Trials] about such corporate and retrospective declarations of guilt'.[28] This was due to fears that declarations of collective guilt could lead to the prosecution of every member of a group regardless of their contribution to the perpetration of the crime. This was one of the reasons the ICC Working Group also rejected the proposal.[29] In particular, Cherif Bassiouni was of the view that:

> [t]o impose international criminal responsibility merely for passive responsibility in an organization stretches the generally accepted principles of criminal responsibility found in most legal systems. Such a proposition would

26 For more general commentary on this point, see Daragh Murray, *Human Rights Obligations of Non-State Armed Groups* (Hart 2016) ch 3.

27 Clapham (n 2) 920.

28 James Owens, *Nuremberg: Evil on Trial* (Headline Review 2006) 13.

29 In particular, the IMT held that:

> [a] criminal organisation is analogous to a criminal conspiracy in that the essence of both is cooperation for criminal purposes. There must be a group bound together and organized for a common purpose. The group must be formed or used in connection with the commission of crimes denounced by the Charter. Since the declaration with respect to the organisations and groups will, as has been pointed out, fix the criminality of its members, that definition should exclude persons who had no knowledge of the criminal purposes or acts of the organisation and those who were drafted by the State for membership, unless they were personally implicated in the commission if acts declared criminal by Article 6 of the Charter as members of the organisation. Membership alone is not enough to come within the scope of these declarations.

International Military Tribunal Nuremberg, *Trial of the Major War Criminals Before the International Military Tribunal* (vol 1, Allied Control Authority for Germany 1947) 256. https://www.loc.gov/rr/frd/Military_Law/pdf/NT_Vol-I.pdf.

> be tantamount to guilt by association which most legal systems reject as fundamentally unfair.[30]

As will be discussed further later in the chapter, it must be questioned what benefits if any would be derived from extending ICL to collective entities. Many types of collective entities are not legally incorporated and generally do not have assets or financial resources in their name. Nor are many overly concerned about reputational damage if allegations are made that they have breached humanitarian/human rights norms, and, in any event, their activities are likely to be already prohibited under the domestic laws of the state in which they operate.[31]

Even if Article 25 of the Rome Statute was amended to include collective entity accountability, how would the trial of a collective entity proceed? What rules of evidence and procedure would apply, and would members (in particular those who are high ranking) be permitted to attend the trial and also give evidence without the fear of being arrested themselves? And finally, how would an international criminal court or tribunal punish a collective entity if it was found guilty? It would seem on the face of it that the concerns of Bassiouni and the ICC Working Group are jurisprudentially reasonable. However, collective entity responsibility seems nevertheless justified from a moral standpoint since the entity may be condoning and inciting the individual member to carry out crimes.[32] As Jann Kleffner contends with regards to non-state armed groups that they 'regularly succeed to creating a climate in which crimes are perceived to be in conformity with, rather than a deviation from, standards of behaviour accepted within such a group'.[33] International bodies such as the United Nations (UN) Security Council and the Special Representative of the UN Secretary General for Children in Armed Conflict rely on naming and shaming non-state armed groups when they breach international law.[34] Their prosecution could perhaps 'enable better implementation of international law . . . by calling on the group to change its practice rather than simply punish the individual and it could be encouraged to develop training and structures to prevent and punish

30 M Cherif Bassiouni (ed), *International Criminal Law: Volume 1: Crimes* (2nd edn, Transnational Publishers 1999) 24. See also Andrea Bianchi, 'Security Council's Anti-Terror Resolutions and Their Implementation by Member States' (2006) 4 *Journal of International Criminal Justice* 1044, 1053.

31 Antonio Cassese, 'The Status of Rebels Under the 1977 Geneva Protocol on Non-International Armed Conflicts' (1981) 30 *International and Comparative Law Quarterly* 424. See also Clapham (n 2) 921.

32 Annyssa Bellal, 'Establishing the Direct Responsibility of Non-State Armed Groups for Violations of International Norms: Issues of Attribution' in Noemi Gal-Or, Math Noortmann, and Cedric Ryngaert (eds), *Responsibilities of the Non-State Actor in Armed Conflict: Theoretical Considerations and Empirical Findings* (Brill 2014).

33 Kleffner (n 2) 246.

34 Clapham (n 2) 921.

[future] violations'.[35] At present, international criminal law does not address these issues. Instead, it ignores the collective entity and only pays attention to its individual members.

b) Accounting for collective entity responsibility in international criminal law

The ambiguity concerning a collective entity's responsibilities under international law towards other subjects of international law is not new. It would seem that the drafters of the ILC Articles were somewhat cognisant of this issue. In 1956, the first Special Rapporteur for the ILC, Francisco V García-Amador contended that:

> It is no longer true, as it was for centuries in the past, that international law exists only for, or finds its sole raison d'être in, the protection of the interests and rights of the States; rather its function is now also to protect the rights and interests of its other subjects who may properly claim its protection.[36]

García-Amador's comments formed part of a discussion that states have a responsibility to guarantee that foreign nationals have the same rights as their own citizens. However, they also suggest that the Commission was of the view that the Articles were to be construed in their broader context in which all subjects enjoy rights and protections under international law. This wider perspective perhaps makes room for considering not only the rights and interests of collective entities but also their duties under international law.[37]

Indeed, the ILC Articles distinguish between primary obligations that derive from specific treaties, customary international law, and other sources of international law on the one hand and secondary obligations that stem from the law of state responsibility on the other. If we consider non-state armed groups in particular, reconciling their responsibilities as collective entities under international law could happen at either a primary or secondary level. Their obligations could be accounted for and enshrined within international law among the primary rules of state responsibility as international courts and tribunals demarcate the specific obligations of non-state armed groups and construct remedies for their wrongful acts. There is some evidence that this is beginning to happen: international courts

35 Bellal (n 32) 306. For more commentary on this point, see Andrew Clapham, 'Non-State Actors' in Daniel Moeckli et al. (eds), *International Human Rights Law* (2nd edn, OUP 2013); Mark Drumbl, 'Collective Responsibility and Post-Conflict Justice' in Tracey Isaacs and Richard Vernon (eds), *Accountability for Collective Wrongdoing* (CUP 2011).

36 F García-Amador, 'Report on International Responsibility' (1956) ii *Yearbook of the International Law Commission* 174, 184.

37 Andrew Clapham, 'The Question of Jurisdiction Under International Criminal Law over Legal Persons: Lessons from the Rome Conference on an International Criminal Court' in Menno Kamminga and Saman Zia-Zarifi (eds), *Liability of Multinational Corporations Under International Law* (Kluwer 2000).

and tribunals have given consideration to the obligations of non-state armed groups under international law.[38] Judges have harnessed the Geneva Conventions as they considered the minimum conditions for ascertaining the duties of non-state armed groups in armed conflict situations. These include, amongst others, defining the degree of organisation a non-state armed group must possess in order for the Geneva Conventions to apply to their conduct, their control over territory, their capacity to gain access to weapons and training, their ability to develop a coherent military strategy, and their capability to generally act as one unit and negotiate agreements such as ceasefires and peace accords.[39] As a result, judges have been cognisant that non-state armed groups have not only 'recognised and respected the international treaties of the United Nations and conventions on war'[40] but also 'issued communiqués assuming responsibility for . . . attacks'.[41]

In particular, Veronika Bilkova argues that the *Case Concerning Military and Paramilitary Activities in and Against Nicaragua* supports her claim that the rules on responsibility for internationally wrongful acts can be extended to non-state armed groups. In particular, she points out that 'violations of primary rules binding on. . . [non-state armed actors] by a conduct attributable to them would constitute internationally wrongful acts entailing responsibility with its classical content'.[42] However, Bilkova does not outline exactly how a principle of collective entity responsibility could be introduced in international law or how international courts and tribunals, in particular the ICC, could approach claims against non-state armed groups. The *Nicaragua* case may imply that non-state armed groups must comply with IHL, but the decision also perhaps supports a separate argument that the decision maker declined to adjudicate on the precise parameters of the duties of non-state armed groups in international law, perhaps for lack of competence or because he or she is limited by terms of reference or by the primary rules themselves.

Perhaps it is understandable that decision makers would be apprehensive about applying rules that were originally designed for states. Moreover, the legal personality of certain types of collective entities, especially non-state armed groups, is likely to be limited since they generally only exist for a short time period, because they are suppressed by the state and are disbanded, succeed in seizing power and form a new government, or create a new state. Such groups thus cannot enjoy rights akin to the permanent nature of international actors but perhaps do not have the capacity to fulfil legal obligations either. So what would be the impact of a finding that a collective entity has committed an international crime? With regard to non-state armed groups, Bilkova posits that they should most

38 *Prosecutor v Haradinaj*, IT-04–84–84-T, Trial Chamber, 3 April 2008, [60]; *Prosecutor v Akayesu*, ICTR-96–4-T, 2 September 1998, [619].

39 *Haradinaj* (n 38).

40 ibid., [69].

41 ibid., [91].

42 Veronika Bilkova, 'Armed Opposition Groups and Shared Responsibility' (2015) 62 *Netherlands International Law Review* 69, 76.

probably be held responsible for the conduct of their members and constituent organs acting on their behalf, but she does not outline how to implement this or acknowledge that the organisational structure of some non-state armed groups can be so ambiguous that it is difficult to ascertain whether these individuals are members of the group in the first place.[43] Thus, determining whether the individual member's conduct can be attributed to the non-state armed group will, at times, be difficult.

Bilkova suggests that a decision maker could perhaps expand an approach suggested by the ICRC called the 'continuous function' test: he or she could take into account whether 'a person assumes a continuous function for the group involving his or her direct participation in hostilities' as a decisive criterion for ascertaining individual membership of the group.[44] Subsequently, he or she could evaluate whether the individual member's performance of this continuous function is attributable to the collective entity. While recognising that there is scant international practice embracing this approach, Bilkova appears not to consider the implications it would have for the doctrine of joint criminal enterprise and also other co-perpetrator liability approaches developed by international criminal courts and tribunals. It also relegates to the background the contemporary realities of collective entities such as non-state armed groups and the fact that the ambiguous organisational structure of some of them means that it can be difficult to pinpoint whether an individual member performs this continuous function for the group. Under this approach, the principle of individual criminal responsibility could run the risk of being ignored as a matter of substance or, at best, becoming part of a spasmodic mishmash of law in which the genesis of how international crimes are perpetrated plays a significant role in some modes of liability and a lesser role in others. No doubt the challenges of consistency and legitimacy caused by multiple competing legal principles are much broader than the particular concerns raised here, but in this context, a prosecutor could find him- or herself stuck between a regime that prioritises individual criminal responsibility and another that impedes it, thus running the risk of forestalling investigations into alleged crimes and prosecutions.

3 Complexity theory: the repercussions for the responsibility of collective entities for international crimes

a) The collective entity as a complex adaptive system

Part 2 of this chapter explored a number of reasons why ICL should be reformed to include a principle of collective entity responsibility. However, none of those

43 ibid., 76.

44 Nils Melzer, *Interpretive Guidance on the Notion of Direct Participation in Hostilities Under International Humanitarian Law* (ICRC 2009) 33.

propositions were entirely satisfying, especially with regard to collective entities such as non-state armed groups. The aim of this section is to examine whether complexity theory can illuminate their ontology further. Complexity theory does not constitute a single body of thought but instead has emerged from different traditions and approaches.[45] It concerns the study of individuals' interactions and the system-wide effects they produce. As a theory, it has created two ways of responding to the matter of change and diversity. Firstly, where the small interactions of individuals lead to bifurcations and new self-sustaining phenomena emerge which the individuals could not have reasonably predicted themselves.[46] The ant colony is a frequently cited example: the individual ant placed on a flat surface will walk around in circles to the point of exhaustion; however, a colony of ants programmed to work together and follow simple instructions can construct amazingly complex nests with underground passages and chambers that are essential for survival.[47] With the ant colony, it is the microscopic interactions between the individual ants that lead to this complex behaviour. Such behaviour can also emerge from the interaction of individuals and the adaptation of a system.

The second way is that, from time to time, an emergent phenomenon like the colony of ants will endure in its environment as a complex adaptive system. Melanie Mitchell suggests that a complex system is one 'in which large networks of components with no central control and simple rules of operation give rise to complex collective behaviour, sophisticated information processing, and adaptation via learning or evolution'.[48] She also alternatively proposed that it is 'a system that exhibits non-trivial emergent and self-organizing behaviours'.[49] Pursuant to the theory, the human body, the environment, and the economy can all be regarded as complex adaptive systems since they are distinct from the entity from which they first emerged.[50] So the key component of complexity theory is its anti-reductionist analytic strategy, which is inextricably linked to a vital

45 Sylvia Walby, 'Complexity Theory, Globalisation and Diversity' (British Sociological Association Conference, University of York, April 2003) 3 <https://www.lancaster.ac.uk/fass/resources/sociology-online-papers/papers/walby-complexityglobalisationdiversity.pdf> accessed 27 September 2021.

46 ibid., 3.

47 The ant colony as a complex adaptive system has been examined considerably in the literature. See, for example, Carl Anderson and Daniel McShea, 'Individual Versus Social Complexity, with Particular Reference to Ant Colonies' (2001) 76 *Biological Reviews of the Cambridge Philosophical Society* 211; Walter Gutjahr, 'First Steps to the Runtime Complexity Analysis of Ant Colony Optimization' (2008) 35 *Computers and Operations Research* 2711; Judith Innes and David Booher, 'Consensus Building and Complex Adaptive Systems: A Framework for Evaluating Collaborative Planning' (1999) 65 *Journal of the American Planning Association* 412; Stuart Kauffman, *The Origins of Order: Self-Organization and Selection in Evolution* (OUP 1993); Stuart Kauffman, *At Home in the Universe: The Search for Laws of Self-Organization and Complexity* (Viking 1995).

48 Melanie Mitchell, *Complexity: A Guided Tour* (OUP 2009) 13.

49 ibid., 13.

50 See, e.g., Eric Beinhocker, *The Origin of Wealth: Evolution, Complexity and the Radical Remaking of Economics* (Random House 2006); Simon Levin, *Fragile Dominion:*

re-examination of the nature of systems, in order to more sufficiently conceptualise the dynamic and systematised inter-relationships between phenomena.[51]

However, complexity theory also has its limitations in that the concept of 'system' is entangled within outmoded conceptions of a self-balancing equilibrium. This has led to some difficulty in delineating the precise boundaries of the modern complex system. As a result, a conceptually cogent theory of a complex system was difficult to ground in reality.[52] However, new theorisations of the system within complexity theory have reshaped the concept so that it can now be applied to the most dynamic and irregular emergent phenomena. Some of these modifications are the culmination of

> simple conceptualisations, such as replacing the conception of parts and wholes with the notion that each system takes all other systems as its environment, while others are more complex conceptions of the relations between systems as well as dynamic conceptions of their uneven, non-linear transformations.[53]

Nevertheless, there are still considerable theoretical and empirical questions about complexity theory, especially whether it can clarify how collective entities such as non-state armed groups work or if the concept can only apply by analogy. However, the theory is still useful since it provides an insight into the non-state armed group and their consequences for the matters examined here. The theory suggests that the non-state armed group is a complex adaptive system that has emerged from the interactions of individuals and the variety of conceptual and social tools such as law, ethics, language, culture, and religion that bolster cohesion among significant numbers of individuals who may share a common objective. The non-state armed group as a complex adaptive system has causal effects in its environment, on its members, and on the interactive processes from which it emerged.[54] As a result, the non-state armed group is greater than its total members since it has the capacity to achieve far more than one individual acting alone.

b) Conceptualising the responsibility of the non-state armed group as a collective entity

The ontology of complex adaptive systems has considerable ramifications for the responsibility of the collective entity in general and, more importantly, for the

Complexity and the Commons (Perseus 1999); Robert Sawyer, *Social Emergence: Societies as Complex Systems* (CUP 2005).

51 Walby (n 45) 3. See also David Bryne, *Complexity and the Social Sciences: An Introduction* (Routledge 1998) 15.

52 Steven Manson, 'Simplifying Complexity: A Review of Complexity Theory' (2001) 32 *Geoforum* 405, 411.

53 Walby (n 45) 3.

54 Jean-Jacques Fresard, *The Roots of Behaviour in War: A Survey of the Literature* (ICRC 2004) 46.

principle of individual criminal responsibility. Since it enforces the actuality of complex adaptive systems, complexity theory arguably supports the claim that collective entities are ontologically distinct and separate from their individual members. So, to the degree to which responsibility necessitates that there is an actor upon which responsibility can be imposed, complexity theory implies that the non-state armed group can be regarded as such an actor because it has causative effects that cannot be devolved into integral components. ICL ignores one of the central premises of systems theory: that collective entites are extensions of their individuals. For ICL's purposes, the collective, like the individual, can be criminally repsonsible.

That said, the ontology of the complex adaptive system indicates that the aperture between the collective entity and the individual is still significant for two reasons. Firstly, complexity theory substantiates that rather anodyne conduct has superfluous consequences at group level. In particular, David Bella asserts that:

> [t]o merely blame individuals . . . is to avoid . . . the essential claim of emergence: that the character of wholes should not be reduced to the character of parts. . . . [Therefore,] outcomes can emerge through the efforts of normal competent and well-adjusted people much like ourselves.[55]

Take, for example, the members of a non-state armed group whose role is to follow the instructions of the centralised command and manufacture of improvised explosive devices. The interactions of individuals following straightforward rules or instructions could result in the catastrophic loss of civilian life. If Bella's contention is correct, then complexity theory helps support the idea that the non-state armed actor must be a focal point of responsibility under ICL as a collective entity.

Nevertheless, if the actions of an individual are indeed inconspicuous but international crimes can still occur at the group level, then the distributive dilemma becomes even more acute. The

> non-linear relationship between the complex interactions of individuals and the phenomena that emerge from those interactions means that in most cases it will be impossible to trace direct connections between an individual and the complex adaptive system from which it is a part and the impacts that system may have in the world.[56]

Considering how complexity theory would posit that the perpetration of an international crime generally stems from the interactions of multiple individuals, it is difficult to delineate why an individual member of a non-state armed

55 David Bella, 'Emergence and Evil' (2006) 8 *Emergence: Complexity and Organization* 102, 103.

56 Chinen (n 3) 723.

group, for example, should shoulder responsibility for that crime alone when numerous other individuals may have contributed towards its commission as well? This implies that even if an individual member conforms with the complex system's behaviour, there may still be no consequential link between that conformity and the crimes that system has committed. The non-linearity between the individual members and the non-state armed group infers that the distribution of responsibility requires a link, no matter how tenuous, between the group and its members. However, complexity theory does not elucidate what this link should be and what criteria need to be met to establish it. Without these criteria, it will be difficult for international criminal courts and tribunals to elucidate how responsibility for international crimes can be distributed to collective entities.

Complexity theory also has consequences for the concept of responsibility. Under ICL, it is deemed pertinent that an individual should bear responsibility for a crime for which he or she understood the potential consequences and, nevertheless, committed the act anyway. However, if an act can lead to unforeseen consequences in the future, why should a person only be considered responsible for that crime and not the group as well? Alicia Juarrero posits that '[s]elf-organization . . . counsels for a wider denotation for the term cause, one reconceptualised in terms of "context-sensitive constraints" to include those causal power that incorporate circular causality, context-sensitive embeddedness, and temporality'.[57] Klaus Mainzer also supports this argument, stating that, in a linear model causation, 'the extent of an effect is believed to be similar to the extent of the cause. Thus, a legal punishment of a punishable action can be proportional to the degree of damage effected'.[58]

However, according to complexity theory, phenomena can emerge from random events, so the principle of proportionate responsibility can be questioned. Complexity theory presupposes that most issues have non-linear characteristics. Indeed, Juarrero asserts that '[a]s the ecological, economic, and political problems of mankind have become global, complex, non-linear, and random, the traditional concept of individual responsibility is questionable'.[59] The same can be said of collective entities like non-state armed groups: the acts they commit in the short term can result in consequences that are felt by the wider international community in the long term. Thus, regard should be given to the context in which responsibility is being applied. While in the short term, the individual member of the non-state armed group will retain some element of control over the effects of their actions for which they can be held accountable, they are also restricted by their environment and the internal dynamics which led to the

57 Alicia Juarrero, 'On Philosophy's "To Rethink" List: Causality, Explanation and Ethic' (2008) 20 *Ecological Psychology* 278, 280.
58 Klaus Mainzer, *Thinking in Complexity: The Computational Dynamics of Matter, Mind and Mankind* (5th edn, Springer 1997) 435.
59 ibid.

emergent behaviour of the group.[60] These limitations have led some commentators to express scepticism about whether a member of a non-state armed group has much autonomy. For instance, Erin Kelly contends that individuals:

> are shaped by environment, genetics, and experience in a way that affects what we perceive as reasons and narrows the horizon of possibilities for action. Environmental, genetic and psychological factors all shape what count as reasons for a person. Recognising this should challenge our confidence that a given wrongdoer was morally capable of doing better.[61]

This is precisely why some scholars who wish to retain some semblance of the concept of responsibility argue that the concept should be constructed. In particular, Anton Schütz states that responsibility 'does not exist prior to its assignment'.[62] However, it is my view, based on the foregoing analysis, that the ontology of complex systems implies that when a collective entity such as a non-state armed group commits an international crime, it is difficult to side-step the criticism that its individual members are unfairly bearing the brunt of accountability for it.[63]

c) *The non-state armed group as a collective entity: an ontology or a legal concept?*

It would appear that complexity theory and its ontology of the complex adaptive system have not been able to answer all our questions. If this is the case, why should we pay any attention to them, especially since international law seems to yearn for us to set questions about the ontology of the non-state armed group to one side? Indeed, the ILC's Articles on the Responsibility of States for Internationally Wrongful Acts would suggest that '[c]ontemporary international law is clearly the work of states, every last word conforms to their wishes. States jealously safeguard their constitutional attribute of independent sovereignty and thereby affirm their monopoly over both national and international matters'.[64] So there would seem to be very little leeway for collective entities such as

60 William Frederick, 'Emergent Management Morality: Explaining Corporate Corruption' (2003) 5 *Emergence* 1, 5.

61 Erin Kelly, 'Reparative Justice' in Tracey Isaacs and Richard Vernon (eds), *Accountability for Collective Wrongdoing* (CUP 2011) 194.

62 Anton Schütz, 'Desiring Society: Autopoiesis Beyond the Paradigm of Mastership' (1994) 5 *Law and Critique* 149, 160.

63 See the San Jose Agreement between El Salvador and the Frente Farabundo Marti la Liberacion Nacional (FMLN), signed by both sides on 26 July 1990: 'Note verbal Dated 14 August 1990 from the Chargé d'affaires a.i. of the Permanent Mission of El Salvador to the United Nations Addressed to the Secretary-General' UN Doc A/44/971 – S/21541, 16 August 1990, Annex ('Agreement on Human Rights').

64 Agnes Lejbowicz, *Philosophie du Droit International: L'Impossible Capture de l'Humanite* (PUF 1999) 292 as translated in Zakaria Dabone; 'International Law: Armed Groups in a State-Centric System' (2011) 93(882) *International Review of the Red Cross* 395, 396.

non-state armed groups in this quandary. At the same time, prosecuting the non-state armed group as a collective entity under ICL would imply that they are international legal subjects, but as discussed in Part 2, there is no clear-cut definition of non-state armed groups, and this is clearly illustrated in the myriad of terms that have been used to describe them.

Liesbeth Zegveld has traced the functional personality of non-state armed groups to determine whether they should satisfy a minimum set of criteria as to their size and power to qualify as legal subjects.[65] However, contemporary international law would posit that the non-state armed group does not have 'a legal status attaching to a certain set of affairs by virtue of certain rules or practices'.[66] Roland Portmann contends that international practice is cognisant of firstly, a formal conception of international personality in which legal rules delineate the criteria for legal personality and secondly, an 'actor conception' in which legal personality is composed of actors who take part in and contribute to the creation of international law.[67] He suggests that it is futile to 'recognise certain entities as international persons: [because] such status in itself does not entail any international legal rights, duties or capacities whatsoever'.[68] It is for international norms to bestow legal rights and obligations upon entities and not the mere fact of international legal personality. On the basis of these amalgamated constructs, even if non-state armed groups could be described as having a legal status, some commentators have sought to argue that they 'do not automatically possess so-called fundamental rights and duties nor are they automatically authorized to formally contribute to the creation of international law'.[69]

Of course, the idea that international law should regard the non-state armed group as a legal concept would be quite appealing, if only because it sidesteps the difficulties with construing the non-state armed group as a sociopolitical object. It has further significance for the issue of responsibility itself. As discussed in the previous section, the majority of the literature has strived to answer whether a collective entity can ever be subject to moral judgment since it is unclear whether the tools we utilise to make moral judgments about individuals can also be applied to entities such as non-state armed groups. Developing a legal conception of collective entities like the non-state armed group would do very little to alleviate the problem since they are regarded as incapable of fulfilling their duties under international law, so it could be said that international law is still not comfortable with regarding a non-state armed group as having the capacity to bear legal responsibility for its wrongful conduct, preferring instead to distinguish them from states under the law and treat their members as mere domestic criminals. As Portmann provides: 'the only consequence directly stemming from international

65 Zegveld (n 6) 134.
66 James Crawford, *The Creation of States in International Law* (2nd edn, CUP 2006) 5.
67 Roland Portmann, *Legal Personality in International Law* (CUP 2010) 176.
68 ibid., 176.
69 ibid., 177. Other views have been put forward in this regard: see, e.g., Daragh Murray, *Human Rights Obligations of Non-State Actors* (Hart Publishing 2016).

personality is the capacity to invoke international responsibility and to be held internationally responsible'.[70]

Classifying a non-state armed group as a legal concept would also have ramifications for the principle of individual criminal responsibility under ICL. A non-state armed group needs individuals to act for it. In turn, if the non-state armed group could be held accountable under ICL as a collective entity, the member's conduct could be imputed to the collective entity. As a result, the member would not always face the consequences for their role in the perpetration of the international crime. This was also a dilemma recognised by Roberto Ago, the second rapporteur for the ILC, with regard to states. However, he averred that the entity to which the individual's actions are imputed must be a legal one and not a sociopolitical entity.[71] If ICL developed to such an extent that non-state armed groups as collective entities could be held accountable for international crimes, states could potentially be held accountable as well. This would have considerable consequences for the utilisation of the principle of individual criminal responsibility under the Rome Statute if the collective entity is deemed to subsume the individual member. Indeed, how would the principle of individual criminal responsibility exist alongside a principle of collective entity responsibility since, from an evidential point of view, pursuing the collective entity would perhaps be a more straightforward option for the Office of the Prosecutor than pursuing individual members. As a result, members of the entity who played a crucial role in the planning, ordering, and commission of international crimes would potentially evade justice, thereby fostering a culture of impunity. It would be essential for ICL to preserve some degree of autonomy and responsibility for individuals who act on behalf of collective entities: in particular, high-ranking members who may have ordered or failed to prevent the commission of international crimes.

Analysing the non-state armed group as a collective entity in legal terms has its benefits but also its limitations. The idea that it could become a legal subject of international law by meeting certain pre-existing legal criteria which it had no role in creating or developing would be a major bone of contention for it. Indeed, many non-state armed groups refuse to be bound by laws that were created by what they perceive to be the 'enemy state'. One could retort by contending that at least some fundamental international legal principles preceded the existence of states, so why not for non-state armed groups as well? Law existed before the Treaty of Westphalia in 1648, but at the same time, it is 'shorthand for the processes in which law and social-political entities interacted well before 1648 and thereafter, not just a single event'.[72] Of course, the debate about whether law or sociopolitical entities existed first is incessant, but modern-day international practice has certainly taken the stance that one precedes the other.

70 ibid., 275.

71 Robert Ago, 'Second Report on State Responsibility' (1970) ii *Yearbook of the International Law Commission* 177, 190 [39]; Kast and Rosenzweig (n 4).

72 Chinen (n 3) 727.

So perhaps it is crucial to reconsider James Crawford's use of the phrase 'state of affairs' to figure out its legal implications. As Mark Chinen points out '[t]erritory, population, government, and the ability to engage in international relations are legal terms . . . but they also purport to say something meaningful about the socio-political and geographic state of affairs to which legal analysis applies'.[73] One could posit that, as an autopoetic system, ICL views the world with reference to its own terms. But even so, the state of affairs should not be relegated to the back burner. As with the relationship between law and ethics, if legal categorisations depart from reality, a number of challenges ensue. There is a danger that ICL could become ineffective because it cannot sufficiently address this reality, or it hazards becoming pointless for this same reason. Both levy a price on ICL's legitimacy. As explored earlier, the reality is that individual members of collective entities bear the brunt of responsibility for international crimes. But if we recognise that the state of affairs is an important component in any analysis of ICL, ontology can perhaps be brought within the fold. With regard to the sociopolitical entity that is the non-state armed group, complexity theory would suggest that its ontology is one of a distinct entity, and its individual members must unfairly shoulder the burden of accountability for international crimes which emanate from the group itself. It is long overdue for ICL to be revamped to embrace this reality.

4 Conclusion

As stated in the introduction, ICL has so far had very little to do with the accountability of collective entities, and this chapter has examined a fundamental consequence of that actuality with reference to non-state armed groups. It has explored the potential impact of certain ideas from complexity theory on the potential future development of ICL: in particular, the challenges that arise from the distribution of criminal responsibility within a non-state armed group to individual members only. Complexity theory highlights how ICL does not fully capture where accountability should lie within non-state armed groups in view of how their international crimes are planned and orchestrated in reality. This chapter contributes to this discussion by providing an ontology of the non-state armed group that complicates ICL's focus on the individual; it is an entity that is not readily differentiable from its individual members. So if ICL is to be effective and achieve its objective of thwarting impunity and deterring future crimes, it must deal with the collective entity itself as well. However, the theory also helps elucidate that any attempt to inter-link individual and group conduct is rife with difficulty: as a complex adaptive system, the non-state armed group could not exist without the interactions of its individual members, but the non-state armed group is also more than the aggregate of its members. Thus, the relationship between the individual member and the collective entity is more challenging to

73 ibid., 727.

delineate than the principle of individual criminal responsibility allows. Unfortunately, ICL continues to overlook this ontology, thereby risking incoherence.

Efforts to develop ICL to include a principle of collective entity responsibility have been and will continue to be challenging at best. This chapter could thus seem quite dispiriting: like a lot of research, it endeavours to illustrate why a particular dilemma in ICL recurs perennially and why any possible strategies to overcome it are likely to fail. Nevertheless, the consequences of only distributing responsibility for international crimes to individual members of collective entities are far-reaching, especially since, for the most part, it is the group as a whole who may be condoning and inciting the individual member to carry out crimes. Therefore, it is, at the very least, useful to consider whether the benefits ensuing from holding individual members of the non-state armed group accountable outweigh those negative consequences and whether there is any means to overcome those impacts, in particular because there may be no rational means to vindicate them.

11 Postscript

International criminal justice futures

Susan Harris Rimmer, Emma Palmer, and Edwin Bikundo

Vale Professor Robert Cryer (2 January 2021)

1 Futures versus Utopia

As we enter 2021,[1] international criminal justice scholars may be feeling distanced from 'Realizing Utopia', the vision for the future of international law edited by the late Judge Antonio Cassese and published posthumously in 2012.[2] The authors in that collection sought 'to discern the potential, in the present legal construct of world society, that might one day be brought to light in a better world'.[3] Judge Cassese was steeped in the *realpolitik* of the politics of international criminal law as the first president of the International Criminal Tribunal for the former Yugoslavia and the first president of the Special Tribunal for Lebanon but did remain, in his own words, an idealist.[4] As he concluded his collection:

> We are comforted in our endeavours by the realization that a new wind of change is currently blowing in the world. As noted above, national and international courts are gradually gnawing at some of the previously unfettered prerogatives of states, with a view to upholding the new values rising in the world society, chiefly those relating to human rights. In sum, the world is rapidly moving and a new ethos is in the offing, if it is not already taking shape.[5]

The authors in that collection dealing with future of international criminal law sought to restrain violence, to struggle for reform, to make modest proposals, to create blueprints for future action. There is serious and justified critique, but there was no sense that the flaws in the project of international criminal justice

1 This chapter was finalised in March 2021.
2 Antonio Cassese (ed), *Realizing Utopia: The Future of International Law* (OUP 2012).
3 ibid., xxi.
4 Antonio Cassese, *Five Masters of International Law: Conversations with R-J Dupuy, E Jimenez de Arechaga, R Jennings, L Henkin and O Schachter* (Hart 2011).
5 Antonio Cassese, 'Conclusion: Gathering up the Main Threads' in Cassese (ed) (n 2) 683.

DOI: 10.4324/9781003087533-14

were so great as to justify disengagement, even from the scholars in the volume more sceptical about Cassese's vision.

This current collection has moved away from seeking agreement about Utopia and an expectation of fertile ground for reform to instead examine the 'futures' of international criminal justice and how it is 'nested' in time and space. Our contributors have highlighted how international criminal justice responds to tensions involving universalism and localisation, technological and environmental change, and, in particular, the non-linear effects of 'justice' and its mechanisms. We acknowledge that sometimes international criminal law should move to the periphery of potential futures, rather than centre stage.

Nevertheless, this collection is offered in the same spirit as Cassese urged: that the starting point is critical engagement and the acknowledgement of the possibility of change. Would any scholar in 2019 have predicted that the Security Council would pass a resolution demanding a general and immediate cessation of hostilities in all situations on the Council's agenda and calling upon all parties to armed conflicts to engage immediately in a 90-day humanitarian pause in 2020?[6] The diversity of interdisciplinary perspectives and approaches showcased here, including international relations, politics, criminology, transitional justice, and development studies, can enrich scholarship on the futures of international criminal justice. Contributors did not explicitly adopt a reformist or specifically critical approach, but instead tackled their respective subject matters in a spirit of inquiry to propose insights into the variety of international criminal justice's multiple possible futures.

And so, as a conclusion to this collection, we wish to reflect on the state of play in early 2021 and note how these events respond to our authors' sense of possible futures.

2 Strife and reform at the International Criminal Court

The International Criminal Court (ICC) faced serious challenges in 2020, from threatened and actual state withdrawals from the Rome Statute, to the debate over the concept of the 'interests of justice' and its role in the Afghanistan investigation. American antagonism to the Court under then-President Trump escalated to the point that the US imposed a travel ban and asset freeze on ICC Prosecutor Fatou Bensouda and a member of her office in September 2020. The ICC responded that the action constituted an attack on the rule of law and an interference with efforts to prosecute grave crimes of concern to the international community.[7]

Debate remained strong about the future of international criminal law in domestic regimes, the promise and potential of regional courts, and the questions

6 UNSC Res 2532 (1 July 2020) UN Doc S/RES/2532.

7 'US under Fire over Sanctions on Top ICC Officials' *Financial Times* (3 September 2020) <www.ft.com/content/f21c253e-5d1f-48ea-9b35-a71c3d111290> accessed 31 March 2021.

of when and where hybrids or specialised mechanisms are preferable.[8] The ICC kept working during the pandemic. As of June 2020, the OTP had 12 situations under investigation: Afghanistan, Burundi, Central African Republic (CAR) I and II, Côte d'Ivoire (CIV), Darfur, DRC, Georgia, Kenya, Mali, Myanmar/Bangladesh, and Uganda. To date, no investigation seems to have been closed, and only CAR I has been completed, though some are hibernated. Nonetheless, the future of international criminal justice seems assured to the extent that a new prosecutor, Karim Khan from the United Kingdom, is set to start his term on 16 June 2021. The current priorities for the prosecutor's investigative division are the investigations in Burundi, CAR II, CIV II, Darfur, DRC, Georgia, Libya (two investigations), and Mali.

In relation to 'new crimes' such as those explored by Rachel Killean and Edwin Bikundo in this volume, in February 2021, Trial Chamber IX found former child-soldier Dominic Ongwen guilty of crimes against humanity and war crimes. These included the 'new' reproductive crime of forced pregnancy (as a war crime and crime against humanity) – new only in the sense that this was the first time it was charged at the ICC.[9]

In a major development, the Independent Expert Review of the International Criminal Court was released at the end of 2020, raising serious issues of accountability and culture.[10] By way of background, in 2014, the Assembly of States Parties to the Rome Statute of the International Criminal Court (ASP) had requested that the Court develop a series of key performance indicators (KPIs) to allow them to assess the Court's performance and ascertain their needs. In 2019, the Court delivered a report on the development of KPIs since then, which outlined significant progress, but there remained room for improvement.

The experts responded to concerns regarding the prioritisation of situations, the difficulties in maintaining hibernated investigations, and the inability of the OTP to close/complete investigations. The report was especially frank about problems in the workplace culture of the ICC. It also brought out the complexity involved in evaluating the ICC's success. The experts could not identify sufficient links between the KPIs established and the strategic plans of the Organs of the Court, except for those in the Registry. An external auditor found insufficient links between the KPIs and budget, and the excessive number of KPIs clouded the ASP's ability to draw conclusions on Court performance. The report recommended that KPIs should be refined in view of two key objectives: assessing the Court's efficiency and its effectiveness.

8 American Society of International Law, 'The ICC and Beyond: Re-Evaluating the Promise of International Criminal Justice' (25 June 2020) <www.asil.org/events/icc-and-beyond-re-evaluating-promise-international-criminal-justice> accessed 31 March 2021.

9 Rosemary Grey, 'The ICC's First "Forced Pregnancy" Case in Historical Perspective' (2017) 15 *Journal of International Criminal Justice* 905.

10 Nicolas Guillou et al., 'Independent Expert Review of the International Criminal Court and the Rome Statute System: Final Report' (30 September 2020) <https://asp.icc-cpi.int/iccdocs/asp_docs/ASP19/IER-Final-Report-ENG.pdf> accessed 31 March 2021.

'Efficiency' encompasses the internal workings of the Court, analysing quantitative data related to the administration of justice such as sitting time, time taken to issue decisions, etc. Analysis of these indicators can be used in improving the Court's operations by guiding budget preparations, forecasting the timing of trials, and identifying areas of underperformance, as well as demonstrating the needs of the Court.

The 'effectiveness' of the Court measures the impact of its outputs, such as its deterrent effect and outcomes for victims and those in affected communities. In contrast with the earlier objective, this is assessed using qualitative analysis, which might be gathered through polls and questionnaires distributed amongst the affected communities. Experts recommended that the Court employ academics and civil society organisations for such ends to take advantage of their existing partnerships with stakeholders such as local communities and regional and international organisations.[11] Our authors also call for the effectiveness of international criminal justice interventions to be defined by the people directly affected at a community level.[12]

3 Notable conflicts

The major conflicts in 2020–March 2021 were those in Afghanistan, Yemen, and Ethiopia – but with significant events in Myanmar, Belarus, and Syria.[13] Major allegations of ongoing crimes were made against China and Sri Lanka.

a) Myanmar

Several international institutions had attempted to 'prevent' future violence in Myanmar through ICC and ICJ actions and a UN commission of inquiry, but it can be argued that both prevention and prosecutorial approaches have essentially failed, so far, to respond to both past violence and its persistent causes and present effects. As developed in Emma Palmer's contribution to this volume, international criminal justice's futures therefore intersect with – and may conflict with – the futures offered by other frames, including those of development and prevention.

A tragic reversal of democratic gains in Myanmar is occurring as we finalise this book. The National League for Democracy (NLD) won about 80 percent of the parliament seats in the November 2020 election, beating the pro-military party, according to the election commission. The army refused to accept the result, citing unsubstantiated allegations of fraud. Widespread demonstrations by citizens have been occurring since then, with 19 deaths of protestors as of March 2021 and many more in the weeks that followed. The UN Security Council was briefed

11 ibid.

12 See further Emma Palmer, 'The Effectiveness of National Human Rights Institutions' Relationships with Civil Society: The Commission on Human Rights in the Philippines' (2019) 25 *Australian Journal of Human Rights* 299.

13 And, as we went to press, Gaza.

after the Myanmar army detained Aung San Suu Kyi and others, handed power to military chief Min Aung Hlaing, and imposed a one-year state of emergency. However, the Security Council could not agree to pass a resolution condemning the 'coup' in Myanmar.

The upheaval in Myanmar has cast a spotlight again on technology and international criminal justice. Eighteen million people in Myanmar use Facebook as the main source of online information. Global human rights campaigners were suing Facebook for promoting genocide against the Rohingya in 2018. The company admitted that the platform was used to promote hate speech,[14] but then Myanmar's military rulers blocked access to Facebook in early February 2020, days after they overthrew the democratic government, for the sake of 'stability'.[15] Finally in February 2021, Facebook banned the remaining Myanmar military and military-controlled state and media entities from Facebook and Instagram, as well as advertisements from military-linked commercial entities.[16]

b) Yemen

A Saudi-led military coalition intervened in Yemen in 2015, supporting government forces fighting the Iran-aligned Houthis. The United Nations described Yemen in 2021 as the world's biggest humanitarian crisis, with 80 percent of its people in need.[17] In his first visit to the State Department as president, Joe Biden stated the United States would end its support for offensive operations in the Saudi-led war in Yemen.[18] This was seen as a reversal of a policy of both the Democratic Obama and Republican Trump administrations.

c) China

According to estimates, more than a million Uighurs and other minorities have been detained in camps in China.[19] In December 2020, the ICC rejected an application from Uighurs in exile to investigate China for alleged genocide and

14 'Facebook Admits it was Used to "Incite Offline Violence" in Myanmar' *BBC News* (6 November 2018) <www.bbc.com/news/world-asia-46105934> accessed 31 March 2021.

15 'Myanmar Coup: Military Blocks Facebook for Sake of "Stability"' *BBC News* (5 February 2021) <www.bbc.com/news/world-asia-55923486> accessed 31 March 2021.

16 Rafael Frankel, 'Un Update on the Situation in Myanmar' *Facebook* (11 February 2021) <https://about.fb.com/news/2021/02/an-update-on-myanmar/> accessed 31 March 2021.

17 United Nations Population Fund, 'After Years of Conflict, Yemen Remains the World's Worst Humanitarian Crisis, a UNFPA 2021 Appeal Shows' (7 December 2020) <www.unfpa.org/news/after-years-conflict-yemen-remains-worlds-worst-humanitarian-crisis-unfpa-2021> accessed 31 March 2021.

18 Ben Hubbard and Shuaib Almosawa, 'Biden to Cease US Aid for War in Yemen, but Ending the Fighting Will Take Time' *New York Times* (6 February 2021) <www.nytimes.com/2021/02/05/world/middleeast/yemen-saudi-biden.html> accessed 31 March 2021.

19 Kelsey Munro, 'Xinjiang Data Project website launch' *Australian Strategic Policy Institute* (25 September 2020) <www.aspi.org.au/news/xinjiang-data-project-website-launch> accessed 31 March 2021.

crimes against humanity, saying it was unable to act because China was outside its jurisdiction.

However, a late 2020 BBC report detailed allegations of systematic rape of Uighur women in Chinese camps.[20] In January, the outgoing Trump administration declared that China had committed genocide in its repression of the Uighurs,[21] a declaration later endorsed by the new Biden administration. China has consistently denied allegations of human rights abuses in Xinjiang and said the camps were not detention camps, but 'vocational educational and training centres'.[22]

d) Ethiopia

Prime Minister Abiy Ahmed, who won the Nobel Peace Prize in 2019, partly for making peace with Eritrea, ordered the start of a military offensive against Tigray in November 2020 after accusing the region's ruling party of attacking a government defence post and attempting to steal artillery and military equipment. A dispute between the federal government and the powerful faction in control of Tigray had been moving towards violent confrontation for some months. The conflict comes as Ethiopia, Africa's second-most-populous nation, faces mounting economic and social challenges amid a volatile democratic transition. The UN Security Council called for greater access to Ethiopia's war-stricken Tigray region, where as many as two million people require humanitarian assistance amid continued hostilities. Although Ethiopia is not a state party, the ICC is nonetheless pursuing investigations in other non-state parties' territories, including Myanmar and Sudan, suggesting that it is theoretically possible that something similar might occur in relation to Ethiopia.[23]

e) Sri Lanka

In a January 2021 report, United Nations High Commissioner for Human Rights Michelle Bachelet said she was 'alarmed' by the worsening human rights situation in Sri Lanka and argued that the Human Rights Council should take steps to confront the increasing risk of future violations. This followed the government of President Gotabaya Rajapaksa withdrawing its support for a 2015

20 Matthew Hill, David Campanale, and Joel Gunter, '"Their Goal Is to Destroy Everyone": Uighur Camp Detainees Allege Systematic Rape' *BBC News* (2 February 2021) <www.bbc.com/news/world-asia-china-55794071> accessed 31 March 2021.

21 'US: China "Committed Genocide Against Uighurs"' *BBC News* (20 January 2021) <www.bbc.com/news/world-us-canada-55723522> accessed 31 March 2021.

22 Hill, Campanale, and Gunter (n 20).

23 International Criminal Court, 'Situations Under Investigation' <www.icc-cpi.int/pages/situation.aspx> accessed 31 March 2021.

consensus resolution seeking justice and reconciliation.[24] Since 2020, the president has appointed at least 28 serving or former military and intelligence personnel to key administrative posts.

The UN report urged improved and close monitoring and preventive efforts from the international community because 'Sri Lanka's current trajectory sets the scene for the recurrence of the policies and practices that gave rise to grave human rights violations'.[25] The report highlights the militarisation of civilian governmental functions, reversal of important constitutional safeguards, political obstruction of accountability, exclusionary rhetoric, intimidation of civil society, and the use of anti-terrorism laws – all representing 'important early warning indicators'.[26]

f) Afghanistan

International observers considered intra-Afghan negotiations that began in Doha, Qatar, in September 2020 to represent a significant development in the Afghanistan peace process.[27] Members of the Security Council welcomed the start of the talks and called on the parties to engage in good faith and to undertake confidence-building measures such as a reduction in violence. Contentious topics included the question of which interpretation of Islam should be used to frame laws in a post-conflict Afghanistan and the place in the negotiations of the 29 February 2020 US-Taliban agreement. According to reports, the 'Taliban has demanded that the Hanafi school of Sunni jurisprudence serve as the principal source of future legislation in Afghanistan, while the Afghan government expressed concern that this could lead to discrimination against religious minorities in the country'.[28] Further, the Taliban indicated that it would not recognise the legitimacy of the Afghan government by insisting that the rules of procedure for the discussions must state that the group is only negotiating with the Afghan government as part of the US-Taliban agreement.[29] The new Biden administra-

24 Office of the High Commissioner on Human Rights, 'Sri Lanka on Alarming Path towards Recurrence of Grave Human Rights Violations – UN Report' (27 January 2021) <www.ohchr.org/EN/NewsEvents/Pages/DisplayNews.aspx?NewsID=26695&LangID=E> accessed 31 March 2021.

25 ibid., 14.

26 ibid., 6.

27 United Nations Secretary-General, 'Secretary-General's Video Message for the Start of Intra-Afghan Negotiations' (12 September 2020) <www.un.org/sg/en/content/sg/statement/2020-09-12/secretary-generals-video-message-for-the-start-of-intra-afghan-negotiations> accessed 31 March 2021.

28 Security Council Report, 'Arria-Formula Meeting on the Peace Process in Afghanistan' *Security Council Report* (19 November 2020) <www.securitycouncilreport.org/whatsinblue/2020/11/arria-formula-meeting-on-the-peace-process-in-afghanistan.php> accessed 31 March 2021.

29 ibid; Clayton Thomas, 'Afghanistan: Background and US Policy: In Brief' *Congressional Research Service* (25 March 2021) <https://crsreports.congress.gov/product/pdf/R/R45122/44> accessed 31 March 2021.

tion has decided to withdraw troops from Afghanistan in September 2021 and remove Taliban members from UN sanctions designations.

Reports suggest that there 'has been no reduction in civilian casualties since the start of the intra-Afghan talks'.[30] Worse, the period between October and early November 2020 witnessed a series of deadly terror attacks and targeted assassinations in the capital, Kabul, and increased fighting in rural areas across the country. Additionally, fighting between the Taliban and the Afghan National Security Forces in several provinces – including Helmand, Kandahar, and Uruzgan – since early October sparked widespread displacement. The UN Office for the Coordination of Humanitarian Affairs also 'verified the displacement of more than 28,000 people in those provinces, with 15,236 people displaced in Helmand alone'.[31] It is important to not just sustain but continue 'the gains made in the past 19 years in the country, including the human rights and constitutional rights of women, girls and minorities', including to prevent further atrocity crimes.[32]

4 Emerging issues

a) COVID-19, climate, and conflict

Security Council Resolution 2532, passed on 1 July 2020, 'demanded a general and immediate cessation of hostilities in all situations' on the Council's agenda and called upon all parties to armed conflicts to engage immediately in a 90-day humanitarian pause. During 2020, the Security Council organised several meetings on the COVID-19 pandemic, centred around Resolution 2532, to assist members to fight COVID-19 in conflict-affected countries. In February 2021, the Security Council held a high-level briefing on COVID-19, with a focus on the UN's role in ensuring equitable access to vaccines, especially in conflict-affected areas.

However, the ability of the Security Council to deal with climate impacts has been slower and less certain than the ability to deal with a pandemic. In recent years, the Security Council has increasingly considered the negative security effects of climate change across many of the 'files' on its agenda. Language on climate change has been integrated into Security Council statements and resolutions on the Central African Republic, Darfur, the Democratic Republic

30 Security Council Report (n 28); see UN Assistance Mission in Afghanistan, 'Afghanistan: Protection of Civilians in Armed Conflict Third Quarter Report: 1 January to 30 September 2020' (27 October 2020) <https://unama.unmissions.org/sites/default/files/unama_protection_of_civilians_in_armed_conflict_-_3rd_quarter_report_2020_revised_13dec_.pdf> accessed 31 March 2021.

31 Security Council Report (n 28); see OCHA, 'Flash Update 9 – Fighting, Displacement and Civilian Casualties in Southern Afghanistan' (18 November 2020) <www.humanitarianresponse.info/sites/www.humanitarianresponse.info/files/documents/files/flash_update_9_south_final.pdf> accessed 31 March 2021.

32 Security Council Report (n 28).

of the Congo, Mali, Somalia, and West Africa. Typically, Council outcomes have focused on implementing 'adequate risk assessments and risk management strategies to cope with the adverse security effects of climate change and other environmental factors in particular situations'.[33] In February 2021, the UK hosted a high-level open debate for the first time, '[a]ddressing climate-related security risks to international peace and security through mitigation and resilience building'.[34] This suggests that environmental issues will remain a focus of international policy, even as international criminal courts – as Killean points out in her contribution – might further explore their scope to tackle this issue. Moreover, it raises the very real possibility that international criminal justice and any form of human activity may have no future at all, unless dramatic changes take place.[35]

b) United Nations Secretary-General prevention reforms

Recent reform measures implemented by UN Secretary-General António Guterres may prove to be more effective in preventing human rights abuses and thereby armed conflict. His reform measures include restructuring Secretariat management to strengthen the UN's approach to crisis prevention and peacekeeping. These measures are intended to streamline the process of crisis prevention; Guterres has placed a priority on systematic reform that 'create[s] a consensus around simplification, decentralization and flexibility' to promote more efficient and effective UN responses.[36] A primary aspect of this strategy is decentralisation of decision making and the simplifying of bureaucratic procedure. Reform is intended to promote more businesslike models within the UN and disseminate decision-making authority amongst managers throughout the Secretariat to promote 'unity of command and purpose; clarity of roles and responsibilities; and empowered delegations of authority'. Reform within the peace and security pillar of the UN emphasises conflict prevention and sustaining peace as well as improving the effectiveness of peacekeeping operations and special political missions. Two new departments will focus on conflict prevention, mediation, resolution, and peacebuilding through 'early warning and response, envoys, regional political offices, offices in support of political processes, mediation and electoral assistance

33 'Climate Change and Security' *Security Council Report* (29 January 2021) <www.securitycouncilreport.org/monthly-forecast/2021-02/climate-and-security-2.php> accessed 31 March 2021.

34 ibid.

35 'Biden's Intelligence Director Vows to Put Climate at "Center" of Foreign Policy' *New York Times* (10 May 2021) <www.nytimes.com/live/2021/04/22/us/biden-earth-day-climate-summit> accessed 31 March 2021.

36 United Nations Secretary-General, 'Secretary-General Designate António Guterres' Remarks to the General Assembly on Taking the Oath of Office' (12 December 2016) <www.un.org/sg/en/content/sg/speeches/2016-12-12/secretary-general-designate-ant%C3%B3nio-guterres-oath-office-speech> accessed 31 March 2021.

support'.[37] This focus on preventing violence – through a range of policy measures and through the direct engagement with political barriers – might be a more transformative approach than justice alone. We note though the tensions inherent in a democratic facilitation approach may not challenge neo-capitalist structures, understanding as John Linarelli, Margot Salomon, and Muthucumaraswamy Sornarajah have written that while human rights might sometimes offer a defence against economic power, they are also 'circumscribed by that power and in important ways reinforce expression of it'.[38]

c) Treaty on the prohibition of nuclear weapons

There may have been one Utopian moment during the consideration of possible futures of international law. The Treaty on the Prohibition of Nuclear Weapons entered into force globally on 22 January 2021. The treaty prohibits the development, testing, production, acquisition, stockpiling, use, and threat of use of nuclear weapons, as well as assistance in and encouragement of the prohibited activities. It obliges states parties to assist any individuals affected by the use or testing of weapons and to take appropriate environmental remediation measures. Because states parties undertake to take appropriate legal measures to prevent and suppress prohibited activity, including imposing penal sanctions, this treaty cannot but be a factor in construing the Rome Statute's provisions regarding unlawful means of warfare.

5 Final thoughts

This review of current events does not lend itself to a clear vision of Utopia but does allow us to examine the concepts of 'futures' and 'newness' in relation to international criminal law and how it is 'nested' in time and space. Questions about how courts, particularly the ICC, are organised; the relationship between the ICC and states; and how that should be measured respond to the concerns addressed by Frédéric Mégret and Shannon Maree Torrens. These issues are embedded within the 'stickiness' of the Rome Statute and the decisions and committees generated by earlier ASP sessions, as well as the older aims and debates about the nature and purpose of justice as political (apology) or otherwise, and its universalism or otherwise. Drawing on debates about how to institutionalise approaches to international criminal law beyond the ICC, Philipp Kastner critiqued the relatively 'new' injection of the concept of resilience into discussions about international criminal justice – in relation to older, recent, and new 'hybrid'

37 United Nations Secretary-General, 'Shifting the management paradigm in the United Nations: ensuring a better future for all. Report of the Secretary-General' (27 September 2017) <https://wedocs.unep.org/bitstream/handle/20.500.11822/22699/SG%20Management%20Reforms%20.pdf?sequence=7&isAllowed=y> accessed 31 March 2021.

38 John Linarelli, Margot Salomon, and Muthucumaraswamy Sornarajah, *The Misery of International Law: Confrontations with Injustice in the Global Economy* (OUP 2018) 266.

models of justice. The impunity for past and ongoing atrocities in the 'recent' conflicts mentioned earlier is rooted in the (often colonial) histories of those conflicts; past attempts to resolve or even secure justice for them; and present intersecting political, environmental, technological, and pandemic tensions. Violence morphs but persists in these shifting contexts, where tensions between peace and justice and development and justice are raised but not resolved, as considered by Palmer. Amidst all this complexity, Killean and Bikundo sought new-but-revised crimes and reparations processes to address persistent international criminal law problems – linking together historic and recent events to propose new directions. In different ways, these proposals are likely to be challenged by their nestedness in 'old' institutions and practices.

Meanwhile as weaponry 'evolves', Eve Massingham and Simon McKenzie and Natalie Nunn also drew on existing and reinterpreted international laws to propose new ideas for the most recent technological separation between perpetrator, weapon, and victim. Anna Marie Brennan argued that the continuing, or even growing, complexity of the entities responsible for atrocities requires new frameworks of liability. International criminal justice does respond to tensions involving universalism and localisation, technological and environmental change, and, in particular, the non-linear effects of 'justice' and its mechanisms. Yet it does not do so in any clear, single, or neat manner, but instead offers experiences, precedents, and methods of practice and inquiry with which to tackle multiple issues as they surface (for better or worse). Our contributors have shown the value in critical engagement and the acknowledgement of the possibility of change in possible futures, including regression.

This exploration of the futures for international criminal justice has revealed the normativity and challenges involved in undertaking such a task without promoting linear understandings of time, identifying the possibility or preferability of particular futures, and even assuming that any future at all may exist as we experience climate, conflict, pandemic, and other risks. Further, identifying consequent challenges and remedies, including institutions and procedures, for an array of potential futures presents further difficulties, including in the 'post'-COVID world. Nonetheless, critical inquiry into the possible futures of international criminal justice remains a fundamental task.

Index

For Product Safety Concerns and Information please contact our EU
representative GPSR@taylorandfrancis.com
Taylor & Francis Verlag GmbH, Kaufingerstraße 24, 80331 München, Germany

www.ingramcontent.com/pod-product-compliance
Ingram Content Group UK Ltd.
Pitfield, Milton Keynes, MK11 3LW, UK
UKHW020011200926
475702UK00014B/1829